The Analysis of International Relations

D1314599

THIRD EDITION

The Analysis of International Relations

Karl W. Deutsch

Emory University

PRENTICE HALL, Englewood Cliffs, New Jersey 07632

Library of Congress Cataloging-in-Publication Data

DEUTSCH, KARL WOLFGANG
   The analysis of international relations.

   Bibliography: p.
   Includes index.
   1. International relations—Research.   I. Title.
JX1291.D48 1988   327   87-25722
ISBN 0-13-033010-8

Editorial/production supervision: Debbie Ford
Cover design: Wanda Lubelska Design
Manufacturing buyer: Margaret Rizzi

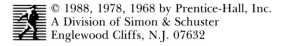
Printed in the United States of America

10   9   8   7   6   5   4   3   2   1

ISBN 0-13-033010-8

Prentice-Hall International (UK) Limited, *London*
Prentice-Hall of Australia Pty. Limited, *Sydney*
Prentice-Hall Canada Inc., *Toronto*
Prentice-Hall Hispanoamericana, S.A., *Mexico*
Prentice-Hall of India Private Limited, *New Delhi*
Prentice-Hall of Japan, Inc., *Tokyo*
Simon & Schuster Asia Pte. Ltd., *Singapore*
Editora do Brasil, Ltda., *Rio de Janeiro*

Contents

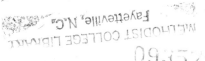
v

Preface

An introduction to the study of international relations in our time is an introduction to the art and science of the survival of mankind. If civilization is killed within the next thirty years, it will not be killed by famine or plague, but by foreign policy and international relations. We can cope with hunger and pestilence, but we cannot yet deal with the power of our own weapons and with our behavior as nation-states.

Possessing unprecedented instruments for national action in the forms of ideologies and weapons, the nation-states have become ever more dangerous vehicles of international conflict, carrying the potential for its escalation to mutual destruction and ultimate annihilation. The nation-state holds the power to control most events within its borders, but few events—or even its own actions—beyond them.

International relations is that area of human action where inescapable interdependence meets with inadequate control. We can neither escape from world affairs nor wholly shape them to our will. We can only try to adjust the world while adjusting to it. Within this limited scope, we must retain and, where possible, enhance our most deeply held values.

As the practice of international relations has become more difficult and decisive, its study has moved to keep pace. The dramatic advances in the field over the last three decades include changes in basic concepts and theories, changes stimulated by a meeting of the newer behavioral sciences of psychology, sociology, and anthropology with the longer established disciplines of political science, history, and economics. These changes in theory have been accompanied by the development of new methods of research, the employment of statistical procedures for analysis, and the growing availability of testable empirical data. Throughout this book, I have tried to introduce the reader to these more recent types of research and analysis. All these changes have made the study of international relations more professional than heretofore, making much—though by no means all—of the older literature obsolete.

But international relations and foreign policy are too important to be left to the specialists. Many young men have thought that world affairs need not concern them, until their draft boards told them otherwise. If our lives are so deeply affected by, and our responses so essential to international affairs, then we must increase our capacity to understand, to decide, and to act.

Knowledge is different from values. Values motivate the search for knowledge and make some of its results more salient to us than others. Knowledge tells us which of our values may conflict, and where and when our means begin to injure and destroy our ends instead of serving them.

My own values are made plain throughout the book. You may share or reject them, or select from among them. I have tried to support all judgments and not to let my preferences deceive me. You may decide for yourself to what extent I have failed or succeeded in this search for realism and reality. You may verify the facts presented here and add others that you might find relevant. It is important that you should try to do this, for we are all bound up in the same enterprise—in the search for a tolerable pathway toward peace and freedom everywhere. It will be a difficult search, but we cannot escape it.

In writing this small book, I have been aided by many people in many ways. Colleagues from whose views I have benefited at various times include Hayward R. Alker, Jr., Gabriel Almond, Kenneth E. Boulding, Richard C. Chadwick, Robert Dahl, Lewis J. Edinger, Bruno Fritsch, Harold Guetzkow, Ernst B. Haas, Stanley Hoffmann, Michael Hudson, Samuel Huntington, Alex Inkeles, Irving Janis, Herbert C. Kelman, Henry Kissinger, U. W. Kissinger, Seymour Martin Lipset, Roy C. Macridis, Richard L. Merritt, James Grier Miller, Joseph Nye, Donald J. Puchala, Lucian Pye, Anatol Rapoport, Rudolph Rummel, Bruce M. Russett, Dankwart Rustow, Burton Spain, I. Richard Savage, Thomas C. Schelling, Erwin Scheuch, J. David Singer, Richard C. Snyder, Harold Sprout, Raymond Tanter, Charles L. Taylor, Robert Triffin, and Sidney Verba. And there are debts to those who have died: Alexander Eckstein, Rupert Emerson, Carl J. Friedrich, Hans Kohn, Harold Lasswell, Daniel Lerner, Robert Marjolin, Talcott Parsons, Ithiel Pool, Joseph A. Schumpeter, Hermann Weilenmann, and Norbert Wiener. No one among these, of course, bears any responsibility for my views or my mistakes.

For assistance in research, computing, and other matters, I am indebted to Irwin C. Bupp, James Chapman, Gordon Fowler, Linda Groff, Chris Kolb, Peter Natchez, Brigitte Rosenbusch, and Philipp von

Stauffenberg. Crucial secretarial aid I owe most of all to Ina Frieser, invaluable during ten years through her understanding intelligence and capacity to organize. Other important help came at various stages from Evelyn Neumark and from Helen D. Alsen, Lucille McKenna, and Karen Salsburg. In preparing the third edition of this book, Chandler Finley and particularly Susanne Schutz were of decisive help, often above and beyond the call of duty.

The first draft of several chapters was written in the ideal scholarly setting of the Villa Serbelloni of the Rockefeller Foundation at Bellagio, Italy. Research utilized in this book was supported in part by the Carnegie Corporation, by Harvard and Yale Universities, by the Mental Health Research Institute of the University of Michigan, by the Science Center Berlin for Social Research, and by Emory University. The Carter Center of Emory University gave important help to the completion of the manuscript of the Third Edition, and so did the coordinator of the Center Fellows, Ms. Dayle Powell. To all of these belong my thanks.

K.W.D.

The Analysis of International Relations

Introduction

As Americans see it, most of the world is inhabited by "foreigners." That is, of the world's 5 billion people, only about 236 million—roughly one in twenty—are Americans. We are a minority of the total population, not only in numbers but also in land area, property, knowledge, and (presumably) power. Large as our country is, we inhabit less than half our continent, which is but one of five. In terms of economics, even by a highly favorable method of counting, we have about one-fourth of the gross national product of the world, and our share of the world's steel production and energy output is still smaller. The same holds for the production of knowledge: only about one-third of Nobel Prize winners in the natural sciences, and a minority of the world's great inventors and discoverers, have been American. All these facts suggest that much less than half the world's potential for political and military power is under our direct national control.

But much the same problem is faced by all other nations: each of them, too, is a minority among the human population. For instance, numerous as they are, the Chinese are less than one-fourth of humanity, and all the East Indians (all counted as a single people) still add up to less than one-sixth. And, large as the industrial might of the Soviet Union has grown in recent years, its population is less than one-seventeenth of humankind, and its income is still only about two-thirds that of the United States, or less than one-sixth of the world total. Every other nation in the world is much smaller still, and hence still much more a minority on earth.

No matter how large or small, however, every nation in the world, including our own, must take very much into account what "foreigners" are doing, and, if it wishes to accomplish more than it can with its own limited resources, it must gain their cooperation. But this is easier said than done, for foreigners can be quite different—starting with such obvious characteristics as appearance. More than two-thirds of the world's people are nonwhite,[1] for example, and by the end of this century that proportion is likely to rise to three-quarters. Furthermore, more than two-thirds are non-Christian. But if Christians are a minority in the world, so are Muslims, Jews, Buddhists, Hindus, communists, Aristotelians, Logical Positivists, and the adherents of any other single organized religion, philosophy, or ideology. They are all minorities among the total population, and indeed, as far as we know, always have been.

People have very much in common in human nature, human needs, and human hopes; but so far we have been incurably diverse in our languages, cultures, religions, philosophies, ideologies, and (most of all) governments. So far, we never have been effectively controlled or managed by a single ruler, a single organization, or a single creed—although in the course of history, as well as in our time, many rulers, organizations, and creeds have tried or claimed to do just that.

Although people are incurably diverse, they are also inescapably interdependent; and in some respects this interdependence has increased in this day of the shrinking world. After all, even the most widely separated people in the world can live at most only half the world apart—roughly 12,500 miles, or about as far as New York City is from Ho Chi Minh City in Vietnam. Most other places on earth are much less far away: Pearl Harbor on Hawaii; Tokyo and Hiroshima in Japan; Omaha and Utah Beach on the Normandy Peninsula of France; Berlin divided between East and West in Germany; Taipei on the island of Taiwan; Seoul in South Korea; the Sinai peninsula between Israel and Egypt; Dacca in Bangladesh; Luanda in Angola; Beirut in Lebanon; Havana on the island of Cuba. The spectacular events that happened at each of these places at some time during the lifetime of the present generation of adults have made a significant difference to the lives of the American people. These events have influenced their business and personal opportunities as well as their taxes, their prices, the value of their money, and the length of the roll call of servicemen killed in open or undeclared warfare on foreign soil.

This interdependence has been increasing fastest in terms of military matters. Every place on earth today is less than two days' flight by jet plane from the farthest other place. By guided missile the distance is approximately 40 minutes. And nearly-instant worldwide communication, long relegated to wireless and pictureless apparatus, now comes in the form of sound plus color images via television relayed by globe-girdling communica-

---

[1]"Nonwhite" includes the black, brown, red, and yellow-skinned peoples—all minority groups themselves within the total population.

tions satellites. (Satellites with powerful cameras have allowed spying to reach new heights, both of altitude and sophistication.)

There are other, perhaps subtler, signs of growing interdependence. The income-tax rate in the United States, it has been said, is set in Moscow, since our government and our voters have felt that we must at least match and balance the military strength and expenditure of Russia. By the same reasoning, additional elements of our income-tax rate have been set in Peking. The governments in Moscow and Peking, however, have claimed that they must at least match and balance each other's power, as well as that part of our power that could be brought to bear against them; and thus it may be said that part of their military expenditures—and hence of the sacrifices of Russian and Chinese housewives—have been determined by political decisions made in Washington, D.C. And what is true of the largest and strongest nations in the world is no less true of the smaller ones. All nations are interdependent in terms of politics and strategy. No nation, no matter how small, can in splendid isolation be master of its fate, master of its blood and treasure; but no nation, no matter how large, can compel all others to do its bidding, nor convert them quickly to its own beliefs.

We are, however, interdependent with the rest of the world in far more ways than simply politics and power. Everybody knows vaguely that science, technology, and medicine are "international," but few of us have stopped to think just what this means. It means, in sober fact, that no people and no country in the world could have reached its present level of technology, prosperity, and health—nor could it maintain its present rate of progress—without the decisive aid of foreign discoveries and foreign contributions. A great leader of American science, the physicist Karl T. Compton, once reminded us that only three of the twelve basic discoveries that permitted the release of atomic energy were made by Americans. That one-quarter of this world-changing discovery was contributed by one-twentieth of the world's population (which is, as we recall, the share of the American people) may well be reason for national pride, but that we depended upon foreigners for three-quarters of this crucial knowledge may well help us to see ourselves in better perspective.

No country could keep many of its own people alive without the help of foreigners. In our hospitals and doctors' offices, thousands of lives are saved daily by the application of discoveries and medicines developed by scientists in other countries. In the last half-century, penicillin was discovered in England, sulfa drugs in Germany, radioactive isotopes in France, insulin in Canada. If all our packages of medicines were brightly labeled with the names and countries of their discoverers, we would get a course in world citizenship at every prescription counter; and if tomorrow all remedies developed by foreigners should lose their power, the number of dead in our streets would be appalling.

But there is another side to the coin: while the countries of the world are becoming more interdependent in regard to strategy and science, and perhaps to foreign policy, they are becoming somewhat less interdependent in regard to language, education, economics, and perhaps domestic politics. Later in this study, we shall survey some evidence that suggests that the relative importance of the old two "world languages," French and English, has been somewhat declining, and that in many regions of the world, a plurality of national—and sometimes regional—languages have taken at least part of their place. In most countries, economic and cultural advancement is accompanied by a rise in the use of their own national language, and also by a decline of the share of students (and hence, later, of leaders) who have been educated abroad. In the world as a whole, the total number of students studying outside their national state almost tripled between 1960 and 1974 from less than 12 million to more than 33 million; but the total number of students in the world more than tripled from 238 to 750 million, so that the percentage of students studying abroad dropped from 4.9 to 4.4 percent. Among American college students, those studying outside the United States in the early 1960s amounted to about 0.5 percent of the total, and this small proportion continued to drop from 0.22 percent in 1974 to 0.16 percent in 1981.[2]

Also, with economic progress and rising populations, the proportion of foreign trade to the gross national product is declining. Modern technology is a technology of substitutes: much of what had to be imported in the past, such as wool or silk, now can be replaced by something made at home, such as orlon or nylon. At the same time, a growing part of the national income is coming to consist of services which are produced in the main within the country, such as housing, schools, health care, and the like. As a result, the exporters and importers, and all the interest groups concerned with foreign trade, now tend to command a declining proportion of the wealth and workforce in each country, and hence a declining share of the potential resources for exercising influence in politics. Yet world interdependence has persisted, and sometimes grown, in regard to some key commodities, such as oil, wheat, and computers; and it has been felt more keenly as their prices rose, often in response to the actions of the nations exporting them. Thus the two sharp rises in oil prices in the 1970s forced many oil-importing countries to commit larger proportions of their national income to foreign trade, since they had to be paid for in part by increased exports. When oil prices again fell somewhat, as they did in 1986, this had considerable effects throughout the world economy, but it did not substantially alter the trend toward increased world interdependence in regard to this commodity.

It is hard but necessary to sum up the overall results of this first look at facts and trends. Every people, every race, and every creed is only a minority in a world of foreigners which is both inescapable and unmanageable. It is in many ways unmanageable because it is so pluralistic and diverse; and it is inescapable because our interdependence with other countries and peoples is very great and very real. In some respects this interdependence has been growing in recent decades, while in other respects it has been declining. In almost every country in the world, there-

---

[2]From data in *Statistical Abstract of the United States 1982–1983*, (Washington, D.C.: Government Printing Office, 1982), pp. 160–161, and *UNESCO Statistical Yearbook 1984*. Vol. III (New York: United Nations), p. 420.

fore, both foreign policy and domestic politics often are being pushed and pulled in several contradictory directions at once, and the safety and prosperity of each country, and even the survival of the human race, may depend on the outcome of these multiple contests.

International relations are too important to be ignored, but they also are too complex to be understood at a glance. We must try to do better. In a medical emergency, all those who have had medical training have an obligation to render first aid and otherwise help as needed. In medicine we know that individuals are victims of illness but also often are major agents in their own recovery. Something similar holds for citizens: they can be victims of politics, but they can also do much to improve them and to improve their own fate and that of their country. We who have the opportunity and privilege of a higher education owe to others the best help that we can give them as informed, competent, and responsible citizens of our countries and of the world; we must do our best to look to the heart of matters and try to help one and all to cope with the recurrent international political crises and emergencies of our time.

But competence here is as necessary as compassion. In medicine, a well-meaning ignoramus is not a doctor but a quack. In an emergency, such a person may endanger the life of a patient. In politics, aroused and zealous but misinformed citizens are a menace who may endanger the liberties and lives of millions, including their own. In our own time, the ruins of Hamburg and Berlin, of Hiroshima and Tokyo, have stood as monuments to the high cost of ignorance in international politics. We must study international relations, therefore, as deeply, as carefully, and as responsibly as our limited time and resources permit. No other subject is as likely to have a direct bearing on what the American statesman Bernard Baruch once called "a choice between the quick and the dead."

This brief book can offer only a first introduction to this study. It will do so in four parts. The first of these will deal with *what* we want to know: the substance of international relations. The second part will ask *how* we can come to know about the actors in world politics. The third part traces the processes of control and conflict among states as they draw them into war, and includes a new chapter on international terrorism and "informal" warfare. The fourth and last part will discuss some of the steps that have been or could be taken in humanity's search for peace and for helpful and effective action.

1

Twelve Fundamental Questions

Much of what we want to know about international relations can be grouped under the headings of twelve fundamental questions. In one form or another, these questions have been asked for many centuries by political scientists, as well as by political leaders and by ordinary citizens. To many of them, there are traditional answers of some kind, usually several; but as in most fields of knowledge, these traditional answers must be looked at with caution. It is harder to get more precise answers to these questions, and hardest to acquire even a little knowledge about them that can be impersonally tested, reproduced, and verified, or else disproved, so that it can be called in some sense scientific. Yet we must try to get such knowledge, and in searching for it, our twelve fundamental questions may help us to keep our search relevant to what we want and need to know.

The twelve fundamental questions with which we shall concern ourselves are these:

1. *Nation and World:* What are the relations of a nation to the world around it? When, how, and how quickly are a people, a state, and a nation likely to arise, and when, how, and how quickly are they apt to disappear? While they last, how do they relate to other peoples, states, and nations? How do they deal with smaller groups within them, and with individuals, and how do they relate to international organizations and to the international political system?

2. *Transnational Processes and International Interdependence:* To what extent can the governments and peoples of any nation-state decide their own future, and to what extent does the outcome of their actions depend on conditions and events outside their national boundaries? Are the world's countries and nations becoming more "sovereign" and independent from each other, or are they becoming more interdependent in their actions and their fate? Or are they becoming both more independent and more interdependent, but in different sectors of activity? What will the world look like in, say, 2010 A.D. in regard to these matters?

3. *War and Peace:* What are the determinants of war and peace among nations? When, how, and why do wars start, proceed, and stop? How did these processes work in the past, how are they working now, and how are they likely to work in the future? How much and what kinds of fighting are people likely to support? When, for what purposes, and under what conditions?

4. *Power and Weakness:* What is the nature of the power or weakness of a government, or of a nation, in international politics? What are the sources and conditions of such power? What are its limits? When, how, and why does power change?

5. *International Politics and International Society:* What is political in international relations, and what is not? What is the relation of international politics to the life of the society of nations?

6. *World Population vs. Food, Resources, and Environment:* Is world population growing faster than world supplies of food, energy, and other resources, and faster than the "carrying capacity" of our environment in regard to tolerably clean air and water and unpolluted living space? Could failures in these regards pose to the "national security" of any nation a threat equal to or worse than that posed by a change in the political or military power of its neighbors? Do these problems pose only temporary "limits to growth," or do they portend a long-term future of poverty and material stagnation for humankind? What would be, in either case, their consequences for world politics, including war or peace, and what, if anything, could be done about them?

7. *Prosperity and Poverty:* How great is the inequality in the distribution of wealth and income among the nations of the world? How great is the inequality in regard to other but related values, such as life expectancy or education? Are economic differences among nations greater or smaller than within them, such as among ethnic or racial groups, or among regions or classes? Are any of these inequalities growing or declining? How fast and by how much? What determines the nature of these distributions and the size and direction of these changes? What could be done to bring about such changes deliberately? How quickly, and by how much?

8. *Freedom and Oppression:* How much do people care about independence from other peoples or countries, and how much do they care about freedom within their own country and nation? What, if anything, are they likely to do about it? When, and under what conditions? What do people perceive as "freedom"—a wide range of choices with tolerance for minorities and for individual nonconformity, or mass submission to majority rule,

to tradition, to some trusted leader, or to some congenial and familiar tyranny? To what extent do they perceive freedom as a value in itself, and to what extent do they see it mainly as an instrument to attain other values which to them are more important? What conditions influence or change such perceptions and such choices? How quickly and to what extent? How great are the differences between the kinds and amounts of freedom which people want in different nations, and in different groups within a nation? How great are the differences in the kinds and amounts of freedom which they get? How far and how fast do these distributions change? When, and under what conditions?

9. *Perception and Illusion:* How do leaders and members of nations perceive their own nations, and how do they perceive other nations and their actions? How realistic or illusory are these perceptions? When, in what regard, and under what conditions? Under what conditions are governments and electorates perceptive, and in regard to what matters are they obtuse or blind? To what extent do national governments function as sources of mass deception, myth, and self-deception? What effect does all this have on the ability of governments and nation-states to control their own behavior and to foresee the consequences of their actions? What is the "error average" of government leaders? How often do they make some major decision about war or peace on the basis of some major error on a point of fact? What could be done, if anything, to make errors more rare and perceptions more realistic?

10. *Activity and Apathy:* What part, and what groups, of the population take an active interest in politics? What part, and what groups, do so in regard to international affairs? What conditions tend to enlarge or diminish these proportions of active participants? How quickly, and in what respects? What broader strata of the population must be considered relevant for politics at some given place and time? What conditions are likely to change the extent of these politically relevant strata? What are the effects of such changes in the amount of actual and potential political participation on the processes of politics and on their outcomes? Particularly, what are the effects of changes in the degree of mass participation in politics upon the conduct and the outcome of international affairs? What kinds of politics and world affairs are likely to exist among populations who are largely limited to subsistence economics and are apathetic about politics? And what kind of national and international politics are likely to develop with a sharp increase in the use of money and in mass communications, literacy, social mobility, and political participation? Obviously, this is a serious problem in developing countries, but it is also a problem for large and advanced countries, such as the United States, France, and the Soviet Union.

11. *Revolution and Stability:* Under what conditions are governments likely to be overthrown? When, under what conditions, and to what extent are entire ruling elites or privileged classes likely to lose all or part of their power and position? What permanent or irreversible changes, if any, are produced by revolutions? When and how are entire systems of law, economics, and society, or entire major patterns of culture, discarded wholly or in part and replaced eventually by other such systems and patterns? How

quickly do these large processes of change occur, and at what cost in material damage and human suffering? Upon what groups in the population do these costs fall, for a short time or for long? What benefits, if any, short-run or long-run, do such changes bring, and to whom do they accrue? How long does it take for political and social stability to be established after a period of revolution? How, with what results, and at what costs to whom? And what are the effects of such processes of revolution, counterrevolution, and eventual stabilization of an old or new political or social order upon the course of international politics? How, in short, can domestic revolutions affect international affairs, and how can foreign influences and international events affect the stability or revolutionary upheaval of the domestic regimes and political systems of particular countries? What, if anything, can governments, leaders, and electorates do about these processes? To what extent can they be influenced or controlled by deliberate action? When, at what cost, and in what direction?

12. *Identity and Transformation:* How, throughout all changes, do individuals, groups, peoples, and nations preserve their identity? What does this identity consist of, insofar as any elements or aspects of their inner structure are concerned, and what difference does it make to their observable behavior? To what extent does an identity of one's own constitute a real need of persons and of groups, and what happens if this need is not fulfilled? To what extent is such an identity of one's own a value in itself, and to what extent is it a condition or an instrument for attaining other values? How is a sense of identity—and how is the reality of identity (that is, the continued meaningfulness of one's own memories to oneself)—acquired, and how is it lost? How thoroughly, how quickly, and under what conditions?

To what extent are persons, classes, elites, governments, peoples, and nations all like leopards, who cannot change their spots, and to what extent are they capable of transformation and self-transformation? To what extent do peoples, social classes, and racial groups learn to identify with the temporary roles of power and privilege which they may have acquired at some time in history, and how deeply can they become addicted to the flattering self-images that often go with them? What happens to their thoughts and feelings, and how are they likely to act, when faced with the impending loss of power and privileged position? Germans in Eastern Europe after World War I, British people in India and Kenya after World War II, Japanese in Korea and Manchuria, the French in Algeria, Portuguese settlers in Angola and Mozambique, white farmers in Rhodesia and South Africa, some white voters in the South of the United States after the Civil War—or the War Between the States as some prefer to call it—all these have had to face the problem in one form or another. Each group has had to choose some kind of response, and these have ranged from peaceful adjustment to bitter last-ditch resistance, and sometimes even all-out war, to preserve or retrieve a threatened position of predominance. And in each case of peaceful adjustment or warlike despair, what other parts of the society and culture of the formerly undisputed power-holders had to be transformed? To restate now our first question in this paragraph: To what extent can peoples, states, and social groups change their behavior, their goals, their inner structure, and their character, and to what extent can they still, throughout these changes, preserve their own identity? What are the effects of the transformation of personalities and groups upon a nation, and of the transformation of a nation upon personalities and groups? Particularly, what are the effects of international changes on national transformation and national identity, and what are the effects of the transformation of one nation, or of some social groups or classes within it, upon other nations and upon the international system?

Clearly it is easier to ask such questions than to answer them. About each of our twelve fundamental questions, many books and articles have been written in the past. A few of these are listed in the reading suggestions. Many more are likely to be written in the future. Yet, if we wish to be introduced to any more thorough study of international politics, we must at least begin to think about these twelve basic questions so as to become acquainted with the problems each of them implies.

Moreover, the twelve questions are interdependent. Whatever answers, or parts of answers, we might find to any one of them will make a difference to our answers to some or all of the others. Each of our twelve questions is a good starting-point but, much as several town gates all lead toward the heart of the same city, so our twelve questions all will lead us deeper into the complexities of our single problem: How so many different nations, while coming into existence and passing from the scene, can live together in a mixture of limited independence and interdependence in a world about which they cannot quite agree but which none of them singly can control, and upon which all of them depend for their peace, their freedom, their happiness, and their survival.

2

Tools for Thinking:
A Few Basic Concepts

In order to make our twelve fundamental questions more manageable, both singly and in their interplay, we must use concepts as tools for cutting into them. Since a concept is a symbol, and a symbol is, so to speak, a command to be mindful of those things to which it refers, it follows that a concept is a kind of command to remember a collection of things or memories. It is an order to select and collect certain items of information—these will refer to facts, *if* they should happen to exist. Hence a concept is a command to search, but it is no guarantee that we shall find.

SOME CONCEPTS ABOUT SOCIAL SYSTEMS

The four concepts we shall start with were proposed by sociologist Talcott Parsons.[1] He derived them from the idea that there are certain fundamental things that must be done in every social system, large or small (that is, in every group, every organization, every country) if it is to endure. First, there is *pattern maintenance:* the system must be preserved in its essential

---

[1]Talcott Parsons, *The Social System* (Glencoe, IL: Free Press, 1951), and *Societies: Evolutionary and Comparative Perspectives* (Englewood Cliffs, NJ: Prentice-Hall, 1966).

patterns—that is, these patterns must be reproduced time and again so as to preserve them over a succession of persons, groups, or generations. In most societies the main function of pattern maintenance is served by households and families; in every society it is also served by many other institutions and agencies, though to a lesser degree.

Second, there is *adaptation:* every organization and every society must adapt itself to its environment, derive its sustenance from it, and adjust to its changes. In every country the chief task of adaptation is performed, according to Parsons, by the economic sector of life and its institutions and activities, including those of technology and science. Adaptation is thus primarily served by the factories, farms, mines, and research laboratories of each country, whether they are under private or public ownership. People adapt to oceans by fishing, to plains by growing wheat on them, and to rivers by building power stations—and such a social adaptation changes the environment as well as the society, for if it changes a hunter into a farmer, it also changes a plain into a field.

Third, there is *goal attainment:* every organization and society has one or several goals which it is trying to approach or attain, or which its members wish to attain, and in terms of which its behavior is being modified beyond the simple requirements of pattern maintenance and adaptation. In every country, Parsons suggests, most of the function of goal attainment is served by the government, and more generally by the political sector, with its processes and institutions. It is through government and politics that most often the human and material resources of a country are gathered and reallocated to the pursuit of whatever goals, peaceful or warlike (ranging from attaining general literacy to conquering a coveted frontier province), that the leaders or the people of the society have accepted.

These three functions—pattern maintenance, adaptation to the natural and human environment, and the pursuit of goals—are not easy to carry on at one and the same time if resources are limited, as they usually are. Yet none of the three can be sacrificed. Every country, every society, and every complex organization, Parsons points out, therefore always faces a continuing and basic fourth task—the task of *integration*. Integration consists in making these different activities compatible and keeping them so, and in making and keeping the expectations and motivations of people compatible with the roles they have to play. The function of integration in most countries is served primarily by their cultural, educational, and religious practices and institutions, but many other elements of society are participating in this task, even though usually to a somewhat lesser degree.

Within each organization or group—that is, within every smaller or larger system—the same four functions are being served. In the U.S. State Department, pattern maintenance may be thought of as being carried out largely by the accounting and auditing services, the personnel bureau, and the security office, while much of the routine work of its consulates and embassies, as well as of its offices of congressional liaison and of public relations (or "public affairs"), may be considered to be serving the tasks of adaptation to various parts of its environment. The task of goal attainment is pursued through the more "political" efforts of our diplomats abroad, through the statements and press releases of departmental spokespeople, through the drafting of international treaties or national legislation proposed by the department, and through the policy-making efforts of its top-ranking officers. The latter, from the Secretary of State on down, also face the unending task of integration—that is, of trying to coordinate and to keep mutually compatible, or if possible even mutually supportive, all the department's numerous activities, bureaus, agencies, and officials, and their efforts.

For the United States at large, goal attainment must be served mainly by the President and Congress, and to a lesser but increasingly significant degree by the Supreme Court. All three branches of the government, however, also have important tasks in regard to pattern maintenance, integration, and adaptation.

At a still higher level, the United Nations is attempting to attain its goals mainly through the work of its Assembly, its Secretary General, and its Security Council. Much of its work of adaptation is carried out through its Economic and Social Council (ECOSOC), and major efforts to serve its integrative function are made through the United Nations Educational and Scientific Council (UNESCO).[2] The task of pattern maintenance largely appears to be left to its member governments and nations, perhaps to a dangerously high degree in times of international tensions.

As these examples show, the four basic functions, to some minimal degree at least, exist in every social system. But they are not always neatly separated in practice, nor are all of them always developed to the same extent. Every stable and identifiable system must have pattern maintenance if it is to survive in at least one unchanging environment. Those systems which are capable of surviving in environments that are varied or changing must develop the function of adaptation. Only systems of some complexity have external goals, and thus the task of attaining them; and only systems of similar or greater complexity may require elaborate facilities and processes of integration.

Two further basic functions become important only in regard to still more highly developed systems. One of these is *goal setting*. While simple goal-seeking systems have built into them once and for all the propensity to approach one goal, or at most very few equivalent or alternative goals, a

---

[2]Since late 1974, however, some highly controversial resolutions accusing the state of Israel of "racism" have been voted in UNESCO by a majority composed of the delegates of the Arab states, most other Third World nations, and the Communist countries, against the negative votes of the United States and some other countries, and against the abstentions of many West European powers. These resolutions were essentially untrue in content; both the political ideology of Zionism and the laws of the State of Israel are indifferent to the inborn and inheritable physical characteristics that we call "race," and according to Jewish religious teaching, anyone may convert to Judaism. By early 1977, Israel became, despite its geographic location, a member of the West European regional group within the UNESCO framework. New conflicts arose, however, between UNESCO and the United States and other Western powers about Third World demands for a "New Information Order" (NTO) which was seen by the West as incompatible with its concepts of press freedom. Further conflicts arose about UNESCO's administration and budgetary policies, leading to the United States leaving UNESCO in 1984, and Britain leaving in 1985.

more advanced system has the ability to set goals for itself in the sense of making changes in the pursuit of a larger repertory of existing goals, and of creating for itself new goals which it had never sought before. "Isolationist" countries, for example, can acquire large military establishments and extensive military goals or "security interests" in distant parts of the world, as England did from the sixteenth to the mid-twentieth century, and as the United States has done gradually since the 1890s, and more rapidly since 1945 and 1965. Conversely, countries may drop, gradually or quickly, some goals which formerly seemed paramount to them. The rulers of England in the sixteenth century dropped their three-centuries-old ambition to rule part of the continental territory that today is France. In the end, they abandoned Calais and began to pursue instead the goals of seapower and of power in regard to some of the lands of the New World. The partial shift of Russian and American attention since the late 1950s, away from competing mainly for influence and bases on this crowded planet and toward the array of goals implicit in the conquest of space (and eventually of the planets), may yet develop into another example of a change in national goals.

There may even be a change in the quality of goals and "vital interests" pursued by a nation. The Swiss in the sixteenth century dropped the pursuit of power over Lombardy; the Swedes in the eighteenth century dropped the pursuit of empire in the Baltic; the British between 1945 and 1965 gave up an empire that would contain by now about 800 million people. Each of these nations, once they did drop the pursuit and preservation of dominion over foreign populations, then shifted to an entirely different set of goals; the cultivation of their domestic affairs, of economic prosperity, and eventually of science, education, and the opportunities and problems of the welfare state.

If a system changes its goals repeatedly and successfully, then it is becoming in one sense potentially greater than the goals which it happens to pursue at any moment, for it may be capable of choosing, pursuing, and attaining greater or more worthwhile goals in the future. This may remind us in a sense of the warning of some philosophers and theologians against "idolatry"—that is, against the worship of passing and transitory things, of small tin gods, as if they were infinite and eternal. In world politics, too, any nation could be tempted toward the idolatry of some partial and transitory goals and interests, and toward forgetting that, if the nation survives, many of its goals will in all likelihood change.

The ability to set goals and to change them is likely to require material and human resources within the system. The greater the range of choice among old and new goals, the larger is likely to be the proportion of resources within the system that may have to be employed in making these choices and setting these new goals, and that may have to be reallocated for implementing their attainment. The latter (the proportion of resources within the system that are available for reallocation to new patterns of behavior) form an important element in the *learning capacity* of the system— that is, in its capacity to "learn" how to behave and to respond to events in its environment in new ways, or at least in different and more rewarding ways.

Some governments, some elite groups, and some peoples in particular historic periods have shown a markedly greater or lesser capacity to learn in this sense than have others. Of the Bourbon monarchs of France, it was said early in the nineteenth century that they had forgotten nothing and learned nothing, even after the social earthquake of the French Revolution; and they were soon thereafter eliminated from French politics. By contrast, the learning rate of the American government and people in the Great Depression of the 1930s, again during World War II, and once more during the "sputnik" crisis of the 1950s, turned out to be unusually high. A decade later, by early 1968, the military crisis of Vietnam, the monetary crisis of the gold value of the dollar, and the crisis of American cities, civil rights and race relations suggested once again that the repetition of past policies might not suffice, and that in the coming decade the political learning capacity of the American government and people might face another period of testing. Indeed the 1970s—with the end of the Vietnam war and the concomitant breakdown of consensus on the nation's foreign policy, the Nixon era that was ended by the Watergate fiasco, global energy crises, a major economic recession, as well as increasingly assertive Soviet and communist geopolitical moves—did bring the country close to a major political crisis, despite some promising political initiatives taken by the administration of President Jimmy Carter, coming to power in 1977. The replacement of the latter by a neoconservative administration in 1981 (with its emphasis on increasing the nation's military capabilities, a monetarist economic recovery program, and a confrontational foreign-policy stance) did resemble a return to the policies of earlier decades, but it indicated also that the American political system was still capable within limits of changing course.

If a very large or crucially important part of the resources of a system is reallocated to a new structural pattern of the system, and simultaneously to a new set or range of goals and patterns of behavior, we may say that the system has become *transformed*. If this transformation has occurred mainly through initiatives and resources from within the system itself, we may speak of a self-transforming system. This function of *self-transformation* is the sixth, and in a sense the highest, of our basic functions of a social system. Any organization or nation that has it, together with the ability to preserve also a significant degree of continuity and identity (pattern maintenance), is more likely to survive, to grow, and to develop, than any that lacks it. Many of the great religious and secular organizations of the world are examples of such self-transformation. The Catholic Church of the Crusaders and the militant popes of the twelfth and thirteenth centuries were very different from the small communities of early Christians who met in the catacombs, and from the state-supervised church of the days of the Emperor Constantine, and again from the present-day Roman Catholic Church that proclaimed at the Second Vatican Council the principle of religious liberty within the state. Yet a great deal of continuity of spirit within it has endured. The same is true of many nations: France, Russia, Japan, and the United States all are now very different from what they were in 1770 or 1780, yet a significant amount of identity and continuity has been preserved in each.

SOME CONCEPTS ABOUT POLITICS

Among the vast number of different human relations, just which ones are *political?* What does politics do that is not being done by other human activities or institutions?

Politics consists in the more or less incomplete control of human behavior through voluntary habits of *compliance* in combination with threats of probable *enforcement*. In its essence, politics is based on the interplay of habits of cooperation as modified by threats.

The *habits* of behaving, cooperating, obeying the law or the government, or respecting some decision as binding, tend to be voluntary for most people. After all, that is what habits are: they become part of our nature and of the way we more or less automatically act. Without these habits of the many, there could be no law and no government as we know them. Only because most drivers stick to the proper side of the road and stop at red lights can the traffic code be enforced at tolerable cost. Only because most people do not steal cars can the police protect our streets and parking lots against the relatively few who do. If a law is not obeyed voluntarily and habitually by, say, at least 90 percent of the people, it becomes either a dead letter or very expensive to enforce, or perhaps, like Prohibition in the 1920s, a noble but unreliable experiment. The voluntary or habitual compliance of the mass of the population is the invisible but very real basis of the power of every government.

But although this compliance is in large part voluntary, it is not wholly so. If it were entirely voluntary, we should be dealing not with politics but with the realm of folkways, custom, and morality. In the area of politics, the compliance habits of the many are preserved and reinforced with the help of the credible *probability of enforcement* against the few who may transgress the law or disobey the government.

Enforcement consists in the threat or the application of positive or negative sanctions—that is, in rewards or punishments. In practice, punishments are used more often than rewards. They are usually cheaper; some people enjoy applying them under any ideological pretext such as communism or anticommunism; and many people like to think that punishments are more reliable. Clearly, where most people are in the habit of obeying law or a government anyhow, it would seem costly and needless to offer them rewards for it; it seems cheaper and more efficient to threaten penalties for the few who deviate from the obedience or compliance of their fellows. Punishments may deter some of the few transgressors from repeating their offense, but it is more important that the fate of those few may deter some others from following their example.

Enforcement usually is not certain; most often it is only probable. But ordinarily the threat it poses is quite enough, together with the compliance habits of most of the population, to keep the proportion of serious transgressions down to a tolerable level. If, for example, six out of ten murderers are convicted and punished, this may be enough to deter many of that fraction of would-be murderers who contemplate murder as a calculated method to attain some gain. And if only one-fourth of automobile thefts were followed by convictions, this might suffice, together with the law-abiding habits of most people, to keep most automobiles unstolen and their theft insurance rates tolerably low. But even the most certain or the most cruel punishments, of course, do not deter that fraction of would-be murderers who are too thoughtless, too confident, or too passionately excited to care or think realistically about the chance of getting caught. Here is one of the several limits to the effectiveness of deterrence against murder in the lives of individuals, as well as against war in the lives of nations.

The conditions that decide the effectiveness of enforcement are thus much the same as those that decide the frequency of compliance (that is, of obedient or law-abiding behavior). First of all, this is to a very large extent the strength of the compliance habits of the bulk of the people and their willingness to give active support to the government in upholding its commands, or in upholding the law. In the second place, there are all the other conditions which influence the relative probabilities of the law-abiding versus the law-breaking behavior to which the threat of enforcement is being applied. If there is hunger among the poor, more people are likely to steal bread. Only in the third place come the size and efficiency of the enforcement apparatus: the skill and zeal of the officers and soldiers and of the judges and the police, and the quality of their weapons and equipment. And only in the last place comes the changing of rules, the passing of new laws, or the threatening of more severe punishments.

Mass habits of compliance, and general social conditions, however, which have the most powerful long-run effects on the behavior of the population, are most difficult to manipulate. Even the size, training, equipment, and morale of the enforcement personnel—the armed forces, the police, the judiciary, and to some extent the civil service—can be changed only slowly and at great cost. The weakest lever of control remains attractive, therefore, because it is the cheapest to move. Passing another law, or threatening a more severe penalty, or being less careful about evidence and about not punishing some innocent people, are much cheaper and quicker, and hence, despite their relatively slight effectiveness, they seem often more inviting than the longer and harder task of bringing about more fundamental changes in the situation.

Politics, then, is the interplay of enforcement threats, which can be changed relatively quickly, with the existing loyalties and compliance habits of the population, which are more powerful but which most often can only be changed much more slowly. Through this interplay of habitual compliance and probable enforcement, societies protect and modify their institutions, the allocation and reallocation of their resources, the distribution of the values, incentives, and rewards among their population, and the patterns of teamwork in which people cooperate in the production and reproduction of their goods, services, and lives.

Rule or Dominion

Once we keep our concept of politics clearly in mind, we can readily understand the two related political concepts of rule or dominion, and of power. By the *rule* or *dominion* of a leader, the German sociologist Max Weber meant the chance (that is, the probability) of being obeyed. Of two leaders or govern-ments, according to Weber's reasoning, the one more likely to be obeyed by a given population has more dominion over them than does the other.[3]

If we carry this reasoning somewhat further, we recognize what T. W. Adorno once called "the implicit mathematics in Max Weber's thought."[4] A probability, strictly speaking, is a number: it denotes the frequency, usually expressed as the percentage, with which events of a certain type (here, acts of obedience to the commands of the ruler) occur within a larger ensemble of events (here, the general behavior of the population). Rule, as defined by Weber, can therefore be expressed as a number; in principle at least it can be measured in quantitative terms.

At the same time, we can see on the one hand the close relation between Max Weber's idea of the chance or frequency of acts of obedience to the commands of a government, and on the other our own concept, discussed earlier as the rate of compliance (that is, the frequency of acts of compliance). The latter (the rate of compliance) is somewhat broader in that it includes also acts of passive submission, tolerance, or apathy, in addition to the more positive acts of obedience emphasized by Max Weber, wherever such more passively compliant behavior plays a significant part in determining the outcome of the political process.

Our concept of *habitual* compliance, however, is somewhat narrower than Max Weber's "chance of being obeyed," for our concept excludes mere acts of submission to the immediate threat of naked force. People obey a robber in a holdup, or a foreign army of occupation, as long as the intruder has a gun pointed at them. These are still cases of Max Weber's "rule" or "dominion," but they are processes of force, not of politics. They become political only insofar as the obedient behavior continues after the robber's, or the invader's, back is turned. Then only, in the interplay of remembered fear and continuing compliance, are we dealing once again with politics.

When we say that politics is that field of human affairs whereupon domination and habitual compliance overlap, we are already implying that politics, owing to its double nature, is apt to be an area of recurrent tension between centralization and decentralization. For domination or rule usually can be exercised more easily by centralized organizations, and threats of enforcement, too, can be manipulated more effectively from a single cen-ter. But the dependable habits of large numbers of people can be created rarely, if ever, through a single center of command alone, and they cannot be created quickly. Habits more often grow from a multitude of different but consonant experiences, repeated over time. The centralized use of threats or force rarely creates, therefore, a durable community of politically relevant habits; it is much more often such a community of habits that provides the possibilities for the exercise of centralized power.

---

[3]Max Weber, *Economy and Society: An Outline of Interpretive Sociology* (Berkeley, CA: Univ. of California Press, 1979).

[4]T. W. Adorno, oral communication, Fifteenth German Congress of Sociology (Max Weber Centenary), Heidelberg, May, 1964.

In a later part of our discussion we shall pursue these matters further, in the context of the processes that determine the size of nations, states, and other political units, and of the migration of power among the various levels of local, national, and supranational government. Here it is only worth noting that these processes, with their vast consequences, have their roots in this double nature of politics itself.

3

Power
and the
Nation-State

Recognizing the dual nature of politics also helps us to realize the limits of the concept of political power. Some brilliant writers have tried to develop a theory of politics, and particularly of the relations among states, largely or entirely based upon the notion of power—among them Niccolò Machiavelli and Thomas Hobbes, and in our own time Hans Morgenthau and Frederick L. Schuman. At the same time, the notion of power as the basis of international politics still is widespread in the popular press, and even in the foreign services and defense establishments of many countries. What then, we ask, is the element of truth contained in this notion, and what are its limits?

In our discussion we shall be concerned not only with the power of nations and of international organizations in the world, but also with the power of governments, of interest groups, of elites, and of individuals, insofar as any of these seems likely to affect significantly some outcome of international politics.

Power, put most crudely and simply, is the ability to prevail in conflict and to overcome obstacles. In this sense Lenin, before the Russian Revolution, posed to his followers as a key problem of politics the two-word question, "Who whom?" It meant: Who is to be the subject and master of actions and events, and who their object and victim? During the 1932 depression, a German protest song called up a related image: "We want to be hammers,

TABLE 1   **Percentage of Total Combat Munitions Output of the Main Belligerents, 1938–1943***

COUNTRY	1938		1939		1940		1941		1942		1943	
United States	6		4		7		14		30		40	
Canada	0		0		0		1		2		2	
Britain	6		10		18		19		15		13	
Soviet Union	27		31		23		24		17		15	
Total: Allied countries		39		45		48		58		64		70
Germany†	46		43		40		31		27		22	
Italy	6		4		5		4		3		1	
Japan	9		8		7		7		6		7	
Total: Axis countries		61		55		52		42		36		30
Grand Total:		100		100		100		100		100		100

*Includes aircraft, army ground ordnance and signal equipment, naval vessels, and related equipment.

†Includes occupied territories.

Source: Klaus E. Knorr, *The War Potential of Nations* (copyright © 1956 by Princeton University Press) Table 1, p. 34, "Percentage of total combat output of the main belligerents; 1938–1943." Reprinted by permission of Princeton University Press.

not anvils," it announced. Who is stronger and who is weaker? Who will get his or her way and who will have to give in?

Such questions as these, when asked about many possible or actual encounters among a limited number of competitors, lead to rank lists— such as the rankings of players in tennis or chess tournaments, of baseball clubs in the world series, of chickens in the peck order of the chicken yard, and of great powers in world politics. The fewer the recent actual encounters that have occurred, of course, the larger the extent to which such rank lists must be built up from hypotheses based upon the past performances and present or expected resources of the contestants.

THE BASIS OF POWER

Power Potential as Inferred from Resources

An example of the relative power potential of two coalitions of nations is given in Table 1. Here, power of the Allied and the Axis countries in World War II is measured, or at least indicated, by the percentage of total munitions which each side produced during each year.

The table reveals that the Axis powers produced far more munitions than the Allied countries in 1938, 1939, and 1940, but that their lead diminished in 1940 and was lost decisively in 1941 and 1942. After this turning point, the Axis powers fell ever further behind until their total collapse in 1945. Winston Churchill summed it up in an image: "the hinge of fate" had swung against them.

A simple ranking of forty-three countries in terms of their short-term military power—insofar as it is indicated by military spending and military power—is presented in Table 2 and Table 3. We may note that in 1983, no one country had more than one-third of total military expenditures; even the United States had only 29.3 percent.

An example of a hypothetical ranking of the long-term power of the major nations for the periods 1950–1973 and 1990–2010, respectively, can be given from calculations (Table 4) of a West German physicist.

The projections to 1990 and 2010 in Table 4 are based on figures of the expected growth of per-capita steel and energy production, and of total population, in each country. For China of 1990 (2010), a population of about 1,100,000,000 (1,575,000,000) and an annual (per-capita) steel output of about 176 pounds (544 pounds) or roughly one-sixth (one-half) the 1973 level of the USSR and one-twelfth (one-fourth) the 1973 level of Japan, are projected. Whether these projections will turn out to be realistic for 1990 (2010), or even any later time, no one, of course, can be sure—particularly after setbacks to the Chinese economic growth in the early 1960s and through the Cultural Revolution in the 1970s. However, for 1982, China's population was estimated at over 1 billion, and its economy resumed its growth after the reforms of the late 1970s and the 1980s. In any case, it seems noteworthy that in the projections, too, the power of the strongest single country, in 1963 and 1973, as well as in 1990 and 2010, is rated as well below half the total power of the first seven countries. Thus, in both periods, the strongest single country will still represent only a minority in terms of world power.

The aggregate power resources of a nation are sometimes called its "power base," since they can be thought of as the basis upon which potential power can be converted to a greater or lesser extent into actuality. A related but somewhat different notion is the concept of a "base value," as defined by Harold D. Lasswell and Abraham Kaplan. According to their reasoning, a power base for action A (where A could be a person or a country) is an amount of some value for actor B, which is under A's control. Actor A, that is to say, controls some possible increase or decrease in B's wealth, well-being, or enjoyment of respect. Since B desires more of this value which A controls, B must try to please A, in order to induce A to let him or her have more of this value. Thus if a developing country needs and wants economic aid to improve its technology, or if a hungry country needs wheat in order to stave off famine, and if the United States or the Soviet Union controls some of the available supplies, then the United States (or the Soviet Union) will have a *power base* for exercising influence over these more needy countries.

It is, of course, another question how effectively the United States government, or the Soviet government, will use this power base or "base value" so as to acquire actual influence and power over the behavior of some or all of those countries in regard to some "scope value"—such as a favorable vote in the United Nations—which the poorer countries control and the richer countries want. A's power in all such cases is based on three things: first, on B's relative poverty and want in regard to some base value

TABLE 2   The Domain of National Power in Terms of World Military Expenditures, 1983
(*At constant 1980 $ prices*)

COUNTRY		U.S. $ (BILLIONS)		PERCENTAGE OF WORLD	
World		637.0		100.0	
1. United States		186.5		29.3	
2. Soviet Union		137.6		21.6	
3. China		35.8		5.6	
4. United Kingdom		29.4		4.6	
5. France		28.0		4.4	
6. Germany, West		27.4		4.3	
Subtotal:	1–6		444.7		69.8
7. Saudi Arabia		23.4		3.7	
8. Japan		10.9		1.7	
9. Italy		10.9		1.7	
10. Argentina		7.3		1.2	
11. Iraq*		6.9		1.1	
12. Israel*		5.8		0.9	
Subtotal:	7–12		65.2		10.3
13. India		5.5		0.9	
14. Canada		5.4		0.9	
15. Netherlands		5.3		0.8	
16. Poland*		5.3		1.1	
17. Iran		5.2		0.8	
18. Germany, East		5.0		0.8	
19. Spain		4.5		0.7	
20. Australia		4.4		0.7	
21. Korea, South		4.2		0.7	
22. Korea, North		4.1		0.6	
23. Sweden		3.9		0.6	
24. Belgium		3.7		0.6	
Subtotal:	13–24		56.5		7.3
25. Taiwan		3.4		0.5	
26. Turkey		3.2		0.5	
27. Czechoslovakia*		3.2		0.5	
28. South Africa		2.8		0.4	
29. Greece		2.8		0.4	
30. Yugoslavia		2.4		0.4	
31. Chile		2.2		0.4	
32. Switzerland		2.1		0.3	
33. Malaysia		2.1		0.3	
34. United Arab Emirates*		2.1		0.4	
35. Pakistan		1.9		0.3	
36. Indonesia		1.9		0.3	
37. Egypt		1.9		0.3	
38. Syria		1.9		0.3	
39. Morocco		1.8		0.3	
40. Oman		1.8		0.3	
41. Norway		1.8		0.3	

TABLE 2 (*cont.*)

COUNTRY		U.S. $ (BILLIONS)		PERCENTAGE OF WORLD
42. Brazil		1.7		0.3
43. Nigeria		1.5		0.2
Subtotal:	25–43		42.5	6.9
Subtotal:	1–24		566.4	88.9
Total in Table			608.9	95.6
Rest of World:			28.1	4.4
Grand Total: World			637.0	100.0%

*1982 data from *The Military Balance 1984/1985* (London: International Institute for Strategic Studies), 1984, p. 140.

Source: *SIPRI Yearbook, 1984; World Armaments and Disarmament* (Stockholm: International Peace Research Institute, 1984; and Philadelphia: Taylor & Francis, 1984), p. 117.

of which *A* controls a relevant supply; second, on *B*'s control of a relevant supply of some scope value which *A* desires and which *A* is trying to get by using its power over *B;* and finally, *A*'s skill and effectiveness in converting the potential of its power base into actual power over *B*'s behavior.[1]

The Weight of Power as Inferred from Results

Power potential is a rough estimate of the material and human resources for power. Indirectly, it can be used to infer how many and how great successes in a power contest a country ought to have, if it uses its resources to advantage. It is possible, however, to reverse this calculation. We can ask: How successful has this actor (this leader, this government, or this nation) been in changing some outcome in the outside world? And we can then infer the "weight" of power from the amount of success. (The four chief dimensions or aspects of power are its weight, domain, range, and scope; of these, weight is closest to the intuitive notion which most of us have when we think of power.)

The weight of the power or influence of an actor over some process is the extent to which that person can change the probability of its outcome. This can be measured most easily wherever we are dealing with a repetitive class of similar outcomes, such as votes in the United Nations Assembly. If it should turn out, as a hypothetical example, that in that Assembly those motions supported by the United States have been passing on the average three times out of four, or with a probability of 75 percent, while those motions not supported by the United States have been passed only 25 percent of the time, then we might say that the support of the United States can shift the chances for the success of a motion in the United Nations Assembly on the average from 25 to 75 percent—that is, by 50 percentage

[1]For more extended discussions see H. D. Lasswell and A. Kaplan, *Power and Society* (New Haven: Yale University Press, 1950), and K. W. Deutsch, "Some Quantitative Constraints on Value Allocation in Society and Politics," *Behavioral Science*, 11, no. 4 (July, 1966), pp. 245–252.

TABLE 3   The Domain of National Power in Terms of Military Manpower 1984*

COUNTRY	NUMBER IN ARMED FORCES (THOUSANDS)	ESTIMATED RESERVES (THOUSANDS)
1. Soviet Union	5,115	5,300
2. China	4,000	5,000
3. United States	2,136	1,440
4. India	1,120	200
5. Korea, North	785	3,300
6. Iraq	643	75
7. Korea, South	622	4,830
8. Turkey	602	836
9. Iran	555	223†
10. Germany, West	495	750
11. Taiwan	484	2,970
12. Pakistan	479	513
13. France	471	393
14. Egypt	460	335
15. Italy	375	799
16. Syria	363	460
17. Spain	330	1,085
18. United Kingdom	326	285
19. Poland	323	500
20. Indonesia	281	—
21. Brazil**	274	1,115
22. Japan	245	44
23. Yugoslavia	240	500
24. Czechoslovakia	207	525
25. Greece	178	350
26. Germany, East	172	635
27. Argentina**	153	250
28. Morocco	144	—
29. Israel	141	328
30. Nigeria	133	—
31. Malaysia	125	61
32. Netherlands	102	175
33. Chile**	96	24
34. Belgium	94	179
35. South Africa	83	157
36. Canada	83	18
37. Australia	72	33
38. Sweden	66	736
39. Saudi Arabia	52	—
40. United Emirates	43	—
41. Norway	37	295
42. Oman	22	—
43. Switzerland	20	625
Total: 1–43		22,747

TABLE 3   (*cont.*)

COUNTRY	NUMBER IN ARMED FORCES (THOUSANDS)	ESTIMATED RESERVES (THOUSANDS)
Rest of World:	2,990	
World Total:	25,737	

Note: * Selected from ninety-eight countries in *Military Balance.* Includes those with defense expenditures in excess of $1.5 billion. Ranked on basis of armed-forces size.

† Source provides estimated range of 220–225 thousand.

** 1983 data for South American countries (*Military Balance*).

The definitions and estimates, often inflated, for paramilitary forces vary from country to country. In six countries, the USSR, the People's Republic of China, North Korea, South Korea, Iran, and Yugoslavia, paramilitary forces are estimated in the millions and may play a significant role in defense against foreign invasion.

Source: The Military Balance 1984/1985 (London: International Institute for Strategic Studies, 1984), p. 140.

points. These 50 percentage points then would be a rough measure of the average weight of the power of the United States in the Assembly during the period under study. (The measure is a rough one, and it may understate the real influence of the United States, since many potential motions opposed by the United States might seem so hopeless to their would-be sponsors that they might not even be proposed, and thus might not enter our statistic.)

The calculation or estimate of the weight of power is more difficult when we are dealing with a single event. What was the power of the atom bomb dropped on Hiroshima on August 6, 1945 (or of the one which cremated Nagasaki three days later) in speeding up the surrender of Japan and in shortening World War II? An outstanding expert on Japan, Professor Edwin O. Reischauer, who in 1961–1967 was United States Ambassador to Japan, concludes that the bomb shortened the war by only a few days.[2] In order to make any such judgment, it is necessary to imagine that the occasion for the event—the dropping of the bomb at a time when Japan already was largely defeated and exhausted, and its government was seeking for a way to surrender—occurred many times. One then would have to try to imagine what would have happened on the average in all those imagined cases in which such a bomb *would* have been dropped, as against the average result in all those imagined cases in which this had *not* been done.

This seems far-fetched, but it is not. Indeed, it is not very different from the reasoning of an engineer as to what caused the breakdown of a particular bridge, or the reasoning of a physician as to what caused the death or the recovery of a particular patient. In all these cases, in order to estimate the effect of what *was* done—and perhaps to estimate what *ought* to have been

[2]E. O. Reischauer, *The United States and Japan*, rev. ed. (New York: Viking Press, 1962), p. 240.

TABLE 4   Some Hypothetical Rank Orderings of the Power Potential of Major Countries*

	1950		1963		1973		1990 (PROJECTION)*		2010 (PROJECTION)*	
1.	U.S.	100	U.S.	100	U.S.	100	U.S.	100	USSR	105
2.	USSR	31	USSR	68	USSR	83	USSR	96	U.S.	100
3.	Britain	13	China	26	China	34	China	43	Japan	50
4.	German Fed. Rep.	10	German Fed. Rep.	14	Japan	28	Japan	42	China	48
5.	France	5	Japan	12	German Fed. Rep.	13	German Fed. Rep.	13	German Fed. Rep.	12
6.	Japan	4	Britain	11	Britain	8	Canada	8	Canada	9
7.	India	3	India	7	India	7	India	6	Italy	6
	Subtotal (1–7)	166		238		273		308		330
8.	China	3	France	6	Canada	6	Britain	6	India	6
9.	Poland	3	Poland	4	France	4	Italy	6	Poland	6
10.	Canada	2	Canada	3	Poland	3	Poland	5	France	5
11.	Czechoslovakia	1	Italy	3	Italy	3	France	4	Britain	4
12.	Italy	1	Czechoslovakia	3	Czechoslovakia	3	Czechoslovakia	3	Czechoslovakia	2
	Subtotal (8–12)	10		19		24		26		23

*Based on the average of the sum of energy production and steel output, times cube root of population, setting U.S. figure equal 100. Formula from Wilhelm Fucks, *Formein zur Macht: Prognosen über Völker, Wirtschaft, Potentiale*. (Stuttgart: Deutsche Verlagsanstalt, 1965), Figs. 37–38, pp. 129–31. These projections for 1990 and 2010 have been calculated on the assumption that the actual rates of growth 1963–1973 would continue without change. The real figures may turn out to be higher or lower. (K.W.D.) Data from *U.N. Statistical Yearbooks* of 1952, 1959, 1964, 1965, 1970, and 1974, and *U.N.Statistical Papers* Series J, No. 1.

done in terms of "good practice"—we convert the unique event into a member of a repetitive class of hypothetical events quite similar to it. We then try to estimate the extent and probability of alternative outcomes in the presence and in the absence, respectively, of the action or condition the power of which we wish to gauge; and we then infer the power of the actor or actors in the situation from the power of the act or the condition they control.

Power considered in this way is much the same thing as causality; and the weight of the power of an actor or actors is the same as the weight of those among the causes of an outcome which are under their control.[3]

Modern governments, compared to those of past centuries, have greatly increased the weight of their power over their own populations. Taxes are collected, soldiers drafted, laws enforced, and lawbreakers arrested, all with a much higher probability than most medieval rulers could have dreamed of. By the same token, the weight of the power of governments of industrially advanced countries usually is much greater than is the case in contemporary countries which are in the early stages of industrial development. Also, among governments of the latter, the weight of domestic power varies widely.

In world politics, on the contrary, the weight of the power of most governments, and particularly of the great powers, has been declining ever since 1945. No government today has as much control over the probable outcome of world affairs as had Great Britain, say, between 1870 and 1935. At present, Britain cannot control its former colonies; the United States cannot control France or Cuba; the Soviet Union cannot control Yugoslavia or China; and China cannot control its neighbors. The attempt by the Soviets to control the politics of Afghanistan through a military occupation in December 1979 seems to provide no lasting guarantee of success. The reasons for this decline in the weight of power of most of the large countries will occupy us later, but the fact seems worth noting now.

On closer inspection, the weight of power may turn out to include two different concepts. The first deals with the ability to *reduce* the probability of an outcome *not* desired by an actor. In domestic politics we sometimes speak of "veto groups" who can prevent or make unlikely the passage of some piece of legislation they dislike. In international politics we find a very considerable veto power formally accorded the five permanent members of the United Nations Security Council by the United Nations Charter. Less formally, we may speak of the power of a nation to deny some territory, or region of influence, to some other government or ideology. Thus the United States in the 1950s successfully denied South Korea to its North Korean attackers, and it denied throughout the 1960s much of South Vietnam to the Viet Cong.

It should be easy to see why this is so. The specific result which we may wish to prevent may not be very probable in the first place. Suppose that a communist guerrilla campaign or a left-leaning political movement in an

[3]Cf. Robert A. Dahl, unpublished paper at the annual meeting of the New England Political Science Assn., Northhampton, Mass., April 25, 1966; and "Power," in David L. Sills (ed.), *International Encyclopedia of the Social Sciences*, vol. 12 (New York: Macmillan, 1968), pp. 405–415.

Asian, African, or Latin American country had roughly one chance in three, or 33 percent, of establishing there eventually a stable communist regime. In that case, an anticommunist intervention by a foreign power carried out with limited power—say with a weight of about 28 percent—could reduce these chances of success for the guerrillas from 33 percent to only 5 percent, and create a 95 percent, or 19:1, probability of their failure. The outcome, which is already moderately improbable, thus can be made highly improbable by the application of even a relatively limited amount of power. In such situations, the change in the probabilities of this particular outcome will seem to us quite drastic, and this limited amount of power will seem to us to have changed considerable uncertainty into near certainty, and thus to have produced spectacular results. Such was the case with British and American support of the Greek royalist government against the communist national liberation movement in the mid-1940s, and the CIA-supported coup against the government of Jacobo Arbenz in Guatemala in 1954, or Prince Sihanouk in Cambodia in 1970.

If the success of the guerrillas and their backers were already highly probable, however—say about 95 percent—then even the negative power of their adversaries might be quite limited. If the weight of their opposing intervention were again 28 percent, it could reduce the probability of an eventual guerrilla victory only from 95 percent down to 67 percent, leaving the guerrillas still with a 2:1 chance of winning. The unsuccessful outcome of the limited United States support for pro-Western factions in Angola from 1975 to the present may have been due at least in part to such unfavorable balances of local strength and motivation. Such adverse local conditions also limited the weight of the power of the United States in its unsuccessful attempts to support Chiang Kai-shek against Mao Zedong's communist movement in the Chinese civil war after 1945; President Batista of Cuba against Fidel Castro in the late 1950s; the South Vietnamese governments from 1965 to 1975; or Shah Reza Palevi against the Ayatollah Khomeini's Islamic movement in Iran in 1978. Similarly, Chinese and Soviet influence crumbled in Indonesia in 1965, in Egypt in 1973, and in Bangladesh in 1975.

The same degree of power also produces still less impressive results when it is applied to promoting an outcome which is fairly improbable in the first place. If we wish to produce a stable constitutional and democratic regime in our imaginary strife-torn Asian, African, or Latin American country, then we might have to remember that only about one out of every twenty of the very poor countries in the world has a stable democratic and law-abiding form of government. India has been one of these rare examples during the last two decades, but there are not very many others. Rather, the great range of alternatives to democracy—such as dictatorships, military juntas, corrupt oligarchies behind constitutional façades, foreign occupation or colonial administration, civilian one-party regimes, successions of *coups d'etat* or civil wars, or combinations and successions of all these—have been much more frequent. But if the chance of democracy in a recently emerged country is only 5 percent, then the application of power of a weight of 28 percent would still produce only a 33 percent probability for the successful establishment of a democratic regime in that country, and would leave us with a 2:1 chance for its failure.

In fact, even this calculation is far too optimistic, for it has assumed without justification that power to promote one outcome can be transformed without loss into the same amount of power to produce another. We all know very well that this is simply not true. The power to knock down a person does not give us the power to teach that person to play the piano or to do calculus or figure skating. The power to bomb and burn a village cannot be completely or easily transformed into the power to win the sympathies of the inhabitants, or to govern it with their consent, and even less can it be transformed into the power to produce among them the many skills, values, and freely given loyalties which are essential for democratic government.

The more highly specific a positive outcome is, the more are the alternatives excluded by it. Hence it usually is more improbable, and thus more difficult to make it highly probable by the application of limited power. Limited power is most effective, therefore, when used negatively as veto power, or as power of denial against some highly specific outcome, because then it is being used (in effect) to increase the already considerable probability of the entire range of possible alternatives to it, with much less or no regard as to which particular alternative will materialize.

The power to increase the probability of a specific positive outcome is the power both of *goal attainment* and of *control* over one's environment. Like all goal attainment and all control, it necessarily implies a high degree of self-control on the part of the actor. A charging elephant can smash down a large obstacle, but it cannot thread a needle. Indeed, it cannot make a right-angle turn within a three-foot radius. The greater the brute power, mass, speed, and momentum of the elephant, the harder it is for him to control his own motions, and the less precise his control becomes. Most of us know something similar from driving: the bigger, heavier, faster, and more powerful our car is, the harder it is to steer. An attempt to measure its power in terms of its performance would give us, therefore, at least two different numbers or ratings—a high one for its power to accelerate, but a low one for its power to stop or to turn.

Does something similar hold for the power of governments and nations? The larger the country, the more numerous its population, and the larger the proportions of its population and resources which have been mobilized for the pursuit of some policy (and, we may add, the more intense and unreserved their emotional commitment to that policy), the greater is likely to be the power of that country and its government to overcome any obstacles or resistance in its path. But national policies usually require more than merely overcoming resistance; often they aim at specific positive results. They often require, therefore, the pursuit of some constant goal through a sequence of changing tactics, or even the enhancement of some basic value through a succession of changing goals. The more people and resources have been committed to the *earlier* tactics, policies, or goals, however, and the more intensely and unreservedly so, the greater is the wealth of the interests, careers, reputations, and emotions thus dedicated, and the harder it is for any member of the government, or even for the entire government, to propose a change. Unless substantial and timely precautions have been taken, therefore, governments may become prisoners of their past policies, and their power may blindly push them into a logjam or a trap.

The United States succeeded in overthrowing the left-leaning government of Guatemala in 1954 and of the Dominican Republic in 1965. The U. S. government under President Nixon considered its interest to have been served by the domestic coup of General Pinochet in Chile in 1973, which it at least encouraged. Another case of successful intervention was the U.S. landing on the island of Grenada—with a total population of 114,000—in 1983. The United States found itself unable, however, to control events first in Cuba (1959–1961), then in Vietnam (1965–1975), and more recently in Iran (1978–1980) and in Lebanon (1984–1985). Similarly Soviet power was not able to preserve stable and dependable Soviet influence in Indonesia (1965), in Egypt (1973), and in Afghanistan (1980–). Current United States engagements in the politics of Nicaragua and El Salvador, so far, have not led to a successful conclusion. The main danger of all such engagements, on whichever side, is that they may escalate into large conflicts, which in the end no one can control.

These dangers tend to grow with the amount of national power and with the intensity of efforts to increase it. Ordinarily these dangers of partial loss of self-control are greater for large nations than for smaller ones, for dictatorships than for democracies, and for times of war and near-war than for times of peace. If these dangers are not guarded against, the weight of power in the long run may in part become self-defeating, or self-destructive.

SOME OTHER DIMENSIONS OF POWER

Domain, Range, and Scope

Over whom is power exercised? The answer to this question consists in the *domain* of power—the set of persons whose probable behavior is significantly changed by its application. The domain of the power of a village chief consists roughly in the inhabitants of his village; the domain of the government of Sweden is largely limited to Sweden but also includes Swedish ships and Swedish citizens abroad. The domains of the government of the United States and of the Soviet Union are limited in many ways to their respective countries—and to their ships, troops, bases, and citizens abroad—but in other and important ways they affect, at least indirectly, each other's behavior, and the fate of most of the world.

Some powers may have domains that cut across national boundaries in other ways. Insofar as Roman Catholics follow the pronouncements of their church in matters of political importance, or in matters where politics and religious doctrine overlap (such as in regard to public policy about population growth and the teaching of birth-control methods), the political power or influence of the Pope reaches into many countries. The same is true for many other religions, since all great world religions teach, explicitly or by implication, that there is a higher moral law and a higher moral authority than the changing policies of any nation-state. Every such religion, in interpreting this moral law, creates opportunities for the exercise of moral leadership, influence, and quite possibly power across the boundaries of nations.

Something similar holds, of course, for some secular philosophies. The degree to which communists in many countries used to follow the directions and policies of Moscow through every change of course has been notorious. Since the emergence of several variations of communist doctrine—such as the Chinese, Yugoslav, and Russian versions, each of which is backed by an established government, as well as the more diverse and multinational Eurocommunist movement—the degree of compliance of communist movements abroad with the commands of any single center of direction has lessened perceptibly. This became especially evident after the dissolution of the coordinating Communist Information Bureau in 1956, but thus far Moscow's influence over its immediate sphere has by no means disappeared altogether. Thus, when the Czechs tried to establish a more liberal socialist version of their own, Soviet tanks and troops occupied their country, in August 1968, and installed a compliant local faction in power. The independent Polish labor movement *Solidarnosc,* too, advocated independent labor unions, demanded improvements in living conditions, and in effect contested the Communist Party's monopoly in the state's organization. It was crushed by a preemptive military self-occupation by the Polish armed forces in December 1981, against a background of extensive Warsaw Pact maneuvers and close Soviet diplomatic control of the Polish government. To a lesser degree, adherents of other philosophies or ideologies, such as conservatives, monarchists, liberals, socialists, existentialists, and adherents of free private enterprise, all sometimes try to exercise some influence or power over congenial or susceptible groups in other countries, and thus to extend the domain of their power.

Essentially, the domain of political power always is the collection of people that are subject and obedient to it. It is more loosely referred to as the geographic area in which power is exercised over most of the population. It is important to be clear which usage is intended. The first (and preferable) meaning of the domain of the power of a government includes only those persons in a territory who obey the government's commands, or at least passively comply with them; while the second, a geographic definition of the domain of a government, would include even the guerrillas on its territory fighting against its rule—at least so long as these guerrillas do not succeed in converting some districts into a stable domain of their own. Thus, while the Soviet Union may have a firm domain of power in terms of the geographic area of Eastern Europe and the Warsaw Pact, it can by no means be assured that most of the population in this territory will obey its commands, or even comply with them only passively.

A third possible meaning of the domain of power might include not only the persons subject or obedient to it, but also those amounts of land, capital goods, and general resources controlled by them. To have power over a hundred paupers, by this reasoning, is less than to have power over a hundred well-equipped people with ample resources at their disposal. This third view of the domain of power comes close to our earlier notion of power defined in terms of a collection of resources.

All three notions of the domain of power have been used if we neglect, for the moment, the possibility of disaffected and rebellious populations and districts in a country; for then we can measure the direct domain of its government in the first sense of the concept by its population; in the second sense by its area; and in the third sense, at least roughly, by its gross national product.

A comparison of the domains of the power of some of the main countries of the world in terms of the first concept of domain (i.e., population) is given in Table 5. This neglects, of course, the populations outside the political boundaries of each country which may yet be subject to its power, but it is still a first approximation worth considering.

We obtain a somewhat different rank list from the geographic concept of domain, as shown in Table 6.

The third rank list of domains of national power, and perhaps in some ways the most realistic one, is in terms of gross national product, as shown in Table 7. Here we find something of a surprise. Although both the United States and the Soviet Union have continued to grow, their joint share in world income has declined, from 48 percent in 1962 to only 34 percent in 1982. In this respect the two "superpowers" are less "super" than they used to be.

The concept of domain could be extended to include the domains of knowledge, technology, and weapons systems. How large a share of the world's scientists at the Ph.D. level or its equivalent are in the domain of this or that government? The United States, with over 100,000 scientists at this level, may have more than one quarter of the scientists in the world. The share of the Soviet Union may well be of the same order of magnitude. Together, the governments of these two giant countries may have under their sway well above half the scientists on this planet—a larger share than their respective proportions of world income. A similar calculation has been carried out in regard to the average annual share of each country in the scientific papers published in the world. The results of this calculation are presented in Table 8. They yield more similar national rank orders and percentage shares than would the counts of scientists, and they may serve as cross-checks and supplements for missing data. Here they show a continuing strength of Britain and a serious lag in Soviet publications.

Another extension of the concept of domain would apply it to weapons systems. Here again, the concept of domain overlaps the concept of resources. Which governments control what sizes of armies, navies, air forces, rocket forces, and nuclear weapons systems? What are the shares of a particular government in the respective world totals for each of these? Some extremely rough and tentative estimates for nuclear weapons are presented in Table 9.

This table shows how, under its assumptions, the rank order of nuclear powers seems to remain constant until a power reaches the assumed

TABLE 5   The Domain of National Power in Terms of Population, 1960–1983

COUNTRY		POPULATION IN MILLIONS			PERCENTAGE OF WORLD TOTALS		
		1960		1983	1960		1983
1. China		654		1040	22		22
2. India		428		732	14		16
Subtotal	1–2:		1082		1773	36		38
3. Soviet Union		214		273	7		6
4. United States		181		235	6		5
Subtotal	3–4:		395		508	13		11
5. Indonesia		93		159	3		3
6. Brazil		72		130	2		3
7. Japan		94		119	3		3
8. Bangladesh		51		95	2		2
9. Pakistan		46		90	2		2
10. Nigeria		44		89	1		2
11. Mexico		36		75	1		2
Subtotal	5–11:		436		757	14		17
12. Germany, West		55		61	2		1
13. Vietnam		30		57	1		1
14. Italy		59		57	2		1
15. United Kingdom		53		56	2		1
16. France		46		55	2		1
Subtotal	12–16:		234		286	9		5
17. Philippines		28		52	1		1
18. Thailand		26		49	1		1
19. Turkey		28		47	1		1
20. Egypt		26		46	1		1
21. Iran		22		42	1		1
22. South Korea		25		40	1		1
23. Spain		30		38	1		1
24. Burma		22		37	1		1
25. Poland		30		37	1		1
Subtotal	17–25:		237		388	9		9
Grand Total:	1–25:	2389		3712	81		80
Rest of World:		609		973	19		20
World:		2993		4685	100		100

Note: Eight Third World countries—China, India, Indonesia, Brazil, Bangladesh, Pakistan, Nigeria, and Mexico—comprised in 1983 more than one-half of humankind.

Source: 1983 data from *United Nations Monthly Bulletin of Statistics, March 1985* (New York: United Nations, 1985), p. 1; 1960 data from C. L. Taylor and D. Jodice, *World Handbook of Political and Social Indicators,* 3rd ed. (New Haven: Yale University Press, 1983), p. 91.

saturation level of more than 10,000 nuclear warheads. However, it also shows, under the same assumptions, five countries already having a nuclear "veto power" by 1967—each of them having by then, that is to say, the ability to deter an attack upon itself by threatening to inflict unacceptable

TABLE 6   The Domain of National Power in Terms of Land Area, 1980

RANK		AREA IN MILLIONS OF SQUARE KILOMETERS		PERCENTAGE OF WORLD TOTAL*	
1. Soviet Union		22.4		17.0	
2. Canada		10.0		8.0	
3. China		9.6		7.0	
4. United States		9.4		7.0	
5. Brazil		8.5		6.0	
6. Australia		7.7		6.0	
Subtotal:	1–6		67.6		51.0
7. India		3.3		2.0	
8. Argentina		2.8		2.0	
9. Sudan		2.5		2.0	
10. Algeria		2.4		2.0	
11. Zaire		2.3		2.0	
12. Saudi Arabia		2.2		2.0	
13. Indonesia		2.0		1.5	
14. Mexico		2.0		1.5	
15. Libya		1.8		1.0	
16. Iran		1.6		1.0	
17. Mongolian People's Republic		1.6		1.0	
18. Peru		1.3		1.0	
Subtotal:	7–18		25.8		19.0
Grand Total:	1–18		93.4		70.0
Rest of World:			39.6		30.0
World Total:			133.0		100.0

*The percentage of world total uses a total land area of 132,951,000 sq. km. (rounded to 133.0), the sum of the land areas of the 142 countries listed in *World Military and Social Expenditures, 1983*. In *World Geographic Atlas: A Composite of Man's Environment,* designed and edited by Herbert Bayer (Chicago: printed privately for Container Corp. of America, 1953), pp. 24–25, we find cited an aggregate figure of 145,616,303.49 sq. km. (rounded to 145.6) for total land area of the world (including Antarctica but opposed to total water area of the world). If one were to use this second figure, the changes in percentage share of the various countries are unimportant. All figures and totals are subject to rounding errors.

Source: Ruth Leger Sivard, *World Military and Social Ependitures, 1983* (Washington, DC: World Priorities, 1983), pp. 33–35.

damage upon its attackers. The fact is, even a dozen nuclear warheads are enough to threaten credibly the destruction of the capital city and much of the central government and metropolitan elite of the enemy country—a degree of damage which most sane governments could not consider an acceptable price for the pursuit of any external or distant objective. But at the same time, not even a threat with 10,000 warheads may suffice to force a country into complete capitulation in its central area and thus into the

TABLE 7 The Domain of National Power in Terms of Gross National Product, 1962, 1973, and 1982

RANK 1982	COUNTRY	GNP IN BILLIONS OF CURRENT DOLLARS			PERCENTAGE OF WORLD GNP			CHANGE IN PERCENTAGE SHARE OF WORLD INCOME	
		1962	1973	1982	1962	1973	1982	1962–1973	1973–1982
1.	United States	556	1,295	3,047	33	27	24	−6	−3
2.	Soviet Union*	256	624	1,212	15	13	10	−2	−3
1–2	Subtotal:	812	1,919	4,259	48	40	34	−8	−6
3.	Japan	56	416	1,190	3	9	10	+6	+1
4.	West Germany	89	349	757	5	7	6	+2	−1
5.	France	79	257	654	4	5	5	+1	0
6.	United Kingdom	89	172	536	5	4	4	−1	0
7.	Italy	53	137	382	3	3	3	0	0
8.	China	60	180	302	4	4	2	0	−2
3–8	Subtotal:	426	1,511	3,794	24	32	30	+8	+8
9.	Canada	39	118	278	2	2	2	0	0
10.	Brazil	15	63	274	1	1	2	0	+1
11.	Spain	13	60	204	1	1	2	0	+1

12. Mexico	15	48	200	1	1	2	0		+1
13. India	33	74	184	2	1	1	0		−1
14. Australia	19	57	169	1	1	1	0		0
15. Saudi Arabia	2	26	158	0	1	1	+1		0
16. Netherlands	16	60	154	1	1	1	0		0
17. Poland*	21	62	140	1	1	1	0		0
18. East Germany*	17	48	121	84	85	79	+1		−6
19. Sweden	16	50	115	16	15	21	−1		+6
Subtotal: 9–19	206	666	1,857	100	100	100		100	
Grand Total: 1–19	1,444	4,096	9,910	1	1	1	1		0	0
Rest of World:	276	731	2,505	1	1	1	1		0	0
World:	1,718	4,832	12,415	12	13	15		1	+1	+2

*In the cases of the USSR, Poland, and East Germany, 1982 data were not available. 1980 data were used from Ruth Leger Sivard, *World Military and Social Expenditures, 1983* (Washington, DC: World Priorities, 1983).

Source: Data for 1962 in K. W. Deutsch, *Nationalism and Social Communication*, rev. ed. (Cambridge, MA; MIT Press, 1966), p. 67 (estimated in gross domestic product for 1962 and 1973 data). Data for 1973 from R. L. Sivard, *World Military and Social Expenditures, 1976* (Leesburg, VA: WMSE Publications, 1976), Table 3. Data for 1982 from *World Bank Atlas, 1985* (Washington, DC: The World Bank, 1985), p. 6. Due to inflation, one dollar in 1982 had the purchasing power of about $0.34 in 1962, and $0.51 in 1973. Purchasing power of the dollar calculated from GNP Deflator in *International Financial Statistics Yearbook, 1984* (Washington, DC: International Monetary Fund, 1984), pp. 596–597. By mid-1987, the international value of the dollar had fallen by another one-third against 1982.

TABLE 8   Contributions to World Scientific Authorship, 1967–1969

RANK		PERCENTAGE OF WORLD TOTAL 1967–69		1983		CHANGE
1. United States		41.7		41.5		−.2
2. United Kingdom		10.2		8.7		−1.5
3. Soviet Union		8.2		6.6		−1.6
Subtotal:	1–3		60.1		56.8	−3.3
4. West Germany		6.9		5.2		−1.7
5. France		5.4		4.4		−1.0
6. Japan		4.2		5.4		.8
7. Canada		3.4		4.4		1.0
8. India		2.3		2.2		−.1
9. Italy		2.0		2.0		.0
Subtotal:	4–9		24.2		23.6	−.6
10. Australia		1.8		2.1		.3
11. Switzerland		1.4		1.20		−.2
12. Czechoslovakia		1.29		.74		−.55
13. Sweden		1.28		1.22		−.06
14. Netherlands		1.08		1.4		.32
15. Poland		.95		.82		−.13
16. Israel		.86		.90		.04
17. Portugal		.76		.07		−.69
18. Belgium		.73		.79		.06
19. Denmark		.57		.60		.03
20. Austria		.53		.47		−.06
Subtotal:	10–20		11.25		10.31	−.94
Grand Total:	1–20		95.55		90.71	−4.84
Rest of World:		4.45		9.29		4.84
World:		100.00		100.00		0

Note: In regard to the number of scientific books published, the People's Republic of China and the USSR were far ahead of the United States in 1981. Perhaps this was also due to the difference between economies of state-supported versus market-oriented publishing, and partly because of the wider opportunities of scientists in market-oriented countries to publish in journals. See data in *UNESCO Statistical Yearbook, 1984* (New York: United Nations, 1984), Table 7.6 and Table 7.7 on book production.

Source: From data by Derek J. de Solla Price, Yale University, presented in C.L. Taylor and M.C. Hudson, *World Handbook of Political and Social Indicators,* 2nd ed. New Haven: Yale Univ. Press, 1972, pp. 322–25. Note: In regard to the number of scientific books published, the People's Republic of China and the USSR were far ahead of the United States in 1981. Perhaps this was also due to the difference between economies of state-supported versus market-oriented publishing, and partly because of the wider opportunities of market-oriented scientists to publish in journals. See data in *UNESCO Statistical Yearbook 1984,* New York: United Nations, 1984, Table 7.6 and Table 7.7 on book production. 1983 data from *Current Bibliographic Directory of the Arts and Science,* 1983 edition, Philadelphia: Institute for Scientific Information, 1984, p. 22.

Source: From data by Derek J. de Solla Price, Yale University, presented in C. L. Taylor and M. C. Hudson, *World Handbook of Political and Social Indicators,* 2nd ed. (New Haven: Yale University Press, 1972), pp. 322–325.

TABLE 9 A Primitive Model of Nuclear Weapons Growth and Proliferation, 1945–1976*

RANK	1945	1949	1952	1955	1958	1961	1964	1967	1970	1973	1976	ESTIMATES OF ACTUAL WARHEADS (STRATEGIC AND TACTICAL) AND NUCLEAR BOMBS 1976
1. United States	2	32	128	512	2,048	8,192	10,000+	10,000+				30,000
2. Soviet Union	—	2	16	64	256	1,024	4,096	10,000+				12,000
3. Britain (2 in 1951)	—	—	4	24	98	396	1,584	6,336	10,000+			500
4. France (2 in 1957)	—	—	—	—	4	24	98	396	1,584	6,336	10,000+	500
5. China	—	—	—	—	—	—	2	16	64	256	1,024	200
6. Country 1	—	—	—	—	—	—	—	2	16	64	256	—
7. Country 2	—	—	—	—	—	—	—	—	2	16	64	—
8. Country 3	—	—	—	—	—	—	—	—	2	16	64	—
9. Country 4	—	—	—	—	—	—	—	—	2	16	64	—
10. Country 5	—	—	—	—	—	—	—	—	—	2	16	—
11. Country 6	—	—	—	—	—	—	—	—	—	2	16	—
12. Country 7	—	—	—	—	—	—	—	—	—	2	16	—

*Assuming annual doubling of output for first three years, and doubling every eighteen months thereafter until approach to saturation level of more than 10,000 warheads. The actual development of nuclear weapons may have been faster in some years and slower in others. It seems plausible, however, that the growth of nuclear stocks in each country starts slowly, then accelerates, and finally slows down near some saturation level.

Source: Adapted from estimates in K. W. Deutsch's multigraph, "A Note on Nuclear Weapons and the Balance of Power, 1945–1965" (New Haven: Yale University, 1966). Estimates for 1976 actual holdings are from a well-informed source. These projections are roughly compatible with the actual data for the United States and China received since 1976 (see Table 10). Estimates for the USSR were thus somewhat understated, and greatly overstated for France and Britain, but the projected trend toward reduced growth rates of nuclear stocks in countries approaching, or having reached, some saturation level seems to have been confirmed by the more recently available data.

39

TABLE 10   World Nuclear Weapons, 1983

	STRATEGIC	INTERMEDIATE	TACTICAL	TOTAL
United States	10,000	1,300+	17,700	29,000
Soviet Union	7,400	3,500	6,500	17,400
United Kingdom	192	96	158	446
France	80	18	165	263
China	4	200	100	304
India		?	?	?
Israel		?	?	?
South Africa		?	?	?
Totals:	17,676+	5,114+	24,623+	47,413+

†In addition, 574 intermediate range missiles (200 Pershing II and 374 Cruise missiles) were deployed in Europe in 1984–1985.

Note: *Strategic*—capable of intercontinental distances and/or intended for use against the enemy's homeland. *Intermediate*—range or combat radius of 1,500 miles or more. *Tactical*—all other shorter-range or battlefield systems, including land mines and artillery shells. *Weapons*—warheads and bombs.

Source: R. L. Sivard, *World Military and Social Expenditures, 1983* (Washington, DC: World Priorities, 1983), p. 15.

surrender of its dominant values, habit patterns, institutions, and elites. In other words, atomic blackmail has its limits. Table 10 shows that by mid-1983 nuclear weapons had spread to India, Israel, and South Africa, and another half-dozen countries seemed likely to follow soon, making the world that much harder for anyone to control.

Nuclear weapons also raise the problem of the *range* of power. This range (as we shall use the term) is the difference between the highest reward (or "indulgence") and the worst punishment (or "deprivation") which power-holders can bestow (or inflict). Though rulers could have many people in their domains, the range of power over some of them might be much smaller than over others. Over those who wanted nothing and feared nothing, who were indifferent to pain or gain, their power would be small indeed.

In the course of recent centuries, the range of the power of governments in domestic politics has tended to become smaller. Extravagant rewards (such as to be given one's weight in gold, or to get the king's daughter in marriage) and extravagant punishments (such as being drawn and quartered, or burned at the stake, or otherwise publicly tortured to death) have disappeared in most countries, and they have become disreputable almost everywhere. Insofar as modern states rely on power, they normally govern not through the range of their power but rather through its weight—that is, through the high probability of the enforcement of their orders. Tyrants who rely mainly for their domestic power on the range of their staggering rewards and cruel punishments are not likely to last very long under present-day conditions.

In recent years, matters sometimes have seemed to tend in a different direction in international politics. Here, governments seem to have increased the range both of rewards they offer and of punishments they threaten, in their efforts to control the behavior of other countries and their governments. Certainly, foreign subsidies and loans are being offered more freely than they were at the beginning of this century, and the threat and practice of aerial bombardment, with its attendant slaughter of civilians, including women and children, has been used by some governments in the 1970s and 1980s including the United States aerial bombardment of Tripoli in April of 1986, on a much larger scale than would have been thought compatible with civilized standards almost 90 years ago, when the international Hague Conventions about the rules of warfare were written and accepted. The threat of wholesale nuclear massacre has further expanded the range of threats now available to the great powers and their rulers, and indeed such threats of nuclear warfare were actually employed, in disguised but unmistakable language, by both the United States and the Soviet Union in the Cuba crisis of 1962.

In fact, however, this temporary expansion of the range of power in international politics has had quite limited effects. The practice of controlling foreign governments through gifts and loans has by now become notorious. Since rival powers are willing to continue at least part of the same subsidies, the governments of most of the third countries have less to gain or lose from switching benefactors, or from calling on two or more of them at the same time. Similarly, any dire threat can be weakened or limited by calling upon the protection of a rival power, or given at least minimal deterrent strength of one's own, by threatening retaliation, or else by the use of hostages as did Iran against the U.S. in 1978–79, and some factions in Lebanon did in 1986 and 1987. As a result, the recent expansion of the range of power in international politics has made any active and ambitious foreign policy much more expensive, without making its fruits more ample or more dependable.

Another dimension of political power that has expanded in recent decades is its scope, an expansion which has had momentous consequences, and is still having them. By the *scope* of power we mean the set or collection of all the particular kinds or classes of behavior relations and affairs that are effectively subjected to it. The scope of the power of parents over young children is very large in one sense, for it includes almost all the child's activities. It is limited, however, in another sense, for even though the parents could control almost all the activities of the child, there are not, after all, very many things a young child can do. The scope of power thus increases with the capabilities of the persons included in the domain of power, in respect to the kinds of behavior subject to it. Political power expands in scope, therefore, whenever additional subject matter or additional kinds of behavior are put under its control. How much weight or effectiveness this control will have is, of course, another question of fact, as was pointed out in an earlier section.

During the past 100 years, and particularly during the last 50, the scope of politics has undergone a vast expansion. Many different activities are now being regulated by governments and laws, and hence by politics, which in the past were left to custom or to individual decision, or which did not exist at all. No medieval king or oriental sultan would have thought to make all children in his realm between the ages of six and fourteen years get up on every working day before 8 A.M. and go to public buildings and remain there for several hours. Yet the modern state, with its compulsory education, school systems, and truancy laws, undertakes to do just that; and such is the weight of its power, based on the compliance and active consent of most of the population, that in all the advanced countries of the world this control is almost entirely effective: almost all children go to school and nearly all adults are literate. In many developing countries, on the other hand, this expansion of the scope of public power and of public services is just now under way; it is part of the great process of transformation which these countries (and with them the majority of the world's people) are now undergoing.

Many other responsibilities and services have been added in recent decades to the scope of government, such as public health and a growing array of medical services; old-age pensions and other forms of social security; public works, including roads, harbors, airports, flood control, and power dams; the regulation and support of farm prices; the regulation of the purity and quality of food and drugs; the development and financing of research and of whole new industries, including nuclear energy, supersonic air travel, rocketry, and space transportation; greatly expanding educational services, from publicly financed kindergartens all the way through the great state universities and their graduate schools; and the vastly expanded burdens of defense.

Each new responsibility of the government, such as a new road system, or public education, or a publicly organized medical service, shifts the distribution of a few additional percentages of the gross national product into the public sector. It raises the stakes of politics. It widens the circle of persons who stand to gain or lose directly from the results of political decisions. It increases the potential and actual politicization of society. And it strengthens the conditions which favor eventually in every country the increasing participation of larger masses of people in politics.

The size and speed of these changes can be seen in the history of such countries as France, Britain, and Prussia-Germany during the last 150 years. Though their statistics are difficult to compare because of national differences in record-keeping, as well as of inaccuracies and gaps, so that at some points one must use estimates, the general outline of the picture is quite clear. In the mid-nineteenth century, the per-capita gross national product in these countries was no more than perhaps $1000 in 1984 money, or less than one-twelvth of what it is today. On the Continent rural and small-town people formed the large majority. Only roughly one-fourth of the population of France—somewhat more in Germany and much more in Britain—lived in cities of over 20,000 inhabitants. More than half of all adults, however, already were literate, and in both France and Prussia at any time about 1 percent of the population—or about 1.7 percent of the population of working age—served in the peacetime standing army. Politics, however, still was a matter for the few. The total expenditures of the central government in each of the three countries averaged below 10 percent of the gross national product, and even the addition of provincial and local government spending did not bring the proportion much higher. If the stakes of politics were relatively small, so was participation. Usually less than one-third of the adult population had the right to vote, and less than one-fourth (that is, less than half of the men) actually voted.

By 1910–1913, on the eve of World War I, per-capita gross national product had risen to perhaps $1050, or nearly one-eleventh of what it was in 1984 money. Urbanization was higher, and literacy was close to 98 percent. The central governments now spent about 13 percent of the gross national product; and perhaps 40 percent of the adult population, or about 80 percent of the men, actually voted. Military participation in peacetime was substantially unchanged, but the war of 1914–1918 was to mobilize every involved population to its depths.

By 1928, the war damage had been more than repaired, and the per-capita gross national product was near $2,600 or better, in 1984 money. Now, however, general governmental expenditures had risen to about 24 percent of the gross national product, and voting participation, including the enfranchised women, was close to 75 percent of all adults. The Great Depression of 1929–1933 enhanced this trend. Per-capita income stagnated or fell, but expenditures rose as more government services were needed. By 1938, total governmental spending in Britain and France was close to 30 percent of gross national product, and it was about 42 percent in Nazi Germany, where it included a frantic rearmament campaign.

After World War II, a new plateau was reached. Once the war damage was repaired, per-capita gross national product rose to about $11,000 in the inflated money of 1984 and it included a greatly expanded social-service sector. Total governmental spending in the countries of the European community now averages over 51 percent of gross national product. Military participation in peacetime has declined slightly, to about 1 percent or less of the total population, but voting participation continues high, at 80 percent or above in most industrialized countries, with the notable exception of the United States and the United Kingdom.

The detailed figures need not be presented here. They show with what relative slowness the world was changing between 1815 and 1914; how rapidly and radically it changed between 1914 and 1980; and how much may depend on the speed and direction of change between 1980 and 2010. This much, though, has become clear already. For good or ill, foreign policy, like all politics, can no longer be made wholly by the few. It must take into account the votes and wishes of the many. The same political evolution, in its great outlines, can be traced in the history of the United States, and indeed in the history of all noncommunist countries that have reached a high level of economic development.

The testimony of this lengthwise-cut through the history of a few countries is generally confirmed by the evidence of a cross-sectional study as shown in Table 11, which compares many countries at or near a single point in time. Together, the long-term trends and the cross-sectional data show that developed noncommunist countries tended to put between 30 and 40 percent of their gross national product through the governmental

TABLE 11   Average Levels of Development and the Rising Stakes of Politics: A Cross-sectional Study of 107 Countries at the Start of the 1960s

1 NUMBER OF COUNTRIES (AVERAGED)	2 DEVELOPMENT (ESTIMATED LEVEL)	3 POPULATION IN MILLIONS (AVERAGED)*	4 GNP (1957) PER CAPITA ($)	5 POPULATION IN CITIES OVER 20,000 (%)	6 LITERATE ADULTS (%)
11	I	105 (10)	56	6	13
15	II	1,359 (91)	87	13	24
31	III	342 (11)	173	21	42
36	IV	733 (20)	445	34	77
14	V	410 (29)	1330	45	98

7 NEWSPAPER (RADIO) AUDIENCE (%)†	8 CENTRAL GOVERNMENT EXPENDITURE (% GNP)	9 GENERAL GOVERNMENT EXPENDITURE (% GNP)	10 MILITARY PARTICIPATION (% POPULATION 15–64)	11 VOTING (% POPULATION, ADULTS)	12 FOREIGN TRADE (% GNP)**
(5)	19	25	0.8	30	43 (35)
(8)	17	23	0.8	49	34 (35)
(23)	26	35	1.7	41	40 (35)
(63)	28	37	1.4	69	36 (27)
(100+)	30	40	1.5	78	39 (43)

*Figures in parentheses are average for all countries, regardless of size.

†Estimated at three per copy and four per set.

**Figures in parentheses are average for middle-sized countries only (5.3 to 37.0 million population).

Source: From data in Bruce M. Russett *et al., World Handbook of Political and Social Indicators* vol. 1 (New Haven: Yale University Press, 1964), pp. 294–298. The rough method of estimating general government expenditures (i.e., the total of central, provincial, and local government spending, but excluding transfers from one level of government to another) as one-third more than central government expenditures probably understates general government spending somewhat at higher levels of development, and generally in the case of federal systems.

sector, and this share of the public sector has tended to rise to 45 percent or more by 1985. Between two-thirds and three-fourths of this (between 20 and 30 percent of gross national product) tends to be controlled directly by the central government of each developed country. The data also show how the modern world has changed from the patterns of nineteenth-century Western Europe. There, and in those days, the rise in urbanization, literacy, and income preceded the rise in voting and in the relative size of the governmental sector. This suggests that in the leading Western countries the productive capacity to satisfy many basic human needs and wants, such as food, shelter, health, education, and a rising living standard, increased before the rise in domestic popular demands and competitive international pressures, as represented by increasing voting participation and rising governmental expenditures. In the developing countries of the second half of the twentieth century, the opposite has happened. The social changes through the initial and partial monetization, industrialization, and urbanization of many Asian, African, and Latin-American countries have combined with the demonstration effects of modern transport and mass communication to stir many people to their depths, long before they have acquired the full educational and productive capabilities of modern life. Accordingly, voting participation, military participation, and the share of governmental spending all are rising now at a much lower level of literacy, income, and urbanization, and thus at a much earlier stage of social and economic development, than they did in the Europe of a hundred years ago. The stakes, the hopes, and the frustrations of political power all are now rising faster, and in more countries, than they ever did before.

In three quarters of the countries of the world, so far as we have data, the nation-state today is spending or reallocating at least one-fourth of the national product, and in the remainder—the world's poorest countries— almost all governments are moving in the same direction. This contrasts with the roughly 1 percent of the world's gross national product which is now being spent by all international organizations together. In spending power alone, nation-states outweigh international organizations by a ratio of more than 25 to 1. Today, and for one or more decades to come, the nation-states are and will be the world's main centers of power. They will remain such centers as long as the nation-state remains people's foremost practical instrument for getting things done.

4

The Limits of Power: Symbol and Reality

By now it should be clear that power is not one thing but many. Or rather, "power" is one single label or symbol which we use to refer to many different resources, relationships, and probabilities. All these, as we have seen, have to do with our ability to change at least somewhat the outcome of events. Beyond this, however, they are diversified indeed, and this diversity is only poorly hidden by the symbol "power" which we are using as their common label.

POWER AS A SYMBOL

Like every other *symbol*, the word "power" is a sort of message ordering us to recall something from memory for further consideration or association in our thoughts and feelings. This is in contrast to a *sign*, which is an order, so to speak, to expect something to be present or to happen in the near future.[1] When we define sharply the collection of memories that are to be

[1] When a doorman announces "The President!" we take it as a sign and expect the Chief Executive to enter, but when a lecturer on government says "the President," we usually take it as a symbol and recall that there is such a person and office, and perhaps various details

recalled with the help of a symbol, the symbol will function as a concept, in the sense in which we have discussed concepts earlier in this book.[2]

Power is a symbol of the ability to change the distribution of results, and particularly the results of people's behavior. In this respect, power can be compared in some ways to money, which is our usual standardized symbol of purchasing power—that is, of our ability to change the distribution of goods and services.

POWER AS A CURRENCY

Just as money is the currency of economic life, so power can be thought of as the currency of politics. Here, power is the currency or medium that makes easy the exchange of more-or-less enforceable decisions for more-or-less dependable support. When a decision is very likely to be enforced by some kind of penalty or sanction, physical or psychic, we think of the decision as "binding"; once it has been made, we say it can be "made to stick." If this decision is one which some people wanted very much, they are likely to support the decision maker—the government or leader—who made it, and in many cases they are likely to give help and support in enforcing the decision they favor.

The basic exchange process of politics from this point of view, as Talcott Parsons has pointed out, is the exchange of binding decisions for support. But in a more developed political system this exchange process, too, occurs in two stages. The leader, ruler, or government assumes general responsibility for making and enforcing many decisions of all kinds; in the extreme case, the government assumes general responsibility for making and enforcing any and all important decisions that might need enforcement. When a prince, a ruler, a party, or a group of revolutionists assumes this general role, we say that they "take power," or "take over," even though it may sometimes turn out later that they lacked the resources, or the capacities, or the concentration of purpose, necessary to hold on to it. If, however, the group or government that is "in power" (in the sense of being in a generalized role of maker of most or all of the more-or-less enforceable decisions) also succeeds in making decisions to the satisfaction of many of those people who count in politics, then these people in turn are likely to give to this government their generalized loyalty. That is, they generally support its decisions, not necessarily because they approve of each particular decision in itself, but because each is the decision of the government— "the law of the land," the decision of "legitimate authority."

Here, power is a symbolic role taken by the government, and ascribed to it by the people, and made credible by an initial minimum of readiness,

---

associated with these. See Susan K. Langer, *Philosophy in a New Key,* 2nd ed. (New York: New York American Library, 1951), p. 37.

[2]See above, pages 14–22.

resources, and capabilities to govern. And this symbolic role of power, together with this real or reputed capability, serves as a currency which mediates the exchange of the many diverse needs and wishes—the "interest"—of the many for the single, legitimate, and widely supported role of decision makers of the few.

To be sure, the similarities between power and money should not be overstressed. As a rule, money is easily divided into standardized accounting units such as dollars, rubles, or grams of gold. Power is not so easily countable and divisible. Votes can be used as counting units in some cases, whether in a popular election or in a close vote in the Senate or in one of its committees, or in the General Assembly or the Security Council of the United Nations. In other cases, power has been counted in units of armed force, such as warships, bombing planes, tanks, soldiers, or divisions.[3] All such counting, however, is far more uncertain, inaccurate, and dependent on particular situations and contingencies than is the relatively smooth and accurate accounting in terms of money, which has facilitated in many fields the development of a more scientific style of economics. No precise parallel for this can be hoped for in politics.

Political science cannot and will not become simply the "economics of power," but it can benefit from the limited similarities between money and power by using them as guides to the deeper similarities and differences behind them. For these similarities, though limited, are by no means trivial. In economics, money represents a person's power to buy, and credit represents a person's reputed power to do so. And what holds here for people also holds largely true for governments. They, too, need money or credit to buy in the world's markets. Similarly, in politics, *prestige* is to power as credit is to cash. This, too, applies not only in domestic politics but also in international affairs. Again, in economic life, people may lose their trust in the notes issued by a bank, or in the paper money issued by a government. When they thus stop believing what a writer on economics has called "the promises men live by," they usually must be shown the power to purchase in its most tangible form: they must be shown gold. Indeed, in international affairs, where trust among governments is somewhat rarer, and its misplacement could be more costly, gold is used more extensively in settling many of the balances of international payments. As gold is to ordinary bank deposits or cash in paper money, so force is to the ordinary forms of influence and power. Much as a show of trucks bearing gold may restore the faltering credit of a bank, so a show of force, such as tanks appearing in the streets of a nation's capital, may restore, at least for a while, the shaky prestige of a government. And so may a demonstration of warships or airplanes near some disputed border, coast, or small third country bolster the strained political position of a great power that has committed itself in an international dispute too closely to the limits of its credibility.

---

[3]"How many divisions does he have?" the late Soviet premier Joseph Stalin is supposed to have asked once ironically about the Pope—apparently not realizing that, for all its imperfections, the reputation of the papacy was to prove more durable than that of many secular rulers.

OVERCOMMITMENT OF PRESTIGE AND THE "ROW OF DOMINOES" IMAGE

The parallel is quite imperfect but it has some sobering policy implications: governments that must continually prove their will and capacity to fight probably do not have quite enough prestige for the policies they are engaged in, much as banks that must constantly supply spectacular proof of their capacity to pay probably do not have quite enough credit for the scale and style of all the business activities they are trying to conduct. An insufficiency of prestige, like a lack of credit, is no trifling matter.

A government is similar to a bank also in that the sum of its commitments is much larger than the sum of its resources. A bank lends out more money than it takes in as deposits—in the United States about seven times as much—because its managers can be fairly sure that not all its depositors will ask for their money back on exactly the same day. If all or even very many depositors *do* want their money back at once—perhaps because they no longer trust the bank—they generate a run on the bank that may break it. Similarly, every government promises to enforce more laws and to guard more objects and persons than it has police, soldiers, and resources to do so. When in domestic politics too many people at the same time disobey the government in too many serious matters, the result is something like a run on the government, which we call unrest or revolution.

Something similar can happen in foreign policy, too. Even an awesomely mighty and wealthy nation's government may enter into so many commitments to defend, develop, or control so many different colonies, satellite countries, or weaker allies, that it simply may not have the wherewithal to do so if its power in more than a few of them should be challenged simultaneously by local uprisings, outside attacks, infiltration, or combinations of all these. Here again a government and nation may find themselves overcommitted, vulnerable to any really serious crisis in their prestige that might precipitate a run by their client countries on all their commitments and promises. To some of the rulers of that great power, their allies and clients may then come to take on the aspect of a row of dominoes: if any one of these smaller countries or regimes should fall because it lacks trust in its great protector, they fear all the others will fall with it. In this way, the "row of dominoes" image often has its roots in a preceding overextension and overcommitment of resources and prestige on the part of some metropolitan power.

Despite this slim link to reality, however, the "row of dominoes" image most often is a fantasy. In most countries and at most times, the stability of domestic regimes and the orientation of foreign policy, foreign trade, foreign credits, and needs for military equipment and spare parts all are determined by many and diverse conditions which usually do not change quickly, nor simultaneously, nor all in the same direction. A marginal change in the military prestige of a great power usually is not enough to change the balance of domestic conditions in each allied country which produced its foreign-policy alignment in the first place, and which continues to maintain it. This large, autonomous ingredient in the foreign-policy alignment of most countries may perhaps explain why France kept so much of her influence in the new successor states of French Africa, even after the French evacuation of Algeria, and why Britain retained so much of her trade and influence in India, in Pakistan, and in many other parts of Asia, even after the end of her imperial rule there in 1947 and after her final loss of control of the Suez Canal in the crises of 1954 and 1956. Similarly, the establishment of a communist regime in Cuba in 1959–1960 was not followed by any stampede to establish similar regimes elsewhere in the Caribbean nor could any domino effects be observed in South East Asia after the retreat by the United States from Vietnam in 1975. In none of these situations of local setbacks in prestige—the French, the British, and the American, respectively—did any substantial "row of dominoes" effect prevail. Most of the time political changes in most countries occur for domestic reasons.

POWER AS A MEANS AND AS AN END

The Politics of Power and the Politics of Growth

Power can be thought of as a means of getting other things that men value. In this sense, the concept of power seems almost self-implied or tautological. To desire any value—wealth, well-being, respect, affection, or any other—necessarily implies desiring the power to get it, somewhat as in much of economic life to desire any good or service is to desire the ability to buy it. As people spend money in economic life to buy what they want, so in politics people spend their power to get what they desire.

But if people only *spend* their money, they end up penniless, and if politicians only *spend* their power, they end up powerless. The thrifty businessperson is an *investor*. He or she spends money on those goods and services (such as valued commodities or capital goods) which eventually will bring in more money than was spent on them. For instance, an investor may buy a factory to produce goods which can then be sold for more money than had been spent on getting them produced. Thus, to *invest* is to *spend* money to *get more* money, in cycle after cycle, again and again.

In politics some people invest in power. They spend their power on other values in such a manner that these values in turn will bring more power back to them. They are driven, as Thomas Hobbes suggested more than 300 years ago, by "a thirst for power after power which only ceases in death."[4] In order to invest thus, they must use the political support which they have at one time, so as to make more-or-less enforceable decisions of such a kind as to get more support; and then they must use this increased support for new decisions that will produce still more support for further decisions, in an expanding feedback cycle, as far as they can carry it.

---

[4]Thomas Hobbes, *Leviathan;* cf. H. D. Lasswell and A. Kaplan, *Power and Society* (New Haven: Yale University Press, 1950), n. 15, p. 95.

In essence it was this that Machiavelli urged his prince to do. A prince who did not wish to lose his realm, he suggested, always had to think and act in terms of power. He had to hoard and increase his resources, not dissipate them; to strive to enhance his own power and prestige and to diminish those of his competitors; to keep the common people passive and content, but willing to fight loyally at his command; to rule by force and fraud, being admired and feared but not hated; and to keep or break his word in quick accordance with whether loyalty or perfidy at any moment would more enhance his power. A prudent prince, Machiavelli thought, should never be neutral in a war among his neighbors, for if he let his weaker neighbor be defeated by some other prince, the strengthened victor would then turn on him. If he helped his weaker neighbor, however, they might jointly defeat the stronger neighbor who was the greater threat to both of them. Or thus allied, even if defeated, the two weaker princes might at least be allies in misfortune. Generally, however, today's ally is tomorrow's enemy, and one's strongest ally is one's greatest threat, for a prince promoting another's power, Machiavelli said, ruins his own. In theory this calculus of power politics was impersonal and inexorable. Every prince and would-be prince—that is, every political actor—had to act out of necessity, since every other prince would do the same harsh things to him; and those who failed to do so, or who mistimed their commitments and betrayals, judging wrongly the intervals in which to spend their power, would soon cease to be princes and would lose all their domains. Much as businesses eventually will be pushed out of the market if they cannot meet their expenses and make their capital grow at least as fast as the prevailing rate of interest, so governments and rulers eventually will be eliminated from the political arena if they cannot make their power grow at least as fast as that of their competitors. Power politics, in short, appeared to Machiavelli as the characteristic of the large political system which in turn determined the characteristics of all competitors surviving in it.[5]

Clearly, Machiavelli's model of an extremely competitive system is one of the great achievements of the human mind. His politician is an intellectual ancestor (or at least a close relative) of the equally competitive "economic man" of Adam Smith and his followers, and of the almost no less competitive animals and plants produced by Charles Darwin's process of "natural selection."

Yet all these models, fruitful as they were in their own day, are only partly true at best. In politics, Machiavelli's model in important aspects is quite false. It is inadequate in a way similar to that in which a mere model of extreme competition would miss the essential core of economics. It is true in economics that buying power for the individual means the power to appropriate goods and services, usually in competition against sellers and against other buyers. But for society as a whole the heart of economics, as Adam Smith already had made clear, is not the power of individuals to appropriate, but the ability of a country or nation to *produce* goods and

[5]Niccolò Machiavelli, *The Prince and the Discourses,* ed. by Q. Skinner (New York: Oxford Univ. Press, 1981).

services, and in particular the enhancement of this productive capacity through the division of labor, increased and speeded through the ability to exchange such goods and services with the aid of money.

Something similar holds for political power. For the individual, it means the ability to command and be obeyed, in competition with rival commands by other contenders, and in competition with the autonomous desires of the audience. For society as a whole, however, politics in any country—and among any group of countries—means the ability of the whole political community to *coordinate* the efforts of its members, to mobilize their support, and to redirect their patterns of cooperation; and, in particular, to do all this more quickly, more widely, and more accurately through the manipulation of power in the interplay of the probabilities of enforcement, compliance, and support.

If this is true, we can already foresee a coming change in much of our political thinking. Economics has shifted from a "bullion theory" that equated wealth with gold, to more sophisticated theories of capital investment and the division of labor, and to theories of economic growth and industrial development. Somewhat similarly, our political theory in time may come to shift from a theory of power to a theory of the interplay of spontaneity and sanctions in the steering and coordination of people's efforts, and in the processes of autonomy and social learning—that is, toward a theory of the politics of growth. Such a theory of political growth and development will be needed for every level of human organization, from the politics of small groups and of local communities all the way to the politics of nations at all levels of economic advancement, and even to the politics of all humankind. Such a theory will necessarily direct our attention to the limits of power. It will make us look to the limits of the scope of power—the things power can and cannot do—and to the limits of its domain, the boundaries where power cannot be relied on to prevail and where the breakdown of political control explodes into war.

The Limits of Power and the Risks of War

At the limits of its domain, as well as at the limits of its scope and range, power declines sharply, and it no longer brings about control. If such control is still needed, its failure causes damage to some or all of the actors involved in the situation, and at least some of them are apt to resort either to force, or else to withdrawal, as the most likely forms of damage control.

In a political system, power is used for all basic system functions—for pattern maintenance, adaptation, goal attainment, and integration, as well as for the higher functions of goal change and self-transformation. Where power fails, any and all of these functions may be endangered. Often, therefore, where compliance and persuasion fail, power is invoked; where power fails, force is called in; where force fails, withdrawal is attempted. Where even withdrawal fails, or is impractical, tensions and frustrations rise within the system, and its functions of adaptation must be improved correspondingly; or else, where adaptation and integration fail, pattern maintenance is endangered and the breakdown of the system becomes imminent.

These are the situations that breed war. Full-fledged war is the organized application of the most intensive and greatest force of which a society is capable. To abolish war, therefore, would be to abolish this "last resort of kings" and one of the ultimate damage controls of society. Yet this must be done, and it must be done substantially within the rest of this century if all-out nuclear war is not to abolish the whole vulnerable civilization of cities and factories on which our lives depend. We must therefore ask when, where, and how nations get into wars and out of them; and we must ask which sources and forms of wars perhaps can be abolished soon, and in fact which ones even now may be in the process of being abolished or of withering away. Before we can ask these questions, however, we must ask who are the actors—the nations, governments, and influential groups taking part in international politics and liable to get into warlike conflicts.

5

Groups and Interests

International politics generally involves groups and states. In all politics, individuals usually act effectively through groups, through other groups on whom they may exert some influence from the outside, or through influencing some government. And many actions of governments can best be understood in terms of the interplay of the interests and efforts of some of the groups behind them.

What makes a "group" and what constitutes an "interest"? A *group,* for the purposes of our analysis, is a collection of persons who are linked by two things: they share some relevant common characteristic, and they fulfill some (at least one pair of) interlocking roles. In other words, in some respect they resemble one another sufficiently to be recognizable as members of a group, and in some other respect they act in sufficiently different but interlocking ways so as to be able to cooperate and act in concert "as a group."

An *interest* in an individual, as well as in a group, is again defined by two things: it means both a distribution of attention and an expectation of reward. If something "arouses our interest," it attracts our attention, and it does so either by giving us at once some rewarding experience, actual or symbolic, or else by arousing in us expectation of such a reward.

To get a reward is to get more of something we value, or else to avoid an otherwise imminent loss of some of it. The substance of such a reward, actual or expected, can consist therefore in any one or several of the eight kinds of basic values that people desire: wealth, power, respect (or status), rectitude (or righteousness), well-being (or sense of gratification), enlightenment (or knowledge), skill, and affection (including friendship as well as love). Or the reward could consist in the expectation of enjoying any one of these values in a particular manner—for instance, safely and for a long time, which we call "security"; or else enjoying it spontaneously and with a wide range of opportunities for meaningful choice, which we call "freedom"; or enjoying it in a manner preserving our "integrity"—that is, our ability to learn autonomously and to govern our own behavior; or preserving our "dignity"—that is, our opportunity to act, learn, and change only at a speed slow enough to preserve autonomous control of our own behavior.

Finally, most people wish to enjoy any desired value "legitimately"— that is, without having to expect that its pursuit or enjoyment will lead them into an intolerable conflict with some other basic values that are relevant to them. Thus most people wish to gain wealth, but not at the price of ruining their health or well-being; they seek rectitude but usually will not bankrupt themselves for it; they wish for affection but not at the price of losing all power; nor do most of them wish for either wealth or power at the price of losing all rectitude or all affection. *Legitimacy* is the expectation of the compatibility or consonance of values. Most people feel a need for it; and they also feel a need, conscious or unconscious, for the compatibility or consonance of their knowledge.

People want *cognitive consonance* so that their world makes sense, adds up to some meaningful and manageable, or at least tolerable, whole. In their quest for cognitive consonance they suppress or reject items of information that do not fit into their image of the world; or they may seek, consciously or unconsciously, for some simplified image of the world that will seem clear, understandable, and consonant to them, and that will relieve their feelings of disorientation, frustration, alienation, and anxiety. An *ideology* is just such an image of the world, or a set of such images, which reduces the disquieting and often painful cognitive dissonance in the minds of the people who hold it. All of us have in our minds such simplifying and possibly more-or-less unrealistic pictures of the world. These pictures most often are partly realistic and partly quite fanciful, but in any case they reassure us through their greater consistency and tidyness. Usually we take them so much for granted that we are not even aware of them. We are sure of our own realism, but we are appalled at the ideological blinkers of other people—or other nations—who disagree with us. The less conscious we are of our own ideology, of our own set of helpful but simplifying pictures of the world, the more apt we are to value and defend them as parts of our own identity and personality. In politics, national and international, many people have preferred losing power, wealth, or life to losing their illusions.

There is a much longer (indeed, perhaps infinite) list, of course, of things which humans value enough to make a difference to their politics. For most practical purposes, however, the eight substantive values (power, wealth, respect, rectitude, well-being, enlightenment, skill, and affection) and the six modal or instrumental values (security, freedom, integrity, dignity, legitimacy, and cognitive consonance) are likely to be at the heart of most of the interests and interest-based policies that matter in international affairs.

Most such rewards are very real to the individuals and groups who seek them. Their judgments of the probability of any such reward following from some particular policy or action, however, are fallible indeed, and their attention to matters and events which they think are relevant may be appallingly misplaced. When a hungry cat concentrates his attention on a mousehole, there usually is a mouse in it; but when the government of some great country has concentrated its attention and efforts on some particular foreign-policy objective, the outcome remarkably often has been unrewarding. Granting that their problems are vastly more complex, it still seems that in judging their own interests, nations and their governments often have done much less well than cats.

During the half century from 1914 to 1964, the decisions of major powers to go to war or to expand a war, and their judgments of the relevant intentions and capabilities of other nations, seem to have involved major errors of fact perhaps in more than 50 percent of all cases. Each of these errors cost thousands of lives; some of them cost millions. The frequency of such errors seems to hold for monarchies and republics, democracies and dictatorships, noncommunist as well as communist regimes. It would be interesting to look for evidence whether present-day governments are any more or less prone to error in perceiving what they suppose to be their interests.

SPECIAL-INTEREST GROUPS

An *interest group* is a collection of persons who expect a parallel or joint reward from some possible course of events, and who are therefore likely, though not certain, to act in some ways in common in regard to what they perceive to be their common chances. This definition enables us to recall the twofold nature of interest, which involves both actual attention and a probable reward, and hence the ever-present risk of misplacing attention and misjudging the probabilities of outcomes and their consequences.

Some of the probable rewards, of course, are fairly obvious. When people buy more milk and cheese, and milk prices go up, most dairy farmers benefit. They receive parallel rewards from the rising prices for their product, and the breeders of dairy cattle and the manufacturers of cream separators, milk trucks, and milk cans also may all gain some share of the joint rewards from the increasing demand for the products of all the industries that cooperate directly in milk production. Accordingly, the dairy industry has long been organized, and has long made known its interests—such as more milk consumption and a higher milk price—to both Congress and the public. As a result, legislators from midwestern dairying states have not been unmindful of their needs.

In the pursuit of this interest, however, the dairy industry has met opponents whose interests conflict with theirs. Within the United States there are groups, such as the cotton growers and the manufacturers of cottonseed oil and margarine, who would benefit if butter were replaced more widely by the "lower-priced spread." This viewpoint is vigorously promoted by their own interest organizations, and it is well understood by many legislators from the cotton-growing states. And not to be ignored is the menace of competition from cheesemakers of Denmark, Finland, Switzerland, Italy, and other foreign countries—competition promoted by governments trying to promote their national exports. Many of our own patriotic cheese manufacturers may clamor for protection, but if we put a high tariff on, say, Swiss cheese, this might make the Swiss retaliate by raising their tariff on American automobiles. And a foreign tariff increase on our cars would hurt the interests of the automobile industry in Detroit, all the way from its executives to the automobile workers' union, and many of the voters for the senators and the governor of Michigan. When a major revision of tariffs is to be negotiated.

Some interest groups may extend across more than one country. American and Canadian farmers, for example, both stood to gain from a foreign policy under which some of their wheat went to Western Europe under the Marshall Plan in 1948–1952; and more recently they stood to gain from a foreign policy that permitted them to sell substantial amounts of grain to the Soviet Union and other communist countries. They then lost from the grain embargo imposed on the USSR by the Carter administration in 1980 in the wake of the Soviet invasion of Afghanistan, and President Reagan's decision to lift the embargo in 1981 was predominantly a response to pressures from these interest groups. Both American and British oil companies are interested in maintaining good political relations with the Arab countries where many of their oil fields and pipelines are located; but Jewish groups in the United States, as well as in Britain, are more interested in economic and political support for the state of Israel in its protracted conflict with its Arab neighbors.

Interest, as this last example reminds us, need not be economic but can cluster around religion, ideology, or any other value people hold. Most individuals have many diverse interests, some of which may be in conflict. A Catholic wheat farmer in Michigan might stand to gain somewhat from increased wheat exports to Poland and the Soviet Union, which might follow from a friendlier United States policy toward these communist-ruled countries; but he might also believe that greater United States pressure on Poland might procure there somewhat more freedom for his church. As a taxpayer he might gain from a cut in defense spending, but as the owner of some land near a defense factory he might gain from increased spending for preparedness. As father of a daughter well employed in a car factory in Detroit, he may wish for tariffs against European and Japanese cars to protect it, while as a consumer he would gain from unhindered car imports.

When people's interests are widely scattered, or when they are immobilized by the *cross-pressures* of conflicting interests, they are unlikely to do much to promote any one of them. They will give little active support to any interest group, and they will have little influence on politics. Those individuals, by contrast, for whom one particular interest is much more salient than most others, are likely to push those interests through their pressure groups, and they are more likely to get at least part of what they want. Carried to the extreme, however, such a pursuit of a special interest would give its practitioners at best more and more influence over less and less of the politics of their country and the world.

MORE GENERAL-INTEREST GROUPS AND SOCIAL CLASSES

Some interests are less narrowly specialized than others. If they still can be pursued effectively and if a large enough array of influence or of numbers of people can be held together in their support, such a diffuse interest will permit to those who share it a considerable amount of influence over a much wider range of situations. It may indeed often produce power of both greater weight and wider scope than a more narrowly specialized interest group could command.

In the noncommunist countries the largest banks, investment houses, and private business corporations, with their relatively well-concentrated top management, their command of high-level talent, their widely diversified holdings, and the high-powered law firms associated with them, usually all are among the most effective interest groups of this broader kind. A list of the United States secretaries of state and of defense, together with many of the people at the undersecretary and assistant secretary level since, say, 1947, would read like a roll call of the major groups of this kind; and much the same would hold for many other countries.

Another general-purpose interest group in many countries is the military, either as a single group or somewhat divided into several services. The military usually favors more defense spending and the acquisition of more powerful weapons. In many countries it favors the acquisition of nuclear armaments, the proliferation of which United States policy has in the past aimed at retarding. The military in many countries favors a more authoritarian posture in domestic politics, and a more vigorous pressing of national territorial or ethnic claims against various neighbors. In noncommunist countries they usually stress their anticommunism, even though experience shows that many such military interest groups or regimes are eager to accept armaments from communist countries. In addition, their readiness to use violence in territorial disputes sometimes endangers or disrupts the unity and stability of the noncommunist world, as occurred in the 1960s, 1970s, and 1980s in the near-war between two NATO members, Greece and Turkey, over Cyprus, and more tragically between India and Pakistan over Kashmir, and over the secession of East Pakistan that formed the new state of Bangladesh.

Often, the military form a part of a broader coalition of interest groups, such as the "military-industrial complex" referred to by President Eisenhower in his Farewell Address in 1961. An important foreign-policy aspect of the opinions of different elite groups consists of their more or less positive attitudes toward armaments and war, and to their use as instruments of foreign policy—with those favoring such policies in the United States often called "hawks" and those opposing them "doves." In a careful survey of over 1,000 high-level American business executives and military officers in March and April 1973, Bruce Russett and Elizabeth Hanson found that the most hawkish interest groups were the military officers, the members of the National Committee of the Republican Party, and the businessmen, in that order; and all three were consistently more hawkish than a general sample of voters.[1] Nine years earlier, extensive interest-group interviews in France and in the Federal Republic of Germany had similarly revealed that hawkish sentiments were consistently highest among the military of these two countries, and next to them among French business executives, while respondents from the German business elite were more differentiated in their sentiments which varied from issue to issue; thus the German business executives overwhelmingly supported general arms control and the United States–Soviet partial nuclear test ban treaty.[2]

Still another important group with common but relatively broad interests is the higher bureaucracy, which counts for much in such countries as France, Germany, India, and also, discreetly but effectively, in Britain.

The most general of these occupational-interest groups are the mass media and the professional politicians. The mass media include mainly newspapers, books and periodicals, radio, television, motion pictures, and to some extent the advertising industry. The attitudes of the media toward politics, and particularly toward foreign-policy questions, reflects a combination of the views of their owners, their advertisers, their readers, and their personnel—in proportions that vary from medium to medium, from paper to paper or network to network, and from case to case. In critical cases, owning a paper is still a great help in making your views prevail in it. Even the owner, however, must be mindful of the trend of preferences among his readers and his advertisers, and of the limited supply of first-rate talent for his staff: in the last two decades, several newspapers in Britain and in the United States, with strong-willed owners who were in some ways out of tune with their times and environment, kept losing money until they ceased publication or were absorbed by competitors, while other periodicals and their more skillful owners flourished.

The politicians are still more general in the interests they represent, but even so their interests, attitudes, and attention patterns differ in many ways from those of the business executives and financiers, or of the military

---

[1]Bruce M. Russett and Elizabeth C. Hanson, *Interest and Ideology: The Foreign Policy Beliefs of American Businessmen* (San Francisco: Freeman, 1975), pp. 59–99, 253.

[2]K. W. Deutsch, *Arms Control and the Atlantic Alliance: Europe Faces Coming Policy Decisions* (New York: Wiley, 1967), pp. 44–46, 53–54, 60–61.

or the civil service. They are often specialists in generality. As has often been said, they must act as brokers among the interests of different groups and regions; and they must produce somehow enough agreement on a "national" interest to attract sufficiently broad support to permit carrying on the government of the country in its domestic and foreign affairs. In trying to accomplish this, politicians often find that it is easier to win broad agreement on foreign rather than domestic matters. For one thing, most voters are only superficially informed by radio and television, and care much less about foreign affairs, whereas they more often have a fairly shrewd idea of their domestic interest and of the probable impact of some proposed domestic policy upon them. Moreover, politics, like all decision making, requires choices which often cannot please everyone, and in such cases it is safer to displease foreigners who cannot vote, and who often cannot retaliate immediately and directly, as an offended domestic-interest group would be apt to do.

Professional diplomats, who must be concerned about the slower but no less real responses of foreign nations, are often worried, therefore, at the ease with which political appointees to the top levels of our State Department, and domestic politicians generally, often produce a national consensus on nationalistic policies that misjudges or disregards the expectable international responses to it. This tendency increases with the size and power of the country, and it is a characteristic weakness of the largest and most powerful nations. The smaller a country, the more skillful usually are the most experienced among its politicians in taking into account the probable international repercussions of their actions.

In recent years, a new and relatively general interest group has been emerging in many developing countries, as well as in some of the most advanced ones, and it may well have come to stay. This new group consists of the universities with their students, faculties, research staffs, and administrations, together with the growing scientific and research institutions and "think industries" outside the universities—such as computer and biological and medical research industries. All of this expanding activity is required by the demands either of a growing technology or of a more complex social and economic organization, as well as of a growing governmental and public-service sector. The resulting growth of the universities and their offshoots is therefore not likely to be reversed, nor even to be appreciably slowed down in the near future.

In the United States, the universities now represent one of the country's larger industries, and together with the rest of education, which they greatly influence, they represent one of the fastest-growing ones. With more than 12 million undergraduates in 1981, about 1 million graduate students, half a million faculty and academic staff, and at least another half million other employees, the universities are becoming a political factor to be reckoned with, even though only one factor among several. In the view of a university professor and former United States ambassador to India, John Kenneth Galbraith, the failure of President Johnson in 1965 to win the support of a large part of the university community of the United States for his policy of escalating the war in Vietnam may have marked a significant change in the foreign-policy process in this country for the decade that followed.

In the developing countries, to be sure, the proportion of university students, faculties, and resources is much smaller, but their political potential often is enhanced by the absence or weakness of most other educated groups, and by the concentration of much of the young, educated leadership talent of the country in the student body of the universities. Although student activities and student politics tend to fluctuate, the political relevance of universities and students in many countries is likely to remain higher than it has been in the past.

Other interest groups with some degree of generality are labor unions, farm groups, and churches. Each of these groups has some primary special interest or group of interests, such as wages, employment, and welfare benefits in the case of organized labor; farm prices and rural services for the farmers; and matters of church support, schools, and public morality for the churches. Beyond this, however, labor is interested in the growth of the economy, the cost of living, the availability of housing, the status of the working person in the community, and the educational opportunities open to laborers' children. Farmers must care about the costs of credit and of transport, and the supply of educational and medical services in rural areas. Churches concern themselves with the entire quality of modern life, including the ethics of the young—which often are a response of sorts to the observed behavior of their elders—and they are concerning themselves inevitably with the relations among the races, as well as with other politically salient issues (such as the ethics of nuclear deterrence or sanctuaries for refugees) that are putting so many of their teachings to the test. To some extent, all these groups represent fairly broad ranges of interests, and many of these impinge more or less directly on foreign policy and on the political climate, increasing the likelihood of war or peace.

All the interest groups named so far are concrete, defined by specific occupations or relationships which leave relatively little uncertainty as to whether a person belongs to a particular group of this kind or not. There is another set of interest groups which is still broader but which is much less sharply defined, leaving far more uncertainty, vagueness, or controversy in its definitions. This is the set of social classes, or in any case, the set of concepts of "social classes." In some countries, such as the United States, some aspects of the class concept (though not all of them) appear somewhat unreal, while in some other countries class looks like an obvious reality. In all countries, however, a good deal of talking and thinking about politics at one time or another has been in terms of class, or has touched upon notions of class. During the Reagan administration, class concepts again emerged as a major issue in the public debate, caused by the extensive cuts in "aid to the poor" and other social welfare programs. Congressional commissions and studies gave evidence of an expanding class of poor people in America, and many of the administration's business incentive programs were accused of making the rich richer, and the poor poorer.[3] In the communist-ruled

_____

[3]See Thomas B. Edsall, *The New Politics of Inequality* (Philadelphia: R. West, 1985).

countries class has remained one of the central concepts of politics. For these reasons classes and the concept of class are definitely relevant to our discussion.

When people speak of social class, they are often referring more-or-less simultaneously to many different relationships. Six of these relationships implied in the common usage of the word "class" are particularly relevant for political analysis.

First of all, "class" often refers to a *general economic interest* which may link a large number of people who occupy parallel positions in the economic process. Thus, all or most landowners are likely to gain if rents and real-estate prices rise and real-estate taxes are kept constant or decline. The "landed interest" appears as a particularly clear example of such a class interest in the writings of Edmund Burke, Adam Smith, and David Ricardo. Similarly, if prices fall and interest-rates rise, all or more creditors are likely to gain, while debtors stand to lose. This common interest of creditors was well known to Alexander Hamilton, and he used it deliberately to strengthen the young federation of the United States. It seems obvious that most employers would gain if labor at all levels of skill were plentiful, working hours were long, and wages were low, while employees and workers would gain if labor were scarcer, hours shorter, and wages higher. Indeed, many employers and many labor unionists incline toward these views.

There is, of course, an opposite "high wage" or "purchasing power" argument to the effect that many employers could make higher profits by selling more goods to better-paid workers; and there is a "labor productivity" argument that many workers would gain if their employers made higher profits which these employers would then invest, according to this argument, in more efficient and productive machines whose more abundant output need not cause unemployment but could lead to greater prosperity for everybody. These arguments, in short, stress not antagonism, but at least partial harmony of interests, among employers and employed.

Just when, under what conditions, and to what extent any of these arguments of "class harmony" or "class conflict" are realistic is still a matter for debate among economists, and the evidence is likely to vary for different periods and countries. In many times and places, however, the clashes of such interests have seemed pervasive and persistent. Noble and serf, landlord and tenant, creditor and debtor, employer and employee, management and labor, property owner and the propertyless, capitalist and proletarian, often have been described as members of opposing classes, and often—but by no means always—have so identified themselves.

Class, however, does not always refer primarily to economic interest. Rather, it often refers to social *status*—that is, to the easier or more difficult access of individuals to the attention, consideration, and respect of other members of the society, and to greater or lesser influence over their actions. The social status of an individual is the degree of that person's access to deference or respect in society. It is the level of preference or priority which is accorded to the individual's messages in the network and flow of communications in society. Depending on local custom, persons of high status are given precedence in entering rooms and passing through doors; they sit at or near the head of the table, or next to their hosts; they are listened to with more attention and less overt dissent. Further, their letters are read and answered first, their telephone calls are put through to the head of the corporation or agency, and their wishes and suggestions are at least somewhat more likely to be heeded. As a socially accepted claim to deference, status includes a secondary ingredient of power; as an accepted claim to respect, it implies a secondary element of righteousness.

As populations grow, peoples are mobilized and communications equipment becomes plentiful, and the pressure of a growing number of messages upon the limited amounts of available time becomes more severe. Communication channels become overloaded, and decision makers over-burdened. The worse the overload, the greater is the need for priorities for those messages that are still to go through, and for those individuals who still are to have access to the powerful or prominent. This process is world-wide, and it tends to increase the potential or actual importance of bureaucracy, hierarchy, and social status.

Social classes are often seen as status groups by their own members as well as by some social scientists. Sociologist Lloyd Warner distinguished six social classes in the United States. He called them the Upper Upper (the old family in the big house in the best part of town), the Lower Upper (the high executive, or professional man, who made his own fortune), the Upper Middle (the local doctors, lawyers, executives, and the like), the Lower Middle (the small businesspeople, officials, and white-collar employees), the Upper Lower (the skilled workers), the Lower Lower (the semiskilled and unskilled workers and rural laborers). He then developed techniques that permitted him to predict with fairly good success into which one of these six groups any individual or family in a small town, or in any local community, would be consigned by their neighbors.[4]

Status is closely related to many kinds of *communication*. Members of the same social stratum or status group often talk and visit more easily among themselves. They often are a bit self-conscious in meeting those of higher status, and they tend to look down upon—or in any case, to be somehow less accessible to—those who seem below them on the status ladder.[5]

Accordingly, social classes often are also communities of more frequent and more freely shared communication. Communicating within one's own class, social scientist Joseph Schumpeter once observed, is like swimming with the current, but trying to communicate across class boundaries often is like swimming against it.

Thus, social classes often constitute something like *subcultures* in their society. The members of a class may live in a particular area in a town, such as the "right" or the "wrong" side of the railroad tracks. They may frequent the same types of places to eat and drink. They may have similar ways of

[4]William Lloyd Warner, *Social Class in America: A Manual of Procedure for the Measurement of Social Status* (Gloucester, MA: P. Smith, 1957).

[5]Despite the great value which Americans put on equality in the 1920s—almost as much as they do today—the status-conscious behavior of Mr. George F. Babbitt has provided some sad and richly comic pages in Sinclair Lewis's famous novel.

dressing, which identify their "blue-collar" or "white-collar" status. They may have similar table manners, courtship habits, and expectations of friendship and of intermarriage.

Out of all these experiences of economic interest, social status, frequency and ease of mutual communication, and the folkways of a common subculture, there may come a perception of a common economic interest, and the acceptance of special *organizations* to promote it. Thus, labor unions are often seen as serving not merely some special interest, but also the general interests of labor.

The perception of a common class interest may become broadened further to a general sense of cultural or historical *mission*. Noble landowners may not only feel that they are defending their interests as owners of large estates, but they may see themselves as the defenders of all the values of aristocracy, and even as defenders of an entire way of life in which the mass of commoners ought to be ruled for their own good by this small class of "the rich, the well-born, and the wise." Members of other classes, too, can develop such a sense of mission. Business executives often see themselves as the champions of free private enterprise, which they would like to spread to some as-yet-unenlightened nations of Asia and Africa, and even, if possible, to some or all of the peoples and countries under communist rule. In many countries, a sense of historical mission has also become part of the ideology of many industrial workers and other members of the poorer classes. Many workers in Italy, France, and other countries have accepted some version of the Marxist theory according to which it is the historic task of the working class to become the ruling class of their nation, and to use a transitional period of "proletarian dictatorship" to transform the economic and social system of their country from a capitalist into a socialist or communist pattern. Obviously, each of these ideologies of historic mission—the conservative aristocrat's, the free-enterprise business leader's, and the Marxist worker's—pictures the world as a good deal simpler than it is. But each of these simplifying visions can become a force in both domestic politics and foreign policy if it takes hold of the minds of a large enough number of people. Whether any such thing will happen depends very much upon the particular conditions prevailing in each country, as well as upon the skill and eloquence of its prophets.

Class means consonance of experiences. What makes a class is the consonance of most of the social, economic, and cultural experiences of its members. What makes a person a member of a class in the consonance of his or her personal experiences in regard to these interests and values—ranging from matters of everyday life to large visions of the world—so that they most often reinforce each other. But such consonance is not equally frequent or strong in all countries, all generations, or all groups of people.

In many countries of the Old World, all six aspects of social class coincided to a large degree for the same groups of persons. Workers were much concerned about lower or higher wages, their social ties, and their housing conditions; and their disdainful treatment by employers and government officials and members of the middle class made them acutely and resentfully aware of their disadvantaged social status. They lived in crowded working-class districts. Their hands were rough from manual labor. Their speech, their manners, and even their cloth caps set them apart. Their unions seemed the chief or only champions of their bread-and-butter interests, and their socialist or communist parties became to many of them symbols of affection and of aspiration—symbols of their pride, their hope, and their sense of a great mission. Where these conditions prevailed, class ideologies and class politics persisted, sometimes for three or four generations, and indeed increased where economic developments exposed masses of newcomers to industry and city life to some such long-lasting combinations of conditions.

In the United States a very different set of experiences has prevailed. Birth into a class has meant less to the life chances of many people; they (or at least their children) often have been able to rise in the social and economic system. New immigrants—more recently from Mexico (often without documents) and from Indochina—kept taking over the least-skilled and worst-paid jobs at the bottom of the ladder, and thus improved the career chances of former occupants of the bottom rung, and so in turn of everyone else on the ladder. American workers, particularly those ambitious enough to acquire a better-paying skill, have been freed by the automobile from the crowding of the tenement districts. Lockers installed in factories have enabled workers to wear their own uniforms only on the job; to and from the job they wear ordinary business or street clothes and cannot be readily identified as belonging to any particular social class or working group. Motion pictures, radio, and television—and the ubiquitous and, in some respects, improving high-school education—have furnished very nearly the same cultural models for all strata of society. Higher wages and shorter hours have offered wider ranges of options, including widespread home ownership, and working on weekends in one's own back yard. Unions, once expected to fight for only the barest economic interests of their members, now are seen most often trying to lay hold of an ever larger share of the profits and benefits of the business enterprises in which their members work. More recently, unions also have been pressing for improvements in the quality of life at the work place, and in times of economic recession they often are pressing for public policies of full employment. To be sure, some of these conditions until now have held to a much lesser degree for many American blacks, either in the southern countryside or in the big cities of the North. For the great majority of their white fellow citizens, however, the issues of class ideology and class mission have appeared increasingly irrelevant; and even the black protest has found expression most often in terms of a distinct people or a race, rather than in terms of class. By now, so many processes have gone so far that it may require a mental effort for many Americans to realize that the conditions for the salience of class politics in many other countries may be quite different.

In spite of what we have just said, however, class perceptions and class attitudes sometimes do exercise a potent (though subtle) influence on the foreign-policy attitudes, and policies also, of even the most advanced and socially well-integrated countries. Our higher living standards make it easy for us to establish sympathetic contacts with many of the middle and upper classes of the world's poorer countries, but we have even fewer direct human contacts with the poor abroad than we have at home. Whatever we hear from our friends abroad about the politics or economics of their countries, we hear most often from friends who belong to their relatively privileged minorities—and experience in Cuba and elsewhere has proven that their grasp of the situation often has been weak. For instance, preference for upper-class contacts contributed to a bias in the treatment of the different regions of Nigeria in the British-designed constitution of that country. British civil servants in the late 1950s found it easier to trust north Nigerian nobles (the Emirs) than the obstreperous and more vulgar commoners of the south and east. When giving a constitution to the newly independent country, they gave the lion's share of power to aristocratic northerners whom they trusted. Within a few years, this arbitrarily selected regime was overthrown, its prime minister was left to die in a ditch, a countercoup followed and a period of instability, violence, and civil war was ushered in that was to claim perhaps one million victims. Similarly, many American business executives and diplomats may be looking upon Latin America through the eyes of their associates in those countries, whose outlook may represent the views of perhaps not more than the top fifth or tenth of their population. And Soviet diplomats, in turn, have at times put more trust in the view of small groups of local communists than in the available evidence of the actual attitudes of the majority of the general population.

Such class biases in perception and policy can be quite real. But they need not be irresistible. Governments have to weigh the interests of their own nationals, and of the classes and elites of other countries. They must do this even if some of those foreign classes and elites seem very similar to, or nearly identical with, their own most influential elites at home. Attention to possible class bias as a source of distortions of reporting (in diplomacy, business, and military affairs) may be an essential precaution in order to protect the national interest.

6

The Power of Elites

Social classes, as we have seen, can be much more directly relevant to the politics of some countries than to those of others. Elites, by contrast, are relevant in every country. By an "elite" we mean a very small (usually less than .5 per cent) minority of people who have very much more of at least one of the basic values than have the rest of the population—usually at least five to ten times as much on the average, in the case of values that can be counted in this way. The members of an economic elite have much more wealth. Those of a political elite have much more power. Those of an enlightenment elite, such as top-level scientists, have and command much more knowledge; and the members of a respect elite, such as high-court judges, or the bishops of a church, are more highly respected. (In the United States they probably do not enjoy five to ten times as much respect as other people, but if we try to measure respect more sensibly on a rank-order scale, social elites emerge even here.)

An elite usually is a much smaller group than a class. The more-or-less underprivileged classes in most societies, of course, are very large. Fully 48 percent of the West German population are wage workers (including the unemployed). The middle classes, too, are large. About 28 percent of the West Germans are members of the lower middle class of small-salaried employees, and 16 percent are members of the self-employed lower middle class in town and country, consisting of small businesspeople, artisans, and peasants. But even the upper middle class of managers, executives, professional people, and substantial property owners still amounts to perhaps 6 percent; and the upper class of those of still greater wealth or higher status is still about 2 percent, or about 200 persons out of every 10,000 of the population.[1] In the United States, too, the upper middle and upper classes make up an even larger proportion of the population. By contrast, an elite in terms of respect or reputation in the United States, such as the persons listed in *Who's Who in America,* constitutes only about .03 percent, or about 3 persons in 10,000. Even if we should include their families, they would amount to less than 1 percent of the population. The elites of wealth, or power, or of any other basic value are of similarly small size—1 percent or less of the population.

As a rough rule of thumb, therefore, we may expect even a large elite to be at most about one-third the size of the smallest social class, and usually its size is more likely to be one-tenth or less. Only for the very top classes in an extremely unequal society does this difference begin to blur. In France on the eve of the French Revolution in 1789, the nobility and the clergy each constituted roughly .5 percent of the French population, so that those classes at that time were almost small enough to be thought of as elites.

In principle, there could be as many different elites as there are different values. In practice, elites overlap, but they do so only more-or-less imperfectly. Scott Fitzgerald and Ernest Hemingway in their dialogue understated the situation when they said: "The very rich are different from you and me . . ." "Yes, they have more money." Many of the very rich also have a good deal of power in politics; many enjoy high status and respect; many are highly educated and rank high in enlightenment and skill. Conversely, top scientists and experts are well paid and usually well respected, but not powerful. Top-level politicians in noncommunist countries, even if they were poor at the start of their careers, sooner or later are likely to become rich; and nowadays they can do so quite legitimately by drawing on their respect and enlightenment rather than their power: their memoirs and other writings earn high royalties, and their purchases of real estate or other investments are likely to be soundly judged and well-informed.

As a general rule, a person who ranks high on any one of the basic values is quite likely to rank high also on other values. This is called the *agglutination* (clustering) of values. In many highly traditional countries, this agglutination of values is high. The rich have high status, and the status elite is rich; and this joint elite has most of the power, enlightenment, and skill, is most often respected and admired, enjoys the relatively best health and physical well-being, and is considered most often righteous in terms of the official ideology or church doctrine prevailing in the country which they rule. To the extent that these conditions prevail in the United States,

---

[1]See Hans-Georg Wehling, "Sozialstruktur und soziale Schichtung," in Eckhard Jesse (ed.), *Bundesrepublik Deutschland und Deutsche Demokratische Republik. Die beiden deutschen Staaten im Vergleich,* 4th ed. (West Berlin: Colloquium Verlag, 1985). For an East German analysis with slightly different figures, see Karl M. Bolte and Stephan Hradil, *Soziale Ungleichheit in der Bundesrepublik Deutschland,* 4th ed. (Opladen: Leske & Budrich, 1984).

they will testify to the existence of what some writers have called a "power elite" or "power structure" in this country. To the extent, however, that values do not agglutinate, or no longer do so, the "power elite" concept is inappropriate or obsolete. In the extreme case, one could imagine a country, or a local community, in which all elites would be completely specific, and no overlap among them would be larger than what could be expected from pure chance. In such a country the powerful would have no significant wealth and the wealthy would have no particular influence in politics; and neither group would enjoy any special amount or degree of well-being, enlightenment, skill, or affection, nor would either group be particularly respected or considered righteous.

Reality in most countries, including the United States, is somewhere between these two poles of complete agglutination and complete nonagglutination of values. Elite status in regard to any one value counts for something in one's chances of getting more of another value, but it does not count for everything. In the United States, there is some impressive evidence that the amount of elite agglutination has somewhat declined. Our elites have become more specialized and more open, some of them to a notable degree, and it seems that the American people are continuing in this process of replacing the old, single, all-purpose elite by a pluralistic array of specialized elites connected by a complex network of communication and bargaining, and more widely accountable to a more highly educated and politically more active population. But this process still has a long way to go.

Indications of similar trends have been observed in other advanced Western countries where a plurality of specialized elites has gained at least somewhat in power at the expense of the older, more narrowly recruited, and more highly integrated elite structure; and something similar may also be happening in the more advanced of the Communist-ruled countries. As a result, there is now in many countries a higher proportion of *marginal* members of the various elites, much as there is now also a larger proportion of marginal members of social classes. That is to say, an even larger percentage of the population belongs at one and the same time to several different groups, oriented toward different life-situations, experiences, and values. This growing proportion of the population, who are in some sense marginal in many or all groups to which they belong, is less likely to respond to the slogans and alignments of class politics, and somewhat more likely to accept the symbols of national politics and national identification. At the same time, however, the experience of being marginal in one's elite or social group tends to make people more critical of prevailing beliefs and practices, and more inclined to reach out for new ones.

As a result, elites are becoming more specialized, more open to newcomers, and less agglutinated in regard to the values and relative privileges which their members enjoy. More among their members are in some sense marginal, vaguely dissatisfied, and sometimes more open to new ideas and to communications from outside their familiar circle of experience. Half a century ago, before and after World War I, many workers in the industrialized countries were class-oriented and somewhat internationalistic in sympathies, while many intellectuals, particularly in Europe, were nationalistic in outlook. Today, however, the working people in most of the advanced countries respond more readily to the symbol "people" than to the symbol "class," and many intellectuals in noncommunist as well as communist countries feel somewhat more uncomfortable in their nation-states, and more critical of existing institutions and national policies—including more often some national policies in world affairs.

Interest groups, if they are large, usually give rise to particular elites who lead them. Most often, these elites consist of the top personnel of the special-interest organizations. Large labor organizations have given rise to an elite of union officials and labor leaders. Business organizations, farm groups, and churches all have produced their own leadership groups and strata. The members of each of these special elites must be acceptable to the members of their larger interest constituency if they are to remain its leaders for long; but at the same time the members of these diverse elites may develop some similar habits, attitudes, living standards, and culture patterns. They may meet each other more often, professionally and sometimes socially. If this process goes far, common attitudes and interests may emerge to unite these diverse leadership groups, together with the more general political and bureaucratic elites, into a broader and more general elite, "establishment," or leading class.

Individual leaders, in turn, are more likely to be accepted by the elite groups on whom they must rely much of the time for support, if they share and express the salient attitudes and desires of the elite members. In much the same way, elites are more likely to be accepted and supported by larger segments of the population if these elites express the attitudes, and do the jobs, which are important to their followers.

Sometimes the day-to-day interests of different elites may diverge when their more basic common interests remain for a time less salient to them. Thus one branch or division of a large chemical firm may be interested strongly in exports, and hence in a policy of freer international trade while another firm or even another division of the same large firm may be interested more strongly in protection of its domestic market against foreign competition. So long as this condition holds, these divergent minor interests may balance each other, so that little effective political action may result. If the situation should change, however, so as to bring major common interests into play—such as those of a wide variety of local and foreign business executives in Chile in 1973, who felt threatened by the nationalization policies of the Allende government—then these various groups may find themselves both aroused and united, and they may then engage in intense and sustained political activity until their major goal is reached, as it was in Chile by the military overthrow of President Allende's government in October 1973. Similarly, of course, leaders and members of diverse labor unions may find themselves united by a perceived threat to social welfare legislation or to the purchasing power of wages through a wage freeze under conditions of continuing inflation.

In the United States during the 1960s, high spending on armaments and a readiness for military intervention had long been favored by the political right and some military and industrial interest groups. These interests, however, had not been shared by consumer industries, department stores, urban and metropolitan real-estate interests, educational, health, and welfare personnel, and many of the mass media catering to audiences of this kind. Some ethnic and religious groups, such as Jewish leaders and voters, had long been a part of this "dovish," arms-control and welfare-oriented coalition, but after the Soviet-supported Arab attack on Israel in October 1973, a considerable part of the Jewish elites and rank and file—perhaps one-third—changed their attitudes. Instead of opposing, they now favored increased military budgets and military commitments to foreign lands. Their power in itself was limited, but where in the past it had partly canceled some of the "hawkish" high-armament and high-risk influences, it now was added to them. As a result, pressures for high arms spending in the United States from several of these major domestic interest groups increased from the mid-1970s. The "hawkish" feelings grew even further due to public frustration over the Iranian detention of American hostages from 1979 to 1981 and the Soviet invasion of Afghanistan in December 1979. The Reagan administration's armament campaign was initially widely supported. It proposed annual defense-budget net increases of 8.1 percent from 1981 to 1987—for a net increase of 59 percent, or a rise of defense spending from 5.6 percent of gross national product in 1981 to 7.4 percent of GNP in 1987. The defense buildup was accompanied by such successful and popular interventionist foreign-policy moves as the invasion of Grenada in 1983 and the bombing of Libya in 1986 in response to Colonel Qaddafi's alleged support of international terrorism. By the mid-1980s, the formerly dominant arms-control and welfare-oriented coalition was left badly weakened. This trend only began to change in the congressional elections of 1986—in which Democrats recaptured the majority of the Senate—and perhaps further with the revelation of the administration's secret arms deal with Iran and the dubious financial practices associated with it.

What had changed was the relative salience of interests. Where earlier dissonant interest had been uppermost in people's minds, now consonant interests were seen as foremost, and mutually off-setting cross-pressures gave way for a time to parallel and mutually reinforcing political action. As a result, political leaders who rode the crest of this change appeared more powerful and popular—so long as this new political climate lasted.

Individual leaders can make a significant difference in the outcome of a chain of events by making a personal decision at some critical juncture. Franklin Roosevelt, Winston Churchill, Charles de Gaulle, Joseph Stalin, Harry Truman, Dwight Eisenhower, John Kennedy, Lyndon Johnson, Richard Nixon, Gerald Ford, Anwar Sadat, Margaret Thatcher, Indira Gandhi, Jimmy Carter, Ronald Reagan, and perhaps Mikhail Gorbachev each in his time has made one or several decisions of this kind. Some leaders have been strained to the breaking point by the burden of decision (as were perhaps Woodrow Wilson and James Forrestal), while other leaders seem to have thrived on pressure, as did Harry Truman during the Berlin crisis in 1948 and over Korea in 1950, John Kennedy during the

Cuba crisis in 1962, Richard Nixon during the Arab-Israeli "October War" of 1973, and Ronald Reagan against Grenada in 1983, Nicaragua in 1983–1987, and Libya in 1986 (but not against stronger adversaries in Lebanon in 1983 and Iran in 1984–86).

Most of the time, however, leaders can only make decisions which are acceptable to their elite collaborators and allies, and to their followers on the intermediate and mass level. The president of the United States, as Richard Neustadt has pointed out, often must act as a broker or mediator among the demands of different powerful interest groups. Only on relatively few occasions is he free within a wide range of discretion to make a critical decision alone. Richard Nixon's attempt to widen drastically the powers of the presidency—and to reduce correspondingly the powers of Congress—ended with his resignation in 1974. Some of his major decisions in the foreign-policy field, however, survived his tenure of office and were official policies of the United States until the end of the 1970s, such as the eventual evacuation of U.S. forces from South Vietnam, Cambodia, and Laos; the *detente*—i.e., the reduction of tensions—between the United States and the Soviet Union; and the improved relations between the United States and communist China. Improved relations with the People's Republic of China still were official policy in 1987.

On some occasions, however, a single leader's decision can be fateful. If it leads to success, the decision maker may be acclaimed for boldness and wisdom. If it is followed by failure, both leader and followers are likely to deny that this was a freely taken decision, insisting that there was no alternative, that no other decision could have been taken under the circumstances of the time. Such simplified versions of environmental or historical determinism have often been a last refuge for unsuccessful politicians.

Leaders sometimes can and do make decisions that change history, but they can do so only within the limits of their resources, their situations, and their minds. Usually, a "strong" leader is not only a person with a firm, decisive personality, but also one with the support of a strong group, or a strong coalition of groups. A weak leader, on the contrary, often is one whose supporters are few, or else are poorly united by weak and inconsistent bounds of attitude and interest.

But there are also limits to leaders' minds. We have already implied that the success of leaders in any situation depends in large part on how well their policies and doctrines fit the needs of their time and place. But leaders have their own personal needs. They are most likely to adopt only those views and policies that jibe with their own as judged according to the extent of *their* experience and imagination, *their* cast of mind, and *their* limited time and inclinations to consider more unfamiliar alternatives. Leaders thus often are—and perhaps must be—sparing in their mental efforts. And, not unexpectedly, perhaps, so are (or must be) the groups that follow and trust them, because the outlook and beliefs of these leaders seem to resemble so reassuringly the thoughts and feelings of the groups that follow them, as well as of the small elites that often form the leaders' immediate environment.

So we see that the leaders are often in part the captives of their external resources, or supporters, and also in part the captives of their own habits and needs for consistency and consonance in their images of the world. More often than by mere economic interest, or by cold calculation of strategy and power, leaders have been moved and driven by tenaciously held images of the world which became the basis of their popularity with masses or elites, as well as the basis of their own self-image and self-respect. Because of momentous decisions to be made on war and peace, and because the freedom to make such decisions is so limited yet so fateful, the existential condition of national leaders in our time often has been close to the edge of tragedy.

7

All-Purpose Interest Groups

If an interest group—for example, stamp collectors, rabbit breeders, or executives in the oil or the aircraft industries—is oriented toward a *single* reward, or a single kind of reward, we say that it has a "specific" interest. In its unity of interest, this type of group is sure to enjoy a certain amount of solidarity. If a group is united by *several* kinds of expected rewards, and hence by several specific interests, its solidarity is likely to be even stronger. And if the common bonds deal with *very many* common rewards and values, this solidarity may become general or "diffuse" among its members; they will now feel united not only in regard to this or that specific interest, but in regard to any and all needs, interests, and values that may come to concern them. And each of them may be willing to help any other just because of membership in this group rather than because of the merits of a particular case.

The relationships among the smallish interest groups known as the nuclear family—consisting normally of husband, wife, and their children—come close to this latter form of solidarity. On a somewhat larger scale, in many cultures today the extended family of kin group has formed a similar all-purpose interest group. In their great days a still larger group, the ancient Greek city-states, approached this feeling of all-purpose solidarity among their citizens. Under modern conditions, the largest all-purpose group whose members can have such a sense of diffuse solidarity is a people, although some of the noblest visions of politics have dealt with the possibility of extending this general sense of solidarity or kinship to all humanity.

A *people* is a group of human beings with complementary habits of communication. Their ways of speaking, listening, and understanding fit together. They usually speak the same language (though the Swiss, the Welsh, the Belgians, the Jews, and some other people have spoken more than one language). Conversely, however, even though they speak the same language, the English, Irish, and Americans belong to different peoples, and the same is true of the several French-, German-, and Spanish-speaking peoples of the world.

What is essential for forming a people is that its members have a community of shared meanings in communications, so that they can understand each other effectively over a wide range of different topics. A common language, though not indispensable, is clearly very helpful to this end, and a common culture which provides the common meanings is decisive. Such common meanings are based on common or interlocking memories given in a common culture, and on common habits of communication learned and practiced in real life.

Such cultural memories and practiced communication habits become part of the personality structure of each individual, and thus of a person's self. Usually, they are learned most easily in childhood, when so much of our habit structure and personality is formed, but they can be learned even late in life (albeit with greater effort and less perfectly). The American people includes many persons who learned to speak, listen, feel, and act more or less like Americans only late in life, but who have become thoroughly assimilated just the same. (This has been a vivid experience for many recent Americans: to feel not merely harbored but included.) Something similar holds true for many other countries of immigration, if they offer newcomers a genuine opportunity to assimilate, closely linked to a substantial gain in the important values in search of which they came.

It is possible, therefore, for an individual to be in transition from membership in one people to membership in another. But it is also possible for millions of persons to belong to two peoples at the same time, if they can communicate and cooperate in both, just as it is possible (within limits) for anyone to communicate meaningfully with more than one partner. Thus, the Scots for over two centuries have been both Scots and British. In early 1977, a majority of French Canadians saw themselves as both *habitants* and Canadians. Many Bavarians are both staunchly Bavarian and intensely German. American blacks may consider themselves members of the black population in the United States, and also as Americans. Their increased interest in Africa, in African studies courses and departments in educational institutions, and the preference of some for the label "Afro-Americans" for their group—all these have proved compatible with their continuing self-identification as Americans.

American Jews feel and act as Americans, but many of them also share significant communications and solidarity with other Jews and with the people of Israel. West Bengalis and Maharashtrians are members of their respective peoples, and at the same time members of the people of India.

As the world becomes more modern, membership in a people becomes more important. The ability to communicate and to understand one another increases the likelihood of mutual trust. It makes for easier cooperation and organization. It facilitates employment and promotion, the extension of credit, the forming of more frequent ties of friendship, and of intermarriage, and thus of family ties and of the transmission of property. In all these respects, membership in the same people links all its members through common bonds not only of communication but also of more probable joint rewards, and thus through expectations of common interest which have some basis in reality.

As life becomes more mobile, competitive, and insecure in the course of a nation's transition to modernity, individuals can rely less on the old security of family and kin, of neighborhood and village, and are exposed even more to the bewildering and threatening changes in the market for their labor, their products, and their necessities. The greater these changes, the more important it becomes to cling to the remnants of security and predictability offered by a common language and culture and common membership in a people. It is this common membership in a people that promises to turn strangers into kin, or at least into friends, and to align them for at least somewhat predictable cooperation and mutual support.

Membership in a people thus coordinates the communications, the expectations, and to some extent the interests of individuals. The more quickly changing and insecure the conditions of their lives, the more salient and urgent will be their needs for such cooperation. As in many cases of social coordination, much of it is based on voluntary or habitual compliance, but some of it can be reinforced by some probability of organized enforcement. Once individuals have come to desire the coordination of their behavior through the common culture of a people—and usually through a common language—they are also likely to desire, support, and demand appropriate common organizations for enforcement in order to make this emerging coordination of their behavior more dependable.

In this manner, the interest in a common culture and language becomes a political interest. The desire to belong to a common people leads to the desire to gain control of an existing government and state in order to implement this interest, or to create a suitable new "national" state and administration where none before existed. As a result, the less than two dozen nation-states in the world of 150 years ago have been replaced by perhaps twice that number on the eve of World War II, and by the mid-1980s by more than 170 nation-states and would-be nation-states still in the process of emerging.

THE MODERN NATION

A *state* is an organization for the enforcement of decisions or commands, made practicable by the existing habits of compliance among the population. Such organized enforcement is an all-purpose instrument. It can serve to reinforce any decision or any command, as long as most of the population will comply or can be persuaded to do so. The more dependable and general such popular compliance, the greater the potential power of the state. This is true of all dimensions of its power: its weight, scope, range, and domain all can be increased with greater popular compliance. Such compliance, as we noted earlier, can be passive or active. It can be based on mere indifference and apathy, or it can include voluntary positive support even at the cost of sacrifice. Such active compliance and support can be increased most readily by solidarity and by persuasion, and thus it can be increased most effectively through the human communication network of a people.

A state can be used to reinforce the communication habits, the co-operation, and the solidarity of a people. And a people through its community of communication, compliance, and active solidarity can greatly increase the power of a state. This is one of the reasons why the combinations of a people and a state in the modern nation-state have proved so powerful in politics, and why during the last 150 years the nation-states have dominated the earth.

If a significant proportion of the members of a people are trying to get control of some substantial part of the machinery of enforcement and government—such as city councils, school boards, or provincial legislatures—we call them a *nationality*. If they succeed in getting hold of significant capabilities of enforcement over a large area—that is, usually if they get control over a state—we call them a *nation*, and ordinarily they will so call themselves.

A nation, then, is a people in control of a state. But people and state need not coincide exactly: some members of the people may live abroad, forming minorities in other states, and members of other peoples may form minorities in this one. In every nation-state proper there is one people more closely identified with the state and with its personnel, and usually also somewhat more favored in regard to political power, respect, and often wealth and other values, than are the other people in that state. This favored nationality need not form the numerical majority of the total population of the state, but in its claims to influence, preference, and deference it is apt to act like one. Often it will call itself "the majority," or it will be called so by observers, while the other groups in the state will be called "minorities" regardless of the actual numbers in each group.

In Spain, the speakers of Spanish form a real majority of the population, and the Basques and Catalans are genuine minorities. But in India, the speakers of Hindi are less than half the population, and so were the Urdu-speaking West Pakistanis within the total population of pre-1973 Pakistan. The Austrians and the Hungarians together furnished not much more than one-third of the Austro-Hungarian Empire that broke up in World War I. Even in the United States, the "white Anglo-Saxon Protestant" old-stock Americans are not a majority but only the largest minority among the population.

The status of a "minority" often depends much less on its numbers than on the presence or absence of discrimination, or on its kind and degree. French-speaking Swiss are a minority of the Swiss people, among whom nearly three out of four speak German, but most of the French speakers are in no way treated as a minority and they willingly identify themselves as Swiss. Where minorities are victims of discrimination in a nation-state, however, they are likely to become alienated from that state, and they often look abroad for friends and protectors, either to help them join with other groups of similar language and culture outside their present state, or else to secede and set up a smaller nation-state of their own. In all such cases, dissatisfied and "unredeemed" minorities can become actors in international politics and contribute significantly to the instability of existing political and social institutions and to pressures for more-or-less drastic change. Thus in South Africa, black people form about 70 percent of the population but are badly discriminated against in the name of *apartheid*.[1] In the few years preceding 1987 the black's riots and resistance to discrimination have cost them more than 1,600 lives, forced the ruling government to declare an almost uninterrupted state of emergency, and gained them increasing moral and political support from the international community—as well as more-or-less substantial attempts at pressing the South African government into changing its domestic policies. The government is supported by a majority of the South African whites, who are 18 percent of the population, but also opposed by the 10 percent "colored" of mixed race and the 3 percent Asians, all of whom suffer from various forms of discrimination.

Out of the resistance of minorities, thus, often grows a degree of sympathy and support for terrorist movements, as among Basques in Spain or Catholics and Protestants in Northern Ireland, which affects international politics and other nation-states far beyond the nation-state's ruling government against which these acts are aimed.

If such a minority, or formerly disfavored group, however, succeeds in setting up its own nation-state, dominated by its members, then it may quite easily find some still smaller minority, or even some other less powerful numerical-majority population, to look down on, to oppress, and to discriminate against. The ancient Romans told the story of a slave set free by his master, who was asked what he would do first of all in his new freedom, and who replied: "Why, buy myself a slave, of course!" Something similar can be said of many nationalists. Indignant about any oppression of their own people, they eagerly look for other peoples to oppress. The habits of privilege and oppression have entered their minds as thoroughly as they had entered the mind of that long-dead Roman slave.

---

[1]In 1985, black people were counted as 18.9 million or 68.4 percent of the officially recognized population. To these must be added about 1 million black workers from 5 black "homelands" bringing the real share of blacks to 72.1 percent. *Fischer Welt-Almanach '86.* (Frankfurt 1985, p. 438).

EMPIRES AND INTERNATIONAL ORGANIZATIONS

When the favored people is a relatively small minority predominating in a relatively large state over many countries and populations, and if they use their predominance in power, wealth, and perhaps other values so as to perpetuate or even increase the gap between themselves and the disfavored majority, then we speak of this large composite state as an *empire*. Such an empire usually includes a dominant or imperial people which supports and defends its government. It also usually has a metropolitan region around the imperial capital and a periphery of subject provinces or colonies which must submit to various forms of economic, military, political, and social exploitation. These latter receive the benefits of the imperial peace, law, and administration, but they must bear most of the costs of empire in peacetime and during the recurrent wars to which empires are liable.

Writers from old imperial capital cities, metropolitan regions, or relatively favored nationalities often are impressed with the splendors, advantages, and benefits of empire, while observers from the provinces and colonies and from the disfavored subject peoples more often tend to note the sufferings, indignities, and costs which empire entails.

In the extreme case, a nation could establish an empire over other peoples so successfully that its own members might all rise in the economic and social scale to the point where the ruling nation within the empire would come close to becoming a ruling class. To turn a nation into a favored class would be indeed the ultimate triumph of nationalism, and such words as *Herrenvolk,* "master race," "ascendancy," "supremacy," and the like, testify to the persistence of the underlying image.

The basis of empires is the political apathy of most of their population. This apathy, it was noted, in turn used to be based upon their backwardness, poverty, and rural isolation and seclusion. All these basic conditions are now disappearing in most countries of the world, even though poverty in many countries has proved most slow-yielding and difficult to overcome. As a result, political apathy has been dwindling, and the foundations of empire everywhere have become increasingly shaky. The epoch of the crumbling of empires has arrived, and there is very little likelihood that this process will be reversed in the near future.

During the Middle Ages, political organization was a matter of five levels: village, district or barony, province or duchy, kingdom, and empire, corresponding loosely and in part to the ecclesiastic divisions of chapel, parish-church, bishopric, archdiocese, and the empirewide or worldwide jurisdiction of the papacy. Much of modern international politics occurs largely on three levels only: the subnational politics of interest groups, minority peoples, and regions; the nation-states, successors to the medieval kingdoms; and the plurality of empires—such as the British, French, Spanish, Ottoman, Russian, and Chinese—that had been prominent in the nineteenth century, only to decline or be replaced by other patterns in the twentieth.

The old worldwide mission of the medieval empire—to unify all peoples at least in symbols and aspirations—has been taken over by a new group, the international organizations. Some of these are highly specific, such as the Universal Postal Union. Others are closer to the character of all-purpose organizations, such as the United Nations, without attaining thus far the general scope, salience, and power of the nation-state. Any and all of them can intervene on occasion in the process of international politics, in ways that will be discussed somewhat later.

The result of the interplay of all these trends and actors is a world of states, buffeted by international competition from without and by competing political pressures and struggles from within. Many of these governments and states are highly armed, all are highly fallible, and almost all are in serious danger of some violent collision. Under these conditions, their survival and that of the international system depends to a crucial extent on the capacities of each state and each government—and generally, of each international actor—for guidance and for self-control.

8

How a State
Controls Itself

Individuals, groups, and nations alike are all said to act, in politics, "in accordance with their *interests*"—that is, according to their distribution of attention and their expectations of reward. We know that their interests may be inconsistent and their own perception of them highly fallible. But in order to understand how states can act in pursuit of what their leaders think to be their interests, we must first understand how a state controls its own behavior. In particular, how is foreign policy made and executed? What is the place of the foreign-policy sector in the total network of national decision making? And when does foreign policy take primacy over domestic politics?

All self-control involves the continuous mixing, blending, analyzing, and selective use of the contents of three separate streams of information. One of these is the stream of messages from the outside world; the second is the stream from the actor's own system and resources (which tells of their status); the third is the stream of messages recalled from memory. Any autonomous (self-steering) system, therefore, must contain within itself three operative information-processing structures (we might say "receptors," "channels," and the like) with which to do the job that combining and balancing these streams require. Only when it is thus properly equipped can any self-steering system—or for that matter any higher organism, any personality system, any social organization, or any government—find, gain, and maintain its autonomy, selfhood, and freedom.

DECISION MAKING: COMBINING NEW INFORMATION WITH OLD MEMORIES

The vast majority of the memories of individuals are stored only in their heads; the memories of states are stored in many places. Of course, the lesser state memories are stored (more or less as individual recollections) in the heads of state rulers and high officials, in the heads of members of state elites, and in the more numerous heads of the members of all the state's politically relevant social strata. But the really important memories are stored in the heads of the entire population, *and* in their culture and language. (These stores of words and images and cultural and moral preferences may imply important biases and predispositions toward certain kinds of responses to certain kinds of events—predispositions of which the individuals concerned often themselves may not be aware until the moment of responding.) They are stored in papers, books, and files; in maps, pictures, monuments, and libraries; in diplomatic reports and policy memoranda; in staff plans for war; in the records of government bureaus and of business organizations; in laws and in treaties. (The government—or the government agency, such as the State Department or the Central Intelligence Agency—which has the larger files will have the "better" memory, if it can find in them quickly and accurately the information that is relevant to the decisions it must make.)

Let us say that a message comes to the United States government about a sudden political crisis in a foreign country. The responsible officer in the State Department has to recall the most pertinent facts: where the country is and what political, economic, and military conditions prevail there; what American interests are involved there in terms of American nationals and investments in the country, as well as in terms of our broader political, economic, and strategic interests; what resources in the way of economic or political influence, as well as in the way of bases, troops, ships, and airplanes the United States may have nearby; and what allies we have in the area. In addition to information about the state of our interests and our armed forces, the officer must remember the state of our domestic political opinion, the views of the president and of Congress, and the known preferences and probable responses of our major domestic-interest groups, of the mass media, and of the national electorate.

To supplement personal memory, this official may draw upon files of earlier reports, on memoranda on current policy, and on other written sources; the officer may consult other officials in the State Department and other agencies, civilian and military, and the official may refer the matter upward for decision to bureaucratic superiors or to the president of the United States, whose own memories and remembered images and preferences may then become decisive in the matter. Between them, these people represent the effective memories of the United States government in making this decision.

On the night of June 25, 1950, the message came to Washington that North Korean troops and tanks had crossed in strength the thirty-eighth parallel into South Korea and that a war had started. During the night, more and more high-ranking officials were called back to the State Department. They remembered—and later repeated—a variety of pertinent bits of information. For instance, they remembered how the Western powers had hesitated overlong to oppose the Japanese aggression against Manchuria in 1931 and against China in 1937, and the German aggression in Central Europe in 1938 and 1939. In pondering the expected effects on world opinion of a communist triumph, and the political and strategic interests of the United States in not letting South Korea be overrun by communist armies, they also remembered that their country had for some time been a reluctant participant in a dangerous "cold war" with the Soviet Union. They remembered too the view, widespread at the time, that Stalin's Russia was continually testing the resolve of the United States, and that larger communist attacks would follow elsewhere if any one should succeed. They recalled the state of American domestic opinion in 1949: the indignation in Congress and among a substantial part of the general public at the communist victory in the Chinese civil war in that year, and at the limited character of the American aid given to the defeated Chinese nationalist faction. And they were aware of past reports of the strength of American naval, air, and military power available in the region from United States bases on the island of Okinawa and in Japan.

Not all these memories pointed in the same direction. Secretary of State Dean Acheson some time earlier had described South Korea as outside the perimeter of major American national defense interests; and some respected military leaders had described an American military engagement there as highly undesirable. These memories, however, counted for very little in the decision process when weighed against the preponderance of memories making for United States intervention, and within a short time substantial American forces were fighting in Korea. Apparently one potentially pertinent set of memories was not recalled by any of these officials during that June night in 1950: the memories of August 1914, when a local conflict between two secondary powers quickly escalated into a great power conflict which engulfed the world. At least none of these officials is recorded as having brought that incident to the attention of the others.[1]

Incoming information also added to the outcome of the American debate on Korea. There was the plea of the South Korean government for help; and there was the willingness of the then secretary general of the United Nations, Trygve Lie, to cooperate in obtaining a vote of the United Nations Security Council during the temporary absence of the Soviet representative (who earlier had walked out on the meetings of the Council in the belief that his absence would have the automatic effect of a legal veto on all

[1]See also Ernest R. May, *"Lessons" of the Past: The Use and Misuse of History in American Foreign Policy* (New York: Oxford Univ. Press, 1973), chapter 3.

important Council decisions under the United Nations Charter), so as to empower the United States to take military action in Korea under the flag and in the name of the United Nations. Finally, there was the impact of the memories and the personality of the president of the United States, who had to complete the decision on which his advisers had substantially agreed; and Harry Truman was not a man to hesitate before a fight that he thought justified.

The bulk of United States opinion agreed with Truman. There was positive rather than negative feedback from Congress and the press, while protests against American involvement in a land war in Asia remained minor and scattered. Outside the country, there was support from America's allies, albeit on a very limited scale, while Soviet opposition to United States intervention in Korea was violent in words but otherwise remained strictly limited chiefly to economic and logistic aid to North Korea. Moreover, the early experiences with intervention soon grew favorable. In October 1950 the United States forces won a major victory at Inchon. The United States government thereupon sent its troops into North Korea for the conquest or liberation of that country; and they advanced across most of it toward the Yalu River and the Chinese border in Manchuria. The original United States decision to resist aggression in South Korea had become transformed into a larger and far more risky undertaking.

FREEDOM AND POLICY:
THE NEED TO MAKE CONSISTENT DECISIONS

Particular decisions arrived at by such an interplay of current messages and recalled memories, as well as by the interplay of foreign and domestic messages, are not inevitable. Though some particular outcome of the decision process may be much more likely than another, the process remains combinatorial and probabilistic in its nature. This also seems characteristic of the autonomy of individuals and groups and of the sovereignty of states—in short, characteristic of self-governing freedom. From decision to decision, its outcome cannot be predicted with complete certainty, neither by any outside observer nor even from within the acting system itself.

Policy is an explicit set of preferences and plans drawn up in order to make the outcomes of series of future decisions more nearly predictable and consistent. Having a consistent policy protects the decision maker from undoing on one day what was done the day before, from undoing on odd-numbered days the work done on even-numbered ones. Similarly, in any cooperative or simply peaceful interactions among states, consistent policies are needed to make the outcome of these interactions somewhat more predictable. The more decisions a government must make, the greater is its need for policy. Once formulated and accepted, such preferences and plans—for instance, for the United States to support and promote the unification of Western Europe—are assigned a preferred place in the memory system of the government and its relevant personnel; and this policy is then given particular weight in the decision-making process, where it may then outweigh the other memories and current messages which conflict with it. Such policies may have to be changed from time to time to meet changing circumstances, but they must not be changed too often if the consistency and effectiveness of the government's actions are not to be reduced or lost.

Tentative foreign-policy plans for the government may be drawn up by one or a few officials. In British foreign policy, a famous memorandum drawn up by Sir Eyre Crowe in 1907 treated Germany, rather than France or Russia, as the most immediate threat to British interests, and British governments acted accordingly during the years that led to World War I. The foreign policy of the United States has had two long-term aims since World War II. One was to prevent or limit the expansion of communist and Soviet influence anywhere in the world. George Kennan, a member of the Policy Planning Staff of the State Department and subsequently United States ambassador to the Soviet Union and later to Yugoslavia, has become known as the author of an article in the magazine *Foreign Affairs* in 1947, signed only by "Mr. X." In it he persuasively urged, and largely initiated, such a policy of "containment" with regard to the Soviet Union and communist influence. But side by side with it, a second U.S. aim was to prevent the conflict with the Soviet Union from escalating into war between the two superpowers or from getting dangerously near to that point. This explains why George Kennan favored containment in 1947 but advocated a policy of *detente* later on. The term had first been introduced by President Kennedy in 1963 when he unilaterally declared the end of the "cold war" and advocated a relaxation of tensions between the United States and the Soviet Union. Consequently, while Kennedy sent additional troops to Berlin in 1961 and stood firm on Cuba in 1962, he then negotiated a partial Test Ban Treaty with the Soviet Union in 1963.

Detente as a long-term aim became a focus of American foreign policy from 1973 under the Nixon-Kissinger-Ford administration. It was yet another form of "containing" the Soviet Union, not by military strength but by the skillful use of checks and balances, pressures and inducements, attempting to build a "structure of peace" on the resulting balance of power. Thus Secretary of State Henry Kissinger and President Nixon favored in the 1970s *detente* with Russia over Berlin, the normalization of relations with the People's Republic of China, and initiated the Strategic Arms Limitation Talks (SALT). President Carter early in his administration continued to stress a policy of *detente,* but then cut off American grain and technology exports to the USSR after the Soviets' December 1979 intervention in Afghanistan.

President Reagan began his first term in office with a rhetoric of confrontation and a willingness to reassert worldwide American military, political, economic, and moral leadership and primacy over the Soviet Union, returning apparently to the assumptions and policy implications of the early strategy of "containment." Accompanying Reagan's verbal declarations was a massive defense buildup—with such new armament programs as the Strategic Defense Initiative (SDI)—and the administration's refusal to adhere to SALT II agreements or achieve substantial progress in the Strategic Arms Reduction Talks (START).

Yet despite such policies, President Reagan met with the Soviet leader Mikhail Gorbachev in November 1985 at Reykjavik to prepare further meetings to reduce conflicts between the two superpowers.

Similarly, both powers have shown relative restraint toward each other over such crises in their respective spheres of interest as in Poland in 1980, Grenada in 1983, Nicaragua in 1984, Libya in 1986, or the ongoing wars in Afghanistan and Indochina. Every recent American president at times has risked looking inconsistent, but each has had to keep serving two foreign-policy goals that were only partly compatible.

One dimension of the self-control of a government consists of how it treats the human beings subject to its power. As a positive note in his foreign policy, President Carter emphasized the priority of *human rights* as a qualification for U.S. support of present and potential allies. The concept of human rights has been established in political discourse since the English and American bills of rights of 1679 and 1776, and the French Declaration of the Rights of Man of 1789. In our time it became almost universally accepted when the United Nations adopted overwhelmingly the Universal Declaration of Human Rights in 1948. The Declaration provides for such civil and political rights as the right to life, liberty, and security of person; the right to freedom of thought, speech, and communication of information and ideas; freedom of assembly and religion; the right to government through free elections; the right to free movement within the state and free exit from it; the right to asylum in another state; the right to nationality; freedom from arbitrary arrest and interference with the privacy of home and family; the prohibition of slavery or torture. And it includes the more controversial economic and social rights to work, to protection against unemployment, and to join trade unions; the right to a standard of life adequate for health and well-being; the right to education; and the right to rest and leisure. The Declaration, however, has only moral authority.

In practice, many people think of human rights as freedom from four kinds of oppression by governments or local powerholders: murder, torture, arbitrary imprisonment, and "disappearance," that is, kidnapping. Some of these infamous practices have become less frequent but in many countries—communist and anti-communist—they still occur too often. President Carter's pressure on the Shah of Iran to have his government respect human rights was unsuccessful until the Shah fell from power—and the Islamic revolutionary regime that succeeded him was often not less cruel.

Since 1948 efforts have been made to enact covenants or conventions (which have treaty-binding powers) rather than declarations. These have been ratified to date only by some U.N. members. Such major powers as the United States have been extremely reluctant to accept treaties internationally guaranteeing human rights, arguing that America's own constitutional guarantees are more than adequate to ensure the protection of human rights for its citizens. Moreover, international protection and enforcement of human rights is often rejected by the ruling government on grounds of national sovereignty. The concept of sovereignty stipulates that the internal affairs of nation-states, including the protection and control of their citizens, are not to be interfered with by other nation-states or by international organizations. This leaves the observation and protection of human rights to private and nongovernmental organizations such as Amnesty International.

Nevertheless, under the pressure of the Carter administration a number of U.S. allies made concessions on human rights. Several military dictatorships in Latin America moved toward a partial "opening" to democracy, and in 1978 an Inter-American Court of Human Rights under the auspices of the Organization of American States (OAS) was instituted.

This trend continued under President Reagan, and by mid-1986 most Latin American countries had become democracies, though probably more in response to domestic than international pressure. Whether human rights will become a consistent theme in American foreign policy, or whether the acceptance and support of "benevolent" anticommunist dictatorships—as advocated by one-time U.S. delegate to the United Nations, Jeane Kirkpatrick and others—will prevail, is as yet, however, uncertain. For reasons of consistency, and as a political weapon, the United States has also directed demands to the Soviet Union and other communist-ruled countries to be more observant of human rights. These demands have produced no major changes in the domestic policy of these countries, but in recent years international influence has probably helped to bring about some improvements in the Soviet Union's treatment of dissidents and led to the release, and often lawful emigration, of a number of these dissidents and other would-be emigrés.

A PLURALITY OF DECISION MAKERS AND DECISION ELEMENTS

Even if clearly formulated, a policy has to be adopted. Just as we can think of the entire United States government as a single decision system with its memory and external and internal intake channels, so also we can think of smaller subsystems within the United States—such as major government agencies like the State Department or the Department of Defense, or the major political parties and congressional groupings—as each forming such a decision system with its own memories and intake channels. Any actual major foreign-policy decision would then be made as the result of the interplay of these several contending domestic actors, and any long-term foreign policy would have to be adopted through a similar pluralistic and competitive process.

The making of foreign policy thus resembles a pinball machine. Each interest group, each agency, each important official, legislator, or national opinion leader, is in the position of a pin, while the emerging decision resembles the end-point of the path of a steel ball bouncing down the board from pin to pin. Clearly, some pins will be placed more strategically than others, and on the average they will thus have a somewhat greater influence on the outcome of the game. But no one pin will determine the outcome. Only the distribution of all the relevant pins on the board—for some or many pins may be so far out on the periphery as to be negligible—will determine the distribution of outcomes. This distribution often can be predicted with fair confidence for large numbers of runs, but for the single run—as for the single decision—even at best only some probability can be stated. To ask of a government of a large nation who "really" runs it—presumably from behind the scenes—is usually as naïve as asking which pin "really" determines the outcome of the pinball game.

A similar combinatorial process, resembling in some ways our pinball game, also may be going on in the mind of any individual political leader or decision maker. He is likely to receive many different messages from the outside world, all bearing on the decision he must make; and he may recall many different items from memory—both memories of facts and memories of preferences—which bear on his decision. No outside observer, nor indeed even the decision maker himself, may be able to say which single outside message, or which single item recalled from memory, decisively influenced the way in which he finally made up his mind, and the course of action which he chose.

Though it is difficult to predict the outcome of a single run on a pinball machine, it is not nearly so hard to predict the distribution of a series of such runs. (Similarly, in rolling two true dice, you cannot predict the numerical value of any single throw, but if you keep making throws you can, according to fairly reliable mathematical odds, expect to get the number seven about one-sixth of the time, and the number twelve about one-thirty-sixth of the time.) Knowing the probability distribution of outcomes or payoffs on a gambling device, such as a pinball machine, would be the basis for your rational strategy if you had to gamble. Knowing (even approximately) the probability distribution of the decisions of a political leader, or of a political organization, a government, or a nation, is to know something about what we call their political "character"; and it is the basis of any rational strategy that could be pursued in regard to them in politics.

POLITICAL GOALS AND GOAL IMAGES

All that we have said so far about political decisions—the bases for them and the predictability of them—does not mean that governments are unlike other groups and organizations—that they do not have *goals* and do not pursue them. Governments certainly do. And some of the most important of these goals are in the field of foreign relations.

Governments may pursue their goals in either a conscious or a machinelike fashion. A *goal* (or *goal state*) for any acting system is that state of affairs, particularly its relationship to the outside world, within which its inner disequilibrium—its drive—has been reduced to a relative minimum. If a state is in some sort of disequilibrium or tension—and most states, like most other acting systems, are in some disequilibrium of this kind—it will tend to change some aspects of its behavior until this disequilibrium is reduced. When the inner disequilibrium is fully or enough reduced, the goal has been reached. The goal-seeking state (or any other acting system that seeks goals as we have defined the term) will tend to repeat those patterns of behavior and to persist in those states of affairs in which its inner disequilibrium will be relatively less, and likewise it will tend to avoid or to forsake quickly those states of affairs in which its inner disequilibrium for one reason or another increases. Any system, organization, or state that behaves in this manner will tend to approach its goal states, or goals, and to stick with them. It will exhibit goal-seeking behavior, and it will seem to be following a purpose, even if the persons within the organization or the state (be it one or the other) should not be aware of it.

Thus a great power, whose Department of Defense is under pressure from its armed services to establish strategic naval and air bases in foreign countries, and which is also under other pressures to minimize both financial costs and political problems with the host nations, may end up putting its overseas bases into some of the world's poorest and most backward countries, where unpopular and corrupt or oppressive governments may be willing to offer strategic sites for such bases to a foreign power most cheaply or with the least insistence on any share in their political control. As a result, a great democracy such as the United States, without any necessary deliberate intention of its leaders, may find itself allied around the world with a remarkable collection of backward monarchies, authoritarian regimes, and military or civilian dictatorships. The *goal image* held in the minds of many national leaders, writers, and voters—the image of the free world as a grand alliance of free countries—describes only very imperfectly the actual short-term *goal* which the United States government tries to approach in seeking such political necessities as compliant foreign allies and strategic overseas bases on the most favorable short-range terms. Similarly, the official Soviet *goal image* to assist "national liberation movements" in other countries is not always in accord with the Soviet military and naval presence in such dictatorial and civil-strife ridden countries as Afghanistan, South Yemen, and Ethiopia.

FEEDBACK AND GOAL-SEEKING BEHAVIOR

In theory, governments (like many other acting systems) could seek their goals by simple trial-and-error. They could try out different kinds of behavior toward their environment, and enter into different situations in relation to it; and they could then stay with those types of behavior and stay in those situations (*goal states* or *goals*) in which their own internal disequilibria or tensions would be smallest. Actually, most governments (like all reasonably effective goal-seeking organizations) can do a great deal better. They can use *feedback* information to guide themselves step-by-step toward their goals.

The feedback process is at the heart of all effective goal-seeking behavior. It consists in sending back to the acting system a stream of information about the results of its own earlier actions. The system thus gets information about the results of what it has just done, and uses this information to modify its subsequent actions. Feedback works in cycles: from *action* to *echo* (that is, to the return of messages about the results of that action), and then from echo to *reaction* (that is—as the next step— either to a repetition of the original action or to an action at least somewhat different from the original).

If the system is more complex, we can think of it as having specific components and subsystems, called *effectors,* through which it acts on the outside world. Soldiers, police officers, diplomats, and administrators of foreign economic aid all can act as effectors for a government, carrying out its orders more-or-less precisely and effectively. Here again, a feedback process may inform the government of just what its subordinates have done and what the results of their actions were; and in the light of this information the government may modify the further commands which it gives to them. At the same time, a shorter feedback process may bring back to the effector component itself (such as to the local commander of the nation's military force in the area) just what have been the results of his preceding action and he may take some corrective steps on his own, without waiting for the next order from his nation's capital. Indeed, much of the art and science of administration in foreign affairs, as in other matters, deals with the problem of how many and what kinds of decisions to allocate to the short-range local feedback circuits of the effector subsystems—the local embassy, the military theater commander, the local economic-aid office— and what kinds to reserve for the larger and often slower feedback channels of the national government, or even of the larger national decision system which may include the legislature, pressure groups, public opinion, and eventually the electorate. (A problem of this kind arose, for instance, in President Thomas Jefferson's quick decision in 1803 to back the decision of the United States representatives in Paris to buy the Louisiana Territory and thus much of the North American continent. This decision could not possibly have been made by any lesser official, such as the United States ambassador to Paris—but even when taken by the president, as it actually was, it was without full constitutional authority and was ratified only subsequently by Congress.)

Feedback signals, we have said, may be used to bring about an increase or a decrease in the intensity and/or frequency of the original behavior that gave rise to them. If the feedback always *increases* the intensity and/ or the frequency of the original behavior, then it is called *positive* or *amplifying feedback;* and it will drive the original behavior of the system higher and higher until some element in the system or in its environment breaks down, or until some essential resource or supply is exhausted. Somewhat as money at compound interest grows slowly but by ever larger absolute amounts, and as a forest fire grows on what it feeds on, so the actions of the members of a crowd in a panic serve as mutual signals, driving them all to more extreme panic behavior. In politics, as Thucydides had already found in Athens in the fifth century B.C., the speeches of competing politicians may drive them to demand ever more extreme strategies in the foreign affairs of their country, going beyond its real capabilities and ending in ruin.

The mutual growls of two dogs at a street corner, the mutual insults of two boys in the school yard, the mutual threats or arms appropriations of two competing great powers—all these may escalate a conflict to ever more intense levels of hostility. Escalation and all other forms of positive feedback are characteristic of incipient runaway situations. If persisted in, they are soon apt to get out of control, regardless of the moderate intentions of the parties who started them. If political actors—whether persons, governments, or nations—are to remain in control of their fate and of their own behavior, positive feedback must be stopped soon, or else it must soon be slowed down to ever smaller increments of behavior, so as to stay within some tolerable limit.

This is to say that positive feedback must be replaced by *negative feedback*, which will reduce or reverse previous behavior enough to limit its outcome. *Negative feedback* is the essential steering process which underlies all keeping of limits and all pursuit of goals. It requires two kinds of information: first, where the goal (or target or limit) is; and second, where and how distant from this goal the actor or acting system is. The feedback of the actual result of the actor's past behavior will then continue or increase that behavior if it is moving the actor closer to the goal, but will diminish or reverse current behavior if it is carrying the actor away from the target.

Negative feedback, then, is the control of behavior at each step or stage, not by good intentions but by its actual results in the stage that went before. In technology, it is the basis of thermostats that keep our homes at an even temperature despite a changing climate, and of the automatic control devices that can land a pilotless airplane or guide a missile to its target. In politics, negative feedback implies information that would suggest that a government continue a policy which appears to be bringing it closer to some clearly defined target-state of affairs, but which would signal a change or even a reverse in its actions if they were moving the government away from its goal.

Although the actual feedback processes in government and politics are multiple and complex, the fundamental concept of feedback is simple enough to be an effective tool to help us recognize, disentangle, and understand the various negative and positive feedback processes we find in practice. And these processes can include more than the direct approach to goals. For example, with the help of data recalled from memory, an actor can pursue a goal around obstacles or through a maze of detours and diversions. To continue approaching a long-range strategic goal throughout a sequence of tactical twists and turns of short-range changes is close to what we call *pursuing a purpose* or *purposive behavior*. Recognizing in each case such purposive behavior among states, and discovering specific message flows and communication channels, together with the particular persons, organizations, and material facilities on which it depends, is a major task of political analysis in international affairs. For as soon as these essential key groups and communication channels (persons and facilities for setting and seeking a particular goal) are drastically changed, or put out of operation, then the large organization or the nation-state which contained them may still continue to exist, but this particular purposive behavior will cease, insofar as it depended on their functioning.

THE MARCH OF HISTORY

Purposes and Causes

Not all of the behavior of political leaders, interest groups, governments, and states is purposive. At all levels—among individuals, groups, and nations—the communication channels and messages directing them toward their goals are not the only ones that impinge on their behavior. Indeed, several goals and several streams of messages from both without and within, may be competing for the limited available communication channels and for the time and attention of decision makers. Some of these competing inputs may be relatively random; and all of them may increase the confusion within the decision-making system and the overload on its channels, facilities, and personnel. This can result in making some part of its output relatively random, and hence cause the whole input-output cycle to be much less predictable in the distribution of its results.

Moreover, all actors depend to some extent on their components which may not be wholly under their control; their behavior can be altered when a critical component fails or otherwise changes. For this reason, national leaders continuously depend (and are judged) on their soundness of body and mind, and the temper of their personality and emotional makeup. Witness such stable American leaders as John Foster Dulles and Dwight Eisenhower, in contrast to those who became eventually incapacitated, unstable, or exhausted, such as Woodrow Wilson, James Forrestal, and perhaps Richard Nixon. Likewise, nations may depend for some of their behavior on crucial subgroups or leaders, and if these fail or change, national and even world history may be changed. The conflict between the army and the communists in 1965 changed the foreign policy of Indonesia; the deaths of Franklin D. Roosevelt and John F. Kennedy were followed by far-reaching changes in some of the foreign policies of the United States; and the deaths of Stalin in 1953 and of Mao Zedong in 1976 each were followed by important policy changes both on the domestic and foreign level in the Soviet Union and the People's Republic of China. No death of an individual leader himself, however, has changed the basic political and social system of a country.

Actors also depend to a significant extent on their environment, which includes the actions of neighbors, partners, and rivals. In fact, the outcome of the behavior of *any* acting system depends to a considerable extent on the actions of other actors and on the larger suprasystem in which it is located. As a result, though each actor may pursue a purpose, the outcome may be one which none of them intended. The time at which an office worker will get home at the end of the day depends not only on his or her hurrying and on the excellence of a powerful car; it may depend crucially on the flow of traffic at 5 P.M. Similarly, the success or failure of a nation's policy depends not only on its own power and on the intentions of its leaders, but also on the larger political and economic situation then prevailing in the world.

To the extent that we can predict changes in the subsystem or in the suprasystem, or at least account for them in an orderly manner, we are inclined to treat them as causes. We then say that this policy was discontinued "because" of the death of a chief executive, or that some other policy failed "because" of the changed international situation. Conversely, if we cannot explain to our satifaction just how and why these critical subsystem and suprasystem changes came about, then we tend to call them accidents.

Together, all these various sources of possible elements of randomness, discontinuity, and unexpected change modify (often quite drastically) the progress of policy and the flow of history; and they also modify the effects of the underlying probabilities, biases, and "mute forces" of history, which in and by themselves often would have indicated a different outcome. As it is, predicting the outcome of international politics often is as hard as predicting the outcome of a game with moderately loaded dice. If they are very heavily loaded, predicting the outcome becomes fairly easy; if their loading is negligible, some few predictions can be made by using randomness as a rule. But if the dice are loaded to a moderate but significant extent without overwhelming all the other factors influencing the outcome, prediction becomes difficult but interesting. Since just this condition seems to prevail in international politics, a better model than either randomness or determinism is needed for thinking about peace and war.

Such a model is also needed to help us deal with the persuasive but conflicting partial theories that have been developed by great thinkers in the past. The Prussian strategist Clausewitz, drawing on the experience of the Napoleonic wars, stressed the purposiveness of war started and conducted by national leaders as "a continuation of policy by other means." The great Russian writer Leo Tolstoy drew the opposite conclusion from the events of the same epoch: wars and battles to him were long series of accidents, least intelligible to those most immediately involved in them. Finally, to the believers in economic and social causes, such as Plato, Karl Marx, and Charles Beard, wars seemed to be caused (as Plato said) by money, or (as Marx and Beard elaborated) by more complex social-class arrangements and group interests.

The Random Walk Model

A helpful tool for dealing with these conflicting theories and facts is the *random walk* model. Imagine a drunken man staggering around the broad, flat ledge of a cliff, taking step after step at random while a horrified but too-busy-to-help mathematician watches him from afar in order to chart and predict his progress. There is an element of determinism in the random walk: the drunkard can only move from where he is, and he can take only one step at a time. Combined with this, there is an element of probability: since his steps are random, they are quite unlikely to be all in the same direction; more likely they will change direction often, and sometimes reverse it. As a result the mathematician, using techniques for analyzing what he calls "stochastic" processes, can calculate his progress. He can say how likely the drunkard is, within a certain number of steps, to come back to his starting point, and on which part of the ledge he is most likely to be at any particular time, and how likely he is to overstep the edge, within what period. If, however, the drunkard should happily be tottering instead all over a hillside, the slope of the hill will add some constant downhill bias to his meandering progress. But again, if this slope is not too steep, the random component in the walk will continue to have an appreciable effect on the outcome.

The random walk of the drunkard has more than a little in common with the policies of great nations and with the march of history on earth. At every step, the walk starts from a position given at that time; it contains an ineradicable random element, which may be either large or small in its effects; and it is subject to modification by persistent deterministic causes, biases, and influences, which can do much to change the distribution of probable outcomes but usually cannot make any single outcome certain. Similarly, national policies and historical processes can only start at one point in time, and from what is given then and there. They, too, are subject to persistent influences, biases, and causal processes, ranging from economic conditions and popular preferences to technical constraints and to the power and resources of particular actors, both within and among nations. Of course, they reflect the purposive behavior and often the deliberately chosen strategies of different participants. But they also include many random or nearly random elements: the random behavior of some components within some or all of the interacting subsystems and systems; the conflicts and collisions among different actors whose strategies may frustrate one another and produce results desired by none; and the interplay among the different system levels, combining perhaps the temper or the headache of a leader in one country with a national crop failure in another; and all of these perhaps with a worldwide business recession or monetary crisis. The disillusioned comment of the author of the Book of Ecclesiastes—"The race is not to the swift nor the battle to the strong, but time and chance happen to them all"—is a fit observation of the properties of random walks and stochastic processes.

Under these conditions individuals and governments must rely less on *assurance* and more on *insurance*—and even this to only a limited extent. Knowing the limitations of their powers to predict, they can endeavor to provide. They can make provisions for possible risks which they can only very imperfectly estimate; they can strive to make the risks smaller; and they can adapt their aspiration levels in foreign affairs to their actual disposable work force and material, as weighed against the resources and reserves which each level of foreign-policy goals would require.

Calculation of Risk and Success: The Theory of "Gambler's Ruin"

Since international politics in today's world includes many aspects of a gamble, the makers of foreign policy—all the way down to the active and interested citizens in a democracy—need to be familiar with the basic idea underlying the mathematical calculation of what is termed *gambler's ruin*. In protracted games of chance, gamblers with small reserve are very likely to be wiped out by the fluctuations in their fortunes, even if the constant house odds in favor of the bank should be quite moderate. Once hit by a run of adverse luck, the smaller gambler is apt to be ruined, and hence not able to profit from any later and more favorable run. The bank with its larger reserves, however, or any similarly well-financed player, can survive even long runs of bad luck, and rely on the chance of doing better at some later stage. The greater the risks and the more uncertain and fluctuating the fortunes of the game, the more likely is the ruin of the small player. The gambler—or the country—with the greater resources can afford more accidents and mistakes, and still stay in the game, while the gambler with scant reserves must be very skillful, and even very lucky, to survive. Indeed, if the game lasts long enough, the bank is apt to break him eventually anyway. This general rule favors large countries against small ones in the uncertainties of conventional warfare. Against the destructive power of nuclear weapons in a major war, however, the reserves of human life even in the largest countries are now quite small.

Rational and responsible policy makers must work within these limitations. As for their countries, they can try to provide them with more generous resources and reserves for expected or unforeseen contingencies. As to their foreign policies, they can insist on leaving themselves broad margins of safety: the random-walk model suggests that if some of their steps are likely to be random, they had better stay well away from the brink of the abyss. Finally, as to acting toward their adversaries, they can stay mindful of the imperfect knowledge and control and the probable random elements among the actions taken by the other side; and if in doubt about their own actions—which will be often—they can hold to the advice of the great conservative thinker Edmund Burke, that the statesman should be in nothing as economical as in the production of evil.

Models of probabilistic processes can do more for the understanding and making of foreign policy than furnish us with general philosophical advice. They can tell us what initial facts, relationships, probabilities, and rates of change we need to know or need to estimate; what model of the process they imply; and, if the model should be reasonably realistic, what most-likely consequences ought to be expected and what less-likely-but-still-quite-possible alternative outcomes ought to be provided for.

Early process models, based on the rates of airplane production and attrition, and on the rates of training losses and recoveries of pilots, were used to predict successfully the outcome of the Battle of Britain in 1940. Other models have been used to simulate the course of electoral campaigns. Such models could be adapted, in the case of an internal civil conflict (using recruitment and attrition rates of guerrillas and government troops, and perhaps also the rates of shift of political sympathies among the rest of the population, and possibly the rate of foreign intervention on one or both sides of the conflict), to estimate the size, duration, and probable outcome of the struggle, and even the probable size, duration, and material and human cost of outside intervention that would be necessary to control it.

Where such calculations were not made, or made poorly, or based on grossly unrealistic estimates, people have died needlessly; and frustrating and disappointing wars have been embarked upon that more rational and realistic forethought could have avoided.

Even at best, however, all such calculations will be uncertain and incomplete for a long time to come. Leaders still will have to make decisions with their hearts and minds; and so we must not underestimate the conceptual and philosophic importance of understanding the random-walk aspects of international politics. That model will remind us that in facing the substantial areas of uncertainty that will remain before us, we shall reveal *which of our own values we shall follow when in doubt:* the values of pride and power or the values of moderation and compassion. Individuals make foreign policy, or accept or reject it in the light of what they think they know and what they think they like. Their foreign policy is apt to change not only with any major change in their cognitive perception of the world, or in their communication and decision systems, but also with any major change in their salient values.

9

How Foreign Policy Is Made

The foreign policy of every country deals first with the preservation of its independence and security, and second with the pursuit and protection of its economic interests (particularly those of its most influential interest groups). Deeply involved with these interests—in the case of the major powers, at least—are a concern with resisting any penetration and manipulation by foreign countries and ideologies, and an unblushing effort to accomplish some active penetration and manipulation of their own. Finally, closely linked to the national security, economic, and clandestine warfare interests of each major power are its policies of economic aid to foreign nations, its efforts to spread its own national and ideological propaganda in foreign countries, and its support of cultural and scientific exchange missions favorable to that end.

THE SEARCH FOR NATIONAL SECURITY

Each of these activities is to some extent an instrument to further some or all of the others, but each also tends to some extent to become an end in itself. Each in time gives rise to formal bureaucratic organizations and informal public- and private-interest groups. Each generates a more-or-less distinct network of information flows, images, and memories, as well as a network of material expectations and rewards. In fact, there are many networks of rewards, including roles, jobs, and careers, appropriations and contracts, and also internalized standards of success and self-respect among the persons involved in this particular branch of the foreign-policy efforts of their country.

The result has been a paradox. The United States and the Soviet Union—and to a significant extent also communist China, Great Britain, and France—are powers so large that no one could abolish their national independence, even if anyone were mad enough to try. Yet it is precisely the United States and the Soviet Union that are spending the most money, labor, resources, and efforts in pursuit of what their governments, elites, and peoples consider their national security. And the three next largest powers follow them closely in their relative levels of expenditure for their national security—although it is not clear who it is that is seriously threatening their national independence.

The explanation is simple. It is a kind of "Parkinson's Law" of national security: a nation's feeling of insecurity expands directly in relation to its power. The larger and more powerful a nation is, the more its leaders, elites, and often its population increase their level of aspirations in international affairs. The more, that is to say, do they see themselves as destined or obliged to put the world's affairs in order, or at least to keep them in some sort of order that seems sound to them. Members of small nations, such as the Norwegians and the Swiss, who have had long experience in preserving their independence, usually have no such idea. It seems natural to them to concentrate their attention and efforts on preserving their own nation in a world whose economics and/or ideologies they do not expect to control in any case. Only the largest and strongest nations can develop some at-least-plausible image of a world which they by their own national efforts might mold, change, or preserve wholly or in large part according to their own desires; and their fears, worries, efforts, and expenditures go up accordingly.

By now, even such large countries as Britain, France, Japan, Italy, and West Germany all have given up the ambition to run the world, and even to gain or retain large empires. They are in fact willing to cooperate with other nations only to a cautious and limited extent, and hope that they do not have to respond (though they will) to a major direct attack on any country that might pose a direct threat to all. The idea of changing or even maintaining the order of the world unilaterally by essentially national decisions and substantially unaided national efforts ("unilateralism," as the late Professor Charles Lerche called it[1]) cannot be entertained seriously today, even as a tempting thought, by any powers other than the United States, the Soviet Union, and possibly communist China. And, even of these three giant countries, probably only the United States is in a position to draft and ship hundreds of thousands—possibly millions—of its population to fight for its world-spanning concept of national security on distant continents; the larger resources of manpower of the USSR and the People's Republic of China are offset by their geographic distance from many theatres and even more by

---

[1]Charles O. Lerche, Jr., *The Uncertain South* (Chicago: Quadrangle Books, 1964).

their lower levels of facilities and equipment for sea and air transportation. Professor Lerche, commenting on this situation in the 1960s, pointed out that "few people at present favor American withdrawal from world affairs. The key distinction is between those who prefer maximum American freedom of action, the 'unilateralists,' and those who emphasize the interdependence of nations for purposes of security and prosperity, the 'multilateralists.' "[2] These two basic foreign-policy orientations have remained important to the present: while President Carter favored a multilateralist foreign-policy approach where possible, the opposite policy—unilateralism—has been more prominent during some parts of President Reagan's two terms in office.

National-security interests and organizations thus predominate in the foreign-policy activities of any large nation.

ECONOMIC INTERESTS IN FOREIGN POLICY

Now we move on to the national interest second in importance to security, and very much dependent on it: the economic, sociological, and psychological structures and processes. According to Marx and Lenin, as well as to J. A. Hobson and Charles A. Beard, we ought to expect economic class or group interests to be decisive, but the evidence suggests a far more complex picture. Important as they are, economic interests do not stand alone, but are linked to political interests which may modify or even override their effects.

In the United States, as in other large countries, such matters as the routine protection of the trade, traffic, and travel of a nation's citizens abroad—and the regulation of the activities of foreign nationals in one's own country—take up only a relatively small part of the activities of the State Department and the other government agencies active in the foreign-affairs sector. More substantial private economic interests in the United States, as in other countries with predominantly private-enterprise economies, are involved in American long-term private investments abroad, such as copper and iron mines, sugar and banana plantations, and telephone companies and other private utilities in Latin America; or oil fields in Venezuela, Libya, Saudi Arabia, and Iran. Table 12 shows a comparison of the gross national product (GNP) of the world's richest nation-states and the size of annual sales of the largest industrial companies of the world in 1979. The order of magnitude of even the biggest of these companies is below the level of most modern industrial states. Annual sales of the largest industrial company are still below the level of the GNP of Sweden, Belgium,

---

[2]The reference to Lerche is Professor Sapin's in Burton M. Sapin, *The Making of United States Foreign Policy* (New York: Praeger, for the Brookings Institution, 1966), p. 48. For the continuing debate on multilateralism and interdependence, see Robert O. Keohane and Joseph S. Nye, Jr., *Power and Interdependence* (Boston: Little, Brown, 1976); Edward L. Morse, *Modernization and the Transformation of International Relations* (Princeton, NJ: Princeton Univ. Press, 1976); and Robert O. Keohane, *After Hegemony: Cooperation and Discord in the World Political Economy* (Princeton, NJ: Princeton Univ. Press, 1984).

Czechoslovakia, and Rumania. On the other hand, the turnover of these major companies clearly rivals the GNP of such nation-states as Venezuela, Indonesia, Pakistan, and New Zealand. The scope and proportions of these corporations, which almost inevitably extend over and across national boundaries, are visible in almost all sectors of the economy. The Exxon Corporation, for example, stations three times as many employees overseas as the U.S. State Department, and its tanker fleet, estimated at 6 million tons, is half the size of that of the Soviet Union. In the nine richest industrial countries, about 30 percent of the industrial workforce is employed by multinational corporations, and these companies employ about 46 million workers worldwide. Furthermore, the average annual growth rate of successful multinational corporations is two or three times that of the United States. In 1978, about 30 percent of international trade was done by multinational corporations, and it is estimated that by the end of the 1980s about 300 large multinational companies will control close to 80 percent of the world's manufacturing assets.

Table 12 also shows that the combined number of top European and Japanese multinational corporations exceeds that of American companies: of the twenty largest multinational corporations in the world, only eleven are American, and nine of the ten largest multinational corporations are oil companies. Table 13 shows that the number of large American companies among the world's multinational corporations has been steadily declining since 1970, and may be continuing to do so.

Nonetheless, the share of American multinational corporations in total sales of manufacturers within the United States, and of the world's gross product has increased steadily. Professor Raymond Vernon showed that the large multinational firms in 1950 accounted for only 17 percent of total U.S. sales of manufacturers. By 1967, the U.S. firms that were then multinational in scope accounted for 42 percent of U.S. sales, and this share had risen to 62 percent by 1974. In the noncommunist world, the first firms classified as multinational in 1950 reported annual sales that amounted to about 8 percent of gross overall product; by 1967 the figure was 17 percent, and by 1974 22 percent. For 1988, the multinational corporations' share of gross world product is expected by some observers to grow to 40 percent.[3]

The gains for American firms from such multinational enterprises are equally considerable. In the three decades since World War II, practically every one of America's largest firms has developed a large overseas network of subsidiaries and branches. The output of these overseas facilities has come to equal nearly 40 percent of home output; and in banking, American businessmen have been writing as much as half their business overseas. In total, the foreign facilities of United States companies are valued at $150 billion and are generating a return flow of earnings to the

---

[3]Raymond Vernon, *Storm over the Multinationals: The Real Issues* (Cambridge, MA: Harvard Univ. Press, 1977), chapter 1. *Author's footnote:* These figures were compiled by Harvard Multinational Enterprise Project. The multinational share in the gross product of the noncommunist world equals about 15 percent of the product of the world as a whole (K.W.D.). Estimate for 1988 from M. J. Taylor, and N. J. Thrift (eds.), *The Geography of Multinationals* (Kent, England: Croom Helm, 1982), p. 147.

United States of $12–15 billion annually. American exports of manufactured goods have become heavily reliant on the overseas subsidiaries of U.S. companies, while American imports of raw materials are also closely linked to overseas networks.[4]

The United States government is expected to protect to a considerable extent the private interests of its citizens abroad, and many of the interest groups just named are sufficiently well organized and politically well connected to make sure that this is done.

The results may be more favorable to United States citizens, however, than they are to foreigners. As private and public loans are repaid by the debtor countries, and as profits from private investments—estimated to be as high as 10 percent on American investments abroad—are repatriated, there is a net transfer of wealth from the developing country to the developed one. For contrary to popular assumptions, multinational corporations secure most of their finance capital in the host countries rather than bringing it with them. One study shows that between the years 1957 and 1965, American multinational corporations operating in Latin America financed 83 percent of their activities with local funds and took 79 percent of their profits out of Latin America. Only about 17 percent of American investments thus presented a transfer of wealth from the richer to the poorer countries.[5] This fact is not often perceived by American newspaper readers, who are more aware of the private and public loans and credit that move from the United States to the developing countries. These capital flows from resource-rich and economically more advanced to less developed countries will have reached proportions of over $1,000 billion at the end of 1986 according to the World Bank. The worldwide economic recession of the late 1970s and early 1980s, creating higher interest payments and lower export earnings, left many less developed countries in Latin America and the Caribbean—but also, for example, Poland and Yugoslavia—unable to meet their scheduled debt repayments; and in mid-1982, international bank lending to Latin American countries had therefore all but ground to a halt. Such countries as Brazil and Mexico—each with external public- and private-sector debts of over $100 billion in 1986—were left on the verge of financial crisis, since they, like the other countries in the area, need a constant inflow of funds to pay off old debts, finance trade, and maintain foreign-exchange reserves.

Many of these countries are heavily burdened by merely having to meet interest payments on these loans and credits extended to them. In 1977, less developed countries paid nearly $40 billion in annual interest and principal repayments, and in 1984 this sum had risen to about $160 billion. Interest payments thus rose from about 10 percent of export earnings to 25 percent. And with another 11 percent committed to repaying principal debts, repayments of less developed countries amounted to more than one-third of their export earnings (and—in the case of Latin Ameri-

---

[4]See Raymond Vernon, "Multinationals: No Strings Attached," *Foreign Policy* 33 (Winter 1978/1979), pp. 121–134.

[5]See Richard J. Barnet and Ronald E. Muller, *Global Reach: The Power of the Multinationals* (New York: Simon and Schuster, 1974), p. 152.

TABLE 12 COMPARATIVE RANKING OF NATIONAL ECONOMIES AND THE LARGEST INDUSTRIAL COMPANIES OF THE WORLD*

RANK (1978)	UNIT OF ANALYSIS	BILLIONS OF DOLLARS	RANK (1978)	UNIT OF ANALYSIS	BILLIONS OF DOLLARS
1	United States	2,107.9	38	Nigeria	35.0
2	Soviet Union	1,253.6	39	MOBIL	34.7
3	Japan	980.0	40	Indonesia	34.0
4	West Germany	638.1	41	Greece	32.3
5	France	469.0	42	Hungary	32.0
6	China	444.0	43	Finland	31.0
7	Great Britain	308.7	44	TEXACO	28.6
8	Italy	260.0	45	BRITISH PETROLEUM	27.4
9	Brazil	187.0	46	Bulgaria	24.8
10	Canada	179.2	47	Taiwan	24.7
11	Netherlands	150.2	48	Philippines and STANDARD OIL (California)	23.2
12	Spain	142.3	49	NATIONAL IRANIAN OIL	22.8
13	Australia	109.9	50	Thailand	21.7
14	Poland	108.3	51	Iraq	21.4
15	India	96.0	52	IBM	21.1
16	Mexico	91.4	53	GENERAL ELECTRIC	19.6
17	Switzerland	88.3	54	Pakistan	19.4
18	Sweden	87.3			

19	East Germany	81.0	55	Libya	19.3
20	Belgium	79.0(1977)	56	UNILEVER	18.6
21	Iran	76.1	57	Colombia	18.5
22	Czechoslovakia	70.7	58	Portugal	18.3
23	Rumania	67.5	59	GULF OIL	18.1
24	Saudi Arabia	64.0	60	CHRYSLER	16.3
25	GENERAL MOTORS	63.2	61	Malaysia	15.7
26	Denmark	62.5	62	IT&T	15.2
27	EXXON	60.3	63	Chile	15.1
28	Austria	58.0	64	STANDARD OIL (Indiana)	15.0
29	Yugoslavia	55.3	65	SIEMENS	13.9
30	Turkey	48.7	66	New Zealand and VOLKSWAGEN	13.3
31	South Korea	47.4			
32	South Africa	46.0	67	Kuwait and TOYOTA	12.8
33	Argentina	45.0			
34	ROYAL DUTCH SHELL	44.0	68	Israel and RENAULT	12.7
35	FORD	42.7			
36	Venezuela	40.0	69	ENI (Rome)	12.6
37	Norway	39.6	70	FRANÇAISE DES PETROLES	12.5

*Data used are the gross national product (GNP) for national economies and national sales for companies. From Theodore A. Couloumbis and James H. Wolfe, *Introduction to International Relations: Power and Justice*, 2nd ed. (Englewood Cliffs, NJ: Prentice-Hall, Inc., 1982), p. 357.

Sources: "The 50 Largest Companies of the World," *Fortune 100* (August 13, 1979). p. 208; and U.S. Central Intelligence Agency, *National Basic Intelligence Factbook* (January 1980).

TABLE 13   The World's Largest Multinational Corporations (MCNs), 1970 and 1979

COUNTRY	1970 NUMBER OF MNCs	PERCENTAGE OF TOTAL	1979 NUMBER OF MNCs	PERCENTAGE OF TOTAL
United States	120	60.9	285	43.2
Japan	13	6.6	98	14.8
Great Britain	17	8.6	72	10.9
West Germany	15	7.6	52	7.9
France	13	6.6	32	4.8
Canada	2	1.0	24	3.6
Sweden	1	0.5	16	2.4
Italy	5	2.5	10	1.5
Netherlands	3	1.5	9	1.4
Others	8	4.1	65	9.8
Total	197	100.0	660	100.0

Note: MNCs with a turnover of $1 billion or more have risen by 335 percent in the 1970s. Italy, France, and the United States are the only countries whose share of large multinational companies has declined. Japan doubled, and Sweden even quadrupled its share. The steep rise of MNCs in other countries is due to the emergence of large companies in such newly industrialized countries as Venezuela, Brazil, Mexico, and South Korea. According to the Harvard Multinational Enterprise Project, already more than 1000 Third World multinational corporations exist, and the findings in *Fortune* show that of the 500 largest non-American companies, 104 are from newly industrialized and less developed countries. Most of these are joint ventures with other Third World countries.

Source: "The 50 Largest Companies in the World," *Fortune* (August 1981).

can countries such as Argentina, Brazil, Chile, and Mexico—to almost one-half of their export earnings in 1983).[6]

In addition to the international flows of commodities or money, American economic interests abroad include the acquisition of titles of ownership of land, buildings, mineral resources, and productive installations. (Such titles are acquired in foreign countries either by American citizens directly, or indirectly by corporations and holding companies in which American capital or business firms are involved.) Finally, American economic interests may include the preservation or acquisition of particularly favorable conditions for buying, for selling, or for establishing credit for American business firms in those foreign countries which are in some ways relatively dependent on the United States. Thus, in pre-Castro days, Cuba obtained many of its imports, such as textiles, from the United States, although these were not cheap in the world market; and Cuba bought relatively little from Japan, even though Japanese goods of equal quality would have been cheaper. And the Japanese themselves in the late 1950s did not push their exports to Batista's Cuba since, as one of their spokes-

---

[6]For a more detailed discussion, see Pedro-Pablo Kuczynski, "Latin American Debt," *Foreign Affairs* 61, no. 2 (Winter 1982/1983), pp. 344–364, and "Latin American Debt: Act Two," *Foreign Affairs* 62, no. 1 (Fall 1983), pp. 17–38.

men said privately, they did not wish to offend the United States by imping-
ing on our favored market.

Even though such conditions seem to lend some support to the classic
theories of imperialism, their evidence must be confronted with a fundamental fact. In the seventy-three years since 1913, foreign investments and
all foreign economic transactions have formed a declining proportion of
the gross national product of all major countries. Similarly, world trade and
the international flow of payments have grown more slowly than has the
world's industrial production, or its production of services. If the classic
theories of imperialism had given an adequate picture of reality, the opposite should be the case. As it is, the annual transactions of all economic
interests and interest groups oriented to foreign trade and investment command only a small and declining share of the gross national product—and
thus probably in the long run, a declining share of political influence and
national attention. In the United States in 1983 this share was about 13
percent; it was about 8 percent in the Soviet Union in 1980.[7] Even if the
latter's collectivist economy had been adapted to the exploitation of its
satellite countries, the amounts would have been marginal.

The evidence seems more nearly compatible with what the late economist and sociologist Joseph A. Schumpeter predicted.[8] In all major countries, the national-security complex of the armed forces, the propaganda,
intelligence, and political warfare services, and the major industries and
special technological organizations supplying a substantial part of their
output to the national-security systems, have tended to form to some extent
a self-perpetuating interest group of their own. In the United States, as in
some other countries, these groups have included the military, the civilian
"defense intellectuals" and strategists, and parts of the arms, aerospace,
and electronics industries. There is reason to think that at least some similar
congealing of occupational, professional, technological, and ideological interests may also have occurred in some sectors of the elites of the Soviet
Union and of communist China. Similar complexes are observable, though
to a much lesser extent, in such middle-rank powers as France and Britain,
and additional interest clusters of this kind eventually may be reemerging
in West Germany and Japan.

SOCIOLOGICAL AND PSYCHOLOGICAL IMPLICATIONS

Some of the rewards sustaining such a "security complex" in each major
country are obviously economic; but to a much larger extent than previously assumed, many of the most salient rewards are sociological and psy-

[7]Calculations by Chandler Finley, based on figures from United Nations Conference on
Trade and Development, *Handbook of Trade and Development Statistics 1983* (New York: United
Nations, 1983); R. L. Sivard, *World Military and Social Expenditures 1983* (Washington, D.C.:
World Priorities, 1983); *Statistical Abstract of the United States 1982–83* (Washington, D.C.:
Government Printing Office, 1982); and *The World Almanac & Book of Facts 1985* (New York:
Newspaper Enterprise, 1984), (data from 1983).

[8]Joseph A. Schumpeter, *Imperialism and Social Classes* (New York: Meridian, 1955).

chological. These are rewards in terms of social status and professional role; of individual and collective self-image and self-respect; of the consistency or "cognitive consonance" of one's previously acquired image of the world; of one's sense of belonging to a group; and of the need to see dignity and meaning in one's past and present actions.

According to Schumpeter, "war hawks" (enemies of the "doves") are a self-perpetuating flock of birds, for he expects that any major interest group with a military or warlike orientation will think up endless rationalizations for warlike policies—that is, for acting out over and over again the patterns of behavior which they have previously learned. President Eisenhower's worried remark in his farewell address about the influence of the "military-industrial complex" in the United States suggests that Schumpeter has not remained alone in his misgivings.

In the late 1960s and early 1970s, mass opinion in the United States moved away from the defense-oriented posture of the preceding two decades and turned against high levels of military spending. In a September 1970 survey, 60 percent of voters under thirty wanted to reduce military spending, whereas only forty-six percent of those thirty and over gave such an answer.[9] This new generation came into the fore in the 1970s, when general public opinion widely supported the Nixon-Kissinger-Ford policies of *detente* between the United States and the Soviet Union and of normalization of relations between the United States and the People's Republic of China. But with the onset of the energy crises and the worldwide economic recession in the mid-1970s, many Americans began to feel increasingly threatened by the Soviet Union's steadily growing military capabilities and expansionist Soviet and communist foreign-policy moves in the face of an apparently weakened defense posture of the United States.

In the 1976 presidential campaign, many of the "hawkish" individuals and groups who had supported the Vietnam war—and generally a more militant foreign policy of the "cold war" type, together with a higher level of armaments—made a new bid to recover their lost or weakened influence; but they failed when President Carter was elected after campaigning on a promise of moderate reduction in military spending and a continuation of much of the policy implications of detente. But while still expressing a strong distaste for sending American troops abroad, Americans also gave gradually increasing support to initiatives for high defense spending from 1973 to 1978; and in the end, events in Iran and Afghanistan brought about the culmination of the public's desire for a stronger defense posture and a tougher stance toward the Russians. This helped bring to power in 1980 a "hawkish" president and an administration whose principal foreign-policy objective was to build up the nation's military defenses and who had promised to make the military-industrial complex once again one of the most favored interest groups in terms of federal budget allocations. The

[9]See Bruce M. Russett, "The Revolt of the Masses: Public Opinion on Military Expenditures," in B. M. Russett (ed.), *Peace, War, and Numbers* (Beverly Hills, CA, and London: Sage Publications, 1972), p. 318.

Reaganites' efforts raised the total defense budget from 23.4 percent in 1980 to 29 percent in 1986.[10]

Yet in 1982 the tide of public opinion began to turn again, and President Reagan's proposals for further massive increases in defense spending met with increasing public and congressional resistance; with concern over the domestic social costs of such a commitment of the nation's wealth and resources to the military sector; and with fear that such a defense posture and tough anti-Soviet foreign policy might also enhance the risk of war. Similarly, the consistently strong noninterventionist sentiment of most of the American public has constrained the Reagan administration's foreign-policy initiatives over such issues as the declaration of martial law in Poland in 1981, the crises in Lebanon and the Falkland Islands in 1982, and the conflicts in El Salvador in 1984 and most recently in Nicaragua since 1984. Only less risky and successful military moves—such as the invasion of Grenada in 1983, and the bombardment of Libya in 1986 (in response to Colonel Qaddafi's alleged support of international terrorist activities)—have been lauded almost unanimously and again given credit and prestige to military interventionist strategies and America's defense establishment.[11] However, the revelation of a deliberate campaign of "disinformation" by the United States government, spreading false news in foreign and American media and rumors of American preparations to attack Libya backfired. It mainly weakened the credibility of the United States, and President Reagan's administration.

Schumpeter distinguished between warlike interest groups which were decisively aided and strengthened by the entire historical, sociological, and ideological structure of their countries and cultures (such as in the cases of Imperial Germany and Japan at the time of World War I) and the far weaker warlike interest groups and elites in such basically democratic countries as Great Britain, where the character of the entire society (in his view) made an early renunciation of empire probable—a prediction which events confirmed. There is little doubt that he would have counted the United States, like Britain, among the basically democratic countries where

[10]Yet the shares of the military in federal spending, national research and development, and labor force in 1986, notably a share of 29 percent of the total federal budget, and 6.8 percent of the gross national product (GNP), had not yet reached the levels of 1961 of 9.7 percent of GNP and 45 percent of the total budget (adjusted for changes in budgetary practice). Only continuation of President Reagan's proposed annual defense budget net increases of 8.1 percent to 1987 would have eventually exceeded the 1961 levels. At the same time, of course, the vastly increased totals of GNP and the federal budget made even the lower percentage figures of 1986 amount to much larger dollar-figures than had been the case in 1961. See "Defense: Smaller Part of a Much Bigger Pie," *International Herald Tribune*, February 5, 1986, p. 3.

[11]For an analysis of recent public opinion trends, see William Schneider, "Conservatism, Not Interventionism: Trends in Foreign Policy Opinion, 1974–1982," chapter 2 in K. Oye, R. Lieber, and D. Rothchild, *Eagle Defiant: United States Foreign Policy in the 1980s* (Boston: Little, Brown, 1983), pp. 33–64. For analyses of two earlier public opinion polls, carried out by the Chicago Council on Foreign Relations in 1974 and 1978, see John E. Rielly (ed.), *American Public Opinion and U.S. Foreign Policy 1975*, (Chicago: Chicago Council on Foreign Relations, 1975), and John E. Rielly (ed.), *American Public Opinion and U.S. Foreign Policy 1979* (Chicago: Chicago Council on Foreign Relations, 1979).

warlike elite groups would at most be quite shallowly rooted and would not long endure. In any case, there is ample evidence that in the nuclear age most members even of military-industrial coalitions of interest groups are not suicidally inclined. There is also evidence that the executives of large corporations who come to serve in the Department of Defense are most often rather level-headed personalities; that the whole American political system is irremediably pluralistic; and that it is, therefore, most often likely within one or two decades to encourage compromise and moderation.

THE IMPACT OF AMERICANS ABROAD

The Department of State

Whether the United States and the world will have these next two decades to survive in will depend, however, in large part on the foreign policy that is made here and now. The instruments that make this policy in the United States are, again, plural. Traditionally first among them is the Department of State, which also has the task of producing some coherence among the activities of other government agencies in international affairs.

In the mid-1980s, the U.S. Department of State employed about 24,000 persons. Though no recent figures have been published, it seems that somewhat more than one-half of these are United States citizens, approximately half of whom serve abroad, as do the over 10,000 foreign nationals employed by the Department.[12] The core of American personnel is about 3,800 professional Foreign Service officers, supplemented by another 4,400 Foreign Service Civil Service officers; and about one-half of all these professionals are serving overseas.[13] The State Department in 1985 had five geographic bureaus that divided among themselves responsibility for most of the areas of the world, and a number of functional bureaus with tasks cutting across the geographic regions. The organization is shown in Figure 1.

Of these bureaus, the geographic ones are the largest and in many ways the most important. Since they deal with different areas and governments, they sometimes develop somewhat different perspectives on certain policy problems. Thus the Bureau of European and Canadian Affairs and the Bureau of African Affairs each may be aware of somewhat different aspects of the problem of the remaining Portuguese interests in Africa. And even though both bureaus are expected to agree on basic policy objectives, they may disagree for a long time about tactics—about what should in fact be done. The functional bureaus, such as Economic and Business Affairs, have less direct influence on general policy in an area, but they must be consulted where their particular competence is concerned.

[12]Data from *Federal Civilian Workforce Statistics: Biannual Report of Employment by Geographic Area* (Washington, D.C.: U.S. Office of Personnel Management, 1983), pp. 114–117.

[13]Data from *Update of the Affirmative Action Plan and Annual Accomplishment Report of Equal Employment Activities, FY 83, Annual May 31, 1984* (Washington, D.C.: Department of State, 1984), and U.S. Department of State, Publication No. 9202, June 1984.

DEPARTMENT OF STATE

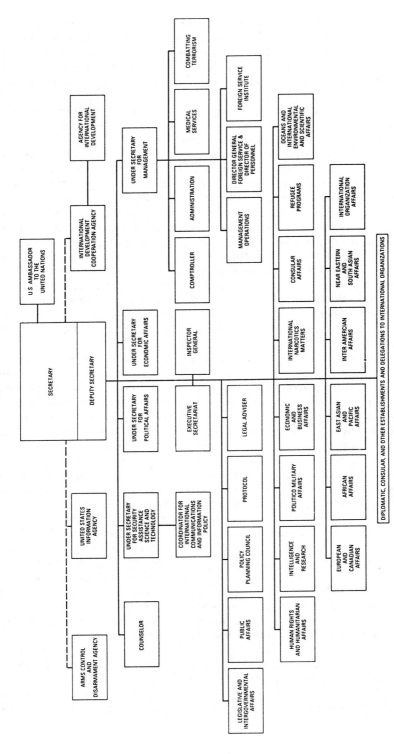

Figure 1 Organization of the Department of State

109

The actual decisions are made in stages. (Of course, only an extremely simplified version can be given here.) Some policy alternatives are implicitly stressed, and others perhaps already foreclosed, by the way the United States ambassador words a report. Another stage comes in the evaluation of this report by the desk officer responsible for dealing with the affairs of that country in one of the Department's geographic bureaus; and policy may take shape in the "position paper" (the recommendation for policy or action) which this officer may draft. This draft is then read by the desk officer's superior, who may endorse, revise, or reject it.

If the revised draft moves on, it goes to higher levels. Then functional bureaus may have to be consulted, clearance from other bureaus may have to be obtained, and meetings may have to be held to adjust the remaining differences of viewpoints. If the draft survives all this (as it usually does), an agreed-on version of a policy decision or directive will have been drafted, acceptable in language—and most often also in substance—to all the responsible officials and bureaus concerned, usually including an assistant secretary of state or a deputy. If sufficiently important, this version then goes up to the undersecretary for political affairs, or still higher to the deputy secretary of state, or even to the secretary of state. Any of these can send the draft back, of course, for further changes, or conceivably could reject it altogether. Otherwise the approved text, with a final checking of its wording, goes to the encoding room and is encoded there and cabled back to the ambassador.

Within the Department, this whole process resembles less the workings of a pinball machine or other mixed device of chance and skill than that of a carefully arranged set of screens or filters. Tradition and precedent can do much to ensure the consistency of new decisions made in accordance with those taken in the past, and Foreign Service officers and the entire State Department can be relied on to pay them very serious attention. A great deal of policy in all countries consists in "getting on with it"—with completing what has been started, and with repeating what has been done before. There is rarely time even among top officials for deep thought leading to radically new departures, and the habit is not encouraged among the junior ranks. In addition, State Department officers at all levels are perceptive of consensus and sensitive to atmosphere. They are usually well aware of unspoken agreements on matters and images that are currently being taken for granted and that mark the subtle boundary between acceptable and unacceptable policy suggestions. In the light of these, they make only those recommendations they feel will survive the sifting process. Crosschecking with other bureaus makes these restrictions still more narrow. Finally, the heads of bureaus and the higher officers in the Department use their memories and judgment to ensure that the emerging policy is consistent with other policies of the Department and with the current overall policies of the government of the United States. In this manner, the Department most often functions as an assembly line of decisions which turns out a fairly dependable product.

The matter becomes more complicated as other executive agencies have to be consulted, such as the Department of Defense, the Central

Intelligence Agency, or the Atomic Energy Commission, each with its own needs and perspectives which may differ somewhat from those of the State Department. The White House staff may add its own viewpoints; and the final policy decision may have to be made in the interagency National Security Council or by the president himself.

The results of this larger executive-policy process are less uniform and harder to predict than were those within the State Department. But the matter is not yet ended. Even the president's decision may require an appropriation from Congress to carry it out. Or it may depend for its success on the support of the press and of public opinion (including nowadays even the opinion polls). Or it may require the support, or at least the acquiescence, of key interest groups, such as big business or labor, or of particular regional or ethnic minorities. And the hard fact is that none of these is under anyone's complete control; they cannot be coerced by even a potent combination of leadership appeal and the skillful use of mass media. If they cooperate, it is only by voluntary consensus.

At this point we may remember the story of the American expert on Soviet affairs who pitied his opposite number in the Soviet Union—for that harried Russian had the much harder task of predicting the next policy moves produced by the inscrutable political processes of the United States. To this we must add the consideration that the outcomes of our policies, like those of the policies of other countries, depend often on the support of other nations, and particularly of our major allies, as well as on the moves made by our adversaries—neither of whom we control. The final result of all these processes is the probabilistic combination of firm persistence, careful planning, massive drift, and random accident which is so characteristic of international politics.

Two semiautonomous agencies within the State Department are the International Development and Cooperation Agency (IDCA) and the United States Information Agency (USIA). Subordinate to the secretary of state, each agency has its own head, hierarchy, and geographic and functional subdivisions. In the mid-1980s IDCA employed about 5,300 persons, and USIA about 8,200. Of these about 3,800 and 4,600, respectively, were United States citizens. A third semiautonomous agency in the State Department, the Arms Control and Disarmament Agency (ACDA), has a smaller staff. Altogether the State Department, with these agencies, employed in the mid-1980s about 39,000 persons, divided about half-and-half between American citizens and foreign nationals. Nearly two-thirds of these, including practially all foreign nationals, are employed abroad.[14] There seems little doubt that this deployment of labor abroad has outgrown the comparable efforts by the Soviet Union, as well as those of any other country in the world.

Even with an effort of this size, however, the State Department does not rank first among the agencies employing and deploying American civilians abroad. The Department of Defense in 1984 accounted for 68

[14]*Federal Civilian Workforce Statistics, Monthly Release, Employment and Trends as of July 1984* (Washington, D.C.: U.S. Office of Personnel Management, 1984).

percent of all U.S. civilians employed abroad by some 45 federal agencies, as against 17 percent employed by the State Department and 14 percent employed by all the rest. In addition, of course, the Department of Defense is responsible for many hundreds of thousands of United States troops stationed abroad, mainly in Asia and Europe.[15] Its organization is shown in Figure 2.

The geographic distribution abroad of State Department personnel and the number of U.S. citizens within each foreign station in 1973 and 1982 is shown in Table 14. The geographic distribution abroad of all United States federal civilian employees and the number of U.S. citizens within each foreign station employed by all U.S. agencies from 1973 to 1982 is shown in Table 15. The rank order of the top twenty countries indicates some of the changes that have occurred since 1945 in the foreign-policy interests and efforts of the United States. For instance, our "special relationship" with England does not seem to be what it once was. Among both State Department employees and other United States civilian overseas personnel, West Germany has assumed first place while the United Kingdom ranks only ninth in State Department and seventh in overseas personnel. Our interests seem concentrated not so much on stable allies as on countries where an opportunity for United States influence and power has combined with a perception of some insecurity or threat. Thus among our State Department personnel abroad, Italy, France, and the Philippines all outrank England. And in the distribution of all U.S. citizens in federal overseas employment, the emphases on possible power confrontation and on Asia have become even clearer: here Korea in 1982 outranked Canada, and the Philippines outranked India and Mexico. Emphasis on deployment of most U.S. personnel abroad seemed to be on action, rather than on listening to or communicating with powers—no matter how large—over whom our influence was small or lacking. The Soviet Union, the third largest and second most powerful nation on earth, did not even rank above twentieth in number of State Department personnel, and did not rank at all on the total number of overseas federal civilian employees. It was "below the chart" for both State Department Personnel and for all reported U.S. federal civilian employees stationed there. In 1982 no more than ninety State Department personnel were stationed there; and employees of other agencies brought the total of United States civilians stationed there to only 125.[16]

The corresponding total of State Department personnel stationed among the 730 million people in India in 1982 was 540; for the over 1 billion on the mainland of China there were 91. Together the Soviet Union, India, and mainland China comprise nearly half the human race and nearly 15 percent of the world's income. Yet these three huge countries in 1982 had stationed in them only about 4.8 percent of our State Department personnel abroad. Both the Soviet Union and the United States seem to have become more aware of the need for more and better channels and

---

[15]*Federal Civilian Workforce Statistics: Biannual Report of Employment by Geographic Area* (Washington, D.C.: U.S. Office of Personnel Management, 1983).

[16]*Ibid.*, p. 116.

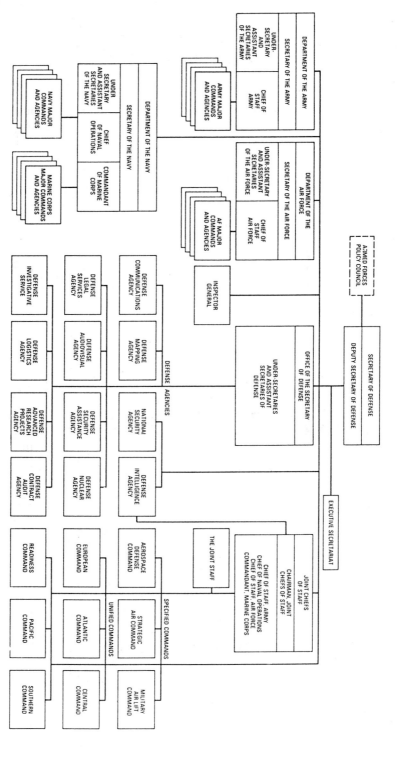

Figure 2 Organization of the Department of Defense

TABLE 14   U.S. State Department Personnel Stationed Overseas (U.S. Citizens and Totals), 1973 and 1982

	1973				1982		
RANK	COUNTRY	TOTAL	U.S. CITIZENS	RANK	COUNTRY	TOTAL	U.S. CITIZENS
1.	Germany (FR)	872	288	1.	Germany, (FR)	751	268
2.	India	714	136	2.	Mexico	565	199
3.	Vietnam (Rep.)	613	139	3.	India	540	104
4.	France	580	186	4.	France	505	189
5.	Italy	566	142	5.	Philippines	495	176
6.	Mexico	555	161	6.	Italy	433	136
7.	Philippines	534	184	7.	Thailand	372	127
8.	Greece	454	128	8.	Greece	361	120
9.	Japan	398	124	9.	United Kingdom	352	119
10.	Brazil	397	143	10.	Japan	329	110
11.	Thailand	365	131	11.	Pakistan	304	92
12.	United Kingdom	346	118	12.	Brazil	284	121
13.	Pakistan	317	75	13.	Belgium	282	130
14.	Nigeria	277	76	14.	Canada	274	118
15.	Belgium	265	138	15.	Egypt	227	78
16.	Canada	232	91	16.	Korea (Rep.)	227	66
17.	Iran	214	68	17.	Turkey	195	82
18.	Morocco	204	51	18.	Israel	194	71
19.	Hong Kong	202	60	19.	Saudi Arabia	193	78
20.	Turkey	199	77	20.	Hong Kong	188	63
Subtotal:	1–20	8,304	1,516	Subtotal:	1–20	7,071	2,447
Rest of World:		8,163	3,153	Rest of World:		7,819	3,188
Grand Total:		16,467	4,559	Grand Total:		14,890	5,635

COUNTRIES BELOW CHART

	1973			1982	
Korea (Rep.)	151	48	Morocco	169	48
Israel	146	55	Nigeria	164	52
Soviet Union	63	63	China (PRC)	91	91
			Soviet Union	90	90
			Iran	0	0
			Vietnam	0	0

"Germany, Federal Republic of," "Republic of Vietnam," and "Republic of Korea" are the official designations for West Germany, South Vietnam (1973), and South Korea, respectively.

Source: Report of Statistics on Employment: By Agency and Citizenship in Foreign Countries, March 31, 1973 (Washington, DC: U.S. Civil Service Commission, Bureau of Manpower Information Systems, Manpower Statistics Division, 1973; Federal Civilian Workforce Statistics: Biannual Report of Employment by Geographic Area (Washington, D.C.: U.S. Office of Personnel Management, 1983), pp. 114–117.

TABLE 15   All U.S. Federal Civilian Employees Stationed Overseas (Totals and U.S. Citizens), 1973 and 1982

1973				1982			
RANK	COUNTRY	TOTAL	U.S. CITIZENS	RANK	COUNTRY	TOTAL	U.S. CITIZENS
1.	Philippines	17,164	1,274	1.	Germany (FR)	28,616	27,849
2.	Korea (Rep.)	13,338	1,222	2.	Panama	15,590	4,246
3.	Germany (FR)	12,522	11,566	3.	Korea (Rep.)	14,753	1,930
4.	Thailand	7,912	610	4.	Philippines	14,142	1,729
5.	Japan	7,130	5,282	5.	Japan	4,567	4,094
6.	Vietnam (Rep.)	6,750	1,378	6.	Italy	4,516	1,451
7.	Italy	4,097	1,073	7.	United Kingdom	3,208	2,086
8.	Spain	2,849	866	8.	Saudi Arabia	1,718	1,359
9.	United Kingdom	2,538	1,454	9.	Portugal	1,425	269
10.	China (Taiwan)	2,112	299	10.	Spain	1,072	895
11.	India	1,485	240	11.	Mexico	1,036	373
12.	Turkey	1,368	479	12.	Iceland	980	192
13.	Canada	1,290	322	13.	India	973	171
14.	Laos	1,276	379	14.	Turkey	959	426
15.	Portugal	1,120	165	15.	Cuba	944	371
16.	Cuba	1,079	220	16.	France	923	304
17.	Mexico	1,067	297	17.	Belgium	906	672
18.	France	1,021	318	18.	Greece	866	362
19.	Greece	968	324	19.	Egypt	759	247
20.	Brazil	953	309	20.	Canada	757	433
21.	Pakistan	760	144	21.	Thailand	692	228
22.	Ethiopia	760	135	22.	Pakistan	517	151
Subtotal:	1–22	89,559	28,456	Subtotal:	1–22	99,919	49,838
	Rest of World:	17,747	6,775		Rest of World:	15,353	6,388
	Grand Total:	107,306	35,231		Grand Total:	115,272	56,226

COUNTRIES BELOW CHART

1973				1982		
Belgium	729	522		Brazil	499	181
Iceland	724	141		Soviet Union	125	115
Saudi Arabia	249	128		China (PRC)	113	113
Panama	247	80		Ethiopia	60	19
Soviet Union	92			China (Taiwan)	52	52
Egypt	nd			Laos	446	
				Vietnam	NA	9

Note: Observe the contrasts between the Federal Republic of Germany and France and between the Republic of South Korea and Taiwan. West Berlin, in 1973 and 1982, had 234 and 183 U.S. citizens, respectively. Figures for the Central Intelligence Agency (CIA) and the National Security Agency (NSA) are not reported and are, therefore, not included in this table.

Source: Report of Statistics on Employment: By Agency and Citizenship in Foreign Countries, March 31, 1973 (Washington, D.C.: U.S. Civil Service Commission, Bureau of Manpower Information Systems, Manpower Statistics Division, 1973); Federal Civilian Workforce Statistics: Biannual Report of Employment by Geographic Area (Washington, DC: U.S. Office of Personnel Management, 1982), pp. 114–117.

institutions of communication. A teletype "hot line" between the White House and the Kremlin was installed after the experience of the Cuban missile crisis, and the State Department personnel stationed in the Soviet Union increased by nearly a third from 1973 to 1982. Even so, the relative scarcity of diplomatic and human contacts between these two superpowers still remains glaring.

Although the distribution abroad of United States diplomats and other government personnel is highly uneven, their numbers are relatively large in all countries where current United States power, influence, and interests are concentrated. Were we to add to the more than 140,000 United States civilian officials abroad the 100,000 business people, the 30,000 missionaries, the 20,000 students, and the approximately 1 million members of our armed forces, together with their dependents, we would finally arrive at Harlan Cleveland's grand total of about 1.6 million "overseas Americans" who are living abroad in any one year in this new period of American worldwide expansion—in addition to the over 8 million Americans traveling abroad each year.[17]

To these 1.6 million relatively permanent overseas Americans there must be added the nearly 105,000 foreign nationals directly employed by the United States government, not to mention the much larger number of foreign nationals employed by American private individuals and corporations. But even then the count is incomplete, for the U.S. Central Intelligence Agency does not publish either its budget—estimated in 1986 at about $9 billion—nor the number of its employees, American or foreign. Even the order of magnitude of its aggregate operations can only be guessed at (it has been estimated as comparable to or larger than the State Department), though some of its indirect operations—often through unsuspecting American or foreign organizations and individuals—have made headlines around the world.

The CIA

The United States effort at organized intelligence operations, combined with various forms of clandestine and psychological warfare, has its roots in World War I, and even more in World War II, when the United States, like all major powers, engaged in a wide range of such activities. After World War II, and with the rise of the cold war, this United States effort was further developed and adapted specifically to offset and overcome the worldwide political pressure of the Soviet Union, its close government allies, and its unofficial allies or instruments, the communist parties of the world. In these parties, together with the international "apparatus" of the Communist International and its successor organization (the Communist Information Bureau) and the numerous "front organizations" and "transmission belts"—as well as in its own military and civilian intelligence organization—the government of the Soviet Union had at its disposal a powerful range of instruments to influence world politics and the internal

---

[17]Harlan Cleveland *et al., The Overseas Americans,* repr. of 1960 ed. (Salem, NH: Ayer Co. Publishers, 1980).

events in many developing or crisis-ridden countries. Despite occasional brief propaganda successes, however, its actual influence in such affluent and stable countries as the United States, Britain, and other English-speaking nations, and in the neutral countries of Switzerland, Austria, and most of Scandinavia, was always very small.

When the United States after 1945 moved into a worldwide contest with these Soviet-directed or otherwise communist-ruled organizations, it acted as Americans often do in contests: it proceeded enthusiastically to mount a much bigger and better effort than its adversaries. In this, so far as one can see into the dark waters of underground warfare, it has succeeded. Today the intelligence and political warfare efforts of the CIA and related organizations are probably larger and better organized than those of the corresponding Soviet or Chinese organizations which oppose them in the world arena. This success has brought with it its own irony. When communist penetration and propaganda appeared to be intensely active and increasingly successful, and the United States seemed passive and unconcerned, nationalist sentiment in many countries saw communism as the main threat to national independence. Many nationalists vigorously opposed Soviet or communist influence and looked to the United States for help. In the late 1960s, when in many countries the United States seemed to be the stronger, more active, and much better staffed and financed contestant, many nationalists abroad were sitting back, or even were fearful lest we gain too much influence over their countries. In the mid-1970s the United States seemed somewhat less active in the global power contest; the CIA faced strong public pressure to refrain from interfering in the domestic affairs of other countries following the publicizing of its covert political-warfare activities in Latin America and Indochina. But by the mid-1970s, however, some domestic and foreign groups again began to urge a more militant and clandestinely interventionist foreign policy upon the United States.

THE IMPLICATIONS OF EXPANSION

Here, and in other sectors of world politics, world economics, and world opinion, the very magnitude of our thrust into international affairs has produced some limiting or countervailing responses from the international environment. As in the case of every other superpower in the past, the essentially unilateral expansion of our power and influence in the world has turned out to be a self-limiting process. "The size and obtrusiveness of American representation," testified a former United States ambassador to the Congo before a subcommittee of the Senate, "sometimes constitute an irritant in our foreign relations that is little recognized by the American public. There are places in which the American mission is as large as the Foreign Office of the host country."[18]

[18]Edmund A. Gullion, "The American Diplomatist in Developing Countries," in Sen. Henry M. Jackson (ed.), *The Secretary of State and the Ambassador*, Jackson Subcommittee Papers on the Conduct of American Foreign Policy (New York: Praeger, 1964), p. 196.

The matter is, of course, not just one of display, such as whether American government personnel in the capital of a foreign country are conspicuously concentrated in one building (as many of them are in London and Mexico City), or whether they are more discreetly dispersed in several smaller ones (as they are in New Delhi). It is a matter of substance; of the greatly increased actual size and power of the American effort to influence the conduct of foreign nations. Nevertheless, we are continuing this ambitious effort. "Indeed," the same ambassador continued in his memorandum to the Senate subcommittee, "this writer hesitates even to call attention to the possibility of reduction in force for fear of playing into the hands of those interested not so much in economy as in fleeing from America's obligations as a world power.[19]

What drives us to this effort, and what maintains this image of our obligations? To what extent is it a network of clear-cut treaty obligations with authentic governments of sovereign foreign nations? To what extent is it the automatic logic of the process of international conflict, in which we and our rivals and adversaries are becoming locked ever more tightly? To what extent is it the popular image of a "power vacuum" out there in the developing countries, which is drawing us irresistibly into increasing efforts and commitments? And to what extent is it the result of our domestic political process, together with the domestic effects of our own earlier commitments?

[19]*Ibid.*, p. 197.

10

The Foreign-Policy Sector

In early 1967, at the height of the Vietnam war, United States secretary of defense Robert S. McNamara was, in the words of a well-informed Washington correspondent, "in charge of 4 million people and $175 billion worth of property, including 5,000 nuclear warheads."[1] The work force directly controlled by the Department then included about 3 million members of the armed forces and 1 million civilians. In 1966 the Department spent nearly $60 billion (not counting at that time the additional funds requested by President Johnson for the Vietnam war); and by March 1967 expenditures for defense stood at $74 billion per year. These sums in each year amounted to more than half the total budget of the federal government of the United States. "The military establishment," wrote Adam Yarmolinsky, a former Deputy Assistant Secretary of Defense for International Security Affairs, in 1967, "is not just the biggest organization in the world; it is bigger by several orders of magnitude . . . than all the other government departments put together."[2] By 1973, with the Vietnam war over, the armed forces had shrunk somewhat, to about 2.3 million; the civilian de-

[1]Douglas Kiker, "The Education of Robert McNamara," *The Atlantic Monthly* (March 1967), p. 49.

[2]Adam Yarmolinsky, "How the Pentagon Works," *The Atlantic Monthly* (March 1967), p. 58; copyright © 1967 by the Atlantic Monthly Company, Boston, Mass. Reprinted with permission.

fense employees still numbered about 1 million; and the nuclear warheads had drastically increased and continued to do so, to an estimated 30,000 warheads in 1976. The budget in that latter year alone exceeded $110 billion—of which about $20 billion was budgeted under other defense-related agencies, such as Civil Defense, National Aeronautics and Space Administration (NASA), and the Veterans Administration. Under the Reagan administration's proclaimed goal of a "rearmed America," the military budget marked a new height after steep increases in defense expenditures from 1980. In 1986, the total defense budget reached almost $280 billion, an increase of about 100 percent over the 1980 defense budget of over $140 billion. These sums amounted to 23.4 percent of the total federal budget in 1980 and 29 percent of the budget in 1986. The size of the armed forces had decreased further to about 1.3 million, and civilian defense employees still numbered about 1 million. Overall, Defense Department employees, military and civilian, and people employed in the defense industry, represented 5.7 percent of the total labor force. The number of nuclear warheads in the United States in 1983 had reached 29,000, and further increases seem likely (although on a less drastic scale than in earlier decades).[3]

This huge block of human and economic effort and concern inevitably generates a vast collection of social, political, and economic interests corresponding to its size. This size, and presumably these interests, equaled in 1967, at the time of the Vietnam war, nearly 10 percent of the American gross national product. After that war, in 1973, they had shrunk in the United States to about 6 percent of GNP and to about 26 percent of the federal budget; rising again to nearly 7 percent of GNP and to about 29 percent of the total federal budget in 1986. This huge slice of the federal pie was more than the total of all United States exports, and was ten times larger than the returns from all American investments abroad. Ninety years ago our defense establishment was considered an instrument for the protection of our interests in the international arena. Today it has itself become the largest interest among them.

The implications were made clear by Mr. Yarmolinsky in 1967. All major decisions made by the secretary of defense and the other high Pentagon officials touching upon matters of policy, procurement, equipment, new weapons systems, strategies, and international arrangements or commitments are subject to pressures and influence from several interest groups, institutional interests, and decision makers. They all

> . . . involve a balancing of values and risks. These are values and risks not only for the country, and often for the world, but also for interest groups within

[3]All figures are given in current dollars. 1980 budget figures from R. L. Sivard, *World Military and Social Expenditures 1983* (Washington, D.C.: World Priorities, 1983), p. 33; 1986 data from "Defense: Smaller Part of a Much Bigger Pie," *International Herald Tribune* (February 5, 1986), p. 3; other data from *Statistical Abstract of the United States 1982/1983* (Washington, D.C.: Government Printing Office, 1982); *Federal Civilian Workforce Statistics: Biannual Report on Employment by Geographic Area* (Washington, D.C.: U.S. Office of Personnel Management, 1983), p. 7, and R. L. Sivard, *World Military and Social Expenditures 1983*, p. 15.

the Pentagon, across the Potomac, and down Pennsylvania Avenue to the Capitol. The pressures for some accommodation of these competing forces are enormous, and in part because of the complexity of the issues, the opportunities for compromise are not inconsiderable. . . . No Secretary of Defense can regularly reject proposals from his military advisers, particularly where both their professional competence and the lives of American boys are at issue; and no analytical arguments will modify the effect of a blanket rejection on the continuing workable relationship between the Secretary and the generals. Indeed, the remarkable thing is not how many compromise decisions are made in the Pentagon, in the face of all the pressures for compromise, but how few.

Within the decision and policy-making process on such defense issues, the military-industrial complex—referred to by President Eisenhower in his Farewell Address in 1961—represents a very powerful and large interest group. However,

> . . . the military-industrial-congressional complex is not a conspiracy. But there are coincidences of interest among the military project officer who is looking for a star, the civilian who sees an opening for a new branch chief, the defense contractor who is running out of work, the union business agents who can see layoffs coming, and the congressman who is concerned about the campaign contributions from business and labor as well as about the prosperity of his district. Each of these constellations of interests wants to expand the defense establishment in its own direction. In the early sixties, the Pentagon was an expanding universe. . . . Resources that were cut out of unnecessary activities could often find employment in areas that needed to be strengthened. A similar situation prevails today [1967]. Until very recently, Army training camps simply were not available for the training of less essential reserves mandated by a congressional lobby, because the training camps were fully utilized readying active forces for Vietnam. But when the war in Vietnam is brought to an end, the pressures of the military-industrial-congressional complex will necessarily be increased.

These pressures from the defense establishment must be effectively balanced and integrated into the political decision-making process by leaders, argued Mr. Yarmolinsky. It is their task to define and restrain the political role of the military-industrial complex:

> The pressures can still be resisted, and there is every evidence that they will be. But it is unreasonable to expect any Secretary of Defense to resist them alone, or supported only by the few people within the Department who are entirely his own men. Over the past six years, the Pentagon has developed the kind of organizational and analytical instruments that permit effective communication between the bureaucracy and the responsible political leadership, and among the elements of the bureaucracy with conflicting institutional interests. Yet the Pentagon's administrators themselves cannot determine the role of the military establishment in the United States, and should not be asked to. It took a national debate over a period of years to demonstrate that the military establishment was inadequate to its tasks and needed major struc-

tural reform. Those reforms have now given the United States more usable military power. The uses that we choose to make of the military establishment, and the limits that are put on its growth and employment, are a large enough subject again to engage the attention of the nation. . . . . [4]

This plea has lost none of its significance in the 1980s with the nation's renewed commitment to strengthening the defense establishment and favoring such interest groups as the military-industrial complex by apportioning almost a third of the federal budget to military and defense-related expenditures. How that interest group's related expansion of influence, prestige, and power will be effectively integrated into the overall political and strategic decision-making process and among other national and domestic interests, remains to be seen in the years to come.

ANOTHER LOOK AT THE NATIONAL DECISION SYSTEM

A Simple Cascade Model

The nation whose attention and decisions are involved here can be thought of as a national decision system, and for some purposes of analysis we can visualize the flow of communications and decisions in a very simplified image as a cascade of five levels. We can imagine that each level is formed by a distinct reservoir of public or elite opinion. Each of these reservoirs is linked to a particular complex of social institutions and status groups. Communications flow more freely within each level than from one level to the other; and they flow more easily from the higher status and power levels to the lower ones, than they do the other way. The communication and action system at each level can be represented by a simple "black box" with only a few labels attached to parts of it, so as to indicate its chief tasks or functions that interest us here: intake of messages and experiences; memory and recall; decision through combining income data with items recalled from memory for determining the output of behavior; and the output of messages and actions that result, and that may return information to the input side of the system and thus modify the next stages of its behavior.

The first of these levels of opinion reservoirs in any Western country is that of the social and economic elite, corresponding roughly to the top 2 or 3 percent or so of the population in terms of property, income, and socioeconomic status—the major owners, stockholders, employers, investors, and top-management executives in the country, with their families, and their major institutions, such as the main business, banking, and investment corporations. These people and institutions do not form a simple monolithic group, but are connected by a dense net of multiple ties, links, and channels of communication. They share among themselves many memories, preferences, styles, and habit patterns of the subculture of the upper classes; and the views, interests, and behavior styles of more specialized subelites are

[4]Adam Yarmolinsky, "How the Pentagon Works," *The Atlantic Monthly* (March, 1967), p. 61.

FIGURE 3   The SocioEconomic Elite Level as a Decision System

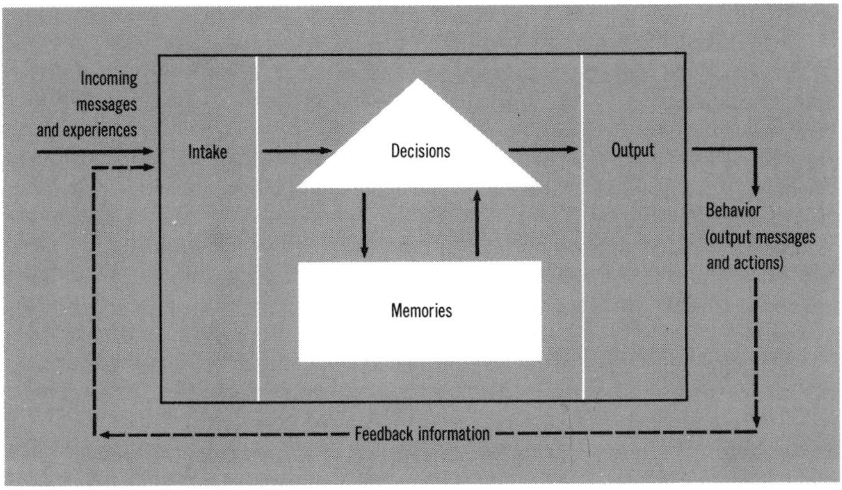

communicated rapidly among them. In addition to its internal communication flow and its shared memories, this elite also receives messages from the rest of the society and from the outside world, and these produce messages and actions directed toward other social groups and to the world outside. We represent it schematically, therefore (Figure 3), by a "black box" with an input sector, an output sector, a set of memories available for recall, and a decision system that will at least produce preferences for, or aversions against, particular kinds of output behavior.

The second level in a highly developed Western society is formed by the political and governmental elite. This elite centers primarily around the national government. It, too, however, is not a monolithic bloc. Within it there are subgroups such as the executive-branch personnel, the legislators, and the judges; the higher elected officials and the higher bureaucrats; and (among this latter group) the civilian and the military dignitaries. There are also the distinctions between the political elites at the national center and in the outlying regions, and the differences among the interests and personnel of national, state, and municipal politics. Finally, there are the distinctions between the incumbents of formal government offices, and the individuals whose share in political power rests on their position in the hierarchy or machine of some party; and there is the real distinction between the political "ins" and the "outs"—although these roles may be reversed when power changes hands. Despite all these real cleavages, there is a good deal of cohesion and communication in the political elite, and together with the bureaucratic and military elites, it does form the government by and large, as well as the most immediate social environment around it. This governmental and political elite again can be represented, therefore, as a communication and decision system with its own memories and decision capabilities, and its own functions of intake and output, similar to the simple scheme shown in Figure 3.

The third level consists of the media of mass communication—particularly the newspapers, magazines, television, and radio, with advertising agencies and the motion picture, phonograph-record, and book-publishing industries as close appendages. This network of mass media can be treated again as a system with its own intake, output, and memory and decision aspects, and represented by another black box similar to those at the preceding levels.

The communications system at the fourth level is much larger and much less cohesive, but no less important. It can be represented by a black box similar to that for each of the other levels, but we must bear in mind that it differs from them in content. It consists of the network of local opinion leaders—the 5 or 10 percent of the population who pay continued attention to the mass media, and to some extent to foreign affairs. These are the men and women who mediate much of national and world affairs to their less attentive neighbors who look to them for interpretations and for models of appropriate attitudes and responses to the distant and unfamiliar events which the mass media bring within their range of vision. If the network of local opinion leaders agrees with the messages and interpretations promoted by the mass media, they can do much to reinforce their impact; if they disagree with them, oppose them, or ignore them, they can do much to nullify their effect. Thus the same nationwide telecast on Africa, or on racial integration in the United States armed forces, could have a very different impact in the North and in the South, depending on the different responses of the opinion leaders (and of the general population) in each region. In mass opinion poll analyses, this "local opinion leader" stratum perhaps can be approximated by segregating the top 5 or 10 percent of respondents by socioeconomic status and education and analyzing their attitudes separately. Alternatively, members of this stratum—or of some subgroup within it, such as local teachers or lawyers—could be identified directly, and a poll taken from a suitable sample among them.

The fifth and largest group formed by the people consists of the politically relevant strata of the population at large, insofar as they are sufficiently accessible, interested, capable, and old enough to have at least a potential influence on politics so that they have to be taken into account in estimating the probable course of political events and the probable outcome of crisis. The politically effective "people" in Western countries equal the total electorate actually voting; that is, to between 50 and 90 percent of the adult population. The electorate (or the mass public) again receives messages, calls on its memories, makes decisions, and produces results in the form of messages and actions.

Four streams of information move downward, in cascade fashion, from higher-level communication systems to lower-level ones. The socioeconomic elite communicates directly with the government and the political system. Many of its members have access to, and influence in, the legislative and executive branches of the government. Many of them also have such

TABLE 16   A Summary of 36 Short-run Influence and Information Flows in a Developed Country (for Fig. 4A–H)

FROM:	TO: 1 SOC.-ECON. ELITE	2 GOVT.-POL. SYSTEM	3 MASS MEDIA	4 OPINION LEADERS	5 POP. (MASS OPIN.)	6 REALITY	7 TOTAL ORIGI-NATED
1. Socioeconomic Elite (3B)	Very Strong	Strong	Strong	Strong	Strong	Weak	5 Strong 1 Weak
2. Gov't.-Political System (3C)	Strong	Very Strong	Strong	Strong	Strong	Strong	6 Strong
3. Mass Media (3D)	Strong	Strong	Very Strong	Strong	Strong	Weak	5 Strong 1 Weak
4. Opinion Leaders (3E)	Weak	Strong	Strong	Very Strong	Very Strong	Weak	4 Strong 1 Weak
5. Population (Mass Opinion) (3Fi)	Weak	Strong	Strong	Strong	Very Strong	Strong	5 Strong 1 Weak
6. Reality (Phys., Econ., Int'l., etc.) (3G)	Weak	Strong	Weak	Strong	Very Strong	Very Strong	4 Strong 2 Weak
7. Total Received (3H)	3 Strong 3 Weak	6 Strong	5 Strong 1 Weak	6 Strong	6 Strong	3 Weak 3 Strong	29 Strong 7 Weak

access and influence in the world of the mass media. They have fewer contacts with, and less direct influence over, the bulk of local opinion leaders; and on the mass of the people their direct influence is least. The government has some direct contacts with, and influence on, the mass media; but its communications and influence are weaker with local opinion leaders and the people. The mass media in turn speak most directly and effectively to the local opinion leaders, who then act as their transmitters or confirmers—and only more rarely as their critics—toward the population. They also speak directly to the people, however, and they do so with still more authority and impact if their messages are paralleled and reinforced by those of the mass media, who often can confer additional status on the local leaders as their spokespersons. The local leaders, finally, communicate directly with the people and exercise their influence parallel with or in opposition to the politics of the mass media. This is shown in Fig. 4 and summarized in Table 16.

Each of the five groups, however, has its own memories and its own measure of autonomy. Each can reject, ignore, or reinterpret many—perhaps almost all—unpalatable messages. Each is capable of innovation

FIGURE 4 (A–H).   Cascade Model of Influence and Information Flows

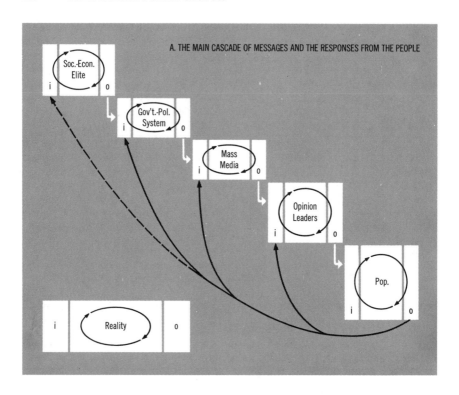

A. THE MAIN CASCADE OF MESSAGES AND THE RESPONSES FROM THE PEOPLE

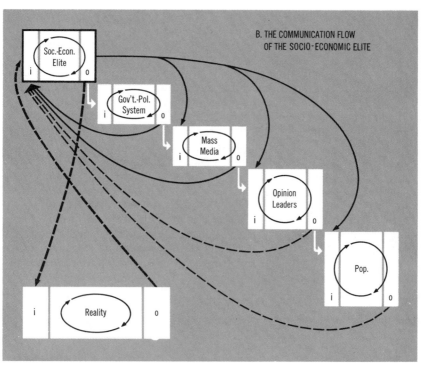

B. THE COMMUNICATION FLOW
OF THE SOCIO-ECONOMIC ELITE

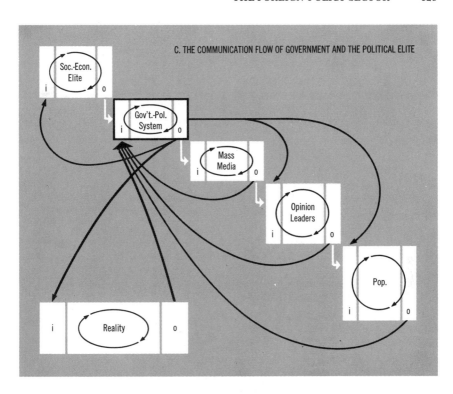

C. THE COMMUNICATION FLOW OF GOVERNMENT AND THE POLITICAL ELITE

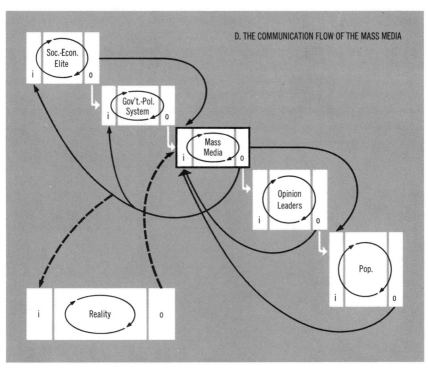

D. THE COMMUNICATION FLOW OF THE MASS MEDIA

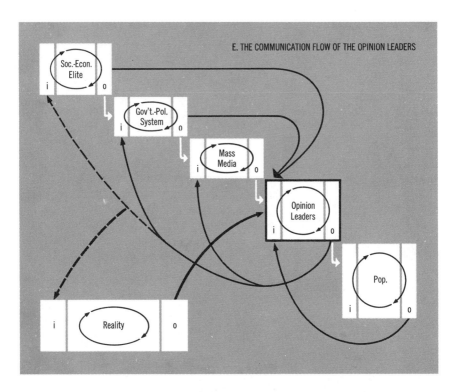

E. THE COMMUNICATION FLOW OF THE OPINION LEADERS

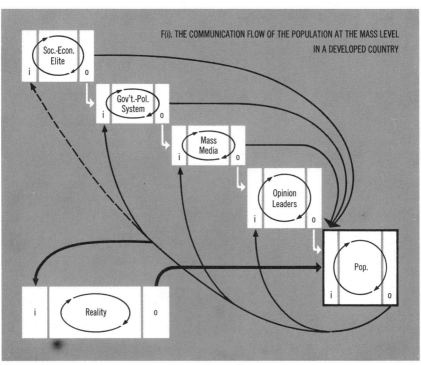

F(i). THE COMMUNICATION FLOW OF THE POPULATION AT THE MASS LEVEL
IN A DEVELOPED COUNTRY

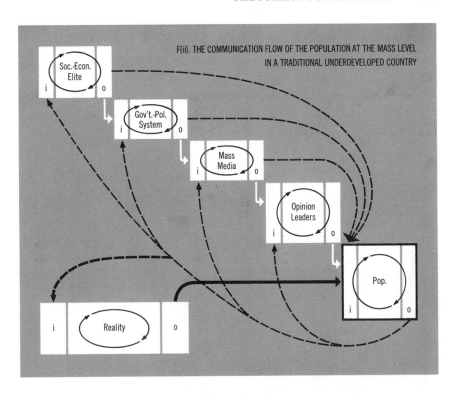

F(ii). THE COMMUNICATION FLOW OF THE POPULATION AT THE MASS LEVEL IN A TRADITIONAL UNDERDEVELOPED COUNTRY

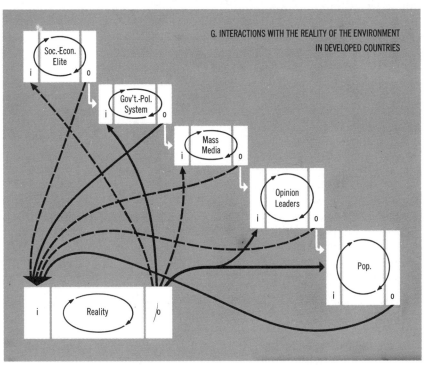

G. INTERACTIONS WITH THE REALITY OF THE ENVIRONMENT IN DEVELOPED COUNTRIES

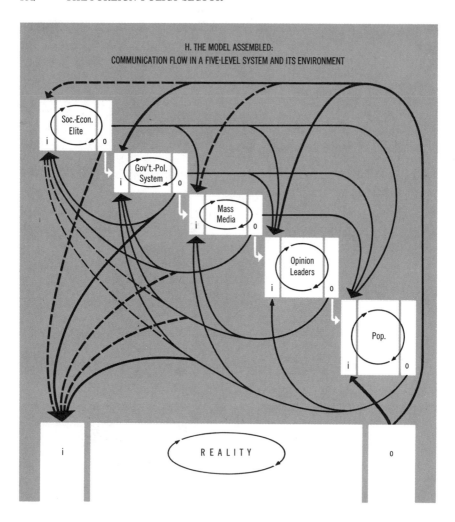

H. THE MODEL ASSEMBLED:
COMMUNICATION FLOW IN A FIVE-LEVEL SYSTEM AND ITS ENVIRONMENT

and initiative. And each can also feed back a stream of information upward to some or all of the higher-level groups.

The people respond to the local opinion leaders by increasing or decreasing their attention and deference to them. They respond to the mass media by giving or withholding their attention, subscription, and patronage. In a democracy, they have strong channels for communicating upward to the government. They have only weak and indirect channels, however, for communication with and influence on the socioeconomic elite, most of whom do not depend on popular favor for income or position.

The local opinion leaders can support, ignore, or oppose the mass media, and to some extent they have similar choices in their actions toward the government and the political leadership of the country. Usually, however, they cannot do much about the socioeconomic elite unless the local and lower-level leaders have become thoroughly alienated from the top elite, or if the top elite should consist largely of conspicuous outsiders or foreigners. But the government and the leaders of the political system *can* do something about the socioeconomic elite. They can defend its privileges and make them appear more legitimate, or they can oppose and reduce its power and privileges through legislation, taxation, and national-opinion leadership and management, and by means of many acts of administration and policy decision.

All together, every one of the five levels of our cascade model is partly autonomous but also partly interdependent with the other levels. Each level is also open to some extent to the direct impact of external reality. When there is an economic recession and people lose their jobs, then they notice it, and so do their neighbors, almost regardless of what local opinion leaders, mass media, and even the government may be saying. The same is true of situations in which people have experienced hunger or rationing, or the mounting casualty lists of a prolonged war. In all these cases, the media and the local and national political leaders can do something to interpret the experiences of the people, but in time the cumulative weight of experience may (though it need not) outweigh the effects of interpretation.

The same holds for the higher levels. Local opinion leaders, the mass media, the government, and the socioeconomic elite all are likely to have some direct experiences with such matters as economic prosperity or depression; the inflow or outflow of gold; the ease or difficulty of emigration; successes or failures in foreign relations or in war; and various advances or frustrations in regard to science, technology, public health, population growth, the improvement or deterioration of the environment, and the conservation or depletion of national resources. Any or all of these can have their effects on the experiences of people at each level of the social communication system, and thus they can influence directly their perceptions of themselves and of the outside world, as well as their trust or distrust of one another. The credibility of a government, a national elite, or a national system of mass media, in the international arena as well as in domestic politics, may well depend in no small part on the extent to which its messages correspond to the direct impact of reality on the populations, groups, and other governments concerned.

Each of these interdependent levels of communication is itself composed of diverse interest groups and institutions, and there are further coalitions among groups at different levels in the communication system. Such coalitions may be found among some national political leaders, some mass media, some local leaders, and some parts of the electorate. All of these may favor a "hard line" or a "soft line" in foreign policy—that is, a greater or lesser willingness to approach the brink of war in the pursuit of their preferred national foreign-policy objectives—while other groups or coalitions may prefer to accord primacy to their domestic goals.

IS THERE A "PRIMACY OF FOREIGN POLICY"?

Complex political communication systems of this kind are unlikely always to accord primacy to either domestic or foreign policy. The great nineteenth-century historian, Leopold von Ranke, spoke of "the primacy of foreign policy," but this notion was better suited to monarchies than to mass societies. Today the elites are still making policy, but policy—at least its requirements and its results—often also makes elites, or else changes their cohesion and their power, as well as the relationships among elite groups.

A modern political communication and decision system of this type also makes it difficult for a country to maintain a very consistent long-run foreign policy. If a single-level elite or interest group were sure to prevail over all others, and if all these others were to remain relatively passive, then this prevailing body could with no special effort develop and maintain consistent international policies for many years. A pluralistic democracy inevitably finds it much harder constantly to exercise influence over, or consistently to submit to, the influence of another nation.

One effect of this plurality of political subsystems and interest groups is that strongly rooted interest groups can be temporarily defeated but are apt to retain the capacity to rise again at the next favorable occasion in a new bid for increased power. Thus the massive military involvement in terms of aid, equipment, troops, and prestige in the Vietnam war initially led to a corresponding increase in power and influence of the defense establishment in the formulation of American military and political foreign policies and strategies. But the failure of these policies in the war, the rising domestic opposition to American involvement in Vietnam after 1968, and that war's unsuccessful end eventually weakened and discredited the military establishment's political influence, as well as that of the large defense-related industrial firms such as the Lockheed Corporation. President Nixon's subsequent policy of *detente* and global military disengagement (the "Nixon doctrine") was in part also a response to and a result of the defeat of these interest groups, and this low point of military influence in American foreign politics, side by side with a low point of the share of defense expenditures in the gross national product, continued through the mid-1970s and the Ford and Carter administrations.[5]

By 1979 the tide seemed to have turned, with public opinion favoring again a stronger defense posture and a foreign policy of toughness and confrontation in response to perceived expansionist Soviet and communist foreign-policy moves and the extremely provocative treatment of American diplomatic hostages by the revolutionary Islamic government of Iran. Much of this public sentiment, exacerbated by television and the mass media, helped to bring to power in 1980 a president whose principal foreign-policy objective was to build up the nation's military defense at an

---

[5]For an excellent study of the long-run changes in the size of these shares of influence and income, see Bruce M. Russett, *What Price Vigilance? The Burdens of National Defense* (New Haven: Yale University Press 1970) and "Defense Expenditures and National Well-Being," *American Political Science Review* 76, no. 4 (December, 1982), pp. 767–777.

unprecedented rate and to reassert American political, military, economic, and moral primacy in the world. The new militant course led to such minor but successful—and widely popular—military moves and far-reaching armament initiatives as the occupation of Grenada in 1983; the stationing of midrange nuclear missiles in Europe from 1984; the spectacular announcement of the Strategic Defense Initiative (SDI), aimed at installing new weapons systems in outer space; and the bombing of Tripoli in 1986 in response to Libya's alleged support of international terrorism. By the mid-1980s, however, this renewed bid for increased military power, privilege, and influence has been met with more resistance from public opinion, congressional leaders, and other interest groups, particularly over the high share of defense expenditures in the federal budget.

The more numerous the elements of plurality, communication, and participation are in a system, the harder it is for its elites and interest groups to stay put, and the more apt to shift is the balance among its levels and flows of internal and external political communications and decisions. In this respect modern democracies are not at all well suited to rule or guide other countries for long periods of time, and they are equally ill suited to submit for long even to the best-intentioned foreign influence or guidance. Britain's relations to the democratic countries of the Commonwealth show something of this difficulty, as do America's experiences since 1954 in trying to influence the policies of France, India, or Israel, and our more recent efforts to influence the military and political course of countries in the process of democratization in Latin America.

But what is true of modern democracies is perhaps also true, to a considerable degree, of all other modern countries. All modernization implies more frequent domestic communications, more differentiated and complex internal systems of communication, larger public sectors, increased popular participation beyond the local level, and a greater likelihood of recurring shifts in the communication and power relations within political systems. Even behind the façade of dictatorship, these shifting processes of politics and communication are at work; they make modern dictatorships no less ill suited to maintain for very long a tight control over distant foreign countries. The difficulties the Soviet Union has experienced in attempting to retain control of the policies of Czechoslovakia, Poland, and Rumania, and her loss of control of Yugoslavia and China, show how shifts within the USSR have combined with changes in the other countries to weaken or dissolve what earlier had looked at least on the surface like a tightly controlled bloc.

Though modern states find it hard to influence or control other states for long periods, their interests often drive their governments to try. The partial interdependence of countries may add urgency to such efforts without ensuring their success. And where interdependence persists, but control efforts fail, and where opposing interests become prominent, conflicts are likely to arise. Here again, international conflict arises out of the failures of control.

11

How Conflicts Arise Among States

At first glance, there are three things we want to know about any political conflict. First, can both sides survive it? Second, will it pass away or will it keep recurring? Third, can it be managed and kept within moderate bounds, or will it escape all controls and become itself the master of the fates of those involved in it?

THREE CRUCIAL ASPECTS OF CONFLICTS

In any conflict between states—and, indeed, in any conflict between political actors of any kind—the three questions mentioned above are crucial. We will consider the implications of each question below.

Bitter End or Joint Survival?

In a "bitter-end" conflict, only one of the two contending actors is likely to survive, at the price of the destruction or practically complete surrender of the other. In a "joint-survival" conflict, both actors are likely to survive, able to quarrel or cooperate in the future. World War II was a bitter-end war; it ended with the surrender of Germany and Japan and with the destruction of their dictatorships, as well as with the destruction of the Fascist regime in

Italy. The Himalaya war between India and China in 1962 was a joint-survival war; so were the wars between India and Pakistan in 1964 and 1971; and so was, as it turned out, the "cold war" between the United States and the Soviet Union, 1945–1963. In all these cases, both sides survived and had to continue to live side by side—as the Russians liked to say, to "coexist"—as best they could.

In bitter-end conflicts, one or both of the adversaries are apt to use strategies of annihilation, aiming at destroying the armed forces and the independence, and sometimes the government, of the adversary state, or at least its capacity to make autonomous decisions. People on one or both sides may then feel that they are fighting for their lives—that is, for their life as an organized self-governing political community—and this may make them willing to use even the most extreme weapons and methods of combat at their disposal.

In a joint-survival conflict, on the contrary, neither side can expect to get permanently rid of its adversary. They will have to face each other again, in peace or in another war; and once they are aware of this as the most likely prospect, people may be more inclined toward moderation during the conflict and toward compromise for its settlement for the time being.

Fundamental or Accidental?

If the conflict is *fundamental*, that is, rooted in some permanent basic structure of one or both of the contending parties, it is likely to recur again and again; if, on the other hand, it is *accidental* or transitory, that is, based on fortuitous and passing circumstances, it may not happen again in the future. The conflict between the United States and the Soviet Union—and generally between countries in which private enterprise predominates and communist-ruled countries where central planning and public or collective ownership prevails—is held to be fundamental, not only by many Marxist theorists but also by many people in the West. Accordingly, they expect it to persist for a long time and to become visible again after each temporary compromise, *detente,* or lull, so long as its root causes will not go away. By contrast, the conflict between the Soviet Union and the People's Republic of China is held by many not to be a conflict between basic social systems but rather one between the political leaders currently in office, or between currents of opinion and ideological interpretation temporarily prevailing in the two countries; once these have passed from power and the ideological frontiers become less distinct, there may be an eventual rapprochement between these two social systems—or such was, at least, the view of many Soviet scholars and American observers in the early 1970s.

Another view would be that the Soviet Union thus far has existed only since 1917, and the People's Republic of China only since 1949. Thus, to date, the world has had not quite seventy years' experience with the simultaneous existence of two distinct, modern social systems (capitalism and dictatorial socialism), and fewer than forty years' with several, if we count the People's Republic of China, Yugoslavia, Albania, Cuba, and Vietnam as distinct social systems of their own. These timespans may simply be too short to judge reliably which conflicts among the opposing systems may be fundamental and which ones are not.

Other scholars have thought to discern other sources of fundamental conflict between states—such as over territories of major strategic or economic importance, over matters of nationality, religion, language, race, or cultural tradition, or over the difference between democracy and dictatorship as forms of government. Many conflicts of these types, however, have not proved permanent between any two particular nations; rather, particular alliances and issues in dispute all have changed from time to time, or ceased to be important, not to return again.

But fundamental conflicts need not destroy either one or both of the antagonists; and a temporary or accidental conflict may do so, if it escalates to a sufficiently high level of violence. This grim possibility leads to the third question.

Manageable or Unmanageable?

Which conflicts remain under the joint control of the parties and stop short of uncontrolled or uncontrollable destruction, and which ones turn the adversaries themselves into the prisoners of a chain of events which neither of them foresaw and none controls? The Korean war of 1950–1952 and the Vietnam war of 1965–1972 remained manageable, so far as the great powers were concerned, in the sense that at each stage the United States, China, and the Soviet Union remained in control of their actions. Their governments could decide whether or not to intervene; if so, with how many and what kinds of supplies, troops, and weapons systems; when to increase or decrease their commitment; and what political and military settlements to accept at the conclusion of their large-scale intervention.[1]

By contrast, the outbreak of World War I was an unmanageable process. Austria, Russia, France, and Germany were racing each other in their efforts to mobilize and deploy their armed forces as fast as possible. Each of these powers then saw the armaments and later the mobilization of its rivals as something inexorably given, which had to be matched or outmatched at all costs. All of them, singly and together, lost control of the events and of their own fate.[2]

To call a conflict "fundamental," then, is to say something about its expected persistence and frequency in the future, and perhaps of the scale and depth of the required structural changes in at least one of the actors or nations, if this conflict were to be abolished. To call a conflict

---

[1]See Townsend Hoopes, *The Limits of Intervention,* 2nd ed. (New York: McKay, 1973).

[2]See S. B. Fay, *The Origins of the World War,* 2 vols. (New York: Macmillan, 1928); B. Tuchman, *The Guns of August* (New York: Macmillan, 1962); B. M. Russett, "Cause, Surprise and No Escape," in his *Power and Community in World Politics* (San Francisco: Freeman, 1974), pp. 173—189; N. Choucri and R. C. North, *Nations in Conflict* (San Francisco: Freeman, 1975), and Miles Kahler, "Rumors of War: The 1914 Analogy," *Foreign Affairs* 58, no. 2 (Winter 1979/1980), pp. 374–396.

"unmanageable," by contrast, says something about the expected difficulties in the way of limiting it, and about the risk of its uncontrollable and destructive escalation.

The United States, the Soviet Union, and China all can live with whatever fundamental conflicts may persist among their economic, social, and political systems, so long as they can keep them within manageable bounds. Over such transitory conflicts as Berlin in 1948 and 1961, and Cuba in 1962, they have shown the capacity and willingness to control and contain conflicts before they become unmanageable. Diplomatic relations, "hot lines" of direct telecommunication between the heads of governments, agreements on partial bans on testing nuclear weapons, advance notification agreements on military exercises, inspection agreements against surprise attack and against test ban violations—all of these have been developed between the United States and the Soviet Union (but much less by China) so as to make any unmanageable escalation of suspicions and hostilities among the great powers less likely.

Our three big questions about the three major dimensions of conflicts—are they bitter end or jointly survivable, fundamental or accidental, manageable or unmanageable?—have dealt only with a few gross external characteristics. What is the inner nature of the conflict relationship? What types of conflict can we discern here, and what are their expectable sources and effects in international politics?

THREE BASIC CONFLICT TYPES

No matter what sort of conflict a state works its way into, it finds itself maintaining some degree of control over not only its own behavior, but that of its adversary. The different types of conflicts can be distinguished according to the various amounts and patterns of self-control and mutual control involved. In the terms proposed by the mathematician and game theorist Anatol Rapoport, the three most important types of conflicts can be called "fights," "games," and "debates."[3] Each type has different background conditions, a different pattern of development, and a different distribution of predictable outcomes.

Some possible relationships between the three conflict aspects discussed earlier and the three conflict types, to be explained below, are shown in Table 17.

"FIGHTS": QUASI-AUTOMATIC TYPES OF CONFLICT

In a "fight" type of conflict, the self-control and mutual control of the actors decline rapidly, for the actions of each actor serve as starting-points for similar counteractions by the other actor. A dog meeting another dog in

---

[3]Anatol Rapoport, *Fights, Games and Debates* (Ann Arbor, MI: Univ. of Michigan Press, 1960).

TABLE 17 A Chart of Conflict Types and Aspects

ASPECTS OF CONFLICTS				TYPES OF CONFLICTS		
1. SURVIVABLE JOINTLY	2. ACCIDENTAL	3. MANAGEABLE	4. COMPOSITE ASPECT	FIGHTS	GAMES	DEBATES
		Yes (M)	SAM		"Pueblo" (1967) and "Maya-guez" (1973) Incidents	"First World" vs. "Third World": "New Economic Order" (1974–)
	Yes (A)	No (M̄)	SAM̄	Arms Race Theories (L.F. Richard-son)		Arab-Israeli Wars: 1948, 1956, 1967, 1973
Yes (S)		Yes (M)	SÂM	U.S.-Indian Wars of 18th and 19th c.	Dean Acheson's "live and let live policy"; H. Kissinger, (1972–77); Soviet "peaceful coexistence" theories after 1947	Convergence theories; changes in thought (Toynbee, Telihard)

No (Ā) "Fundamental"	No (M̄)	SĀM	World War I	
	Yes (M)	ŜAM	U.S. Civil War 1861–65	U.S. vs. Arbenz government of Guatemala, 1954
Yes (A)	No (M̄)	ŜĀM	Mahdi Wars (Sudan, 1885–1898)	
	Yes (M)	ŜĀM		Lenin's and Mao's early views of "revolutionary war" (1917, 1949)
No (S̄) ("Bitter end")	No (Ā)	No (M̄)	ŜĀM	World War II	Christianity-Islam after end of Crusades (1205); Protestant-Catholic wars (after 16th c.)

the street may growl at him; the second dog growls back. The first dog growls louder, and the second still more so. The first dog snarls, and so does the second. In the classic sequence of escalation there follow bared teeth, snaps, and a dogfight. Two small boys at the start of a schoolyard fight may go through a similar sequence: the exchange of taunting looks leads to that of taunting words and gestures, and then to threats, challenges, and counter-challenges, until blows are exchanged and a full-scale fight is under way.

What can be observed among dogs and small boys can also be observed in arms races among nations and in the confrontation of great powers. One nation's level of armaments or armament expenditure becomes the base line for a second nation, which decides to exceed it by some "safe" margin—say 10 percent—in order to feel secure. But this new, higher arms level of the second nation now becomes the basis for the security calculations of the first one, which now tries for its part to spend 10 percent more on weapons than does its rival. Its rival in turn tries to outspend this amount by 10 percent; and so on in a sequence of escalating armaments until one or both of the rivals is exhausted, or until war breaks out, or until there is some highly improbable last-minute change of policy on either side.

In a great-power confrontation, too, each power tries to outbid the other by some margin in its verbal or material commitment at each stage. Moderately worded notes are followed by stiff notes. Notes are followed by movements of ships, troops, or airplanes into locations close to the theater of the quarrel, and perhaps some forces are infiltrated or landed overtly. Shots are fired, followed by a more-than-equal retaliation from the other side. Allied nations step into the picture. And so on, through threat and counterthreat, retaliation and counterretaliation, right up to the brink of all-out war—and perhaps across it.

In their essence, such "fight" type conflict processes tend to be automatic and mindless, like the moves of novice checker players who know less of the game than they think: their every move seems to them obvious and necessary. In fact, often these processes, like the moves of two practiced but still not very skillful checker players, are so swift that they would be hard to distinguish from a reflex. Thus it is that leaders often say "We have no alternative," and that nations that should learn better from experience (as even most novice checker players often do) find themselves involved in what usually seem (to them) to be unavoidable conflict processes, making escape from the evolving sequence of events increasingly more difficult.

In its automatic character, a conflict of this type also resembles a process of nature, and, like certain processes of nature, it can be described by a pair of differential equations. (Mathematical models of such conflict processes have been explored by several natural and social scientists, including Lewis F. Richardson, Nicholas Rashevsky, G. F. Gause, Anatol Rapoport, and Kenneth Boulding.) Typically, such equations include two kinds of terms. Some terms represent processes of *acceleration*—that is, they stand for the accelerating effects which the moves of each actor have on the moves of the other, and possibly also on their own next steps. The other kind of terms, however, represent the opposite effects, which also occur in many conflict situations. These are the retarding or *decelerating* effects, and are in particular the effects making for increasing self-restraint on the part of each actor as the conflict mounts. Such effects include those of rising costs (political or economic), or of growing domestic opposition, or of declining resources—or of several of these combined.

Under certain conditions the accelerating factors will prevail; and an appropriate mathematical model will show that the conflict will escalate indefinitely until the destruction or breakdown of some actor or of some part of the system occurs. And it may even show how soon some such limit or point of breakdown will be reached. Under other conditions, however, factors of self-restraint may grow faster than the factors of accelerating conflict. In that event, the rate of conflict escalation will slow down and the whole conflict system may come to rest at some point well short of the breakdown of the system and the destruction of either of the contending parties. Under such conditions, mathematical models will show when and how competing species of beetles in the same bag of flour will continue to coexist indefinitely; or when and how competing missionary religions or political ideologies will continue in a stable state of competitive coexistence; or when and at what levels of expenditure an arms race may come to a halt. If we can discover and strengthen such factors making for greater self-restraint of the competing states, therefore, even the mindless automatism of "fight" type conflicts may still leave us with some hope.

"GAMES": RATIONAL CONFLICTS CHARACTERIZED BY STRATEGY

A very different type of conflict resembles games in which players maintain rational control over their own moves, though not necessarily over the outcome of those moves; and some of the models of game theory can be applied to them. Many games which we play for recreation, such as poker, bridge, or chess, bear some abstract and limited resemblance to conflict situations in real life—such as business competition, politics, diplomacy, and war; and it is in part for this reason that people have found such games interesting and attractive. In any such game, each player has a scale of utilities, according to which he prefers some outcomes, so long as he plays the game at all. He also has a range of options among different moves which he can make, and he has some set of expectations as to the probable outcome of any move that he may choose.

To play well, therefore, players must know what they want, they must know what they know and what they do not know, and they must know what they can and what they cannot do. Their knowledge of the outcome of their actions is uncertain, for in a typical game the results of one's own move will depend on the move the opponent makes. Often players will not know completely what the opponent can do (the opponent's capabilities, such as the high or low cards the opponent holds), nor what the opponent may decide or plan to do (the opponent's intentions). Faced with such uncertainty, players must base their moves on the most rational possible guess or estimate. Napoleon is said to have advised his generals to base their own military moves on their estimates of their adversaries' capabilities, rather than on their necessarily less reliable estimates of their intentions.

As long as they are "playing the game," the players play to win, or at least not to lose. It is for this purpose that they choose single moves and short sequences of moves, which we call *tactics*, as well as longer patterns and sequences of moves, which we will call *strategy* and in which the tactical moves are included as components. The most rational strategy for a player then is the one most likely to produce a winning outcome or—by another criterion—the one most likely to prevent a losing one. If the payoffs can be expressed in quantitative terms, then the most rational strategy is the one that maximizes net gains, or else the one that minimizes net losses.

Zero-Sum or Fixed-Sum Games

In *zero-sum games,* or, more generally, *fixed-sum games,* the sum of all payoffs to all players equals zero, so that anything any one player wins, some other player or players have to lose. (Chess, bridge, and poker are examples of zero-sum games.) In a fixed-sum game, the sum of all payoffs is fixed at some number which need not be zero but may be larger or smaller. (Here, too, however, the gains of any one player necessarily must be always at the expense of other players.) Zero-sum games, therefore, are a subclass of fixed-sum games, but any fixed-sum game can be turned into a zero-sum game by a simple mathematical transformation, for all the important mathematical properties of zero-sum games and other fixed-sum games are identical. What we shall say here of zero-sum games, therefore, will apply to all fixed-sum games.

Every zero-sum game represents a pattern of unmixed and unrelieved conflict. In a two-person game of this type, whatever one player wins, the other loses. Whatever is good for one, necessarily is bad for the other; and anything that is in any way good for one's adversary inevitably must be to the same extent bad for oneself. More than four centuries before the discovery of game theory, Niccolò Machiavelli used this pattern as a model for his concept of power when he wrote that a prince who advances another's power diminishes his own.[4]

A similar zero-sum notion of power and of the competition among rival states, and particularly among rival ideologies, has survived in some of the more fundamentalist versions of cold war thinking in our time. Whatever is good for, or even acceptable to the West (some "true believers" in militant communism may reason in Peking or Moscow) obviously must be bad for communism; and whatever is good for, or even merely acceptable to, communism (so reason some of our own "true believers" in militant anticommunism) must be automatically bad for the United States. Any step toward moderation, mutual accommodation, or compromise between the

---

[4]Niccolò Machiavelli, *The Prince and the Discourses* (New York: Modern Library, 1940).

United States and the Soviet Union, or between the United States and communist China, on any subject matter, so the "true believers" in the cold war on both sides think, is nothing but the futile appeasement of an insatiable enemy, and a treasonable sacrifice of the interest of one's own nation. Similarly, a variety of zero-sum thinking lies often behind the notion of strategic spheres of influence. Here the world is divided neatly into geographic areas, each of them under the effective strategic control of one of the contending superpowers. If a sphere or region escapes from the control of one superpower, then it must inevitably fall under the control of another power. This argument corresponds to a typical zero-sum situation of irreconcilable conflict and tension. It has been applied to such regions as the Far East, Indochina, Africa, and—particularly with regard to securing energy supplies and winning reliable allies in that area—to the Middle East conflict (where it is assumed that the Soviet Union's success rests in every failed peace initiative of the United States, which in turn is merely furthered in order to gain political and territorial advantages in the Gulf area). Actually, some regions may escape the controlling influence of all superpowers and become independent in their own right, as the People's Republic of China, India, and to some extent other countries such as Vietnam and Egypt have done since World War II. Here as elsewhere, applying zero-sum models to international politics may lead to dangerous illusions and serious misperceptions of regional crises and conflicts.

Strategies and solutions. The world of two-person, zero-sum games is a world of merciless and irreconcilable conflict. By the assumptions of this model, neither the players' motives nor their interest can ever change; they must remain forever hostile. But even this world is ruled by rationality. Players can calculate the average long-run chances of losing or winning in a sequence of repeated plays of the same game. They can calculate the best strategy for this long run; and they can assume, so long as they have no specific information to the contrary, that this strategy will also give them the best chances in a single encounter. Their adversaries, too, can calculate their own best strategy; in turn players can also calculate the best strategy of their opponents. Similarly, in international politics, states can, according to the assumptions of this model, rationally calculate their own best strategy for the long run. If a state makes decisions and moves independent of the decisions of its opponents, the other states, and based merely on the rational calculation of its own best strategy and self-interest, it is said to use *nonstrategic rationality* in the decision-making process. If a state realizes that for the pursuit of its own interests and its best strategy it must take into consideration the interaction of its own choices with the choices and strategies of the other states, then one speaks of *strategic rationality* determining the decision-making process and the moves of states. The strategic pursuit of self-interest may lead one nation-state to forego short-term interests and thus apparently deviate from its best strategy in order to achieve long-term advantages. The concept of strategic rationality also accounts for the ability of nation-states in international politics to choose courses of action which are based on the expectations of how others will behave.

If there is a clear "best strategy" for each player, and if both players can continue to follow their best strategies, we say that the game has "a stable solution." *Solutions* thus are that subclass of strategies from which no player can expect to be able to deviate without loss, and which lead, therefore, to stable outcomes for all rational players.

In fact, it often turns out that such a game has more than one such solution, although the number of stable solutions is likely to be small. By contrast, of course, there are usually very many foolish strategies; but it is worth bearing in mind that there may be more than one stable and viable way for dealing with a situation of conflict. If we think of international politics and more generally of human relations as ways of dealing with possible conflict, then this line of reasoning may suggest to us that there may be a plurality of workable ways to deal with them. Whereas it would be an error to be indifferent to all possible foreign policies or ways of life, it is probably realistic to recognize that a few alternative policies, and even ways of life, are likely to prove stable and viable even though we are likely to consider *for ourselves* only one such policy and way of life, as most consonant with our own values and traditions. These philosophic implications of game theory favor pluralism but not indifference. They suggest that we may choose a group of viable alternative strategies or policies on completely rational grounds, but that our ultimate choice among them sometimes may have to be based on grounds other than pure rationality.

The minimax concept.   Even in the irreconcilable conflict situation modeled in a two-person, zero-sum game, there may be one or several stable solutions resembling in some ways an automatic equivalent of compromise. These are the so-called *minimax* (or *maximin*) solutions. If we assume that our adversary will be as bright as possible and will play to win as much as possible, then there often exists for us some strategy (which we can calculate or discover) by which we can hold to a minimum our own losses, and thus the winnings of the adversary. Where such a strategy exists, it usually requires that we accept either the smallest of the gains available (the "minimum" of the "maxima"), or else the relatively smallest loss (and hence, from our viewpoint, the relative "maximum" gain) from among all possible losses (the "minima").

Game theorists agree that in irreconcilable conflict game situations the safest strategy for a player is to choose either "the best of the worst" or "the worst of the best" of all possible outcomes. They say that where this can be done consistently by a player, the distribution of all possible outcomes of the game for the two players must have at least one "saddle point" at which the minimum of one player's maxima and the maximum of the adversary's minima coincide, and which can be attained by such a strategy. Even in situations where no such "saddle point" exists, a player often can enforce the equivalent of a minimax solution by playing a suitably calculated "mixed" strategy. If a player has, say, four possible strategies, it might be worthwhile to alternate randomly between strategies numbers 1 and 3, but play strategy number 1 twice as often as strategy number 3, and never play strategies numbers 2 and 4 at all. (These arguments cannot be pursued here beyond the extremely crude hints and sketches that have been offered, but they can be studied in fascinating detail in the works of such game theorists as Martin Shubik, Anatol Rapoport, Duncan Luce, and Howard Raiffa, and, of course, in the classic *Theory of Games and Economic Behavior* by John Von Neumann and Oskar Morgenstern.)

Since this prudent strategy we have been discussing (which offers interesting parallels to certain styles of foreign policy) assumes that one's adversaries will do their best, it is not an "offensive" strategy, for it cannot take advantage of any mistakes they may make. Rather, it is essentially defensive. It will protect one player from taking unnecessary risks, and it will represent the best effort in the long run against the best-playing opponent. It is a relentless strategy of firmness and caution: it gives the player who uses it the best possible payoff against any opponent who is as clever as that player and in time it may even wear down the opponent. But it can promise no quick victory, and as a (so-called) "no-win" policy, when employed in international relations it is likely to be unpopular with action-minded generals and impatient civilians. Unpopularity notwithstanding, however, and in spite of the fact that actual foreign policy is made mainly by politicians and diplomats, and not by game theorists, perhaps something of the style of thought of the minimax policy can be discerned in the United States "containment policy" *vis-à-vis* the Soviet Union. This policy, first formulated without benefit of mathematics by George F. Kennan in 1946 and 1947, was pursued by the United States for the better part of two decades and—in its concept of balancing and if necessary resisting the adversary's moves at an overall level of stability—continued to influence the foreign policy approach of *detente* of the Nixon-Kissinger-Ford administration in the 1970s.

Variable-Sum (Mixed-Motive) Games

Not all conflict situations, however, either in daily life or international politics, resemble zero-sum games. They more often resemble *variable-sum games*. These are games in which the players not only win something competitively from one another, but also collectively stand to gain or lose something from an *additional* (or *secondary*) player (whom we may think of as "the banker" in games, or as "reality" or "nature" in certain real-life situations). Such games are, therefore, *mixed-motive games* for their primary players. For these players they are *games of competition*, insofar as these contestants try to win from one another; but they are also *games of coordination*, in that these players will also jointly gain or lose according to their ability to coordinate their moves in accordance with their common interests against "nature" or "the bank."

A prison revolt, from this point of view, would resemble a game of competition between the prisoners trying to escape, and their guards trying to keep them from doing so. Even a few guards can be successful at this, as long as they can prevent the prisoners, who usually are more numerous, from coordinating their efforts. At the same time the revolt would resemble a game of coordination among the prisoners, insofar as they would have to coordinate their moves against their few guards in order to overpower them. It would also resemble a game of competition among the prisoners, insofar as some of them might side with the guards against their fellows in order to obtain preferential treatment while in prison, or to win a partial remittance of their sentence for being among the first prisoners to throw their support to the guards' side. The basic resemblance of this model to many strikes, mutinies, colonial revolts, popular uprisings, or even revolutions is obvious. So is, in international relations, its general resemblance to some problems of collective security, and of the forming of international coalitions against a major power. Sometimes, of course, options and outcomes in international politics are not as clear as they are in such theoretical game models. What one side still describes as an act of cooperation, the other side may already perceive as a move to a defection. Rival parties to an arms control treaty—such as the United States and the Soviet Union in terms of the unratified SALT II treaty of 1979—may see their own deviation from agreements as marginal and harmless, while the greatest threat is seen in any deviation by the other side. In this way, a mixed motive-game can become more similar to a zero-sum game in the perceptions of the adversaries.

Mutual threats: the game of "chicken."   Certain game models of mixed-motive conflict situations have been studied somewhat more thoroughly. One of these is the game called "chicken." In this game (played at some time in the past, according to legend, by some teenage gangs in the United States), two players drive their automobiles on a lonely road at high speed, straight toward each other. The first player to swerve from the middle of the road, so as to avoid a collision, is called "chicken" and is held in disgrace by the rest of the gang; and the more reckless driver who refused to swerve is admired by them as a hero. (According to some commentators, this game bears a more-than-casual resemblance to head-on confrontations in world politics between major powers threatening one another with nuclear war.)

A closer look at the game of "chicken" reveals its underlying mathematical pattern. Each of the two players has a choice between two strategies: (1) "cooperation" with the other player by swerving so as to avoid collision (but at the risk of being disgraced by a decision to at the last minute); or, (2) "defection" from a common interest in survival by driving straight on. If both players refuse to swerve, the result will be their death. If only one player swerves, the other player triumphs. Each player makes a "move" by deciding whether to cooperate or to defect; but the outcome of the move depends not only on that decision but also—and crucially—on the decision taken by the adversary.

In the abstract model of this situation there are four possible outcomes: First, both players may "cooperate" (*CC*) by swerving at the same time, so that neither will be disgraced. Or both may "defect" (*DD*) by driving straight into a head-on collision that will most likely kill or cripple them. Or player *A* may cooperate by swerving while *B* drives straight ahead (*CD*); then *A* is disgraced and *B* is admired by the group. Or, finally, *A* may

Figure 5. Some Examples of Game Models

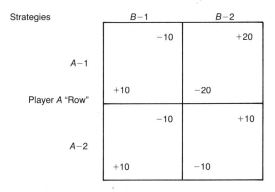

1. *"Minimax"*:

Player B "Column"

| Strategies | B−1 | B−2 |

Matrix of Outcomes: Each cell represents the outcome that follows if *A* and *B* choose the strategies that lead to it. Payoffs to *A* are shown in the bottom left-hand corner, and payoffs to *B*, in the top right-hand corner, of each cell.

Player A "Row"

A−1: B−1 cell −10 / +10; B−2 cell +20 / −20
A−2: B−1 cell −10 / +10; B−2 cell +10 / −10

"Natural" or Minimax Outcome: *A−2, B−2 (−10, +10)*. *A−2* is the best which *A* can do for himself, if *B* does his worst to him; and *B−2* is the best *B* can do against *A*'s best strategy.

2. *"Chicken"*:

	B−1 (C)	B−2 (D)
A−1 (C)	−5 / −5	+10 / −10
A−2 (D)	−10 / +10	−50 / −50

"Natural" or Minimax
Outcome: *CC (−5, −5)*

3. *"Prisoner's Dilemma"*:

	B−1 (C)	B−2 (D)
A−1 (C)	+1 / +1	+20 / −20
A−2 (D)	−20 / +20	−10 / −10

"Natural" or Minimax
Outcome: *DD (−10, −10)*;
Cooperative Outcome:
CC (+1, +1)

"defect" and drive straight on, while *B* cooperates by swerving (*DC*); then *A* is admired and *B* despised.

When driving at high speed in a "chicken" game, neither player has time to see what his or her adversary is about to do, hence each must pick in advance the best strategy and act on it. But which is the best strategy, say, for player *A*? In the game of "chicken," it is clearly *C*, for at best, if *B* also cooperates, the players will get home unhurt and undisgraced; and at worst, if *B* defects, *A* will still get home alive, even though with diminished standing with the gang. The same applies, of course, to *B:* that player's best strategy, too, is to choose to cooperate, regardless of the opponent's choice, so long as that choice cannot be reliably foretold. This choice of *C* for each player is unequivocally rational, as long as for each of them the penalty for double defection (*DD*)—which here is being killed or maimed—is clearly greater than the disrepute and chagrin of the "sucker" who trustingly co-operates while the adversary triumphantly defects (*CD*), and as long as the penalty for the outcome (*DD*) is also clearly greater than the temptation for each player to outwit the adversary by encouraging cooperation so as to encompass the adversary's disgrace and the player's own triumph. Teen-agers, of course, sometimes may be less rational than game theorists are, but the verdict of game theory is clear. As long as the negative payoff for the outcome *DD* is greater than any positive or negative payoff for *CD* or *DC* outcomes, the game is a genuine game of "chicken." It has a rational solution, which is for each player to choose cooperation over conflict. Where a confrontation in international politics should resemble such a "chicken" game, rational statesmen, according to this theory, should choose a "soft-line" rather than a "hard-line" policy.

Another game model of mixed-motive conflict situations is the allegory of the *stag hunt* offered by the French philosopher Jean-Jacques Rousseau to illustrate the possibility of cooperation in the early stages of society.[5] This game model differs from that of "chicken" in that it incorporates the action and moves of more than two parties in a conflict situation. Several primitive hunters happen to come together at a time when all of them suffer from hunger and hence have a common interest in a good meal. The hunger of each will be satisfied by the fifth part of a stag, so they agree to cooperate in trapping one. They position themselves around a stag, and if they continue to cooperate, they will bring the stag down and feast on its meat. But the hunger of any one of the hunters will also be satisfied by a hare, although less so than by a share of the stag. As a hare comes within reach, each hunter has two options: to cooperate and stay at his post—which will be rewarded by a good meal from the stag—or to defect, catch the rabbit for himself, and in so doing permit the stag to escape. Rousseau predicted that the immediate self-interest of one or several of the hunters would prevail over considerations for their fellows or the much larger reward of the stag in the long run.[6] According to classic game theory, however, this multiperson mixed-motive game is much more conducive to cooperative behavior: If the likelihood of killing the stag is high for them, each player's rational choice would be to mutually cooperate and thus gain a much higher reward—the stag and a good meal; the reward for one player's defection or mutual defection at most would be one hare for the first defector.

[5]Jean-Jacques Rousseau, *The First and Second Discourses* (New York: St. Martin's Press, 1964), pp. 165–167.

[6]For a discussion of the philosophical and societal implications of this model, see Kenneth N. Waltz, *Man, the State and War: A Theoretical Analysis* (New York: Columbia Univ. Press, 1959).

Threats and promises: the "prisoners' dilemma." Unfortunately, how-ever, another game model of international conflict often may be more realistic. This is the "prisoners' dilemma" game. According to the story that goes with an explanation of it, the governor of a prison once had two prisoners whom he could not hang without a voluntary confession from at least one. Accordingly, he summoned one prisoner and offered him his freedom and a sum of money if he would confess at least a day before the second prisoner did so, so that an indictment could be prepared and so that the second prisoner could be hanged. If the latter should confess at least a day before him, however, the first prisoner was told, then that prisoner would be freed and rewarded, and he would be hanged. "And what if we both should confess on the same day, your Excellency?" asked the first prisoner. "Then you each will keep your life but will get 10 years in prison." "And if neither of us should confess, your Excellency?" "Then both of you will be set free—without any reward, of course. But will you bet your neck that your fellow prisoner—that crook—will not hurry to confess and pocket the reward? Now go back to your solitary cell and think about your answer until tomorrow." The second prisoner in his interview was told the same, and each man spent the night alone considering his dilemma.

The mathematical structure of this game resembles in some respects that of the game of "chicken." Each prisoner has two strategies to choose from: cooperate with his fellow by keeping silent (C), or defect from him by producing a confession (D). There are again four possible outcomes: (1) CC—both prisoners keep silent and gain their freedom but no cash; (2) CD—the first prisoner keeps silent, but the second defects, sends him to the gallows, and walks off free with a reward; (3) DC—the first prisoner defects and is freed and rewarded, while the second prisoner cooperates and is hanged for his trust; and (4) DD—both prisoners act as hardheaded realists, confess, and spend 10 years in prison.

Knowing this pattern of possible outcomes but not knowing the deci-sion of his fellow, and with no means of communication or coordination with him, which strategy should each solitary prisoner most rationally choose? Classic game theory again has a clear answer; he should defect. At best, defection could bring him freedom and money; at worst, 10 years in prison. Cooperation at best promises him freedom without any money, and at worst, its penalty is more severe: the gallows. So long as he cannot rely on his fellow, each prisoner in his own rational self-interest must choose defec-tion, with its higher rewards and lesser penalties. Accordingly, both prison-ers do so: they confess—and since they are equally rational, they do so on the same day. And so, although they could have walked out free if they had kept silent, they now will spend 10 years in prison contemplating the results of their cold-blooded rationality.

As in the game of "chicken" and the analogy of the stag hunt, the two players would be much better off if they could coordinate their strategies and play CC; but in contrast to the game of "chicken," the players in "prison-ers' dilemma" find it very hard (and, reasoning as individuals, not rational) to do so. Why?

In "chicken" it is rational to cooperate rather than defect, for the penalty for double defection (*DD*) is clearly greater than the temptation to defect from a cooperating partner so as to profit from betrayal. In "prisoners' dilemma," however, the "sucker's" penalty for being betrayed while trustingly cooperating is clearly worse than the penalty for double defection. It seems not rational, therefore, to risk betrayal. Situations of arms control and disarmament, or of deescalation between bitterly opposed ideological adversaries, show somewhat similar characteristics; both sides could reap real gains from mutual trust, but these gains are outweighed by the tempting rewards for successful cheating and by the penalties for being trustful and cheated.

A single play of the "prisoners' dilemma" game has no convincing rational solution, except the somewhat absurd one that both players, by jointly contriving to choose *DD,* should put themselves in prison for 10 years. We could drop, however, the "end-of-the-world" assumption which thus far has been implicit in our model, and which made us pretend that in this game nothing more mattered but a single play. If we shift our attention to the best strategy for a series of repeated plays, the beginning of a solution can be discovered.

The approach to this discovery involves a combination of analysis and experiment. If the two prisoners in our game could coordinate their strategies, they could walk out free, but they have no means of communication. In a series of repeated plays, however, they have one such means, for they communicate something to each other, willy-nilly, through every move they make and through the outcome to which it contributes. Anatol Rapoport and his associates at the University of Michigan have conducted experiments with "prisoners' dilemma" games in which two players had to play 300 consecutive plays against each other. Their published findings are based on the experience of about 100,000 plays, and they are of great interest to all students of conflict among persons, groups, and nations.[7]

Only a few points of these findings can be mentioned here. In the initial play of a typical 300-play sequence, the two adversaries succeed in achieving double cooperation (*CC*) and a joint reward in a little less than 50 percent of the plays. The next 30 to 40 plays are characterized by seeming disillusionment in which they get tough with one another, and their game then usually becomes more competitive, with mutual cooperation (*CC*) declining to about 27 percent, so that both players are now losing heavily. During the next 100 plays, they gradually learn that this cutthroat competition does not pay, and that cooperation does; and during the last 50 plays of the 300-play sequence, they collaborate successfully in achieving the rewarding *CC* payoffs in about 73 percent of their plays.

A possible explanation of these findings is that both players in the early stages employ somewhat more cooperation than defection, but that they are very likely to fail to coordinate their cooperative moves. As soon as this happens, the player who made the cooperative move is strongly penalized by the defecting move of the adversary; and the player is likely to

---

[7]A. Rapoport and A. Chammah, *The Prisoners' Dilemma* (Ann Arbor: University of Michigan Press, 1970).

interpret this as malice and betrayal. The player retaliates by switching to the defecting strategy, and a chain of mutual retaliation follows (from which it takes both sides a long time to recover) until they eventually learn to reach and maintain a substantially higher level of coordination than the one from which they originally started.

The personality of the individual players turns out to have very little to do with the sequence of outcomes of the game. What counts most are outcomes of the first few plays, which seem to produce a powerful "lock-in" effect on further progress of the game. If they set a string of early precedents for hostility, then conflict and mutual penalization will be severe and long, and the recovery of confidence and the learning of more frequent cooperation will be much delayed. If the early moves, on the contrary, have established a setting of cooperation, much of the beneficial effect will tend to persist throughout the later stages.

These findings are suggestive for the prediction and management of international conflict. They would lead us to expect less of an effect from the intentions or the supposed intrinsic characteristics of foreign governments and to pay more attention to the patterns of mutual interactions among governments, including notably our own. It would then be less important to ask, "What did the government of country X intend by this move toward country Y?" than to ask, "What actually happened to country X and Y as a result of this move made by the government of X and by Y's response to it?—and to ask further, "What was the possible lock-in effect for the future, generated by this experience?"

The data also confirm what students of politics would have suspected: that both martyrs and cynics will do poorly at this game. A martyr is a player who always plays the cooperative move C, no matter how often the adversary betrays and penalizes the player by defecting. The data show that such martyrs tend to be shamelessly exploited by their adversaries; martyrs seem to bring out the worst in the opposition. And martyrs tend to remain losers to the end of the game. Cynics, however, who consistently defect, will fare almost as badly. They will soon provoke retaliation, and if they persist in their strategy of defection, they will remain locked in on the penalty outcomes of the DD type and will be consistent losers. The strategy most likely to succeed, it turns out, is: (1) to initiate cooperation; (2) to persist in making cooperative moves as long as they are reciprocated; and (3) to retaliate without fail whenever repeated or frequent defection is encountered; but (4) to renew from time to time thereafter a sequence of two or three unilateral cooperative moves in order to give the adversary a chance to shift to a sequence of mutual cooperation.

More recently, Anatol Rapoport's experiments have been extended and improved, and have concentrated on how a strategy of cooperation can emerge in a repeated, or iterated, series of "prisoners' dilemma" games. Robert Axelrod used computer tournaments to test several different strategies in 200 iterations of the game.[8] Analysis of the results showed

---

[8]Robert Axelrod, *The Evolution of Cooperation* (New York: Basic Books, 1984). For surveys on recent game theoretical advances, see also *Explaining Cooperation under Anarchy: Hypotheses and Strategies*, special issue of *World Politics* 38, no. 1 (October 1985).

that cooperation and even harmony—that is, the absence of incentives to defect—can evolve almost automatically in iterated games and out of seemingly hopeless situations. The simplest of all strategies emerged as the most successful, that of *tit-for-tat,* a strategy of initiating cooperation and then of following whatever move the adversary makes. The experiments showed that the tit-for-tat strategy has four properties that tend to make it successful in enhancing decisions for cooperative moves: (1) it avoids unnecessary conflict by cooperating as long as the other player does; (2) it is provocable—that is, in case of defection of the other player the strategy automatically retaliates; (3) it is forgiving because, having once retaliated, the strategy allows the player to "forget" past defections of the adversary and embark on a new course of mutual cooperation; and (4) it is clear and therefore unexploitable; other players following other strategies will soon realize this and start playing cooperatively. This strategy is thus likely to lead to the evolution of cooperation through practical experience rather than the benevolence of the players.

Robert Axelrod devised four basic rules for success (that is, the emergence of cooperation) in iterated "prisoners' dilemma" games: (1) don't be envious—forgive your adversary, even if he has made a gain in the past; (2) don't be the first to defect; (3) reciprocate both cooperation and defection; and (4) don't be too clever—don't try to exploit the tit-for-tat strategy of your opponent as this will not work in the long run.

Both strategies—that of unilaterally initiating cooperative moves and showing restraint, or that of following cooperative initiatives of one's opponent—need, however, testing in recurrent events in order to accumulate for each player more mutually beneficial outcomes and to decrease the incentives to defect. The evolution of players' tacit cooperation also requires that players have a sufficiently large chance to meet again so that they may, if necessary, add credibility to their threats and promises by executing them, or regain a loss of trust following sudden defections of one party by communication and reciprocal action through the sequence of their behavior. They also need to have a stake in future interactions, a factor which Axelrod has called "the shadow of the future." The higher this stake in the future is, the higher will be the incentive to cooperate as future payoffs will gain more weight and diminish the advantages of a single defection, which could otherwise lead to an extended series of uncooperative rounds. This form of cooperation, once established, can protect itself to a certain extent from invasion of less cooperative strategies. In international politics and diplomacy, such strategies for reciprocal cooperation in a series of events will most likely produce neither a "hard" nor a "soft" policy. U.S. policy and actions during the Cuban missile crisis would not correspond to such a rational strategy of reciprocity and mutual cooperation; they are generally seen as resembling more of a "chicken"-game situation. But in the field of trade conflicts and tariff negotiations, where one country's tariff policy is contingent upon another's and cooperative and retaliatory moves are relatively clear and easy to make, the "prisoners' dilemma" situation is more common and has been used to analyze possibilities for cooperative behavior in trade conflicts.[9]

Another insight from mathematical game models has been that cooperative behavior doubles in frequency when the payoff matrix is prominently and continuously displayed to both players throughout the game. (This effect obtains even when all the players have been told of the payoff matrix at the start of the game, and their gains or losses are reported to them after every play.) This finding may add some support to the view of Immanuel Kant and other philosophers, that fuller awareness of their own situation will make people more likely to behave cooperatively and morally.

Threat games against inequality.   The game models discussed so far and outlined in Figure 5 have been applied primarily to situations where the players are more or less equal and the payoff matrices symmetrical. Interest among theorists in asymmetrical matrices for unequal adversaries has been slower to develop. In the 1970s, however, Anatol Rapoport and his associates have explored a new type of games that focuses on situations of inequality and that has suggestive implications for a large class of cases in international and domestic politics. They consider a game matrix of the kind shown in Fig. 6.

In this situation, the row player A is clearly disfavored and may be called the underdog. If A plays the second strategy, T, then A stands to lose at each play -30 or -20, depending on what the column player B decides to do. If A plays the first strategy A-S, then A gets nothing and submits, in effect, to the supremacy of B; for the favored player, or "top dog," B obviously will want to play B-S and collect a gain of $+20$. But from the viewpoint of individual, short-term rationality, this seems still the best A can do because any attempt to play the alternative strategy B-T will immediately result in a greater loss.

Consider, however, what happens if the underdog A turns stubborn and rebellious and insists on playing A-T. This will cost A a loss of -30 at each play, but it will also threaten the favored player B with a loss of -20, if B continues to play B-S, or, with a smaller loss of -10, if B plays B-T. Once the top dog B discovers that A cannot be shifted from his or her costly and seemingly unreasonable rebellion, then B's self-interest will encourage him or her to shift to playing B-T, so as to keep the losses smaller. Once B does this, however, the underdog A will shift back to playing A-S in order to collect now a gain of $+20$. At that point, in turn, the top dog will shift back to playing B-S, so as to collect once more a reward of $+20$.

The result is at first a merry-go-round of four plays, as shown by the broken arrows in Fig. 6. The outcomes start at SS $(0,+20)$, shift to TS

[9]See, for example William Cline, *Reciprocity: A New Approach to World Trade Policy?* (Washington, D.C.; Institute for International Economics, 1982); Raymond Riezman, "Tariff Retaliation from a Strategic Viewpoint," *Southern Economic Journal* 48 (January 1978), pp. 583–593; and John Conybeare, "Trade Wars: A Comparative Study of Anglo-Hanse, Franco-Italian, and Hawley-Smoot Conflicts," *World Politics* 38, no. 1 (October 1985), pp. 147–172.

Figure 6. A Threat Game Against Inequality (conventions are the same as in Fig. 5)

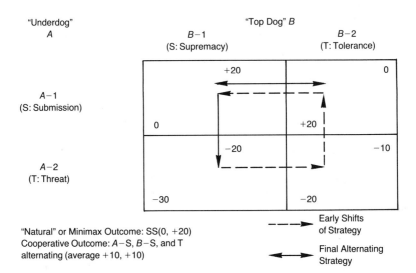

"Natural" or Minimax Outcome: SS(0, +20)
Cooperative Outcome: A−S, B−S, and T
alternating (average +10, +10)

(−30,−20), then to TT (−20,−10), from there to ST (+20,0), and back to SS and another round. The result of the round is a net loss of −30 for *A*, and of −10 for *B*. But sooner or later, *B* will discover that simply alternating moves between S and T would be much better, provided that *A* then will always play S and nothing else. In that case, *A* will collect +20 at every second play—say, at each odd-numbered one—and *B* will collect +20 at every other play—say, at each even-numbered one. In this way, both of them will keep winning at the expense of the bank.

What has happened here? The underdog *A* has discovered a new, long-term rationality as a behavioral guide. The dominant short-term solution SS would perpetuate his or her inferiority. By rejecting it, by threatening the top dog *B* with the outcome TS which could be enforced, and by accepting the costs of carrying out this threat, if necessary, *A* now can compel *B* to concede a number of outcomes ST which give *A* a share of the winnings, up to one-half of the total. (In many actual games, however, top dog and underdog have ended up splitting the winnings not 5:5 but 6:4, respectively.)

Situations of this kind occur in real life. Within a country or a factory, workers may go on strike, at some cost to themselves but in the hope of compelling management to concede a larger share of the profits of the enterprise or the industry to them; this increment in their share may be larger over a period of time than the wages they lost in the strike. In the world market, developing countries that supply some important raw material or fuel, such as oil, may withhold it from the market in order to win a price increase and with it a larger share of the profits from the use of the oil in the oil-importing countries.

According to this model, disadvantaged groups or nations can benefit from such threat tactics, but only within limits. First, there must be a positive payoff in the system that can be shared among the contending parties. Second, the favored side or actor must retain enough of a share of this payoff to make it worthwhile to agree to a concession to the underdog; and third, the costs of the threats and conflicts to the underdog must not be greater than that player can bear, nor greater than what that player can expect to gain over a longer period if the threat and struggle should be successful.

Survival games and protracted conflict.   Three-hundred consecutive plays of the "threat game" or the "prisoners' dilemma" game makes either game more realistic in one crucial aspect. It is no longer an "end-of-the-world" game in which the players have no future and hence no need to consider what future behavior in other players they are inducing by their strategies. Rather, the game is now played more nearly as a *survival game,* in which the reward for success consists in large part in being permitted to continue playing, and the penalty for failure consists in being ruined and having to quit the game—much as in the real-life games of business, party politics, and international relations among governments. The more elaborate game models of the future will have to be conceived of as survival games if they are to resemble real-life business, politics, and international relations, and if they are to be of any use to us in the survival game that all of us are playing for humankind.

Moreover, these survival-game models also need to incorporate the more realistic situations of unequal adversaries and, therefore, more complicated asymmetrical matrices of payoffs; and they need to develop rational strategies such as threat tactics appropriate for each adversary within his or her limitations and capabilities. Under conditions of asymmetry and inequality—which characterize most present-day international relations, in which many smaller and less developed countries are dependent on a few highly developed and powerful ones—one state will be relatively more vulnerable than another. Thus, a conflict or issue for a small country may resemble more of a survival game, whereas for a large, wealthy, or powerful country the same issue may be inconsequential in the long run. Each country will therefore have different preferences for actions and asymmetrical payoff values, and gains and losses from actions will differ according to the position of each country in relation to its adversary. The only cardinal value common to both contending parties can be assumed to be a shared interest in the survival of humankind.

Survival games resemble in some limited ways the simple "fight" models discussed earlier in this chapter, but they differ from these mindless, quasi-automatic processes by providing each of the antagonists with some opportunities for choice. In order to permit us some insight into the complexities of protracted conflicts, however, the following group of models also has to be somewhat more complex. In particular, where game models up to this point assumed that the payoff matrix and the decisions of the two players would completely determine the joint outcome of their actions, the new models explicitly consider the probability of various outcomes and of the ruin of one or another of the players.

Let us assume that there exists some ongoing sequence of probabilistic decisions and that two players have exactly opposite interests in the outcome of each step or play. Thus they may toss coins and place opposing bets on the outcome of each toss, such that whenever A bets on "heads," B bets on "tails." Or they may be two commanders of opposing military forces that are going through a series of clashes, each of which may be won by one side or the other. Or else we may think of the heads of two rival firms that oppose each other in a series of sales campaigns, or the leaders of two political parties that oppose each other in a series of confrontations or elections.

Moreover, let us assume that each rival has only a limited amount of resources, such as chips for betting, or soldiers for combat, or money for advertising, or campaign workers and sympathizers, and that each play or encounter will increase the resources of the winner but decrease those of the loser. The players are free to bet or gamble more or less of their resources on each play, and the crucial questions are, "Which player will be ruined first?"—and hence, "Which one will survive and be counted as the winner?" And further, "Which is the best betting strategy for avoiding ruin, and hence for survival?" Mathematicians call this the problem of "gambler's ruin," but it has its counterpart in real life, not only among gamblers but among armies, parties, and nations.

There are two more points to be considered. The two players may not be equally rich in money or manpower at their disposal. What is the best strategy for a player with ample material resources? What would be the best conduct for his or her adversary of slender means? Moreover, the two players may not be equally skillful or favored by conditions. One of them may be more likely, on the average, therefore, to win each encounter than is the adversary, for the favored player may have greater skill, familiarity with the terrain, popularity with voters, or a more salable product; or the coins or dice may be loaded in that player's favor.

Given equal chances to win each single play, the player with the greater resources is more likely to survive. Given equal resources, the player favored on balance by skill or circumstances is more likely to do so. But how much of an edge in terms of riches or of skill will make how much of a difference to one's chances of surviving one's rival?

Finally, what happens if one player is favored by wealth but the other by skill or the favor of other conditions? How much of an advantage in wealth can be equalized or compensated for by how much of an advantage in skill or favorable circumstances? And how long is it likely to take in such conflicts for the outcome to occur?

All such questions can be answered, in principle, by mathematical models called "stochastic processes" or "models of a random walk between barriers."[10] Only a few results and potential implications can be summarized here.

---

[10]See V. Marma and K. W. Deutsch, "Survival in Unequal Conflict," *Behavioral Science*, 18, no. 5 (September 1973), pp. 313–334, and generally H. R. Alker, K. W. Deutsch, and A. Stoetzel, eds., *Mathematical Approaches to Politics* (Amsterdam-New York: Elsevier, 1973).

1.   An advantage of 1 percent in the likelihood to prevail in each of a series of plays, tosses, or encounters is equal in effect to an advantage of about 7.5 percent of material resources—but this holds only for players whose inequality of material resources is not larger than 4:1.

2.   If the ratio of the resources of one player to those of the rival is between 4:1 and 9:1, the effect of one additional percent of resources is roughly equal to that of 1 percent more likelihood of winning single encounters.

3.   If one player has a superiority of 9:1 or more in resources, as against the rival, every additional 1 percent of resource superiority, will have as much effect as 2 percent of added probability of winning single plays. In short, for moderate inequalities of labor or money, up to 4:1, the effects of popular support, or skill, weigh more than 7 times as much as those of wealth; at intermediate levels of resource inequality, ranging between 4:1 and 9:1, skill and wealth have equal weight; but at high levels of material inequality, above 9:1, added wealth or labor weighs twice as much as added skill, morale, or popular support.

4.   The side favored by its greater likelihood to win encounters, but disfavored by a moderate inferiority in resources, will do better if it limits its commitment of resources to any one encounter and tries to prolong the conflict, such as by a strategy of avoiding large-scale combat, or by guerrilla tactics. If its workforce or resource inferiority is larger than 1:9, however, guerrilla tactics are likely to fail.

5.   The side moderately favored by its ready resources of money or labor, but inferior in its chances to prevail in clashes, will do best by trying to force a quick decision of the conflict by a small number of large-scale clashes, such as through the tactics of *blitzkrieg*, or "lightning war," as used in 1940–1941 by Hitler, and in 1941–1942 by Japan. If the less skillful or less popular side fails to win the quick victory it needs, its eventual defeat may become probable.

Mathematical models with their inevitable simplification cannot replace, of course, an intimate knowledge of real-life situations with their much greater complexity. Game theory is still developing, and even the eighty-seven types of two-party conflicts cited by A. Rapoport have not yet been fully explored for their possible applicability to international politics.[11] Game-theory models for conflicts among more than two parties (*N*-person games) still need to be developed much further, but already they incorporate much more accurately the realities of multilateral international relations and conflicts. Rousseau's allegory of the stag hunt, one of the first models of *N*-person games, demonstrated the problems of control and cooperation, autonomous action, and reciprocal trust that are magnified in conflict situations with multiple numbers of adversaries. Rousseau predicted that in cooperative collective action, even when all participants agree on a common goal and have an equal interest in the outcome, one cannot rely on others. More recent theoretical approaches to *N*-person games deal with the same basic problems and attempt to gain insights into the effect of larger numbers of participants on the robustness of game-theory systems and strategies: Is a stable number of participants required in a conflict situation in order for cooperation to emerge? How do perennial problems of cooperation—such as the sharing and utilizing of public goods—benefit

[11]Anatol Rapoport *et al.*, *The Two by Two Game* (Ann Arbor, MI: Univ. of Michigan Press, 1976). For other important works, see Stephen Brains.

from these mathematical models? It is hoped that eventually strategies for the institutionalization of cooperation can be developed.[12] Future scientists may be able to create highly accurate and dynamic N-person game-theory models with more or less direct applicability to the analysis of international relations. Even if these models can never fully reconstruct complex realities and consider all aspects of the nature of conflict, they can help us to gain analytical insights and to alert us to real-life questions and possibilities we otherwise might overlook. In this way, they can help us to increase the power of our limited capacities to think.

COSTS OF THINKING AND CAPACITIES TO THINK

Another improvement in the models of game theory is critically needed but will be rather difficult to make. To resemble more nearly the realities of politics, both national and international, improved game-models would have to take explicit account of the *costs of thinking* and *decision making*. In classic game theory, it is assumed that players can calculate all possible moves of their own and of their adversaries, together with all their expectable consequences, and that they can do so instantly, completely, and at no cost in time, effort, or resources. Each player may know all the present pieces and positions of the adversary, as in chess; or a player may be ignorant of some or all the cards and combinations which the opponent holds, as is the case in many card games, such as poker; but in any case the classic theory of games by Von Neumann, and Morgenstern assumes that each player should have no difficulty in thinking through, instantly, all the possible combinations of the moves and outcomes which are implied in those facts which he knows.

In fact, of course, this is not true of either chess or poker. Chess is interesting precisely because the time from one move to the next—often one hour in chess tournaments—is far too short for any player (and the mind would be too limited even if the player had a much longer time to think) to go through the whole vast ocean of combinatorial possibilities which the thirty-two chess pieces on their sixty-four squares offer; and the universe of possible poker combinations is similarly inexhaustible within the time limits of the game and the human limitations of the players. The best a player then can do is pick a few promising "candidate strategies" or "candidate solutions" by a mixture of rationality, guess, and intuition, and then spend limited thinking time and calculating resources on analyzing the implications of these few preferred candidate strategies, in the hope that at least one of them will prove acceptable. And the player must make his or her choices knowing the peril.

A similar limitation holds for politics, and for many other human

---

[12]For a discussion of the analytical value of game theory models and their applicability to international conflicts, see Duncan Snidal, "The Game *Theory* of International Politics," *World Politics* 38, no. 1 (October 1985), pp. 25–57, and Thomas C. Schelling, *Micromotives and Macrobehavior* (New York: Norton, 1978).

decision situations. In most of these, the total of combinations of all possible moves and outcomes for all parties concerned is far too great to permit anything like exhaustive calculation within the time available. Under these conditions, it is a delusion to speak of the "optimal" solution (that is, of the "best of all possible" solutions) because the complete range of solutions is more than likely to remain unknown to both players and observers within *any* limits of time available for thought and action. So the search for the *absolutely* best ultimate strategy to win becomes transformed into a search for the best *intermediate* strategy to *search* for the relatively best strategy to win—that is, the one considered the best likely to be found within the given limits of time and calculating resources.

Any effort at search, like all other efforts, has its costs. A choice must be made between potentially better solutions that are more costly to search for and less likely to be discovered, and more obvious solutions or strategies that may be less good but are quicker and cheaper to find. In practical politics, both national and international, time and thinking costs are crucial. The search for the supposedly "best" strategy is apt to stop as soon as *any* acceptable strategy is found at tolerable costs in terms of search and computation, provided that no alternative and equally attractive strategy has emerged. Though national leaders and business executives often believe that they are "optimizing" their strategies (in the sense of choosing the best of all), they are actually only doing what social scientist Herbert Simon has called "satisficing," which is to say, picking the most acceptable strategy among the few alternatives they can survey within the time and resources they can or will spend on the search.

In international politics, the result often is something similar to a "law of least mental effort." Foreign policies must be found, or at least approved, by harassed and busy people laboring under severe pressures of time shortage and communication overload. Any policy that is relatively easy to discover and explain, that fits in well with the previously established thought habits of the relevant decision makers, and that has no obvious major drawbacks, has a good chance to be adopted. Once it has been adopted, moreover, the vast amount of coordination and commitment among very many people, which is needed to implement any major policy, will make it very hard to change. Major foreign policies, therefore, are not always chosen and retained by rational calculation, as the models of classic game theory would suggest, but rather by a partly rational but also partly random process of limited search and limited evaluation, for which as yet no reliable game-theory models have been accepted.

Threats and Deterrence as Mixed-Motive Games

A valuable contribution to the better understanding of international politics has been made by Thomas C. Schelling, who has demonstrated that situations of threat and deterrence can be treated as mixed-motive games.[13] The party who makes the threat (the "threatener") and the party who is

---

[13]T. C. Schelling, *The Strategy of Conflict* (Cambridge, MA: Harvard University Press, 1960).

being threatened (the "threatenee") obviously must have at least one set of clashing interests: the threatenee must be doing something, or about to do something, which the threatener dislikes enough to make the threat in the hope of stopping, changing, or preventing the behavior. Schelling further says that the two parties to the threat also have a common interest in not having the threat carried out. For the threatened action is not only in some sense painful to the threatenee; it is also costly or painful to the threatener. If the threatened action were simply in the threatener's interest, then that person should not threaten it but act. The fact that the threatener prefers to threaten testifies not to kindness but to knowledge of and dislike for the expected costs of the threatened act. Both threatener and threatenee stand to gain something in common, therefore, if the carrying out of the threatened act can be avoided.

This analysis has two distinct implications which sometimes contradict each other. The first is that even in situations of threat and deterrence the two sides retain some common interest. This interest increases with the cost of carrying out the threat. If the contestants are about evenly matched, and if this common cost is larger than the matter they are quarreling about, then deterrence becomes similar to the game of "chicken"; if it is large, but smaller than the prize for which they are contesting, deterrence becomes similar to the "prisoners' dilemma" game. If the adversaries remain more or less evenly matched, but the threat between them becomes more intense (either through greater ruthlessness or through more destructive weapons) while the rewards of victory do not increase, then the deterrence contest will tend to move away from the "prisoners' dilemma" to the "chicken" pattern. The greater the intensity of mutual threats, the less *rational* motivation remains for the contestants to carry them out.

Deterrence, therefore, makes the most rational sense against the relatively defenseless. A severe threat against an adversary who cannot inflict the same level of damage in retaliation threatens him with great costs at small cost to the threatener. This makes it seem inviting, for example, to threaten naval or aerial bombardment against some recalcitrant smaller or poorer country that has no comparable navy or air force to hit back. The more intense the threat (e.g., by threatening to use more destructive weapons, or to direct attacks against more highly cherished objects or persons, or to direct attacks against more highly cherished objects or persons, such as cities, children, or the rulers of the country), the more successful it is supposed to be, according to the theory, against a weaker but still rational opponent.

Even according to classic deterrence theory, however, more intense threats (that is, with more devastating weapons, or against more precious targets) have precisely the opposite effect when they are made against an adversary who can retaliate on the same level of frightfulness, or who has firm allies who are likely to retaliate. The replacement of atom-bomb warheads in their long-distance missiles by much more powerful hydrogen-bomb warheads in the 1950s, therefore, did not make the Soviet's threats against West Germany or Britain more effective because both countries continued to count on protection by the retaliatory hydrogen-bomb power of the United States; and in addition, Britain manufactured some hydrogen bombs of her own. Similarly, of course, communist countries were not overawed by the growing nuclear arsenal of the United States in the 1950s and 1960s, *if* they had great conventional (and soon were also to have nuclear) strength of their own, as did the Soviet Union, or *if* they received Soviet assurances of nuclear protection, as did Cuba in 1962. Neither did they fear if they had vast land armies and at least some Soviet protection, nor if they had acquired some nuclear weapons capabilities, as did China in 1964. There is little reason to doubt that intensified threats of neutronic or biological warfare among the great powers would be similarly useless in extracting any political concessions. As long as both sides remain rational and able to inflict great damage on each other, any intensification of threats will merely decrease their motivation to carry them into effect. Since each side knows this of the other, more intense mutual threats under these conditions decline in credibility and become less effective.

The second implication of Schelling's model deals with just this point. The effectiveness of a threat, according to Schelling, depends not only on its intensity but also on its *credibility;* and this credibility is a distinct aspect of the threat which can be manipulated separately by an astute threatener. Such a threatener, says Schelling, can make a threat more credible by appearing to be partly irrational, and by acting in a partly irrational manner. The threatener does this by making more reckless gestures and by making a commitment to more reckless acts than strict rationality would permit. In one of Schelling's examples, if two automobiles contest for the right of way at an intersection, success is likely to go to the driver who first speeds up the car so much that it could not stop in time to avoid a collision even if an effort were made. This irrational behavior, says Schelling, should force the other driver to slow down to avoid a collision—unless, of course, the other driver (presumably having read Schelling, or at least following the Schelling rationale) also makes a commitment to speeding up until being unable to stop before hitting the antagonist or someone else. In the game of "chicken," by the same reasoning, victory could be gained by the player who throws away the steering wheel of the car, or who flings a black cloth over the windshield while driving straight ahead—unless again the adversary has resorted to the same tactics.

In essence, the tactics studied by Schelling depend on the deliberate creation of a shared risk between the two adversaries. The greater the shared risk created by reckless tactics or by some device that leaves some of the threat to chance (such as by launching a nuclear-armed satellite into orbit, controlled by a roulette wheel; or by engaging in a limited but escalating war which everybody knows could easily get out of hand), the more credible the threat becomes. (And the greater is the rational interest of both parties to escape from this dangerous situation.) And, since the threatener is committed to an irrational persistence toward a goal, the greater now, in Schelling's view, is the rational interest of the threatened party to give in.

The theory of deterrence contains no specific term for the size of the stakes of the contest, which may be momentous or petty, and the hazard of which may be immediate or remote. To the extent that it is true, the theory applies to deterrence confrontations among powers quarreling about some marginal interests, as well as among powers struggling for the existence of their central regions and institutions. It applies as well to the not infrequent cases where marginal interests are misrepresented as vital ones, for purposes of bargaining or of increasing domestic support. Past deterrence confrontations between the Soviet Union and the United States have involved momentous stakes—for example, the very close possibility of thermonuclear war over Soviet attempts to install missile launch pads in Cuba in 1962;[14] and NATO's strategy of "flexible response" threatens nuclear retaliation to a conventional force attack by the Warsaw Pact, a commitment to a more "reckless act" in defense of a central region (Western Europe) than strict rationality would permit. The theory of deterrence also applies to international conflicts involving merely the goals of particular elites or special-interest groups, as well as to those involving the survival of entire regimes, states, or populations. Indeed, in its stress on the potential usefulness of irrational behavior as an aid to the credibility of threats, the theory puts a premium on the ability of a government or nation in such a contest to overrepresent and overestimate its interests at stake. The more credible its overestimation and self-deception about these interests, the more effective may become its threats. Here the theory of deterrence comes close to becoming a theory of self-deception.

The theory of deterrence is interesting and important, but it has grave and potentially fatal gaps. It seems to be widely believed by influential politicians, military leaders, and segments of public opinion in many countries; and it summarizes and synthesizes elegantly and wittily many of the folk beliefs held by these groups. In any case, it has done much to improve thinking on these matters. It has replaced the spirit of crusading with the spirit of calculation; it has taught people always to look at both sides of the gaming board and to consider the real capabilities and possible strategies of their adversary; it has replaced self-righteous fervor with critical reason; and it has taught adversaries to pay attention to possible shared interests as well as to opposing ones.

At the same time, deterrence theory has created its own dangers, both emotional and cognitive. It has encouraged some people to play in their imagination with the lives and deaths of millions, to "think the unthinkable" (as Hermann Kahn put it), and to contemplate almost as easily the "spending" of a "megadeath" (a million lives) as that of a "megabuck" (a million dollars). Among various people it has encouraged some callousness, some hardening of sensibilities, some belief that the end justifies all means, and

---

[14]From the extensive literature on, and the numerous analyses of the Cuban missile crisis in the light of deterrence theory, see, for example, Albert and Roberta Wohlstetter, "Controlling the Risks in Cuba," *Adelphi Paper* No. 7 (April 1965), pp. 3–24; Alexander George and Richard Smoke, *Deterrence in American Foreign Policy: Theory and Practice* (New York: Columbia Univ. Press, 1974), and Richard Ned Lebow, "The Cuban Missile Crisis: Reading the Lessons Correctly," *Political Science Quarterly* 98, no. 3 (Fall 1983), pp. 431–455. But even this seemingly successful case of deterrence has given rise to serious later doubts even among statesmen who carried out those policies in the first place. See e.g. Dean Rusk *et al.*, "The Lessons of the Cuban Missile Crisis," *Time Magazine* (September 27, 1982), pp. 85–86.

some willingness to lower emotional barriers against considering the admitted equivalents of mass slaughter and torture as potential means of public policy. It tends to make us forget that there are means which dishonor any cause that they pretend to serve. In all these respects, it has posed a serious challenge to our most central religious and ethical traditions.

Its cognitive and practical dangers are greater still, because in its present state it is shot through with intellectual weaknesses. Eight of these weaknesses seem worth listing here. Three of these could be remedied relatively easily by a better use of the intellectual possibilities offered by game theory, even in its present state; the other five defects of current deterrence theories seem likely to require more far-reaching changes in our thinking.

The current deterrence theory has a bias for short-run thinking. First, it tends to treat the capabilities of the contestants as fixed, and to neglect the opportunity costs of conflict to each of them. It spends much more attention on what each can take from the other at the points of contact and conflict, than on what each could obtain for the same resources if the conflict were avoided or else limited rigorously for the time being to a holding operation, and the resources saved there were invested more productively elsewhere. In the second place, it often tends to treat the immediate stakes of most of the major international conflicts as bigger than the costs of nuclear war; it thus tends to treat these conflicts as more similar to the "prisoners' dilemma" (which suggests strong motives for distrust and hostility) than to the "chicken" game, although the latter model in some cases may be more realistic.

Third, much of current deterrence theory stresses single encounters or confrontations more than repeated ones, even though the rational tactics for one-shot or "end-of-the-world" games are different from those for survival games. For instance, negotiating after an adversary has started the bombardment of one's territory might seem rational at the moment, but this might invite the adversary to repeat these tactics at the time of the next dispute and thus open the door to a sequence of successive acts of intimidation and stepwise surrender. So, the most rational tactic for any yet undefeated nation might be a flat refusal to negotiate under duress. And, as a matter of fact, for more than a century this has indeed been the customary tactic of most nations not already defeated or hopelessly isolated and overawed into submission.

The five remaining shortcomings of the deterrence theory are more serious. First, current theory assumes that both threatener and threatenee have complete control of their behavior. But this assumption is quite often false. To the extent that the threatener acts irrationally in order to increase the credibility of threats, that actor will thereby almost inevitably *decrease* the credibility of *reassurance* that the threat will certainly not be carried out if the threatenee complies with demands. If the threatener uses reckless tactics, then threats and reassurances cannot be controlled at the same time. But if the threatenee concludes that the terrifying reckless and irrational threatener will do the worst in *any* case, then the threatenee loses any motive to comply. Having nothing to lose, the threatenee may now defy the threatener. By 1939, Hitler had become more credible than he had been in 1936, but now his threats failed to stop France and Britain from going to war against him—not because their governments did not take them seriously (they did), but because they had lost faith in his reassurances.

The threatenee, however, may have even less self-control. Classic deterrence theory neglects to take into account the *autonomous probability* of the behavior that is to be deterred—that is, which the threatener wishes to prohibit. If this prohibited behavior of the threatenee is quite unlikely to occur in any case, then deterrence may work easily, or at least it may seem to do so. But if the behavior to be deterred is ordinarily very probable and frequent, or otherwise backed by strong motives, as in a religious movement, a social revolution, or a struggle for national independence, or against the complete surrender of that independence, then deterrence would have to be extremely powerful to bar it completely; and such attempts at deterrence are most likely to fail. Thus, in the history of military attempts to bomb an adversary into submission or at least a more conciliatory attitude, very few have been successful or able to deter the threatenees from their course of resistance. This was the case with American attempts to "bomb" Hanoi into peace—or at least into negotiations—in the Vietnam war in 1967, and with Mussolini's bombing of Ethiopia, Franco's Nationalists' bombing of Madrid during the Spanish civil war, and allied bombings in Italy and Japan at the end of World War II.[15]

Second, deterrence theory often neglects to calculate *cumulative risk*. Schelling's reckless driver is likely to get the right of way at the first intersection, and thus to pass it quickly alive. Let us suppose that chances of survival are 0.9, or 90 percent. Let us then suppose that the driver continues reckless tactics and that chances of survival and success at every following encounter at intersections are likewise 90 percent. In that case, chances of being alive after two encounters are 90 percent of 90 percent, or 0.9^2, which is 81 percent. Chances of surviving three such encounters are 0.9^3 or 72.9 percent; for four encounters they are about 59 percent, for five encounters they are less than 54 percent, for seven encounters they are less than 50 percent, and they will be halved again for every additional seven encounters. Hence 21 successive encounters would offer our high-risk player only one chance out of eight to stay alive, 49 would provide less than one chance in 100; and 70 would leave less than one chance in 1,000. The fact that each single encounter offered nine chances out of 10 to live is almost irrelevant compared to the deadly effect of cumulative risks. The foreign affairs of nations and states which intend to continue for long periods of time must be governed by methods that more likely than not will let them survive for generations and centuries, and hence through scores of foreign-policy encounters, fraught with some risk of war.

Classic deterrence theory is still more dangerous in its third basic assumption: that both threatener and threatenee—that is, the governments and elites of both countries in a deterrence confrontation—will remain com-

---

[15]See Ernest R. May, *"Lessons" of the Past. The Use and Misuse of History in American Foreign Policy* (New York: Oxford Univ. Press, 1973), chapter 5.

pletely *rational under stress* (such as in a crisis involving threats, fear, uncertainty, fatigue, and communication overload). Experience, as well as a good deal of research in psychology, suggest the contrary; tense, frightened, and exhausted people—including politicians and military personnel—tend to become irritable and aggressive, while their perceptions become less accurate and their judgment becomes poorer. In short, they become *less* rational—even though deterrence theory may advise threateners to stake their own survival on the threatenees' rational responses to their threats.

The fourth of the basic but dubious assumptions of deterrence theory is a hidden one. It is the implicit assumption of some significant *asymmetry* between the threatener and threatenee, particularly when the writer's own country is involved in the contest. American writers on deterrence, as well as some American political and military leaders, assume that foreigners can be intimidated by threats or by demonstrations of ruthlessness which could only infuriate Americans: the foreigner often is assumed almost automatically to be weaker in capabilities, or in motivation to see the conflict through, or in nerve and tolerance of risk. In our age of nationalism, this is a well-known and more-or-less international illusion, much encouraged by almost every government among its citizens. But it can be deadly in a policy of nuclear deterrence.

The fifth basic assumption of deterrence theory is perhaps the most fundamental of all; and it is one which extends to the entire larger class of game models. It is the familiar assumption of *unchanging motives* of the players throughout the game. Rational players, by assumption, must want to win, and they must want nothing else, from start to finish of the game. But this assumption is inappropriate for human affairs, and particularly for politics. We know that individuals, groups, parties, governments, and nations all change their minds; they often do so during some conflict in which they are involved; and some of these changes may be induced by the course of the conflict itself.

This assumption of unchanging motives is particularly important for calculating the probable success of deterrence through calculated recklessness and partial irrationality—the threats that deliberately "leave something to chance"—that have been studied by Schelling. If both the cognitive perceptions and the values of threatenees remain unchanged while they are being subjected to such tactics, then indeed it would be rational for them to give in to them. But this assumption is not plausible. The threatenees' perception of the threateners may change. If threateners try to present themselves as partially irrational—by speeding up an automobile at intersections, by turning off a hearing-aid during negotiations, by pretending to be staggering or drunk while carrying high explosives past an adversary, or perhaps, in the case of the leader of a nation, by deliberately inflaming domestic mass opinion—then it is rather likely that the adversary will *perceive* the threateners as being largely or entirely irrational and thus a blind menace which must be destroyed as soon as possible, at almost any risk. Seemingly irrational or imperfectly controlled threats with nuclear weapons, for instance, might most likely invite a "preemptive" nuclear attack from any threatened party that had the capability for one.

A shift in the *values* of the party who received the reckless threat might work in the same direction. The "Schelling-type" threats work best in situations resembling "chicken" games; that is, situations in which the penalties for mutual noncooperation are clearly much higher than the penalties to either side for giving in; and this is precisely why the more reckless threatener who speeded up the car, or who otherwise was committed early in some irrevocable manner, may expect that the opponent, for reasons of self-interest, will give in about the less valuable point which is at issue in this encounter. In fact, however, the threatenee's values may now drastically change. What matters now is no longer the relatively trivial subject of the original dispute—such as the right of way at the original intersection, or, among governments, some barren and relatively worthless strip of disputed territory in a border conflict—but the threatenee may now assign an extremely high value to *not being subjected to such high-pressure tactics.* "I'll get that road hog if it's the last thing I do," an incensed motorist may mutter; and the government and mass opinion of a threatened country may now prefer to run the highest risks rather than to submit to threats even in an originally trivial dispute. In mathematical terms, the change in the scale of the threatenee's utilities has transformed the original "chicken" type conflict into a genuine prisoners' dilemma, at least for one player, in which the penalty for unilateral giving in (*CD*) has become decisively larger than the share of the joint penalty for mutual conflict (*DD*). If and when this happens, "Schelling-type" threats through irrevocable commitments or deliberate partial loss of control are likely to become self-defeating and potentially self-destructive, and the erstwhile reckless threatener now may be able to survive only by a quick return to tactics of moderation and mutual cooperation.[16]

In the early stages of a deterrence conflict, therefore, both threatener and threatenee can, by their behavior, change to some extent each other's values and perceptions, as well as their own; and they can enlarge or diminish the proportion of interests which they have in common. To the extent that they are thus changing one another's motivations, their contest becomes less of a game and more of a genuine debate.

---

[16]Deterrence theory still forms the central tenet in the strategy for the use of nuclear weapons. Its potentially self-destructive tendencies have in recent years, however, met with increasing criticism. The possibility of uncontrollable escalation of a conflict among powers threatening each other with multiple or only partial mutual annihilation is seen as the more likely outcome of a nuclear deterrence scenario, and the credibility of deterrence in conflict situations that are likely to lead to unacceptable damage in case of an actual nuclear confrontation has been seriously questioned. See, for example, David C. Gompert *et al., Nuclear Weapons and World Politics. 1980s Project, Council on Foreign Relations* (New York: McGraw-Hill, 1977); Hedley Bull, "Future Conditions of Strategic Deterrence," Part I, *Adelphi Paper 160* (London: International Institute for Strategic Studies, Autumn 1980), pp. 13–23; Robert Jervis, "Deterrence Theory Revisited," *World Politics* 31 (January 1979), pp. 314–322, and *The Illogic of American Nuclear Strategy* (Ithaca, NY: Cornell Univ. Press, 1985); and Robert W. Tucker, *The Nuclear Debate: Deterrence and the Lapse of Faith* (New York: Holmes and Meier, 1985).

DEBATES: CONTESTS THAT PERMIT CHANGES OF IMAGES AND MOTIVATIONS

Conflicts in which the adversaries are changing each other's motives, values, or cognitive images of reality, may be called "debates" in the strict sense of the term. Not all exchanges of words or messages, nor all events labeled as "debates," are genuine debates in this sense. Commonly, two high-school debating teams are not trying to change each other's minds on the debating topic which happens to be allotted to them; rather, they are engaged in a game in which they compete in impressing the judges of the debate, and perhaps the audience. In this game they play to win; if a team announced in mid-"debate" that its adversaries had won it over by their arguments, its members might have learned about the topic under discussion, but they would have lost the game. Adversary proceedings in law courts usually have a similar gamelike character. Prosecutor and defense counsel are not trying to convince each other, nor are the lawyers for opposite parties in civil law suits trying to do so. In each case, they are trying to win their case, usually by impressing a judge or a jury; and to the extent that one side wins a verdict, the other side loses. Only the judge or the jury are expected to change their minds as a result of such adversary pleadings; between them, it is assumed (generally with good reason) that the contending parties will do a better job in bringing out all the relevant facts than any single and supposedly impartial investigating officer would be apt to do.

Debates in legislatures have a better chance of becoming genuine debates, and so have negotiations among diplomats representing governments, and the debates of government representatives in international organizations. In each of these cases, of course, the legislators, diplomats, or government delegates are trying to win something for the interests, parties, groups, or governments and nations which they represent. Often they must win something for the interests they represent at the expense of any interests opposed to them, and hence at the expense of other groups or governments. But often it is not entirely known which outcomes or solutions would in fact be most beneficial to the respective interests which each negotiator represents; and the outcomes most favorable to each, and perhaps jointly favorable to several or all of the parties concerned, may yet have to be discovered, and if discovered, then presented for acceptance and agreement.

Genuine negotiations, therefore, are a mixture of a competitive game with a joint voyage of discovery and with a mutual campaign of education toward a mutual appreciation and adjustment of the perceptions and preferences of several or all parties concerned. The long negotiations that led to the partial nuclear test-ban treaty of 1963 between the United States and the Soviet Union—which then was subscribed to by most of the nations of the world with the exception of France and communist China—are an example of such a genuine debate. So are, too, the talks and negotiations that led to the SALT I treaty of 1972 and, after another seven years, the

SALT II treaty draft of 1979.[17] Soberly, in the course of these debates, in addition to the several persistent competitive interests of the various powers, a set of common perceptions and interests also developed, strong enough to lead to decisions which were accepted by almost all countries or the contending parties, respectively, as being in their interests. On the other hand, prolonged debates and negotiations produced little or no changes in attitudes to economic affairs between the rich and poor countries of the world. In the early 1970s, many of the developing countries were trying to promote a debate about a "new economic order" that ought to be established, so as to improve their position in regard to the highly developed ones. And for a time, the attitudes of the Nixon and Carter administrations in the 1970s seemed to suggest that some progress toward a genuine debate—producing genuine changes of attitudes, if not yet concrete results—might be possible even among such unequal partners. The effects of a prolonged worldwide economic recession, however, and a generally less internationalist policy approach in the 1980s seem to have dampened hopes for any early success of this North-South debate.

Though it seems that genuine debates, national or international, cannot be well represented by game models, nor indeed by any of the dumb, quasi-automatic "fight" processes discussed earlier, the precise nature of such debates is not well understood. However, there is a good deal of empirical experience about debates; and elements of insight and practical wisdom have been derived from it. One of these could be called the principle of *mutually acceptable restatement.* According to this principle, a debate is more likely to lead to the discovery of a mutually acceptable and beneficial solution if each side finds out what the other side is actually saying—that is, if it learns to state for itself the case of its adversaries in a form so clear and appealing as to be acceptable to these adversaries themselves.

Another essential step is for each side to find out on which grounds the other side could possibly be convinced of the truth of its own views. After one side has found out what views or pictures of reality its adversaries hold in their minds, they must try to discover the *domain of validity* of each such view. In a dispute between a newly emerged ex-colonial country and its former "mother country," leaders of the new nation are likely to complain about their earlier oppression or exploitation by their colonial masters, while leaders of the former imperial country will tend to stress the former colony's original poverty and the improvements and benefits which their colonial rule brought to the colony's people. Each of these views is likely to be valid for some limited range of facts, but invalid for others. If each side learns to discover the domain of validity, however small, of the seemingly preposterous views of its adversaries, and if they also discover

[17] See John Newhouse, *Cold Dawn: The Story of SALT* (New York: Holt, Rinehart, and Winston, 1973); Strobe Talbott, *Endgame: The Inside Story of SALT II* (New York: Knopf, 1979); and Thomas W. Wolfe, *The SALT Experience* (Cambridge, MA: Ballinger, 1979). The current nuclear arms control dialogue between the Reagan administration and the Kremlin, the Strategic Arms Reduction Talks (START), seemed an exemplary case of nonproductive negotiations until it lead to a treaty to abolish intermediate nuclear forces (INF), signed on December 8, 1987 in Washington, D.C. See also Strobe Talbott, *Deadly Gambits: The Reagan Administration and the Stalemate in Nuclear Arms Control* (New York: Knopf, 1984).

the limits of the validity of their own (seemingly so reasonable) notions, then the likelihood—though not the certainty—of a genuine debate with an eventual fruitful and mutually rewarding outcome is increased.

As these examples suggest, many actual encounters among contending interest groups, parties, nations, or ideologies may have many of the characteristics of debates. If so, then we may expect that time, events, and the results of their own behavior eventually will change not only the fortunes but also the outlook, goals, and values of the contestants. Somewhat in this vein, John Dewey once observed that people do not decide many of their controversies, but get over them. Apart from such small bits of wisdom, however, adequate formal models for genuine debates have yet to be developed.

Actual conflicts among states often resemble mixtures of fights, games, and debates, with this or that element predominating in the combination at different times and places. The art of diplomats, governments, and responsible citizens then consists in managing these international conflicts so as to keep them within tolerable bounds; to safeguard as far as practicable the current national interests while these interests themselves continue to evolve and change; to gain time and strength; and to ensure the national survival.

12

Diplomacy and Coalitions

Any two states in conflict with each other invariably find themselves peculiarly dependent on each other, even though their interests are at odds. This comes about because the government of neither state can get everything it wants without some cooperation (whether voluntary or involuntary) on the part of the other. That is, the one state cannot make (and legitimately claim) a gain against the other, or against a third party, unless the other allows (and tacitly admits to) a corresponding change in its own behavior. Under such conflict conditions, the rulers of each state will, of course, try to make the other state do (and concede the doing of) what they want, by whatever means that seem to suit the situation at the time—and the less embarrassing and costly the means, the better.

DIPLOMACY

First of all, of course, states can negotiate and bargain through the normal channels of diplomacy. Their ambassadors, foreign ministers, and other high-level diplomatic personnel usually are experienced negotiators. They know that to get a favor one may have to give or promise a favor in return; and they know that sometimes they also can put into the scales of bargaining polite suggestions that favors granted earlier to the other country are more likely to be continued if their own government's present wishes are accommodated.

Bargaining of this kind often resembles a game of diplomacy according to the rules of which the perceptions and interests of both parties are treated as given. The diplomats on both sides first have to figure out the most promising strategy for their *own* side, in the light of their estimate of the probable strategy of the *other* side. They then play the negotiating game from move to move, from proposal to counterproposal, as best they can, until either an outcome acceptable to both sides is achieved, or the negotiations fail and are adjourned or terminated.

Sometimes, as we have seen in the preceding chapter, such negotiations even may take on some of the character of a genuine debate or dialogue between the two governments and nations. Each country and government then stands to learn something in the course of the negotiating process. And each party's images of the other, and of external reality, may therefore change somewhat, and so may even some of their initial preferences and values. If these changes tend to make the current interests of each country more compatible with those of the other, then their negotiating positions may converge, and a mutually satisfactory agreement between them becomes more likely. In international politics, however, each nation usually acts as if it had an interest in influencing this process in such a way as to induce as much change as possible in the other nation's views, while accepting as little change as possible in its own. As a rule, each nation prefers to talk rather than to listen; to teach rather than to learn. Each nation thus tries to induce much change in its adversaries or partners, while accepting as little change as possible for itself. (This sort of behavior was defined as the exercise of power—specifically, of net power—in an earlier section of this book.)

The relatively gentlest instruments of this pursuit of power over one or several other countries are influence and propaganda. *Influence* consists of using some of the values and interests of persons and groups within the target country so as to support policies that one's own country is promoting there. *Propaganda* consists mainly of efforts to change the cognitive and emotional image of reality held by some or all of the members of the target country so as to make them more likely to act as the leaders of the propagandizing country desire.

Members of foreign elites can be made somewhat more receptive to the wishes of one's own country if they are educated there, especially in its prestige schools and universities. The influencing country may offer such bait as various honors and prizes to members of the elite of the target country, scholarships to their gifted students, and subsidies to some of their cherished but impecunious cultural institutions. Cultural-exchange programs, libraries, hospitals, visits by eminent poets or scientists may be provided for the same implicit purpose.

Beyond this, more massive efforts at influence may be directed at the mass media of the target country. They may be provided with a flow of suitable news, features, or pictures, free or at low prices; or they may be induced to commit themselves to take most of their international news from one of the more-or-less monopolistic news agencies of one of the great powers, such as Reuter's of Britain, Agence France-Presse of France, Japan's Kyodo News Service, Germany's DNB, the Soviet Union's TASS, and Associated Press (AP) and United Press International (UPI) for the United States. A glance at the initials of the worldwide news agency supplying most of its international news items to the major newspapers of a developing country often is enough to suggest which of the major powers probably exercises most influence in the country. This form of influence by unilateral information flows—and the almost monopolistic position of Western mass media in providing international news to the less developed countries—have caused many Third World countries to demand the creation of a "New World Information and Communication Order" to give their governments more room to influence the inflow of news *to* and the reporting of news *from* their countries, a demand which is seen by the West as incompatible with its concept of freedom of the press and other media.

Other mass media can be used in the same way. For instance, by supplying a large share of the motion pictures shown in a country (usually on the basis of some specific trade or cultural agreement), or a substantial share of its television or radio programs, a large country can greatly increase its indirect influence over a smaller one.

Some methods of influence are more direct. For example, partial control of some foreign mass media can be acquired through manipulation of advertising, or through purchase of ownership or stock. Editors of newspapers can be invited to extended and well-publicized official visits; or editors, like newspapers, can be subsidized discreetly in a variety of ways. Something similar can be done in some countries about some politicians, interest groups, or political factions or parties, and even about some members of the civil service, the military, the police, or the government itself. If any of these are for sale, often there are many ways of buying them quietly, or at least supporting their ambitions; or if their favors are offered freely, they still can be subsidized so as to make them more effective. At these points, of course, influence and propaganda are shading over into corruption, infiltration, subversion, and other disreputable forms of economic penetration or political warfare—but this has rarely stopped governments from resorting to such methods against countries which seemed vulnerable to them, and where major interests seemed to be at stake. In the 1970s, several scandals of this kind received publicity around the world. Several multinational corporations, large and well-known in the United States, had paid very substantial bribes to politicians, officials, and other public figures in foreign countries, as was reported of the Lockheed aircraft corporation in the case of Japan. During the same period, the government of South Korea had paid substantial sums to various members of the United States Congress. The covert political warfare activities of the CIA in many Latin American countries which became publicized in that same period, including attempts to assassinate Cuba's head of government, Fidel Castro, the support of General Pinochet's coup versus President Allende in Chile in 1973, and clandestine activities in Guatemala and Honduras in 1954, caused also considerable public debate on the legitimacy of such intelligence operations. All such attempts may backfire badly, however, if the target government discovers them in time, and if its nation, once aroused, is capable of strong resistance.

Supplementing such efforts at influencing a country from within are ways of subjecting it to propaganda and various forms of pressure from without. The mass media in the influencer country may launch a barrage or a sustained campaign of propaganda against the target government so as to try to make it yield on some matter in dispute. Broadcasts may be beamed from abroad at its population; and even the booming of loudspeakers may be added at some border points. Pamphlets and leaflets may be mailed in, or smuggled in, or dropped from airplanes or balloons; or personal letter-writing campaigns may be organized in the influencer country, directed at presumably susceptible groups among the target population.

Rarely do such propaganda methods accomplish very much unless the target country's policy or government is already on the verge of changing. As a rule, it is far more effective to gain major positions of control or influence within the target country, or to acquire some really major levers for pressure on it from without. For this purpose, it may sometimes help a great deal to have control of major industries or business enterprises in the target country, with all the contacts and channels of economic, political, and social influence that go with them. The British, thus, still have such a widespread unofficial, yet effective, network of economic, political, social, and cultural influence in the Commonwealth countries stemming from their former colonial stronghold in these countries; the United States has a similar network with their multinational business enterprises in the Latin Americas, even if these forms of influence and possible levers for pressure do not primarily serve the aim of controlling the political actions of the target country or subjecting its population to the influence of propaganda. The influencer country may also gain a power position within the target country by supplying essential weapons or communications equipment to the local military or police—who then must send some of their future key officers to the influencer country for training in their use, and who thereafter remain dependent on it for spare parts and for help in the more complex problems of both regular maintenance and periodic updating against obsolescence. Both the Soviet Union and the United States, but also other powers such as France, have made this form of influence by military assistance—or the withholding of it—major strategies of their foreign policies towards their allies as well as adversaries.

Promising but delaying or denying such supplies and help can be a powerful instrument of pressure, particularly in a crisis. So also can be the offer or the refusal (depending on the circumstances) to buy some exports of the target country, which are otherwise hard to sell; or the granting or withholding of a much-needed loan in a time of financial stringency; or the speeding up or slowing down of grain deliveries, after a crop failure in the target country has put a part of its population on the verge of famine. Such tactics of economic pressure have been part of the "cold warfare" between the Soviet Union and the United States since the beginning of the conflict. In 1945, Stalin was refused a $6 billion reconstruction loan by the Truman administration, and NATO has maintained a strategic goods embargo against the USSR since 1948.

But while such economic pressure has proven relatively inefficient between these two large, resourceful, and largely independent countries, the control of supplies to smaller and more dependent countries has been a much more powerful, though not necessarily more successful, instrument of pressure. It was used by the United States, for example, in the sugar embargo against Cuba from 1959 to 1961, the deliberate delay of grain shipments to India under Public Law 480 in 1967, the freezing of Iranian investments and assets in the United States in 1979 in response to the revolutionary government's taking of American hostages, and the food embargo imposed on Poland in response to the declaration of martial law in that country in 1981.

But there are even more drastic means of pressure. Military aircraft of the influencer country may begin to stray more often across the boundaries of the target country, or engage in more extended overflights. In so doing, the influencer's aircraft not only can gather useful intelligence by photographing military objectives, but can show their presence, demonstrate their (and thus their country's) prowess and the target country's timidity or inability to stop them, and encourage the local adherents of the influencer country while demoralizing their opponents. Similar effects can be obtained by warships and aircraft carriers; they have often been used to "show the flag" and to engage in various naval demonstrations off the coast of some recalcitrant country to be overawed, or of some precarious ally to be strengthened. Such was the case in 1984 and 1985, when American warships and aircraft carriers were sent to the Gulf of Mexico and the Pacific Ocean off the coast of Nicaragua; the American military also "showed the flag" in the Mediterranean off the coast of Libya before the bombardment of Tripoli in 1986. Such demonstrations or actions of the government of a greater power against a small country are furthermore likely to give people at home a greater feeling of national pride as well as provide greater popularity to the government issuing such militant threats.

Unfortunately, perhaps, influence over a foreign country can be achieved only to a certain point by mere promises and threats. Beyond that point it is practically impossible to achieve without resorting to some form and degree of war. Before we survey these forms and degrees, however, it may be worthwhile to summarize in Table 18 the various situations that can create within the government of a potential influencer nation a demand for influence over the actions of the government of a potential target country.

In all these situations shown in Table 18 promises can be used to good advantage if they can be made relevant and credible for *B*, the country whose actions are to be influenced. Threats may help in six of the eight cases, and "perhaps" also in the other two, if *B*'s future compliance seems dubious or tardy. Whether threats will succeed or backfire, however, depends not only on *A*'s strength but also on all the conditions and limitations

TABLE 18   Occasions for Country "A" to Exercise Influence Over Country "B"

A PREFERS B TO	PERFORM X PERSUASION SITUATIONS				AVOID X ("PERFORM" O) DISSUASION SITUATIONS			
	1	2	3	4	5	6	7	8
A prefers	X	X	X	X	O	O	O	O
A perceives B as now doing	O	O	X	X	X	X	O	O
A expects B to do later	O	X	O	X	X	O	X	O
A wants to *reinforce* or *modify* B's present behavior	M	M	R	R	M	M	R	R
A should:								
Punish	Yes	Per-haps*	No	No	Yes	Per-haps*	No	No
Reward	No	No	Yes	Yes	No	No	Yes	Yes
Threaten	Yes	Yes	Yes	Per-haps*	Yes	Yes	Yes	Per-haps*
Promise	Yes	Yes	Yes	Yes	Yes	Yes	Yes	Yes

*A should punish or threaten only if in doubt about the predictions about B's future action, or if in doubt about whether B's autonomous change will come soon enough. *Source:* Adapted from J. David Singer, "Inter-Nation Influences: A Formal Model," *The American Political Science Review,* 57, no. 2 (June, 1963), p. 427.

of deterrence theory discussed in the previous chapter, including the credibility of A's reassurances or promises. Similar limitations hold for actual rewards or penalties, for these, too, function among nations as implicit messages, and hence as promises or threats of future actions.

COALITIONS

Often a state can make its promises and threats more credible, and its arsenal of possible actual rewards and penalties larger, by joining a coalition or by organizing one. More generally speaking, coalitions are an essential instrument for exercising influence and power, in international no less than in domestic politics. Most often no single person, group, or nation is strong enough to prevail alone in a major decision; most often each can prevail only with the help of a coalition, or not prevail at all.

Political scientist William H. Riker has developed important theories about such coalitions. He sees politics, elections, legislative voting, and warfare all as decision situations which produce at least two alternative outcomes that are of different value to each participant. All *politically rational* participants, says Riker, prefer the outcome that is most valuable to themselves—

that is, they want to win. Where there are winners, he adds, there must be losers; and therefore, the best model for politics and war is a zero-sum game (which was discussed in the preceding chapter). But whereas money or utilities can be divided in a zero-sum game of economics, this cannot be done in the decisive contests of politics and war; "victory," as Riker sees it, "is an indivisible unit."[1] Rational people, then, are ones who always choose the outcome with the biggest payoff for themselves and who greatly want to win.

How can such dedicated egotists form coalitions? They will do so whenever this pays them more than staying in isolation does. For though victory, according to Riker, cannot be divided, often its spoils can be. In that case, the *rationality principle* predicts that all political actors will join—or try to organize—that coalition that promises them the biggest payoff. Clearly, this must be first of all a winning coalition, because without victory there are no spoils. Among several potential winning coalitions, however, that coalition will be preferable which can distribute the largest amount of spoils, and which can do so among the smallest number of partners.

Political rationality, therefore, as Riker understands it, will lead the political actors to the *size principle:* they will form and re-form tentative "proto-coalitions" in the process of bargaining, and search until some of them finally succeed in forming a *smallest winning coalition,* just big enough to win but small enough to allow no unnecessary allies to claim any part of the spoils.

Since there may be more than one such possible smallest winning coalition, the process of bargaining and search is likely to be long and complex. Rational political actors, such as professional politicians or diplomats, will often spend extra time on negotiations and maneuvering if they have reason to expect that this will give them a better chance of ending up in a more favorable coalition. The direction of their maneuvers is predicted by Riker's *strategic principle: in the final stages of the coalition-forming process, the participants will move toward a minimal winning coalition.* When there are two large proto-coalitions of almost winning size in the "last-but-one" stage of the bargaining, therefore, they probably will not join forces, because the resulting coalition would be too big to offer sufficiently attractive payoffs to its members. Rather, according to Riker, one of the smaller proto-coalitions, or even a single participant, may suffice to turn one of the two large proto-coalitions into a minimal winning coalition. And this small but *pivotal* ally may be paid a share of the coalition's winnings quite out of proportion to the ally's size or weight, but corresponding to the value of that nation's strategic position in this particular sequence of the coalition-forming process.

Often, when the fruits of a victory cannot be readily divided, one of the participants to whom they are particularly valuable may offer various *side payments* to prospective coalition partners, so as to purchase their support. Some of these side payments may come out of the profits of the expected victory: they may consist of changes in a bill or treaty to be enacted, or in commitments to future policies, appointments, contracts, or concessions in the particular territories soon to be acquired by the coalition.

[1]W. H. Riker, *The Theory of Political Coalitions* (New Haven: Yale University Press, 1967), pp. 29–31, 174.

Other payments may come out of what Riker calls the leader's "working capital," such as the present time, effort, and resources or commitments involved in other decisions, beyond the immediate victory now aimed at; and still other payments may come out of what Riker likens to "fixed assets," such as the credibility of the leader's threats, or positive prestige, or *charisma*.[2]

All such side payments have in some sense their costs to the leader who has to give up some things or efforts which have some value for him or her. As side payments to prospective allies go up, therefore, the cumulative value of these payments may become higher than the content of the victory is worth. In that case, a rational leader ought to stop—if it were not for the probability, according to Riker, that winning in itself has acquired a value for the leader, almost regardless of the content or object of the victory. Indeed, says Riker, competitive politics selects the kind of opportunistic leader or politician who has this compulsive habit and desire to win, not for a principle of ideology, but for the sake of winning.

The result is that coalition leaders almost inevitably tend to overspend. They will pay out in side payments more than the spoils of victory are worth to them. Thus they will eventually weaken themselves and build up their overpaid allies. In the end, as Riker sees it, coalition leaders ruin themselves, because the intangible value of winning cannot replace the gradual depletion of the tangible assets they waste on building or maintaining a materially unprofitable empire or coalition. This is one reason, in Riker's view, why empires decline, and why the United States and the Soviet Union will lose in the future a large part of the power they now hold in world politics: sooner or later they will be weakened by this fatal tendency of coalition leaders to overspend on allies. Riker made this prediction in 1967; but by the mid-1980s the collapse of both empires was not yet apparent. Riker was right in that the United States would spend more on its poor and marginal allies than it would get from them. The extent of American military assistance to foreign governments alone indicates that the United States in past decades was very much in the process of coalition-building, giving inordinately high side payments to such committed or prospective allies and anticommunist coalition partners as Western Europe, South Vietnam, Taiwan, and South Korea and, for other reasons, Israel and Egypt. What Riker had not foreseen, however, was that many of these allies—such as South Korea and Taiwan—developed well economically, and Western Europe, subsidized heavily by the Marshall Plan in the late 1940s and early 1950s, became prosperous relative to the United States and now needs no further subsidies from across the Atlantic. On the contrary, private investments from Western Europe and Japan in the United States helped considerably to offset the deficit spending of the Reagan administration on its own arms programs in the 1980s; and in terms of military assistance and commitments, NATO's defense expenditures are shared relatively equally

---

[2]A leader's charisma is the power to elicit spontaneous admiration and compliance from some significance audience or constituency whose members are habituated or predisposed to respond in this manner to the leader's presence, example, and messages.

according to the size and capabilities of its members, with the Western European countries being, for example, responsible for the larger part of the manpower resources of NATO. For the Soviet Union, it is more difficult to assess how much this superpower is depleted by higher side payments to its allies, mainly the Warsaw Pact countries, but increasingly also such countries as Cuba, Vietnam, and Afghanistan, and how much it is profiting from them by taking the spoils of victory. However, such poorer allies as Poland, Vietnam, Mongolia, or Afghanistan clearly need large amounts of economic and military assistance, and in so depleting Soviet assets and resources may seriously weaken the Soviet Union's position as a coalition leader in the long run. For both superpowers, however, there are as yet no perceptible signs of imminent collapse, and Riker's prediction awaits further evidence from future developments.

It might be noted that the tendency to overspend, according to Riker, is also one of the reasons for the basic instability of the international system of sovereign states. A second reason for this instability is the tendency of such an insatiably competitive system to eliminate some of its essential actors.

COALITION THEORY AND THE INSTABILITY OF BALANCE OF POWER

According to the classic *balance-of-power theory* (as reformulated in modern terms by political scientist Morton A. Kaplan), there ought to be at least five great powers, or "essential actors," in the world (since with fewer powers there would not be enough different coalitions to keep the system flexible); and each of these powers would have to obey certain essential rules.[3] A somewhat modified and simplified version of these rules might read:

A. *Rationality:*
   1. Always act to increase capabilities.
   2. Negotiate rather than fight; but fight rather than pass up an increase in capabilities.
B. *Preservation of actors:*
   3. Stop fighting rather than eliminate an essential actor.
   4. Permit any defeated essential actor to reenter as a possible partner; or replace that actor by elevating a previously nonessential actor (*i.e.*, a smaller power); and treat all essential actors as acceptable potential allies.
C. *Preservation of the system:*
   5. Act to oppose any actor or coalition who tends to become predominant within the system. (Hence, if one proto-coalition is close to victory, neutral actors ought to join the strongest of its weaker opponents.)
   6. Act to constrain actors who subscribe to supranational organizing principles.

[3]Morton Kaplan, *System and Process in International Politics* (New York: Wiley, 1957).

Working by these rules, says Kaplan, such a system can preserve itself for a long time; but such a system, says Riker, *cannot* work. Rational actors want to win; they will not support a balance-of-power system when they have an opportunity instead to join a winning coalition; and among five powers, sooner or later there will be such opportunities. Moreover, rational actors certainly will act to increase their capabilities. They will not stop to spare a defeated essential actor, if there is no other way to get a payoff for themselves. Hence, as payoffs in the contest become scarcer, restraints will become ineffective. The same holds for all restraints in rules 3–6: they are based on international morality or long-run self-interest, but both of these are likely to weaken or fade away when immediate decision pressures mount. The competitive system of politics, says Riker, rewards and selects leaders who overreach and overspend and who care more for winning than for principles. Such leaders cannot be expected to care much for any principles by which a balance-of-power system would have to be preserved.

Riker concludes that all such politics are characterized by a *disequilibrium principle*. Political systems whose members act in accordance with the principles of size and strategy must be unstable. They contain forces pressing toward decision regardless of the stakes or content of the decision, and hence toward the elimination of participants, and potentially of the whole system.

Riker's analysis is penetrating but one-sided. In order to highlight some aspects of politics, he has chosen to represent all coalition politics by the zero-sum game rather than by the more realistic variable-sum model. He has emphasized short-run victory and "winning" as single values in themselves, far beyond their substantive content, and remote from the actual context of all other basic values—which are no less important in man's social and political behavior. He has paid a heavy price for this extreme degree of abstraction. In his theory, every victory is final in regard to its spoils. These spoils are grasped by the victors, but no attention is paid to the question of how these spoils were produced in the first place or how they are to be reproduced in the future, for the next round of the process. Where modern economics and sociology, and much of political science, deal with circular flows or feedback processes of messages, services, or values, in Riker's world, transfers of spoils are terminal and one-way only: to the victors. Thus he has written a theory of the politics of appropriation, but not of the politics of production, of cooperation, and of growth—all of which are no less vital.

Regardless of its limits, however, Riker's theory of coalitions represents a considerable intellectual achievement. It offers a model of the process by which coalitions may be formed; it permits the identification of strategic possibilities in this process; it contributes an important criticism of the balance-of-power theory; and it reveals deep-seated sources of instability in the behavior of politicians, national coalition leaders, and leading governments and nations in the international arena.

13

Failures of Controls and Forms of War

If neither national means of influence nor the added influence of an international coalition suffices to change the behavior of a target country, then the power trying to influence it may have to resort to force. The least violent use of force is the blockade—either by land, as imposed by the Soviet Union on West Berlin in 1948, or by sea, as used briefly by the United States against Cuba in 1962.

LIMITED VIOLENCE AS A MEANS OF PRESSURE

If a blockade is not challenged by another power, its enforcement may succeed without bloodshed. But if it is challenged, or if its enforcement fails, or if, though enforced, it fails to change the behavior of the target country, then the would-be influencer nation may either have to abandon its attempt at putting pressure on the target country, or move up higher on the ladder of escalating conflict. And from this level of conflict on upward, some people are likely to be killed.

An obvious way of stepping up the pressure on the target country is the infiltration of saboteurs and guerrillas, who mine roads, blow up weakly guarded installations, and attack isolated officials or local agencies or minor centers of the government. Even if such infiltrators find no significant support among the population, as was the case of Arabs infiltrating into Israel before 1967 from Syria and the United Arab Republic, or of the *Contras* infiltrating into Nicaragua since 1984 to overthrow the Marxist-oriented government, they can maintain an atmosphere of insecurity and harassment, at least in areas close to the border. And if the infiltrators carry more powerful equipment and get some support from among the local population, they can strike more deeply, as did some of the British commando raiders against Nazi-occupied France in World War II and as Arab raiders could do in the Israeli-occupied part of Jordan after the 1967 war.

The greatest effects of infiltration are obtained, however, in situations where the infiltrators serve merely as supplements to or catalysts for local guerrilla forces recruited—and, if possible, led wholly or in part—from within the target country and its population. Here the foreign input of radio, propaganda, armed agents, special equipment, technical expertise, and (perhaps) troops can augment or sustain or even trigger a genuine domestic civil war.

FOREIGN INTERVENTION AND INTERNAL WARS

Foreign pressure or interference can have several different purposes. It can aim at making the government of the target country do something which it otherwise would not do; or it can try to prevent the target government from doing something which it otherwise would do. (The first of these aims was called "X" and the second "O" in Table 18, Chapter 12.) But the influencer country may have more far-reaching aims. It may wish to change the composition of the target country's government, or some of its basic institutions, or to take over part of its territory, or to end its independence altogether. Thus, a communist government may wish to pressure a neighboring target country into admitting local communists to its new coalition government, which alone can end (it is suggested) the foreign-supported violence on its soil; or its pressure may even aim at installing there a full-fledged communist regime, either locally recruited or partly imported from abroad. Conversely, an anticommunist power might put pressure on a communist-ruled target country to relax its dictatorial controls and to grant more freedom and influence to noncommunist or anticommunist domestic groups; or to concede greater local autonomy to border regions where noncommunist or anticommunist sentiments might prevail; or to overthrow entirely the target country's communist government and replace it with an anticommunist regime, perhaps one allied to the West. Bulgarian and Yugoslav support for Greek communist guerrillas in the mid-1940s, and North Vietnamese pressure on Laos and South Vietnam in the 1950s and 1960s, exemplified problems of the first kind; United States support for anticommunist Cuban guerrillas at the time of the Bay of Pigs invasion in 1961 and for the guerilla force called *Contras* in Nicaragua, increasingly overt from 1984, raised problems of the second kind.

The outcome of such efforts depends most often on three things:

1. The sympathies, activity, and vigor of the domestic population of the target country in supporting or opposing its government.

2. The sheer size, kind, and persistence of the foreign input and pressure against the target country or regime relative to the size, resources, and popular backing of the latter.

3. The intervention or nonintervention of additional countries on either side of the conflict.

The relative weight of each of these three factors varies in part with the size of the target country. The larger its population, the larger will tend to be the cost of foreign intervention, and the smaller its effect. In large countries (such as those with over 100 million inhabitants), foreign intervention is particularly costly and unpromising, and the attitudes and actions of the domestic population are apt to be decisive to the outcome of political contests. This was experienced by Western allied support of the "White" antibolshevist armies against the Red Army in the Russian civil war from 1917 to 1921, and American support of Chiang Kai-shek's Kuomintang armies versus Mao Zedong's communist forces on mainland China in the civil war from 1945 to 1949. In small countries (such as those with less than 10 million population), outside intervention, disguised or open, is more likely to carry the day, as did United States intervention in Guatemala in 1954, in the Dominican Republic in 1965, in Cambodia in 1970, and in Grenada in 1983—and as did Syrian intervention in Lebanon in 1976. It takes an unusually well-entrenched government, or unusually strong motivation among a large part of the population, for a small country to retain a type of government that puts it at odds with a powerful next-door neighbor; but at different times and in various ways Switzerland, Israel, Finland, Afghanistan, and Cuba all have shown that it can be done, particularly since a vigorously defended small country may not be worth (to its bigger neighbor) the probable costs of intervention on a scale large enough to bring down its government or end its independence.

Serious international problems are most likely to arise in the case of middle-sized countries (perhaps those between 10 and 50 million in population) such as Algeria, both Vietnams, Yugoslavia, Czechoslovakia, Egypt, Afghanistan, and Poland which may seem small enough to look like easy targets of intervention, yet big enough to appear profitable. If a country of this tempting middle size becomes divided by internal group conflict or incipient revolt or civil war, one or several outside powers may be strongly drawn to intervene, clandestinely or openly, in the hope of some quick gain in the international power contest. Such hopes, however, are likely to be disappointed, particularly if a substantial part of the country's population is strongly motivated to take part in its political struggles. On the other hand, successful acts of intervention in countries with larger populations were in the past facilitated by the relative isolation and political apathy of the mass of the rural populations of these countries.

It is the higher degree of social, political, and potential military mobilization of many present-day countries that makes successful outside interventions in these countries so much less promising. In such cases, the balance of domestic political forces is likely to contribute most to determining the outcome; and the scale of the conflict is apt to be so large as to make outside intervention very long and drawn out, costly, and ultimately unrewarding. Even if the domestic allies of the intervening power should prevail in a country of this inviting but unmanageable middle size, they are likely to conclude quite soon, and often correctly, that they won chiefly by their own efforts, and they may eventually astonish their former protectors by their ingratitude.

In countries of any appreciable size, the relative strength of the three basic factors—the numbers, motivation, and activity of the domestic population; the size and skill of intervention by the outside power; and the abstention or intervention of other foreign powers—will generate one of the three main types of conflict:

1. A civil war, fought and sustained mainly by forces from within the target country, with foreign inputs and pressures playing only a marginal part (as they did in the Russian Civil War of 1917–1921, the Chinese Civil War in 1945–1949, and the struggles in Cambodia after the United States "incursion" of 1970).

2. A foreign attack, carried out primarily by outside troops invading across a national frontier or across the demarcation line of a part of a divided country, with only short-lived and marginal support from local sympathizers and guerrillas (as in the case of the North Korean invasion of South Korea in 1950, and the Soviet invasion of Hungary in 1956 and of Czechoslovakia in 1968).

3. A mixed type of war, in which large domestic rebel forces are fighting against the government of the target country in the manner of a genuine civil war, while at the same time receiving substantial and sustained support from at least one outside power (as did the Viet Cong guerrillas in South Vietnam, who in 1967 consisted of about 230,000 South Vietnamese and 50,000 individuals and troops from North Vietnam; similarly, though to a lesser degree, Afghan resistance forces, supported by the United States and Pakistan, were fighting against the Karmal regime and the Soviet troops supporting it from 1979; and in Kampuchea, the Khmer Rouge factions and the followers of Prince Sihanouk, supported by the People's Republic of China, the United States, and the other Southeast Asian nations, have been engaged in a drawn-out civil war against the Soviet and Vietnam-supported Heng-Samrin government since 1984).

Most of the time since 1945, United States policy toward the first two types of conflict has been clear and relatively simple. It has been to avoid any heavy involvement in genuine civil wars abroad, such as the Chinese civil war, but to oppose vigorously, and even at great cost, any massive aggression across an international boundary or demarcation line, as in Korea in 1950. The majority of the American public would thus massively support United States armed resistance, and even nuclear retaliation, against any Soviet-backed attack across the "demarcation line" between Western and Eastern Europe; but it would not support a Western attack across that demarcation line either. Both these policies have been reasonably popular, within the United States as well as in most of the noncommunist world, where opposition to them has remained minor.

But there is no simple policy for dealing with the third (mixed) type of war, such as the Vietnam war in the 1960s. When simple policies were tried in that case, it soon became evident that they did not work particularly well. Successive administrations in the United States, and particularly President Johnson's administration, tended to describe this conflict as primarily a matter of North Vietnamese aggression against South Vietnam. Domestic and foreign critics, on the contrary, pointing to the four-fifths of South Vietnamese among the Viet Cong, tended to see the contest mainly as a civil war, disregarding the one-fifth of Viet Cong troops coming from North Vietnam, and the presumably much larger share of Viet Cong firepower and equipment supplied from there or from other communist countries. A succession of hard-pressed South Vietnamese governments, all of them already dependent on American support, soon called for ever larger numbers of troops to help them against their foreign and domestic enemies. In 1968, at the height of the Vietnam war, about 543,000 United States troops were engaged in South Vietnam, outnumbering by then its North Vietnamese infiltrators roughly 10 to 1. Also by then, United States air and naval forces had subjected much of North Vietnam to steadily extending bombardment, reaching a peak with the "saturation" bombing, including the use of napalm, in 1972, and a monthly average of 60,000 tons of bombs dropped on North Vietnam alone—as well as extended military intervention in the Indochina war by incursions into Cambodia in 1970 and Laos in 1971. But neither the 230,000 Viet Cong troops nor the government of North Vietnam showed any signs of yielding, and the war in South Vietnam showed no signs of abating—indeed, the overall conflict in the area was continuing to escalate. A war of this kind, it appeared, was unlikely to be settled by either a clean-cut doctrinal definition or clear military victory, but rather by a long and drawn-out sequence of attrition, exhaustion, and eventual compromise—unless it were to be swallowed up in the cataclysm of a much larger war among the great powers. No one wanted such a cataclysm. In 1973 a cease-fire agreement with North Vietnam and Laos terminated the protracted United States military involvement in the Indochina war, and after March 29, 1975, no American combat forces remained in Vietnam. North Vietnamese troops were left in the south, and the formal unification of the two Vietnams into a single communist-ruled country was completed in July 1976. Vietnam was now governed from Hanoi and pursued, at least to some extent, an independent domestic and foreign policy course. Its policies included the extension of tight political and military control over the neighboring countries of Laos since 1975, and Cambodia, then renamed Kampuchea, which it invaded in 1979. The Soviet Union was now left to help offset the greater potential pressure of nearby communist China, which was exemplified by the People's Republic's brief "punitive" incursion into Vietnam in 1980 in response to the invasion of Cambodia. China has thus far failed to deflect Vietnam from its foreign policy course, and the emergence of new conflicts and civil strife in that region indicates that the potential for protracted international involvement and the escalation of regional disputes and mixed-type conflicts into major wars in Indochina has by no means abated.

THE LADDER OF ESCALATION

As pictured by Herman Kahn (and shown in Table 19), a limited war of the type fought in Vietnam early in 1967—that is, a war stopping short of all-out bombardment, massive land invasions, and the use of nuclear weapons— may offer only a temporary resting place on the long ladder of escalation.

In almost every limited war in our time, the great powers are directly or indirectly involved. If all of them accept the outcome of the local limited conflict—win, lose, or draw—then this war becomes for them an "agreed battle." Within its explicit or tacitly accepted rules, the major powers then are free to test both their policies and their (conventional) weapons, as well as the capabilities and motivations of their local allies, but also to accept the eventual local outcome and to pursue thereafter their interests there and elsewhere in its light.

If at least one major power refuses to accept this local outcome, however, then it will break some of the limiting rules rather than accept loss of face or influence for itself, or defeat for its local allies. In that case, it will escalate the war; and unless every great power on the opposing side is much weaker, or much more cowardly, or much more pacifistic, the other side will do the same; and escalation will proceed beyond this major halting point.

From here on, halting points are fewer, and each of them will be less likely to have much effect. Limited conventional war now tends to give way to all-out conventional war, with no limits on military targets in the field. But all-out conventional war strongly favors the rise of a conventional war psychology of the kind familiar from World Wars I and II. Ever more extreme weapons will seem attractive to the elite and mass opinion in the main contending countries, with the ancient rationalization that the most ruthless tactics are now expected to be the most merciful, since they are to knock out the enemy quickly, and thus to save lives. But this logic tends to appeal to both sides; or else the side that first was less ruthless soon resorts to retaliation. The war thus gets ever more destructive, and its survivors on both sides more embittered. Now the resort to nuclear weapons may seem only a question of time, and each side may become determined to snatch every possible advantage by doing sooner what they now think in any case is inevitable.

At first, even nuclear war may remain local. Only tactical nuclear weapons may be used, and only on the battlefield. Soon, however, rocket-borne, intermediate-range nuclear weapons may be used to attack the seaports, railroad centers, and airfields of each side behind the local front, destroying in the process much of the civilian population in their vicinity.[1] (Public opinion may be less shocked at this stage. People already may have become used at earlier stages of the war to large-scale conventional air attacks on civilian populations, and they may not yet be fully aware of the other side's capabilities for nuclear retaliation.)

As one side gets the worst in the local nuclear contest, however, its

---

[1] If the U.S.-Soviet INF Treaty of 1987 should be ratified by the U.S. Senate and carried out by both sides, this particular step on the ladder of escalation might disappear.

TABLE 19   AN ESCALATION LADDER: A Generalized (or Abstract) Scenario

	AFTERMATHS
Civilian	44. Spasm or Insensate War
Central	43. Some Other Kinds of Controlled General War
Wars	42. Civilian Devastation Attack
	41. Augmented Disarming Attack
	40. Countervalue Salvo
	39. Slow-Motion Countercity War
	(City Targeting Threshold)
Military	38. Unmodified Counterforce Attack
Central	37. Counterforce-with-Avoidance Attack
Wars	36. Constrained Disarming Attack
	35. Constrained Force-Reduction Salvo
	34. Slow-Motion Counterforce War
	33. Slow-Motion Counter-"Property" War
	32. Formal Declaration of "General" War
	(Central War Threshold)
Exemplary	31. Reciprocal Reprisals
Central	30. Complete Evacuation (Approximately 95 percent)
Attacks	29. Exemplary Attacks on Population
	28. Exemplary Attacks Against Property
	27. Exemplary Attack on Military
	26. Demonstration Attack on Zone of Interior
	(Central Sanctuary Threshold)
Bizarre	25. Evacuation (Approximately 70 percent)
Crises	24. Unusual, Provocative, and Significant Countermeasures
	23. Local Nuclear War—Military
	22. Declaration of Limited Nuclear War
	21. Local Nuclear War—Exemplary
	(No Nuclear Use Threshold)
Intense	20. "Peaceful" World-Wide Embargo or Blockade
Crises	19. "Justifiable" Counterforce Attack
	18. Spectacular Show or Demonstration of Force
	17. Limited Evacuation (Approximately 20 percent)
	16. Nuclear "Ultimatums"
	15. Barely Nuclear War
	14. Declaration of Limited Conventional War
	13. Large Compound Escalation
	12. Large Undeclared Conventional War (or Actions)
	11. Super-Ready Status
	10. Provocative Breaking Off of Diplomatic Relations
	(Nuclear War Is Unthinkable Threshold)
Traditional	9. Dramatic Military Confrontations
Crises	8. Harassing Acts of Violence
	7. "Legal" Harassment—Retorsions
	6. Significant Mobilization

TABLE 19 (*cont.*)

AFTERMATHS

	5. Show of Force
	4. Hardening of Positions—Confrontation of Wills
	(*Don't Rock the Boat Threshold*)
Subcrisis	3. Solemn and Formal Declarations
Maneuvering	2. Political, Economic, and Diplomatic Gestures
	1. Ostensible Crisis

DISAGREEMENT—COLD WAR

Source: Adapted from *On Escalation: Metaphors and Scenarios* by Herman Kahn, published by Frederick A. Praeger, Inc., Publishers, New York, and Pall Mall Press, London. 1965.

leaders will be tempted to attack the enemy power's (or coalition's) "central sanctuary"—that is, the main national territory with its central regions and main cities. The first attacks from either side may well be mere demonstrations, or they may be "exemplary" attacks, designed to devastate a few specific military targets, industrial installations, or population centers, in order to demonstrate the power of its weapons. From the point of view of the technician, the destruction of the cities of Hiroshima and Nagasaki in August 1945, were such "exemplary" attacks, against which the Japanese then had no power to retaliate. But in today's world, both sides in any major war would have nuclear weapons, and as demonstration or "exemplary" attacks are answered by retaliation rather than surrender, escalation would very likely continue.

Now that each side has demonstrated the terror of its weapons, and its own readiness to use them ruthlessly, it has a very strong motive to destroy as many as possible of the weapons of the other before they can be used. Here the escalating war may enter the stage of "military central wars," with nuclear attacks on military targets in the central territory of each of the contending powers. These may be "counterforce" or "first strike" attacks, aimed at quickly destroying on the ground many of the bombers and missiles of the adversary before they can be launched; here each power may try to beat the other to the draw. But no "first strike" is likely to eliminate all the nuclear weapons of a major power, and its surviving force, for a retaliatory "second strike" against the attacker, may be devastating.

At this stage, "counterforce" war, directed against airfields and missile sites, may give way to "countercity" war directed against people. According to the calculations of some strategists, it would be most rational for each side to destroy at first only one or a few of the cities of its adversary, so as to indicate that the surviving cities now are hostages. But the same rational strategic calculations will suggest that the adversary should do the same: destroy one or a few cities of the enemy nation, so as to hold their remaining cities as hostages. The results may be a "countercity" war in slow motion, in which the two great powers destroy each other's cities, one after the other, in a stately dance of death, until one of them decides to escalate the war further.

For there is still room for escalation. There are some cities which a nation may treasure more highly than others, because they contain sacred religious objects, treasured national relics, irreplaceable art treasures, or many members of the families of the nation's governing elites. And there are, most important in our age of mass politics, the large concentrations of population containing the lives of many millions of the nation. Any or all of these would become targets at this stage for "countervalue" attacks or reprisals. If all or most of them should be attacked, we may speak of a "civilian devastation attack," and if all restraints, and indeed all further efforts at rational political control should cease, and a country should fire all its remaining weapons at its enemy, there would be what some writers speak of as "spasm, or insensate, war." After this—after the last weapon had been fired and the last military resource exhausted—there would be nothing left but the prospect of a lingering death in a vast, poisoned wasteland for most if not all of whatever survivors there might be.

CRUCIAL LINKS IN THE PROCESSES

Our survey began with the effort of one state to put pressure on another. It then surveyed the rising scale of international conflict until the level of limited war had been reached, and then traced its possible escalation to all-out war and the destruction of the major contestants, together with much of their environment. The processes that can link these successive stages of mounting conflict into a fateful chain of events are failures of *perception, foresight,* and *control.*

Failures of perception are familiar to us from our earlier discussion of mass images, media, and the role of governments, which first may strengthen these images and then themselves become influenced by them in their decisions. Attachment to established images of one's own nation and of foreign countries, desire for cognitive consonance, rejection and denial of information that does not fit accepted preconceptions—all these can add up to the equivalent of sleep or blindness for governments and nations. They may fail to see realistically the attitudes and capabilities of foreign populations, and the interests, policies, capabilities, and commitments of foreign governments, until they are on a full collision course with them, and on the way to escalation.

On its way toward collision, a government may be thought of, in a manner similar to that of a ship's captain or an automobile driver, as passing a point of surprise and a point of no escape. The *point of surprise* in an automobile accident, according to a scheme developed for the accident research of insurance companies, is that point in the progress of a vehicle at which its operator first becomes aware of moving toward a collision or other major accident. The *point of no escape* is that point in progress toward the accident when nothing further the driver can do can prevent the crash.

If the point of surprise comes before the point of no escape, the operator might still be able to prevent the crash; if it comes afterward, awareness comes too late and catastrophe has become inevitable.

The same sequences have been traced in the catastrophic collisions of world politics, such as the start of World War I. Some governments in 1914 discovered that they were moving toward a big war, not a small one, at a time when they still could do something to avert it (although, as it happened, they did not do enough). But other governments, such as those of Imperial Germany, Russia, and Austria-Hungary, discovered only too late where events were taking them and were unable to stop their countries' journey to destruction.[2]

If the process of escalation is slower and drawn out over more intermediate stages, the point of no escape comes later. If the rulers of at least one country discover in time that the entire "conflict system" of the contending countries is moving toward catastrophe, they may still succeed in halting escalation. But even if they realize their danger in time, the process of escalation itself may impair their capacity for rational decision making, or in part even destroy it. The national decision makers are now exposed to the tension caused by fear and resentment of the foreign adversary; to the impact of that country's threatening, provocative, or hostile actions; and to the impact of domestic mass opinion and their own patriotic and almost inevitably inflammatory propaganda. Under these pressures, the values and perceptions of the decision makers may change in the direction of more intense conflict, or else the decision makers themselves may now be replaced by others who have fewer inhibitions about vigorously prosecuting and aggravating the conflict.

Eventually, as in a limited war, prowar or proconflict sentiment among the elite, as well as among the masses, may reach a peak level at which it may become stabilized for a time while the limited war is being pressed forward. From this peak level, there are three exits. The limited war may be won, and the proconflict sentiment ends in triumph; or the conflict escalates to all-out nuclear destruction; or else the conflict drags on without victory, and there eventually follows a stage of weariness, exhaustion, or reorientation of desires on the home front. After many young men have been killed, the lives of those who survive often have seemed more valuable; and the aims or demands of the opening phase of a conflict sometimes have seemed curiously irrelevant to those who were still living near its end.

At this stage, domestic political consensus may break down. While some groups are likely to continue to press for war, other groups now may come to oppose it and to press for peace. Alternatively, domestic opinion among all groups and levels may move more-or-less in step, so that domestic conflict is avoided as the foreign war gradually becomes less popular. In either case, elite and mass opinion may now shift toward compromise and accommodation.

---

[2]See Bruce M. Russett, "Cause, Surprise and No Escape," in Russett, *Power and Community in World Politics* (San Francisco: Freeman, 1974), pp. 173–189.

The preceding two paragraphs were written in 1967. Readers may judge for themselves to what extent the actual political developments in the United States during and after the Vietnam war, 1965–1973, resembled the patterns sketched out here. In any case, by the mid-1970s, the United States seemed to have reemerged still as a reasonably well-united country, albeit very much less unanimously supportive of prowar and proconflict sentiments and without a clear foreign policy consensus. This continued to the mid-1980s, with the nation, however, favoring again a more confrontational defense posture and a less accommodating foreign policy approach. How far the mood has changed once more with the loss of control of the Senate by the Republican Party in 1986 and the signing of the Reagan-Gorbachev Treaty of December 1987 (see p. 187, n. 1) remains to be seen.

In other times and countries, some outcomes were less lucky. In the case of a badly exhausted and defeated country, elite and mass opinion may shift further. They may now accept large concessions to the adversary, as many Russians did in early 1918 at the time of the Peace of Brest-Litovsk with Germany. In extreme cases, they even may favor outright surrender, if further resistance against a greatly superior enemy appears hopeless, and if life under the predictable post-surrender conditions appears preferable, as it did to the German and Japanese military leaders who surrendered to the United States and to the other Allies in 1945.

Such a surrender still was an implicit bargain. The defeated country traded its residual capacity to inflict damage on the victor for terms which it expected to be significantly better than it was likely to receive otherwise. Such a surrender, however, requires an effective victor capable of enforcing terms; and it seems unlikely that after any all-out nuclear war between great powers any victor of this kind will be left. Since any great power also seems quite unlikely to surrender short of extreme—and mutual—destruction, discussions about "strategic surrender" are likely to remain quite academic. Discussions of deescalation, and conflict limitation at early stages of great power conflict, should be far more practical. In the last few years, however, a new type of limited, "subcritical" war has developed, with new problems and new dangers.

14

A New Form of Warfare? Terrorism: Old and New

In its wider sense, *terrorism* is the tactic of using an act or threat of violence against individuals or groups to change the outcome of some process of politics.

Classic terrorism aimed at the elimination of individuals. The ancient tactics of tyrannicide have been preached and practiced for many centuries. The murder of Julius Caesar in 44 B.C. and the attempted killing of Adolf Hitler on July 20, 1944, are well-known examples. With the ruler dead, government was expected to change, but often it did not work out that way.

Generally, assassinations of leaders do not disrupt or change political systems. The attack might fail, as did the attempt on Hitler in 1944, or it might succeed, as did the attack on the Tsar of Russia, Alexander II, in 1884; with the main result of having him replaced by Tsar Alexander III while the old autocratic system of government continued. Similarly, the Prime Minister of India, Indira Gandhi, was murdered in 1984, but the Indian democratic system continued with her son Rajiv Gandhi as Prime Minister. When the President of the United States, John F. Kennedy, was murdered on November 22, 1963, his successor, Vice-President Lyndon B. Johnson, was sworn in within one hour, and the main policies of the United States continued.

Speculations, of course, have often pointed in a different direction.

Would President John F. Kennedy have involved the United States less deeply in Vietnam than Lyndon B. Johnson? Or would the pressure of public opinion in the United States of the mid-1960s have produced much the same result under either President? Would the history of the Soviet Union have become different, if Lenin had not been weakened badly by the injuries from Fanny Kaplan's attempt on his life in 1920? Would the communist movement in Germany after World War I have become more effective, if two of its early leaders, Karl Liebknecht and Rosa Luxemburg, had not been murdered by rightist soldiers in January 1919?

We shall never know with certainty, but my own inclination would be to answer "no" or "not much" to such questions. Large populations and large organizations, it seems to me, have a great inertia of their own. They change, but only slowly, and the sudden elimination of one or a few individuals, as sought by class terrorism, has a limited effect, except under quite rare and exceptional conditions.

A second age-old form of terror is that of rulers against some or many of their subjects. "Will no one rid me of this priest?" King Henry II of England is said to have exclaimed before his court, and four knights obligingly murdered Archbishop Thomas à Becket at the altar of Canterbury cathedral. That happened in the 12th century but in the 1930s a play, "Murder in the Cathedral," was written by T. S. Eliot. In the 1980s Archbishop Romero of the small Central American republic of El Salvador was murdered at the altar of his cathedral by agents or adherents, it is widely believed, of the "authoritarian" government of that country.

In the 1970s, the establishment of the dictatorship of General Augusto Pinochet in Chile in a coup was reported to have cost 20,000 lives. In addition a prominent anti-Pinochet exile, Orlando Letelier, was murdered in Washington, D.C., by means of a car bomb by an agent of the Pinochet government who was caught and convicted. In another act of terrorism, two Bulgarian anti-government exiles were murdered, it was reported, by stabs with a poisoned umbrella tip.

The most spectacular and fateful case of the government-supported assassination of a prominent individual was the murder in Sarajevo of the Austrian Archduke and heir-presumptive to the throne, Franz Ferdinand of Este, on June 28, 1914. The murder was carried out by a nationalistic student, Gavril Princip, but the entire operation had been carefully organized and supported by the intelligence section of the Ministry of War of Serbia (a part of today's Yugoslavia). It led to war between Austria-Hungary and Serbia, and then within less than six weeks to World War I—a war, to be sure, that already was expected and prepared for by the governments of several great powers.

Governmental terror has not been limited to attacks on a few individuals. During World War I the Turkish government of Enver Pasha deported 1.5 million Armenians—men, women, and children—on long forced marches. When asked where these people were being sent, a Turkish official was reported to have answered "nothingness." Indeed almost all of these Armenians perished.

AIMS: WHAT TERRORISTS HOPE TO ACCOMPLISH

Sometimes there may be *expressive* terrorism. In this case, terrorists may act just to give vent to their accumulated feelings of bitterness, rage, and frustration. But more elaborate acts of terrorism, particularly against well defended targets, require long preparation and an effective supporting organization. Expressive terrorism rarely finds these resources unless it happens to express the mood of rage of a larger ethnic, religious, or social group—a mood that may not last.

To attract more dependable support, the terrorists must have an aim that at least seems to be attainable. Eliminating some key person, or group, seen as adversaries, may thus be linked to some hope that this will directly produce some large and lasting results—a hope that usually proves unrealistic even if the act of terror itself succeeds.

Since the 19th century, more hopes have been placed in the indirect effects of terrorism. According to the theories of the Russian anarchists Michael Bakunin and Sergei Nechaev, as well as of the Russian movement "People's Will" in the late 1870s and the Socialist Revolutionary political party (SR), in the 1890s, the masses of the people in Russia were already close to a revolutionary mood, and a spectacular act of terror would serve as a signal to trigger off their pent-up emotions and coordinate their actions.

This theory of "signalling" terrorism—of "the propaganda by deeds"—from time to time also won adherents in other countries, such as in Italy, Spain, and Latin America. Terroristic anarchists succeeded in several spectacular assassinations but did not win power in any country in the world.

Finally, terrorists may aim at gaining *attention* and at arousing *fear*. In modern industrial democracies getting attention in the mass media—press, radio, film, and television—is often easily attainable by almost any behavior that is unusual and spectacular enough. Even mild acts of terror—such as the blowing up of mailboxes by separatist nationalists in Scotland, Wales, and Corsica—won much attention in national and foreign media.

Arousing fear in a modern democracy is a more dubious matter. Since people are free to speak, write, vote, and seek office in elections, terrorist groups are automatically suspected of being small minorities who cannot win elections and whose views are too extreme to make them eligible partners for winning coalitions. In short, they are unpopular at the national level. If such a minority then arouses fear through the terrorist acts of some of its members, it soon becomes hated and a likely target of acts of repression. Only if this minority is relatively large, predominant in some distinct territory, and remote from the majority's centers of interest and power, are majorities likely to let troublesome minorities and their territories go. Thus, various combinations of terrorism, guerilla warfare, and a helpful international setting eventually led to the independence of Ireland in 1922, of Israel in 1948, and of Cyprus in 1960.

Terrorism and guerilla warfare. When one side in an armed conflict is not strong enough to put uniformed troops more or less permanently into the field, it may resort to guerilla warfare. Guerillas are not uniformed or otherwise permanently identified. They emerge from the population for some armed strike and melt back into it again. Between attacks they often survive by dispersion, concealment, and near-invisibility, or by retreat into remote peripheral or otherwise inaccessible areas. They destroy local enemy installations and communications, kill or kidnap key personnel, and attack those among the population who collaborate with the enemy or are suspected of doing so. In this manner, they encourage their own adherents, demonstrate that their side is still fighting on, and frighten and dishearten their adversaries.

In such wars of concealment and intimidation, information is both an instrument and an objective of the fight. Knowledge of the plans, locations, and personnel of the adversary must be gained by any means and at any cost—and so must fear be spread among them. The modern rules and conventions of civilized warfare do not apply. Deception and cruelty often become competitive and pervasive as the result of acts of retaliation and counter-retaliation. In the struggle for the control of some territory, wrote two members of the United States Intelligence Community, its inhabitants must be taught to fear the government authorities more than they do the rebels.

In the long run, the outcome of such guerilla-cum-terror campaigns may follow a quantitative model. Each side must recruit fighters and keep them, and it must try to keep its *rate of recruitment* high enough to continue as an effective force. But each side also loses personnel through attrition by battle deaths, wounds, and sickness—and sometimes even more by desertion or muting. If the *rate of attrition* of one side remains higher than its own rate of recruitment then it will eventually disappear. Similarly, if the ratio of recruitment and attrition on one side is more favorable than the comparable ratio on the other side, then the favored side will be more likely to win the contest. Unless other conditions intervene—such as initial force levels, generalship, geography, logistic, or technological advantages—the effect of the recruitment/attrition ratios is likely to prevail.

Here terrorism has not one effect but two. In arousing fear and despondency on the opposing side, it is apt to raise their rate of attrition. But it may also provoke hatred and indignation within the mainstream and this increases their rate of recruitment. If this *provocative* effect of terrorism is larger than its intimidating one, the results may be counterproductive for the terrorist (or more spectacularly terrorist) side.

Some more subtle versions of modern terrorist theories have been trying to deal with this problem. Under one theory, terror acts by revolutionists are not expected to provoke revolution by the masses but repression by the government. The government will then, according to this view, become dictatorial, cruel, and "fascist"—it will be forced to "drop its mask"—and it will become thoroughly unpopular. In this way the government itself will put "the masses" into a revolutionary mood and the revolutionists will get their chance at leadership. But this theory has not worked in any industrial democracy. Governments and privileged classes can be goaded into overreaction, but the terrorists themselves remain unpopular.

And when the repressive regime falls, as it did in Greece in the 1970s, most people want democracy, free speech, and more security in their rights and for their persons. The efforts of small groups in France, Italy, and West Germany to provoke a succession of repression and subsequent revolution have uniformly failed.

MODERN TERRORISM AND SUBLIMINAL WARFARE

Modern terrorism has six prominent characteristics:

1. Acts have become much *more frequent,* reaching hundreds of incidents per year by the late 1970s and early 1980s.

2. Terror is most often directed against *soft targets,* that is, against individuals and installations not prominent enough to be heavily protected. Some prominent individuals have been among its victims. The Prime Ministers of Italy, Aldo Moro, of Lebanon, Bashir Gemayel, of Egypt, Anwar Sadat, of India, Indira Gandhi, and of Sweden, Olaf Palme, were all killed in the 1980s, and Pope John Paul II was wounded. German terrorists of the "Red Army Faction (RAF)" chose victims at an intermediate level, prominent enough to be well known but not enough to be massively protected such as the banker Jürgen Ponto and the Federal Attorney General Martin Buback.

But most attacks have been directed against less prominent targets. At the 1972 Olympic Games in Munich Arab terrorists murdered an athletic team from Israel. In Italy, travellers were killed by a bomb attack on the railroad station at Bologna. Arab attacks on Israeli buses, schools, and civilian aircraft became more frequent. In the late 1970s and in the 1980s hijacking by Arab terrorists of international commercial airliners to Mogadishu, Entebbe, Cyprus, and Karachi occurred, each time with high-profile publicity. Terrorism in Beirut has occupied front pages and television screens in many countries for several years.

3. The perpetration of such acts required preparation, money, weapons, and explosives; places to hide and sanctuaries to escape to. It seems evident that all these have become available on a much larger scale. Modern terrorism is based on more *organizational support* than was the case before the 1960s. Perhaps the 1960s, with the spectacular assassinations of President John F. Kennedy, Attorney General Robert Kennedy, and the Reverend Martin Luther King, Jr., marked a kind of turning point with the world-wide waves of publicity that followed each of these events.

4. The *mass media* reported terrorist events with sensationalism which was used by the terrorists to gain attention for their causes and messages. In this way, the media has become an unintended link in the widening spiral of terrorism.

5. A large part of modern terrorism is *supported by governments.* This is done through money, diplomatic facilities, passports, sanctuaries, experts, training camps, weapons, explosives, and justifying ideologies. The same terrorists who are called "criminals" and "bandits" by the foreign governments whose nationals they attack are hailed as "freedom fighters" or "fighters for national liberation" by the governments who support them. Several Arab states, particularly Libya and Syria, appear to have maintained training camps not only for Palestinians and other Arab nationalists, but

also for various European terrorists whom they regarded as allies. Similar cooperation has occurred among various European terrorist movements and Arab groups in regard to underground international arms trading and transport—again often with the connivance of some government.

Some governments support these activities but they do so within a context of *deniability*—trying to conceal the involvement of their personnel and the traces of their actions. Such attempted concealment may fail. In 1986, a British court of law formally established the participation of London-based Syrian diplomats in an unsuccessful attempt to place a bomb aboard a plane of the Israeli airline El Al which was carrying over 100 passengers. Britain then broke diplomatic relations with Syria and the United States and the German Federal Republic followed suit.

Also in 1986 a court of law in West Berlin established involvement of Libyan personnel in the bombing of a disco in which two American soldiers were killed. President Reagan thereafter ordered the aerial bombing of the Libyan capital, Tripoli, and another city where Libya's President, Muammar Gaddafi, was staying with his family. President Gaddafi was not hurt but one of his children was reported killed in the attack.

On the side of the Soviet Bloc, Bulgaria has been most frequently mentioned in the western press as a major conduit through which terrorist activities have been carried on. The Soviet Union itself, however, has been an overt partner in major weapons deliveries to Syria, Libya, and Iraq and partly with the intervention of Cuban troops, in Angola, Mozambique, and Ethiopia.

On the side of the West, the United States has been the main supplier of weapons, but West Germany, France, and Britain also have been significant sources. Much of this has occurred more or less overtly, through commercial channels sometimes eased by politically motivated credits; or else, as in the United States, as formal or informal military assistance.

But some covert activities of the United States went further. Back in 1961, after earlier United States-supported raids, an invasion of Cuba was launched by a force of Cuban exiles secretly trained and equipped by the government of the United States. That enterprise, begun under President Eisenhower and then Vice-President Nixon, was carried out under President Kennedy, and failed disastrously at the Bay of Pigs. Late in 1962 the CIA was working on plans for the assassination of Cuba's President Fidel Castro, which came to nothing. In 1962 when the Soviet Union agreed to remove its nuclear weapons from Cuba and the United States agreed to end all violent attacks against that country the matter was buried.

Informal and clandestine warfare among the super-powers reached new levels in the late 1970s and early 1980s. In December 1979, Soviet troops entered Afghanistan, which was then ruled by one communist faction. They did so at the invitation of Babrak Kamal, the leader of a rival communist faction, who appeared to have entered the country at about the same time, presumably with Soviet aid. The result was a protracted civil war, that turned into a war of traditionalist Islamic tribesmen against the Soviet-sponsored government in Kabul. The Islamic rebels received continuing support from the United States in weapons and money, and from Pakistan which offered them sanctuaries for regrouping and starting new raids into Afghanistan.

By late 1987 the war was still continuing. In Pakistan there were about 3 million Afghan refugees, Afghanistan itself with its less than 20 million inhabitants was badly devastated, the Soviet-backed regime in Kabul under a new leader, Major General Najibullah, had remained far from popular, and Soviet spokesmen now spoke of their country's willingness to accept a "non-aligned" Afghanistan under a government of national unity, but with Soviet troops remaining there for some years—a proposal still well short of what the other side might find acceptable.

A New Factor: The Islamic Revolution in Iran

In 1978 the pro-United States dictatorship of the Shah of Iran fell. The Shah had dreamed of making Iran a great power and had spent much of the oil wealth of his country on armaments from the United States, monarchical display, and attempts to revive the glories of ancient pre-Islamic Persia. But he had badly neglected the needs of his people. Most remained in poverty and firmly attached to their Shiite version of the Islamic religion. The Shah was toppled by a double revolution, both social and religious, and of these two, the religious one prevailed. Iran became an "Islamic Republic" with its religious leader, the Ayatollah Khomeini, remaining the ultimate arbiter of power thus far. The Ayatollah and the new Iranian government condemned both Russia and the United States as incarnations of Satan, and began to support the export of the ideas of an "Islamic" revolution into other countries. They were particularly successful in Lebanon, where in 1983 an Islamic revolutionist with Iranian connections drove a truck full of explosives into a camp of United States Marines, killing more than 200 of them. President Reagan soon afterward withdrew all United States troops from Lebanon, but pro-Iranian Shiite terrorists kidnapped six American citizens and held them as hostages. The United States imposed an embargo on arms sales to Iran and urged its Allies to do the same.

Elsewhere President Reagan's administration showed itself more warlike. They equipped and financed a force of *Contras*—anti-government exiles—for prolonged guerilla warfare against the left-leaning government of Nicaragua. In President Reagan's view, government of that small country was likely to turn it into a "second Cuba" and a threat to the United States. Its overthrow, therefore, seemed to him a matter of national security. In the course of the same campaign, the CIA had for a short time mined Nicaraguan harbors. The International Court of the Hague condemned this action as illegal, but the United States withdrew from the jurisdiction of the Court before its verdict.

The minings were not resumed, but the *Contra* war went on. The United States Congress, even with the then Republican-led Senate, was reluctant to give President Reagan a blank check for helping the *Contras*. Only $70 million in "humanitarian aid" was authorized.

In the meantime, however, the National Security Council had been partly changed under President Reagan from its function of intelligence evaluation and coordination into an agency for secret operations in the field. This seemed easy and attractive since the Council at that time was more shrouded in secrecy and less subject to Congressional control.

Two officials of the Council—Admiral John Poindexter and Colonel Oliver North—became involved in a complex maneuver. They entered into secret negotiations with some high Iranian leaders and officials whom they believed to be moderate. Iran was to use its influence with the Lebanese terrorists to bring about the release of the six American hostages. The United States would secretly deliver arms to Iran for its ongoing war against Iraq. As a token of earnest a substantial amount of weapons was delivered to Iran before any hostages were freed. Eventually three of the American hostages were released, but the pro-Iranian terrorists in Lebanon kidnapped three others in their place. In the upshot, Iran got a substantial amount of weapons, including 2000 TOW anti-tank missiles.

The aim of the transaction by the United States had not been the exchange of hostages for weapons. After all, this was an act that would reward hostage-taking and something President Reagan had publicly asserted he would not do. Rather the hope had been to divide the Iranian government, strengthen what was believed to be its "moderate" wing, reestablish some United States influence in Iranian politics, and eventually restore a United States-Iranian alliance against the Soviet Union.

This expectation failed. The "moderate" Iranians accepted the weapons and then heaped public abuse on the United States. Officially, at least, Iran remained as unfriendly as before.

But the operation produced money. In 1985–1986, the weapons were delivered to Iran mainly by Israel from Israeli stockpiles, with the United States undertaking to replace them in Israel. Iran paid $30 million for the weapons, but Israel charged the United States only $12 million for the replacement. The rest, perhaps $18 million, was put into Swiss bank accounts under the control of Poindexter and North.

According to some suggestions, these millions were redirected to the *Contras* to finance their war against the government of Nicaragua. This would have been illegal under Congressional legislation valid at the time that forbade spending public money for fighting this war. Moreover, *Contra* spokesmen protested that their side had not received this money but had operated in penury. When asked by members of Congress and by President Reagan to explain the matter fully, both Admiral Poindexter and Colonel North invoked the Fifth Amendment to the United States Constitution, refusing to testify on grounds of possible self-incrimination. At the time of this writing the $18 million has not been accounted for.

President Reagan claimed ignorance of the details of this affair. The head of the CIA, William Casey, also denied involvement, but shortly thereafter had to undergo an operation for a brain tumor, which in effect removed him as a potential witness and was followed by his death. The whole intrigue was kept secret from Congress and from the President's Cabinet, on President Reagan's order. So far, there the matter rests. In the meantime, the credibility of the administration suffered badly, affecting its allies,

Congress, and its own people. Whether the investigating committees of the new 100th Congress will bring more light to the affair and restore some of the confidence lost remains to be seen.

TERRORISM AND SECRET WARFARE AS POLITICAL TRAPS

Terrorism can become a self-perpetuating system. For this situation to develop it requires a significant social group in extreme discontent because many of its members feel politically, economically, or socially oppressed. They may also feel bitterly frustrated in the attainment of some cherished religious, national, or ethnic ambition. Usually there are also some individuals particularly impressed with some real or imagined wrongs who then take upon themselves the role of avengers of that wrong, or the role of leaders in a future mass movement for its abolition, to be called forth by their "pioneering" acts of terrorism.

Most often such terrorists and their acts bring forth counter-terrorism and repression, and these provoke more terrorism. This bloody cycle may continue for a long time until either side is exhausted, the original grievances are dissipated, or more promising ways are perceived to overcome them. Terrorism has existed, on and off, in Ireland for over 130 years, in Italy for about 100 years, and in Spain for about 80.

Terrorism usually changes little and solves nothing. It consumes scarce resources of talent, devoted manpower, thought, and attention. In the long run it most often weakens the side that practices it, and it weakens the country in which it takes place.

Guerilla wars are less long-lived but they may drag on over decades, even without major foreign aid, as they did in China before 1949, and as they still do in parts of Colombia and the Philippines. Sometimes such guerilla wars have turned into mass revolutions and some of these have been successful, but such outcomes are rare.

Terrorism and guerilla warfare can become stronger and more long-lasting if a foreign power intervenes secretly or even openly in their support. Most often this is warfare short of formal war. The intervening power can supply arms, money, equipment, intelligence and expert advice, and even troops though more or less discreetly. At the same time it can conceal and deny much of what it does, withdraw from an unpromising contest with less loss of prestige, and need not put its own country and population on a war footing with all the costs and difficulties this implies.

Such intervention may succeed, even if there is also foreign intervention on the other side of the conflict. In the 1947 Greek civil war the United States and Britain helped the conservative side to prevail although the Soviet Union and Yugoslavia aided the communist and leftist sides. Despite the massive efforts of the United States to aid the South Vietnamese government with 500,000 troops, but without a formal declaration of war in its support, the Soviet Union and China helped North Vietnam and the Viet Cong revolutionists to triumph finally in the civil war of 1965–75.

Most often, however, such conflicts drag on undecided for long periods, even with more or less secret foreign intervention. As of early 1987, the United States was involved in supporting civil war factions in Angola, Mozambique, Ethiopia, Afghanistan, and Nicaragua. The Soviet Union and Cuba supported in these countries the governments on the other side of the conflict. In all these protracted conflicts, no clear-cut victory for either side and its allies was in sight.

Terrorism is a trap for political movements that practice it. It uses up their key personnel, resources, and attention. It makes them less able to discover what should be done about the real problems of their peoples and their countries, and less able to make the compromises and coalitions necessary to get it done. In time, it distorts the personalities of their leaders. It makes them less sensitive, less caring, and more brutal and intolerant even toward one another. In all these ways, its opportunity costs are devastating.

And the governments that support terrorism and secret warfare? Their opportunity costs, too, are high. Not just the costs in manpower, treasure, and equipment but the more important costs in thought and attention, realism, morality, and in the time of their leaders that might be put to better uses. In the end, secret wars may become overt, and small wars may turn into large ones. One big escalation might be quite enough to put an end to the superpowers—and to much of the rest of mankind as well. The possible gains from such conflicts are out of proportion with their possible risks and likely costs. If the contest for armaments and power resembles a drug of nations, secret warfare resembles an act of shooting the poison into their veins.

Luckily, many drug addicts have survived and learned to control their habit or to get rid of it. Similarly, many nations have succeeded. Perhaps the biggest and strongest powers may yet be equally lucky.

15

Some Alternatives to Escalation and Warfare

Even where one state has not succeeded in controlling the behavior of another, escalation toward all-out conflict still can be either slowed down or halted—perhaps even reversed. Under certain conditions (to be discussed later) it can in fact be avoided altogether. It is possible to make conflicts rare and weak, even between closely interdependent countries or peoples, and to make collaboration so frequent and rewarding that it may initiate a chain of events leading to some form of stable and lasting political integration.

One class of strategy to deescalate tense conflict situations has been proposed by the social psychologists Charles E. Osgood and Morton Deutsch and the sociologist Amitai Etzioni.[1] In their view, any government wishing to mitigate a conflict should make a limited but unmistakable unilateral conces-

---

[1]See Charles E. Osgood, "Graduated Unilateral Initiatives for Peace," in *Preventing World War III*, eds. Q. Wright, W. M. Evans, and M. Deutsch (New York: Simon and Schuster, 1962) pp. 161–177; Morton Deutsch, "A Psychological Basis for Peace," in *Preventing World War III*, pp. 369–392; Amitai Etzioni, *The Hard Way to Peace* (New York: Colliers, 1962).

sion or gesture of conciliation, or even a small number of such acts or gestures. If the adversary nation should reciprocate by some counterconcession or conciliatory gesture, the first country should initiate another small but clear step toward improved relations; and if this were answered in kind, still another step should be initiated, until the entire conflict has been reduced to a safe level, or even until it has been replaced by some degree of mutual tolerance, cooperation, and—eventually—friendliness.

If the first initiative toward deescalation or greater friendliness should be rebuffed, this theory suggests that the more conciliatory country should under no circumstances escalate the conflict, but merely wait for a time. If attacked, it should defend its interests at the existing level of contention or hostility; but it should soon seek and take another limited unilateral initiative toward conciliation. The basic idea is similar to the one suggested by Anatol Rapoport's experimental data for the prisoners' dilemma game (see Chapter 11). It is to avoid both martyrdom and cynicism: to resist attack, but to continue offering the adversary clear and repeated opportunities to shift to a sequence of mutually cooperative moves.

Though this strategy may work sometimes in international relations, as it has worked in labor relations and in some other relatively small-scale conflict situations, its success at the present stage of international politics cannot be relied on. After all, drives toward conflict most often have existed in *both* states. Usually they have been embodied in much of their social and political structure, in their earlier economic decisions and investments, in the commitments of their political and military leaders and elites, in the images in the minds of their elites and their masses, and in the expectations and trains of actions to which all these have given rise. To stop these trains of actions, to undo commitments, to reverse specific orders and major policies, to cancel government contracts, to take back political promises, to disengage the reputations of parties and leaders, to disappoint expectations and interests, to upset domestic and international compromises and policy agreements— all this is painful, costly, and often fraught with severe risk. The country that is suddenly trying to deescalate a foreign conflict may find itself subjected to severe domestic strains and conflicts; and its rulers and elites may fear the domestic costs of "giving in," or even of deescalation, in a foreign conflict, more than they fear the political and military costs of a mounting foreign confrontation.

These domestic dangers are greater if the unilateral concessions to a foreign adversary are large or sudden, and they are still greater if these are not matched fairly soon by some visible concessions from his side. Repeated limited step-by-step initiatives, tempered by waiting for counterconcessions and by resistance to and limited retaliation for any new attacks by the foreign adversary may go far to reduce the risks of bringing on a domestic political crisis, but may not eliminate it altogether. For success, genuine good will to deescalate abroad would have to be combined with skill and competence in domestic leadership.

INTERNAL TRANSFORMATION OF ONE OR BOTH PARTIES
TO THE CONFLICT

Since conflicts are often brought on by processes implicit in the internal structures of one or both of the clashing countries, a change of these structures might end such conflicts and also end their recurrence. Radical internal transformation of competing countries has often been advocated, therefore, as the best way—and by some, as the only way—to abolish war. Jean-Jacques Rousseau believed that absolute princely rule in the states of eighteenth-century Europe was the root cause of wars. He rejected, therefore, as impracticable the project of his contemporary, the Abbe St. Pierre, for a League of Princes to keep the peace; only by abolishing the absolute monarchial regimes, Rousseau thought, could peace be made secure. (Alexander Hamilton would not have believed this. He pointed out in *The Federalist* that in history, "commercial republics," such as Carthage and Venice, had proved as warlike as, or more warlike than, aristocratic monarchies.) In due course, absolute monarchies disappeared from most of Europe and the rest of the world, but the nation-states that succeeded them proved no more peaceful than their predecessors.

Whereas Rousseau had hoped to abolish war by abolishing absolute monarchies, Marx and Lenin hoped to end all wars by abolishing the capitalist economic system—and with it, as they expected, eventually all class rule. With the end of conflicts among classes, Marx believed, there would be an end to conflicts among nations. Since 1945, a plurality of communist states has emerged, and this hope, too, has begun to be tested by experience. Although communist governments usually claim that class conflicts within their countries have been largely ended, and that their relations to other communist countries are fraternal, the dictatorial state machinery in each of the countries has not yet "withered away," nor does it show any signs of soon doing so; too, international relations among communist countries, particularly those with different shades of communist doctrine, have been rich in political and economic conflicts, although by the mid-1980s no major wars had broken out among them. The communist hope of avoiding short-of-war conflicts among communist states has thus been disappointed, as in the conspicuous cases of the Soviet occupation of Hungary in 1956, and Czechoslovakia in 1968, and recently, the pressure on Poland to declare and maintain martial law from 1981 to 1985—as well as in the serious Sino-Soviet border clashes in 1969 on the Amur and Ussuri rivers, and the "punitive" invasion of Vietnam by the People's Republic of China in 1980 in response to that country's intervention against the Pol Pot regime and the invasion of Cambodia in 1979. Another sign of disappointed hopes for stable peace among communist regimes has also been the stationing of troops on both sides of the Russo-Chinese border from at least the 1960s, but the verdict on their hopes to avoid major intercommunist warfare indefinitely has as yet remained open.

If no radical internal transformation of states thus far has abolished the danger of war, the fear of such radical transformations often has made the danger worse. Threatened elites and favored minorities (such as those of Germany, Italy, and Japan in the 1930s) sometimes have deliberately preferred conflict abroad to the prospect of intolerable change at home. Their fears and resentments of threatening domestic changes have made them irrationally defensive and aggressive, seeking everywhere around them conspiracies and threats and striking out finally in blind panic and fury against some foreign rival or target.

From the viewpoint of preserving peace, less sweeping changes in the domestic social systems and politics of states might be both safer and more effective, particularly if such limited changes can be carried forward unremittingly. Such limited changes would have to be generally in the direction of increasing the capabilities of each nation for conflict tolerance and conflict management. They would have to aim within each country at increasing the adaptability and cohesion of its political system, at its capability for integration and for the effective change of at least some of the nation's goals, and even at its capability for further national self-transformation and development.

Such limited and partial internal transformations of states and nations (toward more effective conflict management and the pursuit of less dangerous and more rewarding goals) have been more frequent in history than one might think. England had been embroiled in land wars on the European continent from the thirteenth to the fifeenth centuries, holding during much of the time such port cities as Bordeaux and Calais, winning resounding victories at Crecy and Agincourt, burning Joan of Arc and devastating France, and spending considerable blood and treasure in the process. The English military and political commitment to the continent may well have seemed irreversible to many of her leaders. As late as the mid-sixteenth century, Queen Mary the Catholic was said to have died with the word "Calais" on her lips. Yet in fact the commitment was by then almost ended. Calais, and with it the last English strong point in France, was soon abandoned, and England turned away from the pursuit of land power on the continent to the more rewarding pursuit of sea power all around the world.

The shift was immensely beneficial for England, to whom it brought four centuries of unprecedented growth, power, and prosperity. But the shift was made possible, or at least easier, only by the coming to power in England in 1485 of a new dynasty, the Tudors, with a greater interest in ships and naval affairs, a new coalition of supporters (based on Wales and some of the formerly less influential elite groups and families in England), and a new view of administration and government. Later on, after 1536, the shift was further aided by the rise of a new issue, the Protestant Reformation, which overshadowed the old images of an English commitment to the continent. The shift became complete when in 1555 English Protestantism finally triumphed with the accession of Queen Elizabeth I.

Other examples cannot be traced here in detail. But the shift of the Swiss Confederation in 1515, from an exhausting pursuit of power over Lombardy to a less costly and more rewarding policy of neutrality, limited westward expansion, and internal development would show a similar pattern. Here, too, the shift was facilitated by a relative shift in influence in favor of those old and new members of the Confederacy (such as Bern, Fribourg, Solothurn, Basel, Schaffhausen, and Appenzell) who had little interest in Lombardy, along with a relative decline of influence over the Confederation as a whole on the part of Cantons (such as Uri and Schwyz) most immediately concerned with the affairs of Lombardy. Here, too, eventually, the Reformation brought in a new set of problems and conflicts which made the earlier Swiss commitment to power politics in Lombardy soon seem unimportant and even irrelevant.

Sweden's abandonment in the eighteenth century of her former great power policies in the Baltic area and at the edge of the land mass of Russia was similarly prompted by the mounting costs of unending land wars against Russia. And the United States' efforts to bring Canada into the Union, pursued in fits and starts from the American Revolution and the Articles of Confederation until the War of 1812, were abandoned after that war and its unsuccessful campaign against Canada. The United States–Canadian frontier was demilitarized in 1819 and remained substantially unchallenged thereafter, while United States policy shifted fully to the more rewarding pursuit of westward expansion.

The conflict between France and the Arab nationalists of Algeria may have been deescalated by a similar process. France shifted in 1962 from protracted and unrewarding land warfare in Algeria since 1954 to a more effective pursuit of her interests in much of the rest of Africa and in Europe, as well as to the economic and technological development of France herself and the nuclear equipment of the French armed forces. This shift was made easier by the partial replacement of the institutions and leadership groups of the Fourth French Republic by those of the Fifth, including notably President de Gaulle and his party, and by the replacement of some of the old colonial-war-minded generals by new and more technically oriented military leaders.

The United States in the late 1960s was beginning to face the possibility of a choice between increasing pursuit of land power in Asia and a more vigorous pursuit of European and Atlantic integration, more economic aid to developing countries, and expansion into outer space, with an attendant growth in its overall scientific and technological capabilities and resources. Under its Constitution and the two-party system, such a shift could be easily and smoothly accomplished, once public opinion at the mass and elite levels should come to demand it. Already by the mid-1970s, United States commitments on the Asian land mass had been terminated by the policies of Presidents Nixon and Ford, with the sole major exception of South Korea, where United States troops continue to be stationed. The withdrawal from Vietnam, Laos, and Cambodia had been backed by a large bipartisan majority of Congress, as well as by a preponderance of public opinion. During the first few months of the Carter administration in 1977, preparations were made for the gradual withdrawal of American ground troops from South Korea, but this policy was never implemented in the wake of other international developments such as the unresolved Iranian hostage crisis and the Soviet invasion of Afghanistan. These events helped to bring about a renewed shift in public opinion at the mass and elite levels towards favoring an increase in American military power, and a determination to stem the tide of Soviet and communist expansionism in the Near as well as the Far East. Here occurred perhaps once again a change in the nation's international goals and interests, hand in hand with a shift of perhaps 10 to 15 percent of the voters to more conservative views on domestic matters. Whether these new policies and the foreign policy orientation towards larger international goals will prove more rewarding remains to be seen in the years to come.

REDUCTION OF MUTUAL CONTACTS

As the schematic presentation in Fig. 7 suggests, conflicts tend to arise among countries which have a high degree of interdependence and mutual transaction, but who have opposite interests, so that there is a "negative covariance" in their rewards: many outcomes which are rewarding for one country are frustrating or penalizing for the other. Conflicts among such countries can be reduced by reducing the extent of their mutual interdependence, and by cutting down the flow of transactions among them. As mutual contacts decline, so may occasions for quarrels.

The traditional policies of ancient China seem to have followed some such principle when its rulers built the Great Wall and kept down most contacts with the outside world until the early nineteenth century. Japan's rulers under the Tokugawa Dynasty from the sixteenth to the nineteenth centuries pursued a similar policy of isolation from the outside world. In the course of the nineteenth century, both China and Japan had to give up these policies of seclusion, but until that time they had enabled both countries to avoid major external wars for several centuries, in striking contrast to the far more warlike history of countries like contemporary France.

In the Western world such policies of conflict reduction by the reduction of the absolute level (or at least the relative importance) of contacts among potential enemy countries have been used more rarely. Some sentiments of this kind may have contributed to the mood of George Washington's Farewell Address in 1797, when he realistically advised the country to keep clear of the contemporary political quarrels and entanglements of the Old World; and they were revived once more under very different circumstances in the isolationist mood of many Americans between 1932 and 1941, with less fortunate results. Communist governments have been more inclined to reduce contact across the boundaries of their countries—a particularly dramatic example of this was the building of the Berlin Wall in August 1961—but they have done this less to reduce foreign conflicts and more to maintain and tighten their domestic control within each of their countries. It is possible, however (though not certain), that this policy may have prevented at least some international frictions and clashes which otherwise might have occurred. Berlin, in the mid-1980s, seemed a somewhat calmer city than it had been in the two decades after World War II. Particularly the four-power agreement over Berlin of 1971, though unable to achieve a consensus on the political and legal status of the divided city, has

Figure 7   Covariance of Rewards or Interests Between Countries

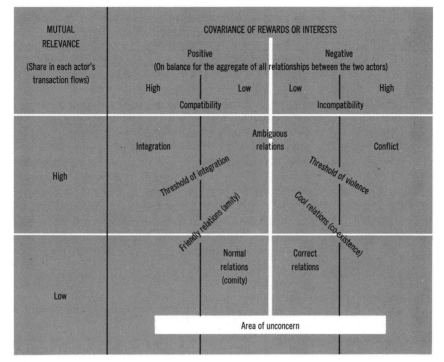

Source: Reproduced from K. W. Deutsch, "Power and Communication in International Society," in *Conflict in Society,* Ciba Foundation Symposium, A.V.S. de Reuck and Julie Knight, eds., London, 1966, p. 302.

facilitated and legitimized contacts and relations among the two governments and the two peoples of Germany, and has reduced the conflict potential over the city among the major controlling powers.[2]

REDUCTION OF ANTAGONISTIC INTERESTS
AND STRENGTHENING OF CONSONANT INTERESTS

If mutual contacts cannot be reduced, conflicts can be made less probable by reducing some or all of the mutually opposed interests in the countries concerned. How and at what price this can be done depends on the nature of each interest. Countries engaged in keen economic competition can each shift to a different line of specialization, or to a different market or geographic area of primary interest. Political objectives can be readjusted, and

[2]See Ronald A. Francisco and Richard L. Merritt, *Berlin Between Two Worlds* (Boulder, CO, and London: Westview Press, 1986).

alternative and less conflict-laden foci of attention can be created for public opinion in each country.

Threats and grievances can be removed; for example, the Soviets abstained from stationing ballistic missiles in Cuba and removed missile launch pads under construction there in late 1962, at United States insistence; and real or pretended fears can be calmed, as were Cuban and Soviet fears by United States assurances, given at the same time, that there would not be any further United States-supported invasion attempt against Cuba, following the abortive one at the Bay of Pigs in 1961. After these deescalation measures (and with a continuing low level of United States-Cuban contacts), tension in the vicinity of Cuba from 1962 to mid-1986 remained markedly reduced, despite minor tensions over the inflow of more than 35,000 Cuban refugees and expellees into the United States in 1980, and the initiation of anti-Castro broadcasts from "Radio Marti," a new U.S.-influenced government station, under the Reagan administration.

Even if neither contacts nor clashing interests can be reduced significantly, conflicts still can be reduced by increasing the salience and weight of parallel or interlocking interests among the countries concerned. Within each country, such positive bonds of interest to the other country often can be made to outweigh the negative and mutually clashing interests that make for separation or hostility. Where such common interests can be found and can be made to predominate in the relation between two countries, these countries are apt to move toward friendly mutual relations, and perhaps even toward some higher stage or degree of political integration. The improved relationships since the 1950s between France and West Germany, after two centuries of enmity, are a conspicuous example. The same logic governs West Germany's policy towards East Germany, and has determined Western Europe's relations to the Soviet Union and Eastern Europe in the 1970s and early 1980s. They were hoping to build on interlocking and consonant interests in the field of economic and trade relations, particularly in such areas as raw materials and consumer and technology goods, a structure of mutually beneficial interdependence that might some day, if not lead to some form of political integration, at least outweigh their negative and mutually clashing interests, reduce the potential for conflict among the two blocs, and eventually enable some form of peaceful cooperation and adjustment.

The best hope for moving in this direction may be in a combined strategy of both internal and external change for the countries that may remain locked in conflict or move toward correct relations or even integration. Among the concerned, such an approach would imply making dissonant interests less weighty and salient, while making consonant ones more clearly perceived and stronger. It would require shifting the foci of public attention away from conflict and, if possible, toward cooperation. Within each country, it would mean isolating and weakening all groups, elites, institutions, and interests making for aggravated conflicts, while strengthening and joining into coalitions all those groups and interests making for international peaceful adjustment and cooperation.

All this may well imply considerable political change within most or all of the countries concerned, and within some of them these changes would have to reach fairly deep into their political structure. Yet these changes may be most effective for peace if they stop well short of total revolution, and if they avoid arousing extreme and potentially war-engendering fears and resentments in hitherto favored but now threatened elites and interest groups.

Most of all, such a strategy of conflict-reduction and potential integration would have to aim at increasing each nation-state's capability for conflict management, for tolerance of threats and ambiguity, and for goal-change and self-transformation without loss of identity and of essential values and traditions. This would require a redefinition of a nation's role in international politics, as well as a redefinition of many political roles within each country. Most often it also would require a redefinition of the image of the world held by a nation, or by its leaders and its politically relevant strata; and it usually would require some change in national self-perception—that is, in the politically and culturally accepted image which a nation has of itself, its values, and its goals.

In the course of history, as we have seen, a few nations have succeeded in undergoing such partial transformations and reducing the threat of some (though not all) international conflicts to their existence or prosperity. But today, such successes are necessary for many nations, more reliably and sooner. New or improved instruments may now be available to attain these results and deserve to be studied; and most promising among these potential instruments are international law, international organizations, and the various forms of federalism and supranational integration.

16

Integration: International and Supranational

To *integrate* generally means to make a whole out of parts—that is, to turn previously separate units into components of a coherent system. The essential characteristic of any *system,* we may recall, is a significant degree of interdependence among its components, and *interdependence* between any two components or units consists in the probability that a change in one of them—or an operation performed upon one of them will produce a predictable change in the other. (In this sense, a lock and a key that fits it form an integrated system: turning the key will "turn" the lock.) Usually, a system as a whole also has *system properties* which are absent in any one of its components alone. (A proper lock-and-key system can be used to control the opening and locking of a door; a lock by itself or a key by itself cannot.)

Integration, then, is a relationship among units in which they are mutually interdependent and jointly produce system properties which they would separately lack. Sometimes, however, the word "integration" is also used to describe the *integrative process* by which such a relationship or state of affairs among formerly separate units is attained.

Political integration is the integration of political actors or political units, such as individuals, groups, municipalities, regions, or countries, in regard to their political behavior. In politics, integration is a relationship in which the behavior of such political actors, units, or components is modified from what it otherwise would be (i.e., if these components were not integrated). In this respect, integration can be compared to *power*, for we recall that power can be thought of as a relationship in which at least one actor is made to act differently from the way that actor would act otherwise (i.e., if this power were absent).

The *domain* of integration, like that of power, consists of the populations of the geographic areas integrated. Like power, integration also has *scope*, which is the collection of different aspects of behavior to which this integrated relationship applies. Thus England and Wales are integrated not only politically by means of all the many policies of a modern welfare state, but they were integrated until the early twentieth century also in regard to religion through the Church of England, which from 1536 until 1914 was supported by their common state and headed by its monarch. But in the United States (which are integrated in very many other respects), there is no such official religious integration among the states (which may have as different traditions as have Massachusetts, Maryland, Utah, Nevada, and New York). And the members of the United Nations are integrated in regard to a still much smaller set of tasks.

Political integration also may be compared to power in regard to its *range*. We may think of this range of integration as consisting of the range of rewards and deprivations for the component units, by which an integrated relationship is maintained among them. This range may be moderate in the case of some minor international organization which is only of marginal importance to its members, so that its success can bring them little gain, and its dissolution, or their secession from it, only little loss. Or this range of positive and negative integrative sanctions can be large, including vast joint rewards and prospects in case of success, and severe penalties for failure or secession. This was the case from 1776 onward, when the populations and elites of the states of the United States faced—and won—the rewards of integration in terms of independence and the joint settlement of the western lands, and eventually of a continent. A failure of integration, on the other hand, would have threatened them with the loss of independence, the establishment and persistence of different European colonial regimes in various parts of the divided continent, and the ravages of both civil war and international wars waged within their territory.

Whether a given range of rewards and penalties will actually prevail in a given political environment is, of course, another matter. In the case of power, as we recall, we spoke of the *weight* of power as actors' probability of overcoming resistance, and as their ability to shift the probability of relevant outcomes in the environment. The case of integration—the notion of the weight of power—is paralleled by the concept of *cohesion*, or *cohesiveness*.

An integrated system is *cohesive* to the extent that it can withstand stress and strain, support disequilibrium, and resist disruptions. Its cohesion, or cohesive power, could also be measured by the sustained shift which the system produces in the probabilities of the behavior of its components (as against the way in which they probably would behave if they were not integrated in the system). The greater the strains an integrated system can survive, the greater we may estimate to be its cohesion. Thus the cohesiveness, or consolidation, attained by Germany and Italy, respectively, after the national unification of each in the nineteenth century, is indicated by the fact that none of their component regions tried to secede after the disastrous sufferings of either World War I or World War II, while comparable strains contributed in 1918 to the breakup of both Austria-Hungary and of the British-Irish union.

Differences in these four dimensions of integration—domain, scope, range, and weight—help us to distinguish different types of integrated political communities:

A community with a general domain we call *universal*, such as the Universal Postal Union in principle, and nearly so in practice, in contrast to a *particular* community, whose membership is restricted to particular countries (such as the Arab League, or the Benelux customs union of Belgium, the Netherlands, and Luxembourg). In terms of *scope* we distinguish *specific* communities, communities limited to some specific subject matter or service, as against *diffuse* communities, each of which is expected to do more or less whatever is needed or demanded by its members. Usually, limited capabilities of international organization force a choice. An organization can perform a specific service for a universal clientele, such as the International Telecommunication Union (ITU), which coordinates international telegraph services among a large number of countries, and which is open to all qualified nations who apply. Or else an organization or community can undertake a diffuse responsibility for a wide variety of services limited to a particular group of regions, states, or countries. The United States, under the Articles of Confederation (1781–1791), was a community of the latter kind, and it became still more so under its federal Constitution (ratified in 1791).

Before we survey some of the different types of international organizations or communities which are generated by such differences in domain and scope, we must first be clear about the meaning of the concept of "political community." A *political community* is a collection of political actors whose interdependence is sufficient to make a substantial difference to the outcome of some of each other's relevant decisions. According to the minimal definition, community is simply a relevant degree of interdependence, and hence an objective fact, regardless of whether the governments or populations involved are aware of it or not. Two players in a game, or two states in competition or conflict, are members of one political community in this minimal but real sense, and, whether they like it or not, the outcome of what each of them does will depend to a significant extent upon the actions of the other.

If the two units, groups, or states concerned are aware of their interdependence, and perhaps also of its limits, they may modify their behavior accordingly. They may then act as members of a community and adopt the competitive and/or cooperative roles appropriate to the particular kind of interdependence—economic, strategic, or political—in which they find themselves involved. If it is mainly a *community of conflict*, so that outcomes rewarding for country *A* are frustrating or penalizing for country *B*, they may act as rivals or adversaries; if their rewards run parallel and depend on the coordination of their actions, they are in a positive *community of interest*, and may try to cooperate. Whether in cooperation or in conflict, however, they will now act as members of a community—rather differently from the way they would otherwise have acted.

Communities of conflict lock their members (whether individuals, groups, or nations) in a relationship in which mutual conflict predominates either wholly or to a large extent. Interestingly, however, although usually they produce little or no integration among the "traditional" or "hereditary" adversaries within them, it turns out (as many students of history and psychology have observed) that people and nations tend to copy in many ways the very things they hate. Some of the most Anglicized Irishmen, the Irish patriot George Russell (who wrote under the pen name "AE") once pointed out, were those who professed the greatest hatred of England.

Most often, nations are involved with one another in a community characterized by a variable-sum or mixed-motive contest. Their interests are then in some important respects opposed, but in other respects they stand to gain from coordinating their behavior. In such cases, it helps both parties if there is some conspicuous "prominent solution," acceptable to both, around which they can coordinate their expectations and their actions. A simple form of such coordination often is supplied by international custom and international law.

INTERNATIONAL LAW

A *law* is a general rule which covers a specific class of cases, and which is backed by a probable sanction, stated in advance and widely accepted as legitimate among the population concerned. *National law* usually derives its sanction from the enforcement machinery of the nation-state, and its legitimacy from the community of communication, memories, and political culture upon which popular acceptance and support of each nation-state are based. Within the nation-state, enforcement machinery and sentiments of legitimacy are available *for general purposes* (that is, for whatever purpose or need that may arise) and thus are diffuse in scope. Within the international system, they are not.

International law can be thought of, therefore, as both the most universal and the most specific form of international organization. Like all law it applies only to specific matters. But as a rule, it has no dependable permanent machinery behind it. There is also (ordinarily) much less of a common international political culture, except at most within a thin top layer of diplomats, international lawyers, and some other elite members particularly concerned with international affairs. National messages, symbols, and perceived interests are much more salient to most members of the general population of every country. As a result, perceptions of the legitimacy of international law tend to be relatively weak, and perceptions of national law and interest relatively strong. Nonetheless, international law has not only survived, but actually has increased, over several centuries, and in general it cannot be

broken without serious consequences. International law gets its sanction—
that is, the equivalent of a significant probability of enforcement—from the
significant probable cost of breaking it.

The boundary between international law and international custom is
blurred, therefore—unlike the sharper boundary between legal and political custom and statutory law within each nation, but still somewhat like the
earlier blurred boundary between unwritten customary law and written law
or precedent found in the early stages of development of many legal systems (such as Roman Law and the English Common Law), and in the law of
contemporary developing countries in transition from traditional to full-
fledged modern law.

Custom saves time, trouble, and uncertainty. It prefabricates many
decisions; it reduces the burdens of communication and decision making; it
coordinates the expectations of different actors; and it helps to make the
future more predictable. Law is custom which is widely perceived as being
legitimate, and which is backed by probable sanctions against a few transgressors. Law does what custom does, only more so—more precisely, more
intensely, more reliably. Moreover, law is explicit, and it is usually rational
(that is, retraceable in its operations, step by step). It is, therefore, usually
amenable to logic and often to combinatorial manipulation which permits
its elements or rules to be put together in new ways so as to cover new
problems. From the outset, it creates classes of cases included or excluded
by its provisions. Therefore, it can be used to include new cases under old
categories, or it can be extended by analogy to new classes of cases. Law is,
therefore, not only potentially more powerful and more precise than custom, but also more flexible and more capable of development.

International law has all these properties and possibilities. Whether
arising out of custom or out of treaties, it serves the nations to coordinate
their mutual expectations and behavior *in their own interest.* The first and
foremost sanction behind it is not merely the self-restraint of the actors but
also the realization of much greater cost and trouble for all parties concerned if international law did not exist, or if it were generally disregarded.
The situation resembles that of the matter of traffic rules, such as driving
on the right-hand side of the road in most countries, which are usually
more troublesome and dangerous to disobey than to obey.

The ancient rule of international law which provides that the persons
of ambassadors must remain inviolate is a good example. Ancient tyrants
sometimes executed foreign ambassadors whose messages displeased them.
Usually the rule of such tyrants did not last long. Any modern nation that
would dare to execute ambassadors would have to expect that no foreign
nation would send them ambassadors in the future, and also that its own
ambassadors might have to expect similar treatment abroad (which doubt-
less would make a career in their diplomatic service rather unattractive). In
short, ill-treatment of foreign ambassadors and other diplomats leads to
much more trouble than it is worth.

A seeming exception was the Iranian occupation of the United States
embassy in Teheran in 1978, and the imprisonment of most of its diplomatic personnel as hostages for more than 440 days until January 1981.

Although the rule of diplomatic immunity had clearly been broken and many governments expressed their protest over this, Western powers other than the United States—whose diplomatic matters were carried out by the Swiss embassy in Teheran—continued to send ambassadors and other diplomatic representatives to Iran. The revolutionary government in Iran profited from this move by increased popularity both domestically and among many Third World Countries, while the prestige of the United States government was gravely damaged. American attempts to free the hostages by a helicopter raid failed in a sand storm in the Iranian desert. President Carter than canceled the mission in an act of uncommon political courage and thus prevented further escalation of the conflict that might easily have become uncontrollable. But these Iranian advantages were transitory, and the United States administration's freezing of Iranian banking accounts and assets, amounting to $8 billion, in the United States and several other Western countries, proved in the long run an effective means of retaliation, and helped to bring about negotiations on the release of the hostages, which took place on January 20, 1981. The United States continued to block arms sales to Iran on the grounds of that country's support for international terrorism, and it tried to persuade its allies to do likewise. This policy was secretly reversed in 1985 and 1986 by the Reagan Administration which sent arms to Iran without informing Congress in the hope to win Iran's cooperation with the United States and to obtain the release of six U.S. hostages held in Lebanon by forces believed to be under Iranian influence. By September 1986, the attempt has failed and given rise to a scandal in American politics.

There have been several attacks on foreign embassies and their occupants in various parts of the world, but in general the rule of respecting ambassadors has held for more than a thousand years, with very few exceptions, even though there has been no world government or world court and police in existence to enforce it. The self-enforcing aspects of this rule have on the whole proved sufficient.

More numerous than the ill-treatment of foreign ambassadors, however, is in our days the expulsion of diplomatic staff and ambassadors, often on charges of espionage activities, which has become a popular gesture between the United States and the Soviet Union with regard to the other country's diplomatic mission, but also, for example, with the United Kingdom. The United States has also shown concern over the misuse of diplomatic privileges by the large number of United Nations ambassadors and their staff in the United States. Although such gestures do not directly infringe on the rule of diplomatic immunity and are often used merely for demonstrative effects, they may over time cause diplomatic relations with their more or less autonomous channels of communication to become more difficult and subject to political manipulation, and hence less reliable at times when they are most needed.

As a rule, however, the self-enforcing character of international law requires either an *approximate equality* in the power positions of the parties (permitting tit-for-tat tactics between them), or else an expectation of possible future *role reversal* between them (permitting tit-for-tat tactics in the probable future). If the two sides in an international cause are about equally strong, each can retaliate effectively for what the other may do. In repeated encounters under such conditions of approximate symmetry, simple self-interest will reward actors who learn to coordinate their behavior and to avoid mutually penalizing clashes.

Even if the two sides are not roughly symmetrical in power and position, they may have to expect that in the future their roles may become reversed. Nazi Germany had air superiority in 1939 and 1940, and exploited this superiority in bombing the cities of Warsaw and Rotterdam, with their civilian populations, in disregard of the international law which until then had prevailed. But soon, from 1942 onward, Germany had lost her air superiority; the precedent of the heavy bombing of cities which she had so recently established now turned heavily against her, and American, British, and much of world opinion now accepted the saturation bombing of Cologne, Hamburg, and finally, without military necessity, Dresden. These bombardments had little military effect but claimed about half a million German civilian victims. It is one question whether this retaliation was probable under these circumstances, and another question whether it was morally right.

In general, most nations do well to consider the possibility, and indeed the probability, of role reversal in the future. The nation that stresses its sovereign right to stop and/or search all ships in its coastal waters, and is tempted to extend its own definition of "territorial waters" to beyond the traditional three-mile limit as far as twelve miles out—as the United States did back in the Prohibition days of the 1920s, or the Soviet Union in 1960—may find later on that this principle, if adopted by other countries and extended to 200 miles (even if only as an economic or fishing zone), can work against the interests of its own fishing industry. This had been done by eight Latin American countries by 1971, as well as Indonesia and the Philippines. Retaliation followed then by other states, such as the United States, which established an exclusive fishing zone of 200 miles along their coasts in 1977. Since then, international codification of the law of the sea has somewhat legalized such practices, and the United Nations law of the sea treaty of 1984 permits the extension of territorial waters to 12 miles, and of economic zones up to 200 miles. Several countries with large maritime interests such as the United States, the United Kingdom, and the Federal Republic of Germany have, however, neither signed nor ratified this treaty so far. More serious examples apply to international legal restraints on warfare, such as the treatment of prisoners or of open cities, or the use of chemical, bacteriological, or nuclear weapons. Whatever weapons or methods of warfare one nation uses, particularly if it uses them repeatedly, are likely to be used some day against its own people. The long-run advantages of having been the first to disregard an international legal restraint usually turn out to be much smaller than they seemed at first, and the long-run costs and disadvantages are belatedly discovered to be far more heavy. The biblical rules which warned "It must needs be that offense comes, but woe to him through whom it comes," and "As you measure unto others, so it shall be measured unto you," had a thousand years of political experience behind them when they were written;

and the experiences of the many empires and kingdoms that have risen and fallen in the thousands of years since then have only served to confirm their long-run validity.

It is perhaps more difficult for Americans than for others to appreciate the full weight of the biblical consideration, history-proven though it be, because their own historical experience thus far has been so different, and indeed in large part exceptional. Much of the early American war experience was against Indians, who usually were inferior in strength, and against Britain (in 1776–1783 and 1812–1815), which was too distant and preoccupied to apply her full strength. The wars of 1848 against Mexico, and 1898 against Spain, were waged against conspicuously weaker countries, while World Wars I and II against Germany were waged in alliance, so that in each case the American troops met the German forces on the ground relatively late in the war, when much of the German strength was already weakened or occupied elsewhere, and the American push could force an early decision at a relatively low cost in casualties. The fight against Japan in World War II was perhaps the most bitterly fought American war of the past 100 years; and here, too, the United States defeated a country that had only about half its population and less than one-twentieth of its capacity to produce steel. In no foreign war since 1815 has the United States mainland been invaded or its cities bombed. The vast majority of Americans have no personal experience of seeing their own cities and houses become a battleground, an experience that has been unhappily commonplace in many other countries.

It seems natural to many Americans, therefore, to think of all-out war as meaning victory and not disaster; to call for a bigger war and for the use of ever more destructive weapons when they feel frustrated in some limited war far from their shores; and to feel impatient of all international legal and diplomatic restraints on what they believe to be their country's powers, while paying little or no realistic attention to the long-run costs. This is indeed a natural response to the unique experience of our past, and it seems most popular among those groups in Congress and among our electorate who are most strongly oriented to the past—but in the last decades of the twentieth century this response could be suicidal. For in the age of intercontinental ballistic missiles, the entire mainland of the United States is within range of thermonuclear warheads; and for every disaster that we could inflict upon the Soviet Union, some no-less-intolerable disaster could be inflicted upon us. Many of our past international power relationships were asymmetrical and left us with memories making many of us impatient of international law and national policies of self-restraint. But today our most important power relationship, that to the Soviet Union, is a symmetrical one for many practical purposes. In this world of "mutually assured destruction (M.A.D.)," new and onesided armament initiatives such as President Reagan's Strategic Defense Initiative (SDI), designed to launch weapons into outer space, have no assurance that by the time of their deployment—expected to be the year 1995 for the SDI weapons—counterweapons will not exist. In the meantime, the major effect of such initiatives seems to be one of destabilizing the existing superpower relationship and of fueling the arms race between them. Furthermore, as time goes on and other nations acquire larger stocks of nuclear weapons and the means for their delivery, international law and national policies of self-restraint will become increasingly relevant to everyone's survival. Mutual reduction of nuclear forces, as agreed upon in the Reagan-Gorbachev INF Treaty of December 1987, point in a more hopeful direction.

In the future, international law will also be of increasing importance in the general context of international relations. If severe violations of international law tend to arouse moral condemnation, smaller violations are likely to increase disorder, confusion, and collisions that may escalate into conflict. The few major powers so far have been powerful enough to afford to disregard these costs, and the lesser powers have often had little choice but to give in to these violations. But with the spread of technology, economic and military capabilities, and the social and political mobilization of the peoples of many countries, many smaller powers are now experiencing an increase in their power and capabilities, while the major powers are increasingly forced to take this diffused international power context into account in their decisions and actions. As the power differential between the countries of the world declines, the relevance of international law increases; and with the growing awareness of the finiteness and scarcity of global resources, it is becoming more important to know how, for example, territorial waters, national air space, and deep sea access are defined, and how the world's natural resources can be not only shared and exploited, but also preserved and protected. International agreements, and jurisdiction by international law, will be necessary to achieve an enlightened use of the global commons, as well as an international order governed by self-restraint and collective enforcement of commonly agreed on principles.

Self-enforcement through bitter experience, and self-restraint through exercising foresight, are not the only sanctions behind international law. Lesser but not negligible sanctions are the pressure of world opinion (which German governments ignored to their sorrow in two world wars), and the revulsion of domestic opinion from deeds of their own government, which are perceived as illegitimate, and which may lead to a quiet but effective withdrawal of popular support and of the support of important sections of the country's social, cultural, political, and technological elites. In addition, flagrant violations of international law may bring about adverse actions by third countries, and various disadvantages and penalties in international organizations. No responsible government could afford to ignore the cumulative effect of all these processes.

The Machinery of International Law

All this does not mean, however, that it is always easy to determine just what the international law is in a given case, any more than one can always determine easily the content of national law (or "municipal law" as the international lawyers call it) on a disputed point. Much of international law is laid down in international treaties and conventions, such as the United Nations Charter, and the Human Rights Convention. These bind directly, of course, only those nations whose governments have signed and ratified each document; but if sufficiently widely accepted, notably by all great powers, they also indicate the consensus of the international community of states. Beyond this, there are codes and collections of international law, the consensus of experts, and the precedents created by earlier international awards or acts of adjudication.

Disputed points may be settled by *direct diplomacy*—that is, by negotiation and bargaining among the parties directly concerned. If this process fails and leads to deadlock and the danger of escalating conflict, third countries may be brought in. Their participation may be limited to *good offices,* such as providing hospitality and a neutral meeting-ground for the next round of negotiations. Or they may act through *mediation,* offering suggestions or proposals for a possible compromise. These latter are listened to by the contending parties in proportion not only to their perceived intrinsic merit but also the power of the nation whose government proposes them.

If the two parties to a dispute bind themselves in advance to accept the decision of a third party, mediation is replaced by *arbitration.* The arbitrator may be a government, or a panel of individual arbitrators. Often three or five arbitrators are chosen by the two parties from some existing list of trusted experts. Such a list is maintained as the Permanent Court of International Arbitration at The Hague (which is, therefore, not a court of law). The powers of the arbitrators and the limits of the case to be decided are established in each case by an agreement among the parties to submit this case, or sometimes this class of cases, to the arbitrators. The same agreement also states the principles according to which they are to decide—such as strict law, or else considerations of equity.

If the case is to be decided by *strict law,* it is most often submitted to the International Court of Justice (ICJ). This Court, in the words of the United Nations Charter, is "the principal judicial organ of the United Nations." It is the almost unchanged successor of the former Permanent Court of International Justice, and thus it has been functioning in effect since 1920. Members of the United Nations are bound by the statutes of the Court, but the Court's jurisdiction depends in many cases upon the consent of the parties, and is further limited by many reservations by the member nations. The Court has no means to enforce its judgments, but once states submit to its jurisdiction, they usually obey its decisions, though there have been some exceptions in cases involving either the cold war or the Union of South Africa. More recently, in 1986, the United States rejected the verdict of the Court when it was found guilty of having violated international law by the mining of international ports in Nicaragua in 1984, and refused to pay reparations demanded by, and accorded to the government of Nicaragua.

Efforts to extend drastically the compulsory jurisdiction of the Court have been resisted by the United States as well as by the Soviet Union and many other countries, and they have thus far failed. If such efforts should succeed at some time in the future, they would turn the World Court into a more general-purpose instrument of control, and thus make it far more diffuse in scope. If the Court at the same time would retain or expand the universality of its domain, it would require much greater capabilities in order to cope with its expanded tasks in both domain and scope; and such greater political capabilities at the international level have yet to be developed.

FUNCTIONALISM: INTERNATIONAL OR SUPRANATIONAL
ORGANIZATIONS FOR SPECIFIC PURPOSES

Functionally specific international organizations open to all or nearly all nations differ from international law in their stronger permanent machinery, in their greater stress both on making limited new rules and decisions, and on the implementation and administration of policies. Some of these are nongovernmental organizations (NGOs), such as the International Red Cross (stemming from the first International Red Cross Conference at Geneva in 1863), which concerns itself among other things with disaster relief, the furnishing of emergency medical supplies, and the care of prisoners of war.

Most of the important international organizations of this kind, however, are composed of governments and hence are called Intergovernmental Organizations (IGOs). Such organizations include the Universal Postal Union (UPU, 1874), the International Telecommunication Union (ITU, 1932; successor to the International Telegraph Union, 1865), the International Civil Aviation Organization (ICAO), and others. Somewhat broader functions are exercised by such organizations as the International Labor Organization (ILO, 1919), the Food and Agriculture Organization (FAO, 1945), the World Health Organization (WHO, 1948), and the United Nations Educational, Scientific and Cultural Organization (UNESCO, 1946). These and several other "specialized" agencies of the United Nations are coordinated, very loosely to be sure, by the United Nations Economic and Social Council (ECOSOC). This council, which also has the task of discussing basic economic and social issues, has sponsored some important departures toward setting new standards of national and international behavior through its Convention on the Prevention and Punishment of the Crime of Genocide, adopted in 1948 by the United Nations General Assembly, and its Convention on the Suppression and Punishment of the Crime of Apartheid, adopted in 1973, both of which many countries have yet to ratify.[1]

The theory of *functionalism* in international relations is based on the hope that more and more common tasks will be delegated to such specific functional organizations and that each of these organizations will become in time *supranational,* that is, superior to its member governments in power and authority. In this way, says this theory, the world's nations will gradu-

---

[1]Both conventions, in force since 1951 and 1976, respectively, have not yet been signed by the United States; they have been signed by the Soviet Union and eighty other states in the case of the Convention against Genocide, and the Soviet Union and twenty other states in the case of the Convention against Apartheid. The Human Rights Convention, adopted in 1948 by the overwhelming majority of the General Assembly of the United Nations, has only recently been signed by the United States by means of a Resolution in Congress in 1984.

ally become integrated into a single community within which war will be impossible. But this hope seems rather uncertain. All these organizations are limited mainly to the exchange of views and of knowledge, the making of studies, the drafting of recommendations, and the rendering of technical assistance to governments requesting it. They cannot legislate. Although the old principle of unanimity usually has been replaced in these organizations by majority voting, their decisions do not bind any government until it has ratified them. (Only some technical agencies have a limited rule-making power; thus air-safety standards set by ICAO, and regulations by WHO to prevent the spread of epidemics, become binding on their member nations unless they give notice to the contrary within a specified time.)

Neither do these agencies have the power to tax, nor do most of them have any effective powers of sanctions. Their governing bodies are composed of instructed delegates of governments who must say what their governments have ordered them to say. Unlike members of a national legislature, these delegates, even if they should arrive at a consensus, cannot vote a decision and bind by it those who sent them. They are, so to speak, one-way representatives. They represent their governments to the international organization, but they cannot also represent effectively the will of this organization to their constituents, as national legislators can and sometimes do.

Perhaps most importantly, classic functionalism, as formulated by David Mitrany, envisaged the treatment of these international or supranational functions and services as technical matters, nonpolitical in nature, and well removed from the clamor and pressures of interest groups, nations, and the masses of the population.[2] But this view is more likely to prove a source of political weakness than of strength. Most of the time, the present international organizations can do no more than communicate with governments which remain free to deny their international officials all access to their territories at any time. Except for technical assistance missions in the field, the international civil servants cannot deal directly with the people whom they are to serve. They are hampered in receiving and answering direct communications from the public, and even more in doing anything about them. Under these conditions, popular loyalties to international agencies and symbols are unlikely to grow, and the appeal of nationalist images and symbols is unlikely to weaken.

Most of the national elites prefer it just this way. Their members have no desire to weaken their own power over their national societies by permitting the serious promotion of any competing international loyalties by which their own domestic power could be weakened. UNESCO—where each nation has an equal vote and hence the Third World has a majority—soon was discouraged from following through on its original assignment to create a new international ideology and set of symbols. Neither the Soviet leaders nor the major Western governments cherished the thought of fos-

---

[2]David Mitrany, *A Working Peace System* (Chicago: Quadrangle Books, 1966). For a case history suggesting an opposite conclusion, see Robert J. Lieber, *British Politics and European Unity: Parties, Elites and Pressure Groups* (Berkeley, CA: University of California Press, 1970).

tering potential competition. The United States and Britain even withdrew from that organization in 1985 and 1986, respectively, because of its alleged administrative inefficiencies and, perhaps more important, its alleged anti-Western ideological orientation and politically biased decisions on such issues as the creation of a New Information and Communications Order, disarmament and human rights, and the Middle East conflict, leaving UNESCO deprived of major financial contributions, which in the case of the United States had amounted to about a quarter of the organization's budget.

Similarly, the Food and Agriculture Organization was refused in 1947, at that time chiefly by the Western countries, the effective powers over international food prices and supplies. It has remained an organization devoted to studies, recommendations, and a modest amount of technical assistance, while the decisions about the allocation of the world's grain and other foodstuffs, and the potential political power that goes with them, have remained in the hands of the governments of the main food-exporting countries, such as the United States.

Functionalism often is also at odds with the growth of modern technology. The larger the technical resources set into motion by one seemingly technical decision, the more likely are its consequences to reach beyond the limits of any one technical specialty. When aircraft were relatively small, decisions about landing rights and the location of airports could be left to air traffic specialists. With the coming of big multiengined jet planes and large supersonic aircraft like the Anglo-French *Concorde,* such decisions also involve problems of aircraft noise, real estate values, city planning, civic protests, municipal politics, and even politics at the national and international level, such as between France and the United States in 1977 about landing rights for the *Concorde* near New York. Inevitably, such comprehensive decisions ever more often tend to exceed the competence of any one group of technical specialists. They must be dealt with on the general—that is, the political—level. Here technical and political obstacles to international functionalism may reinforce each other. The greater the potential power of an international organization, the broader and more functionally diffuse becomes its potential influence; and the greater usually also becomes the resistance of national societies and elites to let this potential international power grow. The closer an international agency comes to touching the core of the sovereignty of a nation, the more severe this problem may become. The International Monetary Fund (IMF) and the International Bank for Reconstruction and Development (IBRD) touch upon the freedom of each nation to manage its national currency as each national government sees fit. The Fund even has some power of sanctions, since, under certain conditions, it can refuse financial support to, and even block the credit of, uncooperative governments. The United States, as the largest financial contributor, has 20 percent of the votes in the IMF, and the top five members, comprising countries of the industrial West, have together over 40 percent of the votes. But just for these reasons, further extensions of the powers of the IMF to act and to bind its 148 members, at the price of a further cut in their sovereignty, are apt to be quite difficult to accomplish. The hope for a "spill-over" effect, which would lead from one specific integrated service or function to a widening demand for creating additional international institutions and integrating additional functions and services, has not been fulfilled to any large extent among organizations of this type.

Classic functionalism, to be sure, had a different ideal. Highly specific functional agencies, Mitrany hoped, would enter into direct contact with the people they served in each country. Their services would somehow remain nonpolitical, but they would win, through their performance, both increasing elite acceptance and popular support. Among the universal and functionally specific international agencies, as we have seen, to date very few, if any—except perhaps the World Health Organization and, among international nongovernmental organizations (INGOs), the International Red Cross—have moved very far in this direction.

17

Universal General-Purpose Organizations

Among the many goals which individuals and governments pursue, the broadest and most common is *security*. It is the basic mode in which most other values, such as wealth, well-being, affection, and "the rest," are enjoyed with the expectation that they will last for at least some time; and to many people it is also a value in itself. But since it is both a manner of and a condition for enjoying many other values, its meaning often is ambiguous.

Most often and most obviously, security to most people means the security of life and limb for themselves and their loved ones; and thus it means peace and the maintenance of peace. But security can also mean the security of wealth and property, even if this wealth should be based on a partial but real conflict of interest between creditor and debtor, landlord and tenant, employer and employee—a conflict which may reach the intensity of a latent war in some developing countries and sometimes in the poorest regions and urban quarters of countries that are otherwise counted as rich. Or security can mean the security of symbols and institutions, of positions of class and role, of images and habits, of ideology, and culture, of claims to respect and self-respect. To most people, some or all of these seem worth defending; and since the nation-state so often has been manifestly inadequate to safeguard these, people have turned their hopes to international organizations for their protection.

To preserve the peace requires the ability either to forestall force or to overcome it; and to safeguard the security of other values usually requires the same ability. To preserve security thus means to control and organize power, and hence to have the capacity to influence the allocation of many values and the pursuit of many purposes.

A federal or international organization to preserve "only" peace and security, therefore, may look like a special-purpose organization in form, but it would be a general-purpose organization in substance. Its charter and its personnel may solemnly promise that it will not interfere in the "domestic" or "internal" affairs of its member states, but in the long run, its intentions are less important than its capabilities. If it is weaker than one or several of its members, the organization will not be able to keep or restore peace in the face of their defiance, but if the organization is stronger than its members, it is likely to be strong enough to intervene from time to time in any and all of their affairs as it may choose. If there is disagreement as to just what are "domestic" matters, a stronger federal or international organization will be more apt to make its view prevail; and its superior strength may eventually determine how gaps or disputed passages in its charter or constitution are to be interpreted.

Thus far, the main problem of every international organization for the maintenance of peace and security has been its weakness rather than its strength. In each case the organization has remained weak precisely because most of its members feared its strength, and because they feared the possibility that this international or federal organization might become a mere instrument for the power and hegemony of one or a few of its strongest members, somewhat as a holding company often serves as an instrument to enhance and multiple the power of a well-organized minority of stockholders against all the rest.

In international organizations aiming at a worldwide membership, the differences among members are apt to be greatest, and so are their mutual fears. Accordingly, though projects for peace-keeping organizations or alliances including most or all states have been recurring ever since Pierre Dubois proposed such a project in 1310, and international congresses advocating such ideas have been held since the 1840s, it was only after World War I that an actual organization of this kind, the League of Nations, came into existence. Only then did governments and nations begin to be more afraid of war and international upheaval than of one another, and only intermittently and fitfully since the founding of the League have they continued to do so.

COLLECTIVE SECURITY AND THE LEAGUE OF NATIONS

The League of Nations was founded in 1920 with the purpose to protect peace and the new international distribution of rights and territories that had resulted from the global upheaval. Article 10 in its Covenant obligated the members to defend the independence and territorial integrity of each of them, but it ultimately left each nation to decide whether and how to fulfill this obligation.

According to the principle of *collective security,* all members of the League were to act together in resisting any peace-breaking nation by imposing economic and, if necessary, military sanctions on it. They were to do this regardless of whose ally the peace breakers might have been; for the defense of the new status quo through collective security, so it was hoped, was going to replace the old system of alliances and the balance of power, which had led to World War I. During the two decades that followed, almost every then-sovereign nation at one time or another joined the League. The handful of exceptions included Afghanistan, Bhutan, Nepal, Yemen—and the United States.

The United States, under the leadership of President Woodrow Wilson, had since April 1917, actually been one of the chief sponsors of the League and of its Covenant, of which a preliminary draft was published in February 1919, at the Paris Peace Conference. Concessions to nationalist sentiment in the United States, and particularly in the Senate, soon seemed to be essential. In accordance with proposals by former United States President William Howard Taft, the draft Covenant of the proposed League was modified to protect the domestic jurisdiction of members, to require unanimity for all political decisions, to assure to each nation the right of withdrawal, and to reserve the Monroe Doctrine and thus to keep the worldwide organization and the non-American members of the League out of the settlement of any disputes within the Western Hemisphere. Each of these modifications was designed to reduce the legal powers of the world organization and to preserve and strengthen those of the nation-states of which it was composed. Nonetheless, President Wilson failed to obtain ratification of the Covenant in the Senate. With the defeat of Wilson and the Democratic Party by President Warren G. Harding and the Republicans in 1920, the project died. The United States never became a member.

The League was governed by a Council in which the great powers of that time predominated. These were primarily France and Britain, but they were joined by such other "permanent members" as Italy, Japan, and eventually Germany (1926) and the Soviet Union (1934), and by nine nonpermanent members elected by the Assembly of the League, so as to represent all the main geographical areas of the world. The Assembly, including all members, was the other chief organ of the League; and there was a secretariat with a staff of about 750, headed by a Secretary General.

In the course of its existence, sixty-six political disputes were submitted to the League. It dealt successfully with thirty-five of them, but failed in the most important ones. Successes predominated in the early years of the League (1920–1925) and in its heyday (1925–1932). Though the United States remained outside, it drew somewhat closer to the League from 1927 onward, when France and the United States launched the Briand-Kellogg Pact, by which each signatory nation solemnly renounced war as an instrument of national policy. The pact was joined by many other nations, and marked a new low for the declining moral prestige of war, though not yet a turning point in its continuing occurrence.

The members of the League remained profoundly divided by their interests and ideologies. France and Britain wished to retain the territories and privileges they had won in World War I. France, which had gained Alsace-Lorraine and (temporarily) the Saar basin on the European continent, wanted collective security arrangements to be tight and rigid; Britain, whose gains were overseas, preferred such arrangements to be loose and flexible; and in their rivalry the two countries succeeded, between the two World Wars, in destroying most of one another's influence on the continent of Europe. Germany's elites and a majority of her voters wanted her to make new and larger gains, and after Hitler's seizure of power in 1933 a militant German policy was directed toward these ends. The leaders of Italy, particularly after the Fascist seizure of power under Benito Mussolini in 1922, and the leaders of Japan desired territorial gains which their countries had failed to make in World War I. These three "Axis powers," as well as some lesser powers, strove to upset the status quo which the League was to defend against all threats of "external aggression."

The Soviet Union's attitude was more ambiguous. For the time being, its rulers were willing to accept the diminished frontiers of their country as they had emerged from World War I. They hoped for greater gains in the future from the growing economic and military strength of their vast and rapidly industrializing country, and from the eventual appeal of its revolutionary ideology to the poverty-stricken masses of China, the rest of Asia, and other developing regions—and even some day (so they hoped) to the workers of a depression-ridden Western world. The Soviet government thus had no interest in defending the status quo, but it was in no hurry to risk an all-out attack on it. Rather, it felt more immediately threatened by the new militancy of Germany and Japan, and by joining the League in 1934, it sought an alliance with the status-quo powers.

The original concept of "collective security" as an alternative to the old system of alliance politics soon faded out. As an end in itself, collective security never was salient enough for governments and peoples to override the national interests and cost considerations of each nation-state. And as a means to other ends, alliances seemed better suited. Soon "collective security" became a label attached to any alliance system opposed to any other (which of course was similarly labeled by its members).

But all alliances remained precarious. Germany, Italy, and Japan insisted on revision of the territorial status quo. France and Britain alternated between attempts at resistance and moves toward "appeasement" through buying off the revisionist powers by concessions, or through deflecting their expansionist pressures in the direction of third countries. The United States, with no substantial territorial interests at stake, long remained aloof; and between the Soviet Union and the Western powers there remained an abyss of ideological hostility and mutual suspicion.

The League could not be stronger than the unity of the great powers who between them made up most of its strength. From 1931 onward, the major failures of the League began. In that year, it failed to take effective action against Japan's attack on China in Manchuria. In 1935, it voted to impose limited economic sanctions on Fascist Italy, whose armies were invading Ethiopia, but it did not even vote to try to stop the flow of oil to the Italian war machine; and the feeble sanctions ended in failure by 1936.

Although not all observers saw it at the time, the years 1935–1937 were the turning point in the fate of the League. In those years, it was the focus of world attention. It could have become the rallying point and the unifying symbol for world opinion and for the coordinated action of many powerful governments against the threat and practice of aggressive war by the revisionist powers (Germany, Italy, and Japan). For reasons of its own, the Soviet Union in that period was interested in collaborating with the Western powers, and the aggressor powers at that time were much less strong, relative to the West (as well as to Russia), than they were to become later in 1938–1941. If the League had succeeded in those crucial years of 1935–1937, World War II could have been prevented, or at least it could have been stopped by defeating the aggressors much sooner, with much less loss of life than eventually occurred.

But for reasons of their own in each country, both governments and mass opinion in all major Western countries hesitated throughout the period of 1935–1938, until the years of opportunity were lost. President Franklin D. Roosevelt, in a famous speech at Chicago in 1937, called for "quarantining the aggressors," but neither mass opinion nor elite opinion backed him up, and he had to wait another four years for majority opinion to come closer to his view.

Thus the League failed, and the world moved step by step to World War II and the 50 million deaths it was to claim. The League did nothing to stop the massive intervention of Italy and Germany in their attempt to overthrow the Spanish Republic in the Spanish Civil War (1936–1938), nor did it do anything about Japan's attack on Shanghai in 1937, or about Hitler's forcible absorption of Austria and Czechoslovakia in 1938 and 1939, nor about Hitler's all-out attack on Poland in the latter year, which started World War II. By then the Soviet Union, too, had come to disregard the paralyzed League. Abandoning the frustrating search for an alliance with the West, Stalin in August, 1939, concluded a sudden and utterly opportunistic "nonaggression pact" with Hitler; and in the fall and winter of 1939–1940 Stalin's armies occupied parts of eastern Poland, the Baltic countries of Esthonia, Latvia, and Lithuania, and finally eastern Finland, all on the grounds of either "liberating" their populations or of safeguarding Soviet national security. The Finns fought back, and this time the League acted by "expelling" Russia. It was a gesture without effect, its moral force destroyed in advance by the League's passivity in the face of the far more extended and spectacular aggressions of the Axis powers.

Thereafter, the League became politically insignificant. The alliance between the Western powers and the Soviet Union, vital to their interests, did not come about until France had been overrun, German bombs had fallen on London, and attacking German tanks had reached the outskirts of Leningrad and Moscow. By then, in late 1941, the United States was moving toward increasing aid to the allies; but it remained for Japanese bombs falling on Pearl Harbor on December 7, 1941, and for a German declaration of war on the United States on the next day, to make the United States a full, and soon a leading, member of the alliance which in time was to give rise to the United Nations.

THE UNITED NATIONS: WORLD ASSEMBLY OR WORLD GOVERNMENT?

When the formal organization of the United Nations was founded in June 1945, its general purposes were stated in the preamble to its charter. There, in language bearing traces of many compromises, "We, the peoples of the United Nations" declared themselves "determined" to pursue four major aims:

1. "To save succeeding generations from the scourge of war"
2. "To reaffirm faith in fundamental human rights, in the dignity and worth of the human person, in the equal right of men and women and of nations large and small"
3. To maintain "justice and respect for the obligations arising from treaties and other sources of international law"
4. "To promote social progress and better standards of life in larger freedom."

The first two aims, peace and human rights, appealed to human desires aroused by the war in almost all countries. The third, "justice and respect for obligations," could be understood to protect the new status quo to be established by the peace treaties, and also perhaps property rights in foreign countries on the part of nations, business firms, and individuals, insofar as such rights were covered by international law. (But the actual words of the preamble only said that the signers were determined "to establish conditions" under which such justice and respect for international obligations "can be" maintained.) The last aim linked the "social progress" and higher living standards, emphasized by the Soviet Union and some of the poorer countries, to "larger freedom," stressed by the Western powers. More than the League of Nations, the United Nations showed the marks of the ideological compromises characteristic of the era of the modern welfare state.

The United Nations, of course, was not a superstate. Like the League of Nations before it, it left untouched the sovereignty of its members. Article 2 of its Charter described the organization as "based on the principle of the sovereign equality of all its Members" (Art. 2.1), and explicitly denied to it any authority "to intervene in matters which are essentially within the domestic jurisdiction of any state" (Art. 2.7). Just what matters were "essentially within" this domestic jurisdiction was left undefined; in practice the government of each member state insisted on making this judgment for itself whenever it became involved in a case which it considered important.

In recent years, many Third World countries have argued that such jurisdictional principles and the present system of international law do in fact cement the asymmetrical relationship between developed and developing nations. In their demand for at least approximate equality in the formulation of international law and principles of justice, these countries maintain that much of traditional law is Western law, and is as such merely reflecting the hegemonic interests of Western nation-states, and oriented towards maintaining the present status quo of Western control of much of the power and wealth in the world community. The principle of sovereignty, for example, thus upholds international stability and order at the expense of achieving some form of international economic and social justice and progress, and a radical redistribution of wealth at the international as well as subnational level of countries. Political and theoretical as much of this jurisdictional discussion is at the present, the need to develop new principles of jurisdiction and international law that take into account a future world increasingly dominated by numerous lesser powers rather than a few major Western states will be one of the major concerns of an organization such as the United Nations with its commitment to democratic principles and aspiration to universal membership.

The General Assembly

In contrast to the League, the Assembly of the United Nations has the power to make decisions by majority vote. "Important questions," such as the admission or expulsion of member states, the suspension of their rights and privileges, the election of member states to major United Nations bodies, and the making of "recommendations" to member states and/or to the Security Council "with respect to the maintenance of international peace and security," require a two-thirds majority of the members present and voting (Art. 18.2). Other questions, "including the determination of additional categories of questions to be decided by a two-thirds majority," are to be made by a simple majority of the members present and voting (Art. 18.3).

About the crucial questions of war and peace, the Assembly cannot act. It can only consider, debate, and recommend, and it may not even make recommendations concerning any matters of international peace and security while they are being dealt with by the Security Council. In the fall of 1950, during the Korean War, the Assembly passed a United States-supported resolution, "Uniting for Peace," which was designed to enable the Assembly to initiate action by its members, if the Security Council should be deadlocked by disagreement among the great powers. As more new states have entered the United Nations, however, the majorities in the Assembly have been more often led by the countries uncommitted between the United States and the Soviet Union; and its majority votes on such issues as the remnants of colonialism, or the racial policies of the Republic of South Africa, or of Rhodesia (since 1980 Zimbabwe), have often become inconvenient to the Western powers who have then, predictably, shown little inclination to act on them. In general, each great power has professed great zeal in implementing Assembly votes or recommendations when they suited its national policies, but no zeal at all when they did not. By mid-

1986, the Assembly had not yet moved very far toward becoming a more effective instrument than it had been three decades earlier.

Similarly, the Assembly's power to "consider and approve the budget of the Organization" (Art. 17.1), and to apportion "the expenses of the Organization" among the members (Art. 17.2), has not developed into any full-fledged power to tax. When the Assembly voted for the intervention in 1961–1962 by a United Nations force in the troubled affairs of the Congo (Leopoldville)—i.e., the former Belgian Congo and today's Zaire—the United States approved of the action, exercised considerable influence in its execution, and favored the assessment of each member of the United Nations with a proportionate share of the cost. France and the Soviet Union refused to pay, on the grounds that the action (which they had opposed) could have been taken legally only by the Security Council (where their adverse votes would have stopped it), and that it was illegal to assess them for an action taken in a manner circumventing their veto right in the Security Council. The United States for a time tried to get an Assembly vote which eventually would have suspended from voting in the Assembly all nations not paying their assessment, just as if they had failed to pay their regular dues (Art. 19). Many of the Assembly members, however, were reluctant to accept this new interpretation of the Charter; and the United States itself had to consider what its response would be if some day an Assembly majority, perhaps a coalition of developing countries and the Soviet bloc, should authorize some governments to start some expensive undertaking in the name of the United Nations, and then assess the United States for a substantial portion of the cost. In any case, by the mid-1980s the project of having the Assembly assess unwilling great powers for special enterprises backed by it had been quietly abandoned. An international organization with an effective taxing power (which in the end would fall most heavily upon the richest countries) was at best still in the future.

In 1987, pressed by its large budget deficit, the U.S. announced it would pay only two-thirds of its contributions to the U.N., although they were fixed by treaties the U.S. ratified earlier. The last word in that affair, however, had not yet been spoken.

The Security Council

The heart of the United Nations' capacity to act is in the Security Council. United Nations members "confer on the Security Council primary responsibility for the maintenance of international peace and security, and agree that in carrying out its duties . . . the Security Council acts on their behalf" (Art. 24.1). If the Council can act, the United Nations can; if it cannot, they can only make gestures. This was foreseen from the start. While the Assembly was to debate, the Council was to act. The Charter speaks of the Assembly as making "recommendations"; it empowers the Council to make "decisions" (Arts. 25, 27, 39, 41, 44, and 48).

Under the Charter, these decisions include decisions about life and death. The Council has the power to "determine the existence of any threat to the peace, breach of the peace, or act of aggression," and to "decide what measures shall be taken . . . to maintain or restore international peace and security" (Art. 39). Such measures, as envisaged by the Charter, include "complete or partial interruption of economic relations and of rail, sea, air, postal, telegraphic, radio and other means of communication, and the severance of diplomatic relations" (Art. 41). These measures are to be carried out by the member states, when called upon to do so by the Council. "Should the Security Council consider," however, that these measures "would be inadequate," it has the right to act directly. "It may take such action by air, sea or land forces," says the Charter, "as may be necessary to maintain or restore international peace and security" (Art. 42). In short, the Council has the legal power to enforce its decisions, if need be, by warfare. For this purpose, all members "undertake to make available to the Security Council, on its call and in accordance with . . . special . . . agreements," suitable armed forces and facilities (Art. 43.1), and: "In order to enable the United Nations to take urgent military measures, members shall hold immediately available national air-force contingents for combined international enforcement action" (Art. 45).

All this legalized enforcement machinery can be set in motion, moreover, to enforce any political disposition or solution on which the Security Council may decide in dealing with any situation which in its judgment is threatening the peace. The Security Council, to be sure, "shall act in accordance with the purposes and principles of the United Nations" (Art. 24.2), but it is its own judge in this matter. No other body within or outside the United Nations can override its decisions. Indeed, the United Nations General Assembly is explicitly barred even from making any recommendation about any situation (e.g., political or military) while the Security Council is dealing with it, "unless the Security Council so requests" (Art. 12.1).

Taken together, these are extremely sweeping powers, almost wholly unchecked from outside, but checked from within the Security Council, almost to the point of paralyzing it, by the inability of its members to agree on many decisions of importance.

The crucial dilemmas of world politics are realistically reflected in the voting procedures of the Council. The Council has five permanent members (the United States, the USSR, the United Kingdom, France, and China), and since its 1963 enlargement, ten nonpermanent members elected by the Assembly for two-year terms. The permanent members were the actual or potential great powers of 1945; and by 1965, they had become the five powers then possessing nuclear weapons, albeit still in very unequal amounts. The heart of the functioning of the Security Council, as envisaged by the Charter, is in the unanimity of the five permanent members. The "concurring votes" of all the permanent members are essential for all decisions of the Security Council except procedural ones, which may be carried by the affirmative votes of any nine Council members (Art. 27).

Due to this "principle of unanimity" among the great powers, each permanent member has a *veto right* built into the Charter. Against its vote, or even without its concurrence, no substantive action may be taken. The veto power of each of the five permanent members extends not only to "material" issues (that is, presumably substantive ones) but also to the class of issue a question pertains to; but the decision on the official procedure of the Security Council cannot be vetoed. In 1950, when the Soviet Union boycotted the Security Council meeting on the North Korean attack on South Korea, the United States was authorized, in effect, to resist the attack on behalf of the United Nations. This decision was taken without the "concurring vote" of the Soviet Union and hence, all members of the Council, as prescribed in the Charter. It caused some subsequent jurisdictional and political controversy, but since then abstentions or absence from Security Council votes by one permanent member are no longer considered vetoes. The Soviet Union, most likely to be in a minority in a Council vote, has used its veto right most often by far, but the Western powers, too, have used it on occasion, and in recent years the number of United States vetoes and threats of vetoes have increased, particularly in the early 1980s, when American foreign policy shifted from the more conciliatory policy of *detente* to the more militant "containment" of Soviet and communist influence. Thus, when the Security Council, which had convened at the request of Nicaragua, reached a decision to condemn the invasion of the Antillan island of Grenada by a multinational force which in effect consisted of 95 percent American troops, in October 1983, the decision was vetoed by the United States, and so United Nations intervention was made impossible. On November 2, 1983, the General Assembly also overwhelmingly voted for a resolution demanding the immediate halt of military intervention and the withdrawal of foreign troops from Grenada; but since the United States proved unwilling to submit to these decisions, no results came from these initiatives.

This voting arrangement reflects a basic fact, not only of the world of 1945, but also of the larger world of 1986. Then, as now, it has been manifestly impractical to coerce either the United States or the Soviet Union to do anything important against its will; and it seemed clear that Britain, France, and China were similarly uncoercible, or soon would be. But if these five powers can agree, and if they care enough, so the drafters of the United Nations reasoned, they can muster enough force to stop quickly any war or threat of war anywhere in the world. The age-old problem of stopping or controlling the warlike propensities of all people and all states was thus replaced by the much smaller problem of discovering ways of producing coordination among only five countries—a problem which, though still very difficult, clearly seemed more manageable.

East-West Conflicts in United Nations Politics

The potentialities for collaboration among the major powers, envisaged by the designers of the United Nations Charter, to date have been realized to only a small extent. The cold war kept the United States and the Soviet Union on opposite sides on most questions. Its end in the late 1960s mitigated their rivalry, but has not abolished it. The renewed period of tension and hostility between these major powers in the early 1980s demonstrated the persistence of this conflict, and it might at some future time become even more intense again. Thus far, each power has used the United Nations primarily as an instrument to serve its own interests, and to carry out geopolitical confrontations in this continuing competition. Peace initiatives and policies of peaceful cooperation, deescalation, or merely increased communication have come about largely through the actions and decisions undertaken outside the United Nations by individual governments and statesmen.

Neither of these two superpowers, nor indeed most other members of the United Nations, has thus far shown any deep commitment to United Nations intervention or United Nations supranationalism as ends in themselves. Western powers have urged or favored United Nations intervention in countries and situations where it has seemed likely to weaken communist influence, or forestall its extension, such as in the case of northern Iran (1946), Greece (1946–1948), Korea (1947–1953), Hungary (1956), Lebanon (1958), Laos (1959), and the Congo (now Zaire; 1960–1963). But where the Assembly majority has urged United Nations measures against the colonial policies of a Western ally, such as Portugal, or France, or against the racial unrest of regimes closely linked to the Western financial and economic system, such as Rhodesia (now Zimbabwe) and the Republic of South Africa (from the 1960s to this day), Western powers have been far more reluctant. The Soviet Union, of course, has generally tended to take the opposite side in each question, modified by its general distaste for supranationalist institutions which would be dominated almost inevitably by noncommunist majorities. Thus, from 1945 to 1955, a large number of Soviet vetoes were cast in the Security Council to block the admission of new members supported by the United States. These abated only with the eventual admission of members from both major alliance blocs such as Albania, Bulgaria, Hungary, and Rumania, as well as Austria, Ireland, Italy, Japan, Portugal, and Spain. Since 1955, the organization has achieved its goal of global membership and nearly complete representation, including the Chinese People's Republic (since 1971), and the two German states (since 1973).

Even where the United States and the Soviet Union have found themselves in limited agreement in the United Nations, as they did in such cases as those of the establishment of Israel (1947–1949), the independence of Indonesia (1947–1949), and the Suez War (1956), antagonistic East-versus-West alignments eventually have recurred in these regions. Some of the more recent conflicts, such as the Sinai War of 1973 between Israel and Egypt, the bloody Lebanese civil war of 1976, and the protracted civil war in Nicaragua since 1984 have been largely kept out of the United Nations bodies, apparently by tacit consent of the great powers.

All things considered, East-West conflicts tended to increase in United Nations voting until the late 1960s. A careful study shows that in 1947 they dominated about 45 percent of votes in the Assembly; this rose to about 65 percent in 1961, and was expected to reach over 70 percent in the late 1960s. But with the period of the "cold war" gradually giving way to a period of peaceful coexistence between the United States and the Soviet Union, and the policy of *detente* evolving in the early 1970s, East-West conflicts have tended to decline somewhat in importance since then, and at least until the beginning of the 1980s. Conversely, in the earlier period, so-called "North-South" issues between developed and underdeveloped countries declined from about 20 percent of the Assembly votes in 1947 to about

12 percent in 1961, and were expected to fall below 10 percent in the late 1960s.[1] But in the 1970s and the 1980s, North-South issues again became somewhat more salient, and voting confrontations have become much more frequent between the countries of the highly industrialized West and those of the Third World.

The continuing bipolarity in terms of East-West issues has been accompanied, however, by a growing multipolarity of interests and of voting successes on the part of different voting blocs. More often than in the early years of the United Nations, the great powers now are finding it expedient to make alliances with special-interest blocs of lesser powers, by accommodating them on particular issues most salient to them. As a result Arab, African, and Soviet groups in recent years have been more often successful in the Assembly, and perhaps also in other organs of the United Nations.[2] To the extent that this has happened, the United Nations seemed to be moving toward a kind of two-party system in which the leading powers of the West and East blocs respectively must compete by offering concessions to lesser powers in order to hold their coalitions together and to attract needed additional support. Under such conditions the great powers can destroy the United Nations through rigid and closed-minded policies, or they can save the organization and develop it by increasing their powers of perceptiveness and flexibility. The emergence of a majority of smaller states—altogether there are now 157 United Nations members, besides the Soviet Union and the United States—and hence a multipolarity of interests in the decades since World War II have contributed to the loosening, and perhaps even the disintegration, of the major blocs in East and West. In the East, China and the Soviet Union became bitterly divided, and today, such communist-ruled countries as Rumania, North Korea, and reunited Vietnam try to describe themselves as "nonaligned." In the West, the European Economic Community is increasingly following a common foreign policy course more independent of, and at times even contrary to, the interests of the United States. And in the "Third World," the roughly 100 developing countries have formed an increasingly active majority in such bodies as the United Nations Conference on Trade and Development (UNCTAD) and hope to represent a "neutral bloc" of nonaligned countries that in effect form a major third power among the alliances of the East and the West.

North-South Issues in United Nations Politics

With the lessening of East-West tensions and conflicts in the United Nations, and that organization's growth in membership of non-Western countries, the ideological confrontation between the United States and the Soviet Union over issues of war and peace became less important on the agenda of United Nations activities in the 1970s. Similarly, conflicts between a market-oriented so-called "Free World," with countries almost all

[1]Hayward R. Alker, Jr., and Bruce M. Russett, *World Politics in the General Assembly* (New Haven: Yale University Press, 1965), pp. 134–137, 276–279, and 289–293.

[2]*Ibid.*, pp. 293–297.

rich in terms of average per-capita income, and the centrally planned economies of such large communist countries as the Soviet Union and the People's Republic of China, have also become less sharply focused. The communist camp has become increasingly divided between poor and relatively rich countries with the joining of such new members as Cuba, Vietnam, Ethiopia, Angola, and Mozambique, but the People's Republic of China and North Korea are also considered to be poorer countries. Economic contrasts also persist in many regions of the Western industrial countries such as Sicily, or Scotland. But the overall much larger division of the world into an underdeveloped "South" of humankind and the highly industrialized countries, noncommunist and communist alike, of the world's northern hemisphere has come to play an increasingly important role in world politics.

This change was reflected in the shift of the bulk of United Nations activities in the 1970s to such areas as economic development, technological regulation, and cultural and social coordination of the organization's worldwide programs. In the United Nations budget of 1983–1984, not even 5 percent were devoted to the security sector, whilse almost 35 percent were spent on socioeconomic activities. The promotion of social progress and better standards of life, as set down in the preamble to the Charter, for all members of the United Nations would require some redistribution of resources to be a major function of the United Nations in order to reduce the global inequality in wealth and income.

The gap between rich and poor is wide indeed. The poorest countries of the world such as India, the People's Republic of China, Bangladesh, Ethiopia, and Ghana were reaching an average annual per-capita income of not more than U.S. $440 in 1982, whilse the richest countries such as the United States and Switzerland had an average annual per-capita income of $13,160 and $17,000, respectively, in 1982; the oil exporting countries widened this gap even further with, for example, the United Arab Emirates reaching an average annual per-capita income of $25,000 in 1982.

In past decades, the general increase in world income has largely taken place in the industrial countries; and this inequality even increased again sharply in the early 1980s, with the industrial countries of the West, comprising about 20 percent of the world's population, taking over 70 percent of the world's income, and the less developed countries of the South, comprising about 80 percent of the world's population, receiving less than 15 percent. Similarly, differences in child mortality, life expectancy, literacy rates, access to elementary education, and other basic indicators of the standard of life are still very large today, although they are much smaller now than they were at the beginning of this century, or at the end of World War II.

The United Nations so far has been able to make only limited progress on these matters, and the global redistribution of resources has been one of its least successful functions. But being at best a rudimentary form of global government, it does not possess either the means of taxation or other forms of revenue production that would allow it to undertake large-scale programs; nor does it have the power to force national governments and the highly industrialized countries to give up their vested interests.

The international institutions developed to facilitate cooperation and compromise on these socioeconomic matters—such as the World Bank, the International Monetary Fund, the United Nations Development Program, and the General Agreement on Tariffs and Trade (GATT)—have been criticized by many developing countries as being dominated by Western capitalist interests, and as perpetuating in effect neocolonial relationships in the economic sphere. They have demanded instead the direct linking of trade to workable plans of economic development, and have voiced these demands repeatedly at the United Nations Conference on Trade and Development (UNCTAD), which meets in plenary session every four years since 1964 and maintains a permanent secretariat in Geneva to coordinate its activities with the GATT secretariat there. It is authorized to report to the Third-World-oriented and -dominated United Nations General Assembly, rather than to ECOSOC (which is dominated by the Western industrial countries), and comprises almost all countries of the world, and hence a majority of Third World and communist nations. UNCTAD and the "Group of 77" (with a membership of 120 developing countries by now) have been accused of vagueness and rhetoric in their demands, the best known of which is that for a "New International Economic Order" (NIEO), which is to be based on premises of economic justice and balanced planetary growth, and is designed to redistribute the wealth of the world economy in the direction of the poorer states.[3]

The Declaration and Action Program on the NIEO, adopted by the General Assembly in 1974, included demands for the preferential treatment of less developed countries in economic affairs (in order to repair damages done by Western industrialized countries in colonial and neocolonial times); greater official intervention and regulation in such areas as commodity prices, food stock-piling, investment codes, and financial and exchange rate policies; increased industrialization of the less developed countries; increased transfer of capital, investments, and technology to these countries; increased participation of developing countries in global services such as international transportation and communication; and an expansion of multilateral aid, with 7 percent of the gross national product of developed countries to be devoted to official development assistance (at the beginning of the 1980s, the actual percentages of the gross national product devoted to development assistance were 0.7 percent for the OECD countries, and 3.0 percent for the OPEC countries).

It is evident that the less developed countries lack the power to impose these far-reaching demands upon the unwilling industrialized states; and where the global economic system has undergone major changes, and reforms reflecting these demands were implemented, they were accepted by the industrial states because they realized that such reforms would

[3]See James H. Weaver, and Kenneth P. Jameson, *Economic Development: Competing Paradigms—Competing Parables*, DSP Occasional Paper No. 3 (Washington, D.C.: The Agency for International Development, 1978).

strengthen the whole international system and so benefit them, too. The hope remains that leaders of industrialized states will largely on their own accord choose the path of enlightened realism and adopt policies which, in the short run, do not maximize the advantages of the rich states but rather nurture and subsidize the struggling economies of the Third World.[4] However, the impact and results from such important nongovernmental initiatives as the "North-South Commission," chaired by the former West German chancellor Willy Brandt and including many prominent Western public figures as well as Third World statesmen, suggest that in spite of some substantial intellectual progress and wide recognition of the existence of a shared interest of humankind in the global improvement of social and economic conditions, actual progress is painfully slow, and the much-heralded "North-South dialogue" so far has not significantly altered the world system.[5]

The Key Position of the Secretary General

The changing position of the United Nations Secretary General will be one indicator of the direction in which the world organization will be moving; the universality of membership and representation in the United Nations may well be another. The first Secretary General, Trygve Lie of Norway, incurred the hostility of the Soviet Union in 1950 for favoring an interpretation of the United Nations charter which was substantively attractive but legally doubtful. Then (at the time of the North Korean attack on South Korea) Lie as Secretary General had accepted a crucial vote of the Security Council deputizing the United States, in effect, to resist the attack on behalf of the United Nations. But this vote had been taken in the absence of the Soviet delegate (who was then boycotting the meeting in protest against the nonrecognition of communist China); and thus, lacking the "concurring vote" of a permanent member of the Council, as prescribed in the charter, it was considered illegal not only by the Soviet Union, but by jurists in many countries, including some highly respected international lawyers in the United States.[6] At the time, the view of Lie and the Council majority prevailed. The Korean war was fought under the United Nations flag, and the North Korean attack was thwarted; the cease-fire and armistice of 1953–1954 left the territories of both North and South Korea substantially unchanged; and no Soviet delegate has been absent since then from a meeting

---

[4]See Richard E. Feinberg, *The Intemperate Zone: The Third World Challenge to U.S. Foreign Policy* (New York: Norton, 1983). For a summary of the reforms that were undertaken in the 1970s, see C. Fred Bergsten, "North-South Relations: A Candid Appraisal," in *Papers of C. Fred Bergsten, 1980* (Lexington, KY: Heath and Co., 1981). See also Joan E. Spero, *The Politics of International Economic Relations.*

[5]Willy Brandt *et al.*, *North-South: A Program for Survival* (Cambridge, MA: M.I.T. Press, 1980).

[6]For a good example of the controversy, see Leo Gross, "Voting in the Security Council: Abstention from Voting and Absence from Meetings," and Myres S. McDougal and Richard N. Gardner, "The Veto and the Charter: An Interpretation for Survival," *Yale Law Journal*, 60, no. 2 (February, 1951), pp. 209–257; 258–292.

of the Security Council. But at the end of his term, Trygve Lie was not acceptable to the Soviet Union for reelection.

Lie's successor, the Swede Dag Hammarskjold, was acceptable to all the great powers. During his term of office, the membership of the United Nations was greatly enlarged, and issues of rapid decolonization came to the fore, as did the use of United Nations forces to keep the peace in local conflicts. The first such force was used in the Gaza Strip between Egypt and Israel, from 1956 to 1967. A larger United Nations force, drawn from India, Ireland, Sweden, Yugoslavia, and a number of African nations, was used in 1960 in the Congo, where Hammarskjold lost his life in an airplane crash.

The third Secretary General, U Thant of Burma, was the first non-Westerner to become the chief executive officer of the world organization. As in the case of his predecessors, the degree of support which his recommendations in international disputes received from the great powers was limited indeed. The United States had turned down U Thant's repeated calls for a unilateral halt in its bombing of North Vietnam—a halt which he hoped might open the way (as he saw it) to an early cease-fire and to negotiations to settle the Vietnam conflict; nor had the government of North Vietnam made any effort to encourage a United Nations settlement of the conflict. United Nations mediation efforts in the Arab-Israeli conflict after the withdrawal of its peace-keeping force from the Gaza Strip in 1967 remained also unsuccessful; but a peace force stationed in Cyprus from 1964 to 1972 was able to intervene successfully in the conflict between the Greek and Turkish groups of Cyprus. During his two terms in office, the United Nations Treaty on the Non-Proliferation of Nuclear Weapons was also signed, but U Thant nevertheless announced publicly his fear that the world might well be on the way to World War III.

In the 1970s, the Middle East conflict continued to be in the fore of international politics and several United Nations debates, to which the Palestine Liberation Organization (PLO) was admitted in 1974; but a clear settlement of the conflict remained out of sight. The United States had withdrawn its forces entirely from Vietnam, Laos, Cambodia, and largely from Thailand by the mid-1970s, albeit more on its own accord than through United Nations intervention.

The new Secretary General, Kurt Waldheim of Austria, continued the conciliatory policies of Dag Hammarskjold and U Thant, but with limited success, and was repeatedly blamed for not backing one or another party in a dispute with sufficient vigor—for example, over such issues as South Africa's policy of *apartheid* and towards Namibia, or the repeated United States vetoes against the admission of reunited Vietnam to the United Nations until 1977. During Waldheim's terms in office, however, the United Nations began to address such significant and far-reaching global issues as the world's ecological preservation and the management of its natural resources at various conferences such as the World Conference on the Protection of Man's Environment in Stockholm in 1972, which was followed by the establishment of the United Nations Governing Council for Environmental Programs (UNEP), whose report on the state of the world was published in 1983. UNESCO also initiated two international research programs on "Man and the Environment" and "Man and the Biosphere." The United Nations Food Conference in Rome in 1974 was spurred by the decrease in world grain production in 1972—unprecedented since World War II—and several severe famines in the wake of worldwide droughts and floods; in consequence the International Fund for Agricultural Development (IFAD), a specialized agency within the United Nations system, was established in 1976. Also during Waldheim's term, the draft convention of the United Nations Law of the Sea Treaty was drawn up after eleven years of negotiations and eleven conferences. It was signed in 1984 by 151 states, even though not by the United States, the United Kingdom, and the Federal Republic of Germany. Controversy about Dr. Waldheim's full war-service in Hitler's armies surfaced only after his second term at the United Nations, but did not prevent him in 1986 from being elected president of Austria by a plurality of 46 percent of the votes. The new Secretary General, Javier Perez de Cuellar of Peru, coming into office in 1982, aroused less controversy and proved to be more active than his predecessor. Whether his efforts to settle the civil war in Central America through a kind of "shuttle diplomacy" will succeed, however, the future will have to show.

Issues for the Future: Membership and Tasks of the United Nations

In the mid-1980s, membership in the United Nations had become nearly universal, with 160 of the 178 nation-states of the world having become members of that organization. Since 1971, the government on the island of Taiwan is no longer recognized as the government of China, and the People's Republic on the Chinese mainland with its over 1 billion people now enjoys official United Nations recognition. In 1973, the two Germanys were admitted to the organization, and in 1977, reunited Vietnam became a member, and of the few remaining smaller countries outside the United Nations, countries such as Zimbabwe, Belize, and Brunei joined in the early 1980s. North Korea and South Korea, however, as well as the neutral countries of Liechtenstein, Monaco, and Switzerland have only observer status as nonmember states, but contribute financially and participate fully in many of the United Nations agencies.[7] Every Secretary General of the United Nations thus far has recommended the adoption of the principle of universality, according to which every government in effective control of a country ought to be a member of the United Nations. For a long time, the Western powers, and particularly an influential part of domestic opinion in the United States, have been extremely reluctant to recognize any communist regimes established after World War II. Only in 1955, several communist governments, Albania, Bulgaria, Hungary, and Rumania, were admit-

---

[7]The Swiss stayed outside the United Nations so as to protect their country's complete neutrality with its important implications for international finance and banking. In a plebiscite in early 1986, only half of the population cared to vote on whether their country should enter the United Nations; but of these, two-thirds staunchly rejected the idea.

ted to the United Nations, along with the anticommunist dictatorships of Spain and Portugal, and other countries of the Western bloc such as Ireland, Italy, and Japan.

Throughout the history of the United Nations, two themes can be traced: the search for centralizing power and the search for pluralistic communication and accommodation. Greater centralizing power would require strengthening majority rule, abolishing the great powers' vetoes, increasing the powers of the Secretary General, and widening the compulsory jurisdiction of the Permanent Court of International Justice. It also would require the development of a United Nations military force, and of United Nations powers of taxation. However, as long as the nations of the world are as different from one another as they are now, the nation exercising paramount influence in the United Nations, whether it happened to be the United States or any other, in effect would rule the world.

There is no realistic prospect that anything like this will happen in the near future. But there is a second way, suggested by the late Senator Arthur Vandenberg in 1945. It is to make the United Nations the town meeting of the world, where all issues can be brought out into the open, and where governments can learn how to manage differences of interest and ideology, and how to avoid head-on collisions. Here the United Nations also can help newly emerging nations to learn their new roles in world politics and to become, so to speak, "socialized" into the international system. In these respects, the United Nations since 1945 has been remarkably successful. If one recalls the bloody emergence of the Balkan nations in the nineteenth century, and contrasts it with the United Nations era since 1945, one may realize the difference. Never before in history have so many new nations emerged as now, with so relatively little loss of life (Nigeria's civil war in 1968 was a major tragic exception, and this was an intranational, not an international conflict.)

But at the same time, the platform of the United Nations and its affiliated organizations has been turned increasingly often into an instrument of political and psychological warfare. The Arab states have found the support of the newly active majorities of Third-World countries, aided by the Soviet bloc, for passing one-sided resolutions condemning Israel in the continuing conflicts stemming from the wars of 1967 and 1973. The result has been a vicious spiral: Israel's reluctance to return the Arab territories, conquered in 1967, is enhanced by the added fear for its existence which these resolutions generate.

United States policy in these matters has not been completely consistent. Secretaries of State from Henry Kissinger to George Shultz tried to find and promote compromise solutions, acceptable to both sides, but also tried to deny the Soviet Union any share or influence in any such Near East settlements, even though its consent may eventually prove to be necessary. In the 1970s, in protest against anti-Israeli resolutions, passed by UNESCO, the United States withheld its financial contributions to that organization and even left UNESCO in 1985 partly for that reason. However, much larger aid in money, and sometimes in weapons, is furnished by the United States to such Arab states as Egypt, Saudi Arabia, and the United Arab Emirates, by whom those resolutions had been actively promoted. Whether these complex and often secretive methods of negotiating with both sides would eventually produce a peaceful and stable settlement between Israel and her neighbors remains yet to be seen.

All these considerations show that a worldwide general-purpose organization is still far away. Even the United Nations is neither quite worldwide nor fully able to serve general purposes. It now includes almost all of the human population; but it is so limited in its actual tasks, resources, powers, and support that it cannot be called supranational, only international. It is at best the common servant of most of the major national governments in the world, and it is the master of none. Nor has it replaced all of them commonly in any one major political task or function. In order to find genuine *supranational* government (responsible for many or all major tasks of government and empowered to override the component governments on at least some matters of importance), or for the full-fledged delegation of at least some important task or function of government to an international organization, we must turn to particularistic international organizations.

18

Regional Organizations as a Path to Integration

Particularistic international organizations are usually limited in their domain to something vaguely called a "region"—that is, to a few countries united by some geographic, cultural, or historical associations, or by economic and financial ties, or by political liberal-mindedness and similarity of social institutions, or by some combination of all these. Experience in creating and developing such "regional" and/or "functional" associations, it has been hoped, may teach governments and peoples to appreciate the benefits of international integration, and to develop the integrative political habits and skills necessary to practice it successfully on a larger scale and for a broader range of tasks.

Quite a few such regional organizations are now in existence. Each of them deals with a small number of functions for a limited number of countries—usually not many more countries nor many more functions than the ones with which they started. Perhaps in the early stages of each such organization, a few countries and/or functions were added, and sometimes there were confident expectations of their continued growth. In fact, however, growth usually soon either stopped or slowed down greatly. Eventually each organization reached some kind of plateau on which it continued to function and survive (except for a few regional organizations which became dormant or defunct—such as, for example, the South-East Asia Treaty Organization [SEATO] in the late 1960s). Occasionally, some regional organizations later on entered again into another phase of growth in membership or scope, or both; and some regional organizations may achieve such phases of new growth again in the future.

Perhaps the largest and most important regional organizations were those formed after World War II in Western Europe. The *Organization for European Economic Cooperation* (OEEC) was founded in 1948 to provide a forum in which the plans for using the American Marshall Plan and for the national economic reconstruction and development of sixteen European nations could be coordinated. Its successor, the *Organization for Economic Cooperation and Development* (OECD), with twenty-five member states, is larger, and also includes the United States, Canada, and Japan, but its powers are limited to the making of studies and recommendations. OEEC and OECD are special-purpose organizations, limited to economic matters. Even thus limited, however, perhaps they have helped, together with other international organizations, to prepare the groundwork for successive reductions of tariff barriers among the world's industrial countries. In the late 1960s, the so-called "Kennedy Round" of negotiations brought about agreements to reduce these barriers on the average by about one-fourth of their original amounts; but in the 1970s and 1980s there were still intermittent disputes about trade matters between the United States and its European partners. Thus in the 1970s, United States pressures forced European automobile manufacturers to raise the prices of their small cars in the American market; Italy resorted to temporary trade limitations to protect the value of her currency; and in the 1980s, protectionist moves with regard to exports and imports of highly subsidized steel and foodstuffs from the Common Market have caused bitter resentment among competing groups. No sustained common monetary policy for all countries of the OECD, or even for Western Europe, was arrived at. Nor was there any concerted effort to stem the world-wide recession of the late 1970s and 1980s. From President Carter's efforts to use economic summits to tie together a "locomotive strategy" for lifting the world economy out of lingering recession to the monetary summit of February 1987 to stop the slide of the value of the dollar, all such efforts showed that a good deal of economic nationalism had remained alive.

THE NORTH ATLANTIC TREATY ORGANIZATION

An international body with a smaller domain but somewhat greater powers is the *North Atlantic Treaty Organization* (NATO) which comprises the United States, Canada, Britain, and thirteen continental European countries, including, since 1982, Spain. These include, however, some countries rather far from the Atlantic Ocean, such as Greece and Turkey.

The main concern of NATO is the coordination of military capabilities of its members, and hence the management of power. To some extent, therefore, it could become an organization serving general purposes. When it was founded in 1948, its main task was to coordinate the armed forces of its members in order to ward off any possible Soviet attack upon Western Europe, whether in the form of military invasion, escalating border conflicts, or Soviet-supported internal revolts. Its core was in a kind of exchange of military commitments. The United States promised to use its nuclear weapons (which then were still a United States monopoly) to protect its European allies; and these allies committed themselves to furnishing much of the troops and part of the conventional equipment, as well as the territorial bases and facilities, for the joint defense effort under a joint command.

In practice, this joint command was most responsive to the policies of the United States, which continued to control the main part of the nuclear "sword" of the alliance, and traditionally claims the chief office of the Supreme Allied Commander for Europe. At the same time, however, NATO provided the political and legal framework for the rearmament of Western Germany. By the late 1950s, the German Federal Republic had come to supply the largest single ingredient of NATO's "shield" of conventionally armed ground troops. A lesser but substantial contribution to both "sword" and "shield" has come from Britain, while France gradually withdrew her troops from NATO in 1966. The Organization was then compelled to remove its troops and installations from French soil, and to move its headquarters from Paris to a small town near Brussels, Belgium. But France has remained a member of the North Atlantic Treaty and takes part in NATO's planning and coordinating activities, and by the mid-1980s, French informal collaboration with NATO had improved again. In April 1986, a principal NATO ally, the United States, was officially denied the use of French airspace for the approach to Libya and the bombing of Tripoli, but this was technically not a NATO operation. Similar partial membership now exists still for Spain, which has not yet integrated its troops under NATO's Supreme Command, and Greece, which in 1985 withdrew from some of NATO's organizational bodies and military exercises on the grounds of NATO's allegedly preferential treatment of Turkey.

From the outset, NATO had considerable powers to plan, coordinate, and arrange agreements with its member governments for the deployment of troops, ships, and aircraft; to conduct maneuvers; to provide a common NATO command for the forces put at its disposal by its member nations; and to propose agreements to these members for the raising and upkeep of such forces. NATO has no power, however, to compel any country to provide the forces for which the Organization may ask. The target level of thirty divisions in Europe under NATO command, agreed on in the early 1950s, was surpassed only in 1982. In 1984, there were thirty-eight divisions under NATO command in Northern Europe, which many military observers saw as in need of further enlargement. During the years of NATO's existence since 1948, however, no European country has fallen under communist rule, or has been the victim of a major communist attack. In 1975, the anticommunist dictatorship of Portugal was overthrown by a communist-supported internal uprising—at least partly due to the long and unsuccessful colonial war in Africa by the previous regime—but the communists remained a minority at the margin of power, Portugal remained a NATO member, and by mid-1976 a government of Prime Minister Mario Soarez with a clearly noncommunist character had emerged from a general election. If a communist seizure of power anywhere in Western Europe had been quite unlikely to happen in any case, then the efforts put into NATO could have been put to better use elsewhere; but if it is believed that at some time between 1948 and 1968 intense Soviet pressure on a Western European country undefended by NATO would have been likely to occur, then NATO may claim some of the credit for having prevented it.

In any case, the likelihood of a direct Soviet attack on Western Europe has seemed remote since the late 1960s. Once the United States and the Soviet Union could inflict intolerable damage on each other, both governments seemed unlikely to choose a course leading to national suicide, and the credibility of their threats and promises of nuclear action declined. Indeed, after the Cuba crisis of 1962, NATO's European members grew less fearful of Soviet threats; and the Soviet occupation of Czechoslovakia in 1968 shook their attitude but did not reverse it. They still relied on United States nuclear protection—but expected it to be based on American self-interest rather than on any abstract commitment to the NATO alliance for its own sake.

Under these conditions, NATO as a primarily military alliance system was likely to decline somewhat in importance, unless it could be broadened in scope to include political and economic matters. In all these respects, moreover, the United States would have to become an ally more nearly equal to the others in letting itself be outvoted on occasion, and in subordinating its national judgment to the collective judgment of the community. In the years 1965–1968, the unilateral United States decision to run the worldwide risks of escalating the war in Vietnam, without the backing of a majority vote either in the United Nations or of its NATO allies, showed how far the United States still was from being fully integrated either in the United Nations or in the Atlantic Alliance. After the end of the Vietnam war, however, United States ties to NATO improved, and with the increase in the naval and military power of the Soviet Union in the 1970s, many Europeans gradually became more inclined to look upon membership in NATO as a reinsurance for their national independence. In 1976 the Italian Communist leader Enrico Berlinguer even stated that his party, if it should enter a government coalition in Italy, would support Italy's continued membership in NATO, but this suggestion drew highly negative reactions from the majority of Italian parties and from the governments of the German Federal Republic and of the United States.

With the decline of the era of *detente* in the late 1970s and early 1980s, and more confrontationalist moves on both sides of the alliances—but not in Western Europe, which continued to adhere to the policy orientation of *detente*—many people in Western Europe began to question again, as they had done in the 1950s, NATO's current military policy of "flexible response," envisaging the use of nuclear weapons in response to a nuclear as well as a *conventional* force attack by the Warsaw Pact. Criticism also came from former top members of the United States defense establishment.[1]

Opposition reached a new height over NATO's decision of December 1979 to deploy a new generation of "theater nuclear forces" (air-launched cruise and Pershing II missiles), capable of reaching most of European Russia and Moscow within minutes, in response to the Soviet deployment of a new generation of medium-range ballistic missiles, the SS-20. This decision, though taken collectively, was followed by a widespread Western European peace movement, demanding a nuclear-free and possibly neutralized zone in Western Europe. Though substantial, this opposition was eventually rejected by majorities on both sides of the Atlantic. European voters and governments remained unwilling to support a buildup of conventional forces in Europe to compensate for a possible dismissal of NATO's strategic nuclear option, and left the United States largely alone to implement its proposed massive defense buildup in order to counter any Soviet military threat unilaterally, if necessary. The INF Treaty to abolish such forces on both sides signed in December 1987 by the U.S. and the Soviets, would if ratified and carried out, make this whole situation more manageable.

Complaints about the imbalance of burden sharing within NATO, and thoughts about a reduction of U.S. troops stationed in Western Europe, however persist on the American side, while Western European doubts about the readiness of its major ally to risk nuclear annihilation in defending its allies and Western European territory similarly persist. But even so, the Alliance in the 1980s has withstood such disputes and tensions. It even may be passing to a new stage of more equality among its members, as well as the sharing of responsibilities in the task of collectively ensuring security and military stability in Western Europe.

With regard to other political and economic matters, NATO has also experienced disputes and minor conflicts among its members. But first and foremost, NATO is only a defense treaty against aggression from Eastern Europe. It does not obligate its members to support each other in any conflict outside the NATO area, such as the Persian Gulf, although this was strongly supported by the United States in the case of the Iranian hostage crisis in 1978, and the Soviet invasion of Afghanistan in 1979. Nor is it even a dependable instrument to maintain peace among its members. Greece and Turkey fought each other over Cyprus in 1967 and 1974, and by the mid-1980s the conflict was by no means resolved; and Iceland and Britain skirmished over fishing rights in 1972 and 1975, and temporarily broke diplomatic relations in 1976. But these minor conflicts have so far been successfully contained and prevented from escalating into serious wars; and the Alliance has withstood major cleavages over issues and crises arising among its members or in the general international arena.

In general, the prediction of psychologist Jerome Bruner in 1944 that the American people would not fully join an organization which they could not dominate still remained to be disproved more than thirty years later.

---

[1]See for example McGeorge Bundy, George F. Keenan, Robert S. McNamara, and Gerard Smith, "Nuclear Weapons and the Atlantic Alliance," *Foreign Affairs* 60 (Spring 1982), pp. 765–766.

They were loyal members of NATO, as it then stood (as they also were loyal members of the United Nations), but they expected their will to predominate. They were more inclined to ask what NATO and the United Nations could do for the United States, than what the United States could do for either of these organizations. Eventually, if NATO was not to decline, something more would be needed from the United States, as well as from the other members; and by late 1987 it was not at all clear whether this something more would be forthcoming. But if the United States seemed too large, too self-preoccupied, and too different from its Atlantic partners to merge its identity at any early date in any kind of Atlantic union, were not the countries of Western Europe smaller and in greater need of union? And were they not potentially more like-minded about what kind of integration they wanted, and how it was to be achieved?

EFFORTS AT UNIFYING WESTERN EUROPE: THE EEC COMPLEX

The years 1946 to 1949 saw the shaping of the basic ideas of unifying Europe which were to influence European politics for the next three decades. In September 1946, in a famous speech at Zurich, Sir Winston Churchill proposed for the ills of Europe a "remedy" which, as he said:

> ... if it were generally and spontaneously adopted, would, as if by a miracle, transform the whole scene, and would, in a few years, make all Europe, or the greater part of it, as free and happy as Switzerland is today.[2]

To Sir Winston, the nature of "this sovereign remedy" was clear: "We must build a kind of United States of Europe. ..." He seemed equally clear about the method. "The process," he said, "is simple. All that is needed is the resolve of hundreds of millions of men and women ..."[3]

Sir Winston's deceptively simple rhetoric was likely to appeal to four groups of experiences and aspirations which were widespread in the Europe of 1946. The first was security. The nations had failed to protect their peoples from the ravages of World War II, and a United Europe, it was hoped, would do better, and would also protect them from the apparent threat of communist expansion. The second was prosperity. Europe's national economies were damaged and impoverished by the war; and earlier, they had proved extremely vulnerable to the Great Depression of the 1930s. A United Europe, it was thought, would be economically more stable and more prosperous, perhaps soon attaining both the market size and the per-capita income level of the United States. The third issue was liberty and mobility. People had chafed for years under wartime rationing of goods

---

[2]Sir Winston Churchill, speech at Zurich, September 1946, reprinted in Andrew and Frances Boyd (eds.), *Western Union: A Study of the Trend Toward European Unity* (Washington: Public Affairs Press, 1949), p. 109.

[3]*Ibid.*

and under national restrictions on the movement of persons, goods, and capital, which had been intensified during the depression and the war. Many people now desired "a United Europe, throughout whose area the free movement of persons, ideas and goods is restored."[4] The fourth was power. The nation-states of Western Europe had visibly lost much of their power. Those which had had colonies had lost some of them and were likely soon to lose the rest; and no Western European nation in 1946–1948, except England, counted for much in international politics. A United Europe might restore to its peoples jointly much of the power, and perhaps some of the possessions, which they had separately lost.

Although these four considerations—security, prosperity, mobility, and power—appealed strongly to some and mildly to many throughout Western Europe, they never became an urgent concern of the mass of the people, or even of a bare majority, in any country. Against the event of attack, Western European security was protected by national alliances in principle, and by the United States in practice. Prosperity was restored by the economic reconstruction of the nation-states and national economies under the Marshall Plan (1948–1952), again with very substantial aid from the United States, and the economic depression of 1972–1976 proved worse in the large market of the United States than in the smaller markets of West Germany and Switzerland. Free mobility of persons and goods was never established, since it would have dismantled effectively the control of the national states over wages and price levels, tax and interest rates, employment levels, living standards, and the rate and direction of economic growth; and no supranational institutions were created to take over these tasks of control, much less to fulfill them in a manner responsive to the varying popular desires in each country. (However, passports and visas among Western European states gradually ceased to be required. European passports became available in 1985 to those who wanted them, and travel and tourism among them have increased to a spectacular extent.) Finally, the Western European countries did not regain their power during the next two decades, either jointly or severally. They lost most of the rest of their colonies, but found themselves more prosperous; and their peoples showed little inclination to make any sustained sacrifices for a new pursuit of empire or power, under either national or European auspices.

Nonetheless, modest advances were made in all four directions; and they were facilitated by the rise of a number of new European institutions which proved viable, even though other projected institutions failed and all European institutions had been conceived originally with more ambitious aims. From the outset, each of these European institutions had been intended to be *transitional*. Though limited to some specific task or function, and often to a particular group of European countries, each new institution was meant to create new needs for further integration and new political attitudes, interests, and habits facilitating further steps toward it. Eventu-

---

[4]"Message to Europeans," adopted at the Congress of Europe, The Hague, May 8–10, 1948; cited in A. H. Robertson, *European Institutions* (London: Stevens & Sons, Ltd., 1959), p. 11.

ally, so the "Europeans" among the West European leaders hoped, this integration would be one for general purposes, similar to that of a nation-state, federal or unitary. And it would eventually cover all of noncommunist Europe and even perhaps, so it was hoped, lure in time some of the currently communist-ruled East European countries away from the Soviet bloc and into Western Europe.

The major efforts toward European integration began with the *Treaty of Dunkirk* (March 1947) between France and Britain, which was a treaty of alliance and mutual assistance against any possible renewal of German aggression, but which also included a pledge of mutual cooperation in the general interests of the prosperity and economic security of the two countries. This was followed by the first announcement of the Marshall Plan in June 1947, the formation of the Committee on European Economic Cooperation by Britain, France, and fourteen other European countries in July 1947, and the signing of the *Convention on European Economic Cooperation* in April 1948.

In the meantime, Western governments had become alarmed by the formation in September 1947 of an international communist body, the *Cominform*, by the Communist parties of the Soviet Union and the other communist-ruled East European countries. This was followed in December 1947 by the proclamation of a communist-led "Provisional Democratic Government of Free Greece" (which eventually proved unsuccessful), and in February 1948 by a communist coup d'état in Czechoslovakia which established firm communist control in that country. One Western response to these events was in the form of two military agreements: the *Brussels Treaty*, a military alliance signed in March 1948 by Britain, France, and the "Benelux" countries (Belgium, Netherlands, and Luxembourg), and initially known as "Western European Union" (WEU); and the *North Atlantic Treaty*, signed in April 1949, which created the North Atlantic Treaty Organization (NATO).

STEPS TOWARD EUROPEAN FEDERALISM

In May 1949, the Statute of the *Council of Europe* (CE) was signed, providing for a Consultative Assembly, meeting in public (the so-called "European Parliament" at Strasbourg), and the Committee of Ministers, meeting in private. The Consultative Assembly until 1979 was composed of representatives elected by the national parliaments, or appointed by the governments of the twenty-one member states, but voting as individuals—which often means, in practice, along party lines. It was intended to be a sounding-board of European opinion, which it was also expected to help to formulate and lead; but its powers are limited to making recommendations (by majority vote) to the Committee of Ministers. The Committee of Ministers in turn can do no more than make recommendations (but only by unanimous vote of the Ministers or their Deputies, acting in each case as instructed representatives of their governments) to the member governments; and these national governments alone have the power to take any action. "European" opinion thus may at most propose, but each nation-state disposes.

In 1950, a *European Payments Union* (EPU) was established within the framework of OEEC. This was done to facilitate multilateral trade and financial transactions within the trading area of Western Europe and the sterling area, at least until such time as full convertibility of the currencies of a sufficient number of OEEC member nations could be achieved, so as to make EPU unnecessary. The setup worked as planned: EPU did facilitate multilateral European trade in the 1950s, and by the end of the decade had passed out of existence, after the main European currencies had become more or less freely convertible in the international money market. Whether EPU could have been used to prepare the groundwork for a common European currency (which was achieved only partly in the 1980s) is another question. In any event, all major governments (and, presumably, their peoples) then preferred to keep the control over their national currency (and hence much of their national economic life) as much as possible in their own hands; and EPU was dissolved.

In the spring of 1950, there was also launched (by the French Foreign Minister Robert Schuman) the *Schuman Plan* for pooling the control of the entire French and German production of coal and steel in a common market under a joint High Authority with executive powers, based on a deliberate transfer of sovereignty by the participating states; and this new organization was to be open to other European countries. The High Authority was to be responsible to a parliamentary assembly; legal matters were to be decided by a Court of Justice; and the national governments were to be represented by a Council of Ministers. Within its field of competence, the new organization was to be *supranational*—that is (according to our previous definition of the term), it was to supersede or override the decision-making powers of the national governments of the member countries. Its immediate political goal was to keep France safe from any possible revival of German nationalism and militarism in the course of German rearmament, plans for which had been in the making ever since NATO had come into existence, and which soon was to become more salient under the impact of the Korean War. Far beyond this, however, Schuman described his plan in May 1950 as "a first step in the direction of European federation"; and in August he expressed his confidence that "it will rapidly lead us on towards the complete economic and political unification of Europe."[5] By April 1951, a treaty creating the *European Coal and Steel Community* (ECSC) was signed by "the Six"—France, the German Federal Republic, Italy, and the three Benelux countries—and, duly ratified by all, it entered into force in July 1952. A third of a century later, in 1986, ECSC still existed, with some new responsibilities for allocating recession-caused cutbacks and the setting of minimum prices in steel and coal productions among its members, but it still received little or no power over oil, gas, and electricity.

Two months before the ESCS treaty, in May 1952, the foreign minis-

[5]Walter Hallstein, *United Europe: Challenge and Opportunity* (Cambridge, MA: Harvard University Press, 1962), pp. 11, 62.

ters of the Six had signed an even more far-reaching treaty (also proposed by France) which was to find them merging their armed forces in a *European Defense Community* (EDC) under a supranational authority similar to that provided by ECSC. This treaty was designed to permit German rearmament, but only within the framework of a European army. At the same time, however, it also would have replaced the French army (or rather the ensemble of French armed forces) by a European one, and thus eliminate France's military arm as a potential force in the national politics of its mother country. Large segments of the French right and left united in opposing this prospect. Although the other five member nations of the Six ratified the treaty, it was defeated, and the EDC project buried, in the French parliament in August 1954.

An even more ambitious draft treaty for a *European Community* (EC), which earlier had been called the *European Political Community*, or EPC, was worked out in 1953 by a European "ad hoc assembly" (composed of the ECSC Assembly with some additional French, German, and Italian delegates); but this draft treaty was never even signed by the governments of the Six, and it died stillborn.

European Functional Institutions

If European federalism ground to a halt in 1953–1954, at least European functionalism made some progress. A *European Productivity Agency* (EPA), a *Customs Cooperations Council* (CCC), a *European Conference of Ministers of Transport* (ECMT), and a *European Council for Nuclear Research* (CERN) were created in 1953; and a *European Civil Aviation Conference* (ECAC) came into existence in 1955. (A number of European organizations and their varied membership of states are shown in Fig. 8.)

In an attempt to compensate for the setbacks to European military and political unification, important efforts were launched for promoting European unity in economic matters, at least among the Six. In March 1957, their foreign ministers signed the *Treaty of Rome*, providing for a *European Economic Community* (EEC) and the gradual establishment of a *European Common Market* with the eventual free movement of goods, persons, services, and capital among their countries, to be achieved step-by-step over a period of twelve to fifteen years. At the same time, a second treaty was signed, establishing among the Six a *European Atomic Energy Community* (EURATOM), more far-reaching than CERN. Both treaties were quickly ratified, and EEC and EURATOM came into being on January 1, 1958. By 1967, the Common Market was, in legal terms, somewhat ahead of its original schedule: four-fifths of the tariffs among the Six on manufactured goods had been abolished, and agreements on the regulated production and marketing of an important range of agricultural products had been reached. Already by the mid-1970s, European public opinion had come to take the Common Market for granted. Within its limits, functionalism had been successful.

The nature and limits of this success deserve attention. For the first time in history, war within Western Europe is being looked upon by its

Rank of Countries	ECPT	ECAC	OECD (1)	ECMT	Council of Europe (6)	NATO (2)	CERN (5)	ESA	European Communities (3)	WEU	EFTA (4)	Rhine Commission	Nordic Council	Benelux	Out of 14 Possible Members
1. Belgium															12
2. Netherlands															12
3. France															11
4. Germany															11
5. United Kingdom															11
6. Italy															10
7. Denmark															10
8. Luxembourg															9
9. Norway															9
10. Sweden															9
11. Switzerland															9
12. Greece									(3)						8
13. Spain									(3)						8
14. Austria															7
15. Iceland															7
16. Ireland															7
17. Portugal									(3)						7
18. Turkey							(5)								6
19. Finland											(4)				5
20. Cyprus															3
21. Malta															2
22. Yugoslavia			(1)				(5)								1
Out of 22 Possible Members	21	20	19	19	20	14	13	11	10	7	6	6	5	3	

Out of 14 Possible Members: Belgium, Netherlands, France, Germany, United Kingdom, Italy, Denmark, Luxembourg, Norway, Sweden, Switzerland, Grece, Spain, Austria, Iceland, Ireland, Portugal, Turkey, Finland, Cyprus, Malta, Yugoslavia

Notes:

1. Also U.S.A., Canada, Japan, Australia, and New Zealand. Yugoslavia is a full member as regards economic policies, scientif and technical matters, agriculture and fisheries, technical assistance and productivity. Yugoslavia has observer status in other matters.
2. Also U.S.A. and Canada.
3. Turkey has associate status; Portugal and Spain became members in 1986.
4. Finland has associate status. The Convention has been extended to Liechtenstein.
5. Turkey and Yugoslavia have observer status.
6. Also Liechtenstein.

Abbreviations:

BENELUX	Belgium, Netherlands, and Luxembourg	EFTA	European Free Trade Association
CERN	European Organization for Nuclear Research	ESA	European Space Agency
ECAC	European Civil Aviation Conference	NATO	North Atlantic Treaty Organization
ECMT	European Conference of Ministers of Transport	OECD	Organization for Economic Co-operation and Development
ECPT	European Conference of Posts and Telecommunications	WEU	Western European Union

governments and peoples as illegitimate and improbable, and as not worth preparing for in any major way. In this sense, Western Europe has become a security community. It can still be threatened from without, but its population does not feel threatened from within by any of their Western European neighbors.

At the same time, Western Europe has remained politically pluralistic. A fear of social or class conflicts rather than of national ones, however, has remained alive, chiefly in the Mediterranean countries of Western Europe. Its states have retained almost all their sovereignty in political and military matters, a fact which President de Gaulle demonstrated in 1963 and again in 1967 when he vetoed Britain's attempt to enter the European Economic Community. Only after President de Gaulle's retirement did Britain join the EEC in 1973. Similarly, other countries have refused to let themselves be outvoted on important matters within the EEC and on a number of decisions concerning Common Market agricultural policies that would have been more unfavorable to some governments—such as those of the Federal Republic of Germany and Britain, and the interest groups and farm blocs they represented.

Today, in the late 1980s, Europe's currencies, its national economies, its labor markets, and its capital markets have not yet become one. To be sure, from 1913 to about 1957 there had been a trend toward the structural integration of the economic and social fabric of Western Europe, as shown by the growing proportions of cross-boundary trade, mail correspondence, travel, and university attendance within the area. After 1957–1958, however, this trend halted. The structural unification of Western Europe reached a plateau on which it stayed for more than a decade. Further increases in several major kinds of intra-EEC transactions since 1958 were no larger than could be accounted for by the effects of prosperity and random probability (or chance).[6]

If greater integration is to occur, a new generation might have to wield political influence; perhaps that generation that was of university age in 1948–1950, a time when the European drive was launched and unity was widely hoped for. In the mid-1980s there were at least a few signs of new efforts in this direction. Overall, the most significant advances were probably made in economic and trade matters. For example, negotiations in the GATT rounds are now undertaken by the EEC rather than individual national governments. In July 1978, a common currency system, the *European Currency Unit* (ECU), a "basket" of nine currencies (excluding the British pound sterling, as Britain has not yet joined the system) was established to facilitate stable exchange rates among its members as well as non-EEC currencies; an extensive credit system was created similar to the Special Drawing Rights of members of the IMF. Thus, some

[6]For data see Karl W. Deutsch, Lewis J. Edinger, Roy C. Macridis, Richard L. Merritt, *France, Germany and the Western Alliance* (New York: Scribner's, 1967), pp. 218–251, and Charles L. Taylor and David Jodice, *World Handbook of Political and Social Indicators*, 3rd. ed. (New Haven, CT: Yale Univ. Press, 1983), pp. 226–229; and for survey data on the attitudes of the very young, see Ronald Inglehart, "An End to European Integration?" *American Political Science Review* (March 1967), pp. 91–105.

of the goals have been fulfilled which the European Payments Union of 1950 had only aspired to then. But even this European currency system has not yet achieved complete European economic harmony in which member states could, for example, help to check inflation in other member countries. Further, there are as yet widely diverging political and fiscal approaches to exchange rate policies among the "monetarists," such as France and the Benelux countries, and the "fiscalists," led by the Federal Republic of Germany. The agrarian sector of the Common Market, for which a further currency unit, the *green* ECU (with a value usually 10 percent higher than that of ECU) was established, has in consequence been plagued by increased bureaucratic intervention and compensatory exchange payment problems for imports to the EEC. Nevertheless, these continued efforts at structural economic integration are significant. They show that the process of the integration of Western Europe is continuing, albeit with very slow progress.

The political integration of Western Europe has progressed at least in terms of institutional developments. Direct elections to the European Parliament, the Consultative Assembly, were agreed on after long negotiations; they were held in 1979 and 1984 among the ten member states, although with the somewhat discouraging participation rate of voters: in 1979, only about 60 percent of Europeans cared to vote, and in Britain, only 32 percent of the eligible voters went to the ballot boxes. The Parliament still has no substantial powers: it can help to initiate European legislation; it controls the EEC Council, the Committee of Ministers, and the special commissions (all of whom it can dismiss by a majority vote); and, perhaps most important, it can help determine and veto the EEC's annual budget. Over time it is hoped that its direct popular mandate will increase its prestige and authority, and that some real increase in power might then follow.

The Committee of Ministers, with its division of foreign policy and agriculture, has continued to be one of the central organs within the Community. The representatives of the national governments of member states decide on policy proposals made by the EEC Commission, which is responsible for overall planning and the coordination of policies within the EEC, and formally independent of national member governments. The Committee can veto or change the Commission's proposals, but their proposals in turn are still subject to the acceptance of their national governments. The divisional ministers of the Committee meet regularly to coordinate their policies and those of the European Council, which was established in 1974 and is responsible for the summit meetings of European heads of state at least three times annually in order to discuss questions outside the EEC's normal institutional competence. To date, the Council appears to have been relatively efficient in delegating problems and postponing them until the next meeting—particularly those concerning the Community's common agricultural policy, which in the mid-1980s was in desperate need of reform in the face of unrealistically high price guarantees and large-scale surplus production and storage problems. In 1986, for example, the EEC stored over 1 million tons of surplus butter and about 750 million tons of milk powder; productions of fruit, wine, and meat have had to be destroyed regularly or sold at prices far below production costs on the world market. Although the problems are glaring, reforms have repeatedly been resisted by such countries as Britain and the Federal Republic of Germany; for example, in 1985 these countries gave in to pressures from their farm lobbies and blocked effective reform measures suggested by the EEC Commission.

Nevertheless, there have also been moves towards increased cooperation and joint initiatives among the members of the EEC. The Community increasingly favors a common coherent and coordinated foreign policy orientation: the Community has favored initiatives in such areas as the Middle East, with the Near East declaration of 1973 supporting the Arab side in the Middle East conflict, and the "Euro-Arab dialogue" since 1975. In Latin America, the Community supports the negotiation efforts of the Contadora group and peaceful settlement of the civil war in Nicaragua. The Community also favors a common policy approach towards the government of South Africa to eliminate the system of *apartheid* there.

Furthermore, with such functionally oriented joint technological and research ventures as the research program EUREKA, the space rocket *Ariane,* and the joint development of aircraft, such as the *Airbus,* and military equipment, the European Community is gaining in prestige and a set of shared aspirations. Through these it is becoming increasingly independent from its major economic competitor, the United States. Overall, integrated and unified Europe has proved attractive and successful enough to attract associate members not only in its geographic vicinity—such as Algeria, Austria, Finland, Morocco, Portugal, Sweden, Switzerland, and Turkey—but also among some sixty African, Caribbean, and Pacific states under the Lome agreement of 1975; and trade agreements exist with such countries as Egypt, Iran, Pakistan, Mexico, Uruguay, Brazil, and Argentina. Thus, the EEC has become one of the largest economic powers in the world in the remarkably short period of time since the end of World War II. Although European unity has not been progressing swiftly like a river, it has moved slowly like a glacier—and it has kept moving.

OTHER EFFORTS AT REGIONAL INTEGRATION

Supranational integration elsewhere has remained weaker than in Western Europe. The *Organization of American States* (OAS), founded in 1948, successor to the Pan-American Union and heir to a tradition of inter-American sympathies (but also of some Latin-American misgivings and resentments of United States economic and political preponderance). Theoretically it has thirty-three member states, but Cuba has been de facto excluded, and the position of Nicaragua is precarious. It is far less integrated than Western Europe in terms of mutual transactions, popular loyalties, and effective institutions; today the OAS is primarily politically oriented towards the preservation of peace and security in the Americas, including mediation and arbitration efforts (with the use of sanctions to enforce its decisions) during conflicts among its members, and collective action against outside aggression. This, however, did not lead to OAS-intervention in such conflicts as the Falklands/Malvinas war between Argentina and Britain in 1982, or the United States invasion of Grenada in 1983.

The institutional framework of the OAS includes a General Assembly which since 1970 decides on the policies of the OAS, and the Council of Foreign Ministers which, according to the Rio Pact of 1947, convenes at the request of at least one member for consultations and, if necessary, intervention in military disputes. So far, however, there have been no major wars, and there are no major military confrontations among Latin American states—with the exception of Central America where civil war and foreign intervention have become intermingled. In South America, even the long-standing conflict between Argentina and Chile over the Beagle Canal at the southern tip of the continent was finally settled in 1984, with the mediating assistance of the Pope.

The *Arab League* has had predecessors in the Arab Congress of 1913 in Paris, the Arab Conference of 1937, and the Pact of the League of Arab States of 1943. The Arab League was founded in 1945 in Cairo as a loose unification of several Arab states, Egypt, Iraq, Jordan, Yemen, Lebanon, Saudi Arabia, Syria, and Palestine, which has been represented by the Palestine Liberation Organization (PLO) since 1976. Egypt was expelled from the League in 1979. To date the Arab League has no important supranational organs with important supranational functions, and, because of its complicated voting system with veto rights for every member, no substantial formal and institutional mechanisms for decision making exist.

The Arab League has united its member states in terms of a common heritage of language, culture, and (to a large extent) religion; common distrust of outside powers, Western as well as communist; and a common hostility to the state of Israel. Its central political aim since 1943 has been the recognition of Palestine as an independent state. Unity among its members began to crumble when President Anwar Sadat of Egypt launched a unilateral peace initiative, in the course of which the Camp David agreement was signed in September 1978, and the Egyptian-Israeli peace treaty followed in March 1979. In reaction, Egypt, the most populous and militarily strongest country in the League, was expelled from that Organization in 1979; a number of Arab States, Syria, Iraq, Libya, South Yemen, and the PLO, who saw their position in the conflict with Israel weakened, founded the "Panarabic Front for Steadfastness and Confrontation."

More conservative states such as Morocco, Jordan, and Saudi Arabia then had to show solidarity with the Arab cause against Israel; but their more constructively oriented "Peace Plans" for the Near East, the so-called Fahd-Plan of 1981 and the Charta of Fes of 1982, as well as their founding of the Gulf Cooperation Council in 1981 to ensure economic and political stability among its member countries have been unable to produce substantial results; there have been no other major initiatives launched recently.

Similarly, the existing links have also not sufficed to sustain major undertakings in other political and economic areas. The Arab League has lacked the power and influence to ensure an equitable distribution of oil revenues among the richer and poorer Arab countries. Nor has it been able to prevent the Arab states from experiencing major military setbacks in 1948, 1956, and 1967; the limited military success of Egypt and Syria against Israel in the brief Sinai War of 1973 was followed by a compromise cease-fire agreement. With the Egyptian-Israeli peace treaty of March 1979, Israel returned the Sinai peninsula to Egypt, and by mid-1986 only minor territorial adjustments and disputes remained to be settled between the two countries.

Nevertheless, developments on both sides may in the future again escalate into military confrontation. The policies of the conservative Likud government in Israel in the early 1980s—with the annexation of Jerusalem and the Golan Heights, the uncompromising claim on Judaea and Samaria, the bombing of an Iraqi atomic reactor in 1981, and the invasion of Lebanon in June 1982—all have increased and solidified Arab hostility toward the state of Israel. In Egypt, President Sadat was murdered in October 1981, and his successor, President Mubarak, has kept the peace, but with a conspicuous coolness toward Israel.

Other conflicts within and among Arab states have also been mounting. Since 1983, the PLO itself has been split into a more conservative faction under Yassir Arafat; Arafat negotiated for a time with King Hussein of Jordan, whose peace initiatives in the mid-1980s could have contributed to the settlement of conflicts; however Hussein discontinued talks with Arafat in 1986. While Arafat seemed willing to accept some compromise with Israel, a radical faction of the PLO under Abu Nidal, backed by Syria, has rejected any compromise and even negotiations with Israel; so far it is not at all clear which faction will eventually determine the policy course of the PLO.

Syria, as well as Libya and South Yemen, also supported Iran in the war with Iraq, which broke out after the Islamic revolutionary movement under the Ayatollah Khomeini had overthrown the regime of the Shah in Iran in 1979. The Arab League expressed its solidarity with the aggressor, Iraq, against the non-Arabic, Islamic government of Iran. But an end to the war, either by defeat of one side or through mediating efforts of the League, was by late 1987 not in sight. Thus the war continued, with its unrestricted methods of warfare—including the deliberate bombardment of civilian centers, the use of chemical weapons, and the recruitment of children to serve as troops in battle. The war even threatened to escalate when both countries began to attack international ships in the Persian Gulf in 1984 and thus endangered the flow of oil to the rest of the world. The United States in response offered air cover to the ships of friendly gulf-area nations, but at the request of the Gulf Cooperation Council eventually abstained from such intervention in the region.

Similarly, the drawn-out bloody civil war between Muslims and Christians in Lebanon has so far claimed tens of thousands of victims, and others have been killed in armed clashes between Shiite and Sunnite Moslem factions. In early 1987, the pro-Syrian groups of Palestinians and others in Lebanon were excelled in extremism by a Hezbollah party under Iranian influence whose adherents were involved in kidnappings of United States citizens and other acts of violence. When in February 1987, Syria sent 7000 of its own troops into Beirut, torn by unending civil war, this was widely regarded as a possible contribution to stability. Here, too, radicalization of the conflicts seems more likely than a peaceful settlement in the future. Direct outside intervention in the Near East, such as by the United States bombing of Tripoli in April 1986 in response to Libya's alleged support of international terrorist activities, are most likely to add further potential for escalation of these regional conflicts, as well as help to solidify the Arab front against Israel and those states supporting a compromise settlement. By late 1987, the Gulf war was nowhere close to being at an end, nor had the Palestinian question been settled in a satisfactory way. With such a multitude of conflict and further conflict potential in the region, among the members as well as with nonmembers of the Arab League, regional integration is at most at a rather early stage; and many of the positive links among the Arab states still have to be forged in the future.

The integration of the various countries of the *Soviet bloc* has remained less complete than the apparent strength of its two major regional organizations, the *Warsaw Pact* and the *Communist Organization for Economic Cooperation* (COMECON) would suggest. The Warsaw Pact was founded in 1955 officially as a response to West German rearmament and the establishment of NATO. The Pact was founded on the basis of existing friendship treaties and military assistance agreements between the Soviet Union and Eastern European states; its members include Bulgaria, the German Democratic Republic (since 1956), Poland, Rumania, the USSR, Czechoslovakia, and Hungary. Albania left the Pact in 1968. The Pact was established for the duration of thirty years, and was extended in 1985 for a further period of twenty years.

Officially, the Warsaw Pact is a defense treaty for immediate collective action against outside aggression, and for the maintenance of peace and security within the region. De facto, it also ensures that the communist system is maintained in the member states according to Soviet doctrine; the Soviet Union's effective monopoly on the Supreme Command of the Pact forces and in other important decision-making bodies, as well as its stationing of Soviet troops in the German Democratic Republic (GDR), Poland, Hungary, and Czechoslovakia indicate that its decisions can be backed up by military force if necessary. This has occurred repeatedly, for although warfare within the communist world would be considered illegitimate, bitter disputes with vehement mutual abuses, sometimes followed by direct military intervention, have been part of the history of the Warsaw Pact. Such was the case between the Soviet Union and Yugoslavia from 1948 to 1953, between the Soviet Union and communist China since the 1960s, and between the Soviet Union and Hungary in 1956—a conflict that was ended by the occupation of that country by the Red Army. Similarly, the dispute between the Soviet Union and Czechoslovakia in 1968 was ended by the occupation of the country—this time, however, Bulgaria and the GDR sent troops under Soviet command (an action in which Rumania refused to participate). In the 1970s, the exchanges between the People's Republic of China and Albania remained verbal, but communist China did not hesitate to invade communist Vietnam "punitively" in 1980 following that country's invasion of Cambodia in 1979. This Chinese action had no clearcut success, however, and the Vietnamese still were in Cambodia in late 1987.

The economic vehicle of Soviet bloc integration, COMECON, was founded in 1949 as the counterpart to the OECD. It has not developed, however, any supranational organs and has neither executive powers nor control over a common market. In the main, its members, Albania (until 1962), Bulgaria, Cuba (since 1972), the GDR, Mongolia, Poland, Rumania, Czechoslovakia, Hungary, the USSR, and, since 1978, Vietnam, coordinate their national economic policies through bilateral agreements. Their common aim is an international division of labor within their group, the joint development of infrastructure and transportation facilities, and increased technological and scientific exchange. Cooperation agreements exist with Finland, Iraq, Mexico, and Yugoslavia (an associate member since 1946); and other countries, such as Afghanistan, Ethiopia, Angola, the People's Republic of China (until 1966), Yemen, Laos, North Korea, Mozambique, and Nicaragua (since 1983) have or have had observer status. Its institutional organs are the Council, which has convened regularly since 1954, and a permanent executive committee, for whose decisions unanimous votes are no longer required since 1979, as well as several permanent commissions. Member states are obliged to consult each other in general economic matters; however, since the COMECON summit meeting of 1984, the Soviet Union has begun to emphasize its unilateral leadership again and has obliged its members to increase intra-COMECON trade at the expense of existing East-West trade relations.

Thus, at least for a time in recent decades both the Warsaw Pact and COMECON seemed to have become looser as the communist regimes in Poland, Czechoslovakia, and Rumania, became somewhat stronger and more confident (and as such countries as Yugoslavia and Albania left these regional organizations altogether). However, it has also become apparent that as instruments of control and pressure the Soviet Union will uphold the Pact and COMECON at almost any cost to keep its military and economic alliance in Eastern Europe stable and consolidated—and the USSR will certainly not shy away from repression of its allies' attempts at more national self-determination and independence.

Though reliable data are scarce on transactions among communist countries comparable to those on Western Europe, they suggest that a pluralism of nation-states has been persisting in the communist world. With the rise of a new generation in these countries, liberalism and nationalism may increase further below the surface of conformity. Governments will then have to choose between accommodation and repression. Whether such coercive measures will in the future be able to give cohesion to the region and eventually lead to substantial political, economic, and military integration among the Eastern European countries remains to be seen.

In any case, pressures for change are apt to continue in most Soviet-bloc countries and, in the period of leadership of Party Secretary Mikhail Gorbachev in 1986 and 1987, within the Soviet Union itself.

International initiatives toward limited liberalization in the Eastern bloc, such as those leading to the Helsinki Agreements of 1975, or the increased possibilities for ethnic and religious minorities as well as dissidents to emigrate from the Soviet Union, have added to these pressures. The susceptibility of national governments to such international pressure has generally remained below the level many Western countries had hoped for. When limited steps toward liberalization began in the Gorbachev era, they seem to have been due mainly to developments within the Soviet Union.

Supranational integration elsewhere in the world has progressed far more slowly and to a much more limited extent. In economic affairs, at least temporary integration appears to have been most successful in other regions of the world, although so far moves for substantial and structural integration have not followed. The *Organization of Petroleum Exporting Countries* (OPEC) was founded in 1960 to unify and coordinate members' petroleum policies and to safeguard their interests generally. Its thirteen member states in 1985 included Algeria, Ecuador, Indonesia, Iraq, Iran, Kuwait, Libya, Nigeria, Saudi Arabia, Venezuela, and the United Arab Emirates. These countries were producing some 30 percent of the world's petroleum at the beginning of 1983 (compared with 45 percent in 1980, and a peak of 55.5 percent in 1973), and were estimated to possess 67 percent of known petroleum reserves, and 32.8 percent of known natural gas reserves.

OPEC was most successful in collectively setting and controlling the world market price of oil in 1973, when the price of a barrel of oil was increased by 130 percent to 30 to 35 dollars and supplies drastically shortened. This caused major oil shortages and energy crises in the economies of the world and a massive transfer of wealth and investments to these oil-exporting countries. With the global economic recession of the mid-1970s and the implementation of at least rudimentary energy conservation programs by many advanced industrial states, the position of OPEC began to weaken: many of its members de facto broke the organization's price and production policies, and this trend continued when oil prices fell further in 1983 to a low point below $12. Consequently, the official price for a barrel of oil had to be lowered again and new production quotas and export limitations were agreed on, with a hoped-for target price of $17 to $18, though by early 1987 many of these policies were again broken by many of OPEC's member states. Thus, the organization seems to have shown only limited cohesion, cooperation, and integrative potential in times of economic recession and competition. Nevertheless, the collective income of its member states, though now reduced, is still a major factor and influence in the world's economy. Plans are underway for an OPEC Bank; OPEC's Fund for International Development—reaching over $8 billion in 1982, with another $890 million available for lending operations, a further $30 million for development assistance (extended primarily to Arab states), and additional payments of $425 million to the International Fund for Agricultural Development (IFAD)—is a major instrument of influence particularly in the Third World. It exceeded, for example, the amount of assistance aid given by the OECD countries by over 400 percent at the beginning of the

1980s. The lowering of the international value of the U.S. dollar by about 40 percent in 1986–1987 may have further reduced the purchasing power of many funds and revenues of OPEC countries.

In the Southern hemisphere, organizational efforts at regional cooperation, if not integration, have included the *Colombo Plan for Cooperative Economic and Social Development in Asia and the Pacific*. The Colombo Plan was initiated in 1950 by seven Commonwealth foreign ministers with the aim of raising the standard of living in Asia and the Pacific by means similar to those employed by the United States-funded Marshall Plan for the reconstruction of Western Europe in the mid-1940s and early 1950s. The Colombo Plan now has twenty-six member states, including such nonregional members as Canada, the United Kingdom, and, since 1951, the United States. Initially the Plan was rejected by many South Asian countries who suspected yet another colonial and imperialist venture by these major powers. The major powers have indeed become the major financial contributors; for example, Japan and the United States have contributed the most to the total of almost $3.5 billion given in bilateral assistance and over $590 million extended in technical assistance payments in 1984 to such countries as Bangladesh and India, who are the recipients of the largest amount of aid. There is, however, no centralized programming or a common fund to finance national development projects. And the major aims of the Colombo Plan—programs for increased technical cooperation and the transfer of intermediate technology, capital aid operations in support of national development plans, a drug advisory program, and the technical education of teachers and students from these regions—have had little in the appearance of neocolonialist ventures. Their contribution to greater regional integration efforts, however, has as yet remained limited and a shadow of the original plans as well.

The *Andean Group,* also known as the *Andean Subregional Group* or the *Andean Common Market,* was founded in 1969; it aims at a Latin American common market through intraregional liberalization of trade and the establishment of preferential trade arrangements, common tariffs, and the removal of tariff barriers. The Group has formally established supranational institutions with supranational executive powers over its members, which now include Bolivia, Ecuador, Colombia, Peru, and Venezuela. Chile left the Group in 1976. The Group's institutions include a Commission as the principal political organ, several councils, a Committee of Foreign Ministers, and, since 1979, a Latin American regional parliament and an Andean Judicial Tribunal, all of which are modeled on the institutions of the EEC. Structural integration of these Latin American countries has not advanced as far as in Western Europe yet; to date, the Group has been most successful in facilitating economic integration through a reduction of tariffs among its members as well as the coordination of exchange rate and currency policies. The Group's Reserve Fund, with initial capital of $240 million, is authorized to invest in the Andean Development Corporation, and is intended to help harmonize the exchange, monetary, and financial policies of the Group countries as well as assist member countries with balance-of-payments problems. By 1980, tariff reduction on manufactured goods traded between Colombia, Peru, and Venezuela was almost complete, although agreement on a common external tariff had not yet been reached. Since 1984, however, Colombia's import ban on goods from the Andean Group has practically halted efforts at an intraregional zone of preferential trade; intraregional trade, which had grown from $90 million in 1969 to $1.3 billion in 1982 (which was still less than 5 percent of their total foreign trade), has declined by about a third since then. Furthermore, to date the planned intraregional division of labor, the Group's industrial cooperation and development plans, and the common approach to capital investments by foreign companies under the Andean Foreign Investment Code of 1971 have not materialized or been sufficiently supported by the Latin American member states. Political differences have also threatened the operations of the Group. Bolivia almost withdrew in 1980 following criticism of its government by other members of the Group; Ecuador suspended its membership temporarily at the beginning of 1981 following border disputes with Peru. In general, however, the economic and institutional initiatives taken so far reflect the initial stages of economic and political integration of the EEC and may in the future generate more substantial political unification in the region.

The *Association of South-East Asian Nations* (ASEAN), founded in 1967 in Bangkok, is so far still a very loose regional organization aimed at accelerating economic growth, social progress, and cultural development in the region—thereby increasing its stability. Its members now include Brunei, Indonesia, Malaysia, the Philippines, Singapore, and Thailand, with Sri Lanka currently applying for membership. ASEAN has no major supranational institutions and has coordinated its activities chiefly through summit meetings and ministerial conferences. Special commissions have been established to coordinate moves toward preferential trade arrangements among its members (by 1982, however, only about 3 percent of the value of intra-ASEAN trade was acccounted for by preferentially traded items) and with such major trading partners as the European Economic Community and Japan. Special commissions also have been set up to facilitate joint action in international markets and to further the development of intraregional transportation and industrialization.

Since the end of the Indochina war and the emergence of reunited Vietnam—that is, Vietnam as a military power seeking to extend its influence over its neighboring countries and perhaps as far as Thailand—the ASEAN states have increasingly taken coordinated political and diplomatic initiatives. For example, ASEAN sponsored the United Nations Conference on Kampuchea in 1981 to counter this hegemonic pressure and to maintain and promote a "zone of peace, freedom and neutrality" in the region. ASEAN, however, was only designed as an economic and diplomatic forum, and a military alliance has never appeared feasible in achieving such goals. Such initiatives towards maintaining regional peace and stability, together with the area's economic potential, may well lead from economic and political cooperation to more substantial moves towards integration and unification, despite the region's geographic extension and disjointedness. A regional organization of smaller nation-states capable of balancing and offsetting the influence and interference of major powers such as the People's Republic of China and the Soviet Union in the vicinity of ASEAN may develop.

Regional, political, and linguistic differences and divisions have been major barriers to substantial political integration on the sub-Saharan continent of Africa. The *Organization of African Unity* (OAU) was founded in 1963 by the then thirty-two independent states of Africa after attempts at the establishment of a more integrated Union of African States (with plans for an African Military Command and an African Common Market) had failed in the late 1950s. The OAU now includes members from the forty-nine independent African states and the disputed state of Western Sahara; Morocco and Zaire left the Organization in 1984. The central aims of the OAU are: the promotion of unity and solidarity among African states; the furthering and coordination of efforts to improve living standards in Africa; the defense of the sovereignty, territorial integrity, and independence of African states; the eradication of all forms of colonialism and *apartheid* from Africa; and the promotion of international cooperation according to the principles of the United Nations Charter.

Relations among member states of OAU are to be based on the principles of sovereignty, noninterference in internal affairs of member states and hence in the status quo, the peaceful settlement of disputes, the condemnation of political subversion, dedication to the emancipation of dependent African territories, and a general international stance of political nonalignment. One of its principal organs to enforce these principles is the Assembly of Heads of States and Government, whose annual meetings define and coordinate the policies of the OAU; its resolutions require a two-thirds majority vote to be implemented. The Council of Ministers, composed of the foreign ministers or other designated representatives of all member states (who are, however, responsible only to the OAU), meets at least twice a year to confer on preparation for meetings of the Assembly, the implementation of its decisions, the budget of the organization, and matters of intra-African cooperation as well as general international policy.

In addition, there is a General Secretariat plus several specialized permanent commissions on such issues as economic affairs and defense matters. A Commission of Mediation, Conciliation, and Arbitration is to hear and settle disputes by peaceful means brought to it by the parties concerned, the Council, or the Assembly; however, each party to a dispute may refuse to submit to the jurisdiction of the Commission. The Commission's jurisdiction was accepted in the case of the Ogaden war in 1977, where the Commission reaffirmed the inviolability of colonial boundaries. The Coordinating Committee for the Liberation Movements of Africa provides financial and military aid to nationalist movements in dependent countries. So far, the OAU has supported such movements in Rhodesia (now Zimbabwe), Angola, and Namibia, and mandatory economic sanctions were imposed on South Africa in 1981 to persuade its government to negotiate on Namibia's independence.

Other activities of the OAU have included initiatives towards increased cooperation with the Arab League and Organization of Arab Petroleum Exporting Countries (OAPEC) on oil supplies and increased aid to African states. But political divisions over such issues as the OAU's support of the Arab League against Israel and Egypt, of Morocco and Polisario over the Sahrawi Arab Democratic Republic (Western Sahara) in 1982, and more recently the crisis in Chad have so far made progress towards integration in other areas slow at best. Repeated initiatives toward a joint African defense force have to date not materialized; but an African peace-keeping force, comprised of troops from Nigeria, Senegal, and Zaire, was active in the Chad conflict from 1981 to prevent the proposed merger of that country with Libya, press for the withdrawal of all foreign troops, and supervise elections to be held there. By 1987, however, neither the conflict in Western Sahara nor in Chad had been settled with the mediating efforts of the OAU.

In its political and mediation activities, the OAU is hindered by many of its principles legalizing political action that are difficult to reconcile with the realities of African politics. For example, the maintenance of the territorial status quo and hence of former colonial boundaries is often in conflict with the ethnic and geographic division of Africa. Its opposition to political subversion and commitment to the principle of nonintervention makes it almost impossible for the OAU to deal with the frequent attempts by outside powers to support or bring about coups in its member states; nor can the OAU deal with outright foreign military intervention, as in the case of French and Belgian paratroop operations in Zaire, and Cuban and Soviet intervention in Angola in the mid-1970s. The existence of 40,000 Cuban troops and 11,000 French troops on African soil at that time exemplified a major problem of African states and the OAU: how to rid the continent of foreign influence while allowing a member state to exercise its sovereignty by calling upon external support for defensive purposes. Controversies have also existed on the tolerance and recognition of governments brought to power by mercenaries as well as such actions among member states as Tanzania's intervention in Uganda and the overthrow of its dictator, Idi Amin.

Disagreements exist also on the general international political orientation of the OAU, although there have been moves towards following initiatives taken by the Movement of Nonaligned Countries. For example, a Pan-African News Agency (PANA) was founded in 1979 to become more independent of the dominating influence of Western news media; and in 1981 the OAU Ministers of Justice approved the establishment of an African Charter on Human and People's Rights with an African Commission to investigate violations of human rights; the Charter is, however, still subject to ratification by a majority of OAU members.

To date, the OAU is the most conspicuous result of the search for unity among the emerging states of Africa; but its major function so far has been to serve as a sounding board for African opinion on the problems of colonialism, racial discrimination, and foreign economic, political, and military intervention in Africa. Being still occupied with settling the problems arising from its colonial past, the OAU has as yet far to go to develop an integrative momentum towards future African unity and integration in such important fields as economic affairs, the maintenance of regional peace and stability, and an effective political representation in the world political arena. Further development of this regional organization seems likely to occur in the decades to come.

The *Movement of Nonaligned Countries* has developed geopolitical perspectives on several important fields of international relations, but has lagged behind in developing substantial integrative organizational and institutional structures to allow for a more coherent supranational organization to take part in international debates. The Movement as yet has no formal organization, having emerged gradually from the Afro-Asian Solidarity Conference in Bandung, Indonesia, in 1955 and the meeting in 1956 of three statesmen of nonaligned countries: President Nasser of Egypt, President Nehru of India, and President Tito of Yugoslavia. Membership in the Movement grew from 25 member states at the first summit conference in Belgrade in 1961 to 101 member states, 18 observer states, and 25 participating "liberation movements" and international governmental as well as nongovernmental organizations at the conference in New Delhi, in 1983.

Within the Movement, the "Group of 77" represents the economic interests of to date 124 developing countries; it was founded in 1964 on the occasion of the first United Nations Conference on Trade and Development. Another major group within the Movement is that of the neutral and nonaligned states of Europe that has been in existence since the Helsinki Conference on Security and Cooperation in Europe. The central political aims of these nonaligned countries are: the promotion of equality among the world's nation-states and the upholding of the principle of peaceful coexistence; demands for an end to all forms of colonialism, racism, and imperialism; a New International Economic Order (NIEO);[7] and complete disarmament with the redistribution of defense expenditures to development assistance. The Movement opposes any bloc formation or form of political or military alliance which it sees as endangering international peace and stability.

The Movement has no formal institutional structure. Policy formulation and coordination usually take place at summit conferences and at the annual ministerial meetings to prepare joint action in the United Nations General Assembly. A coordinating bureau in New York regularly organizes meetings at the level of United Nations ambassadors. If the Movement has so far advanced little beyond a forum for discussion and a sounding board for the grievances and demands of the world's smaller and underprivileged nation-states, it has nevertheless shown limited capacities to develop a unify-

[7]See pp. 000–000.

ing ideology and political orientation with which diverse countries from different regions of the world have been able to identify, and have supported in consequence. If much of this support has remained rhetorical or vague, it still does exemplify that efforts at integration and unification of nation-states with similar economic, political, social, and military interests had by the late 1980s become worldwide and world-spanning phenomena.[8]

[8]For more detailed discussions of international governmental and nongovernmental organizations, see Union of International Associations (eds.), *Yearbook of International Organizations 1985/1986,* (New York: C. K. Saur, 1985); *The Europa Yearbook 1985: A World Survey.* Vol. 1: *International Organizations* (London: Europa Publications, 1985); and S. J. Tisch and L. L. Humphrey, "Inter-governmental Organizations," in A. S. Banks (ed.), *Political Handbook of the World: 1983* (New York: McGraw-Hill, 1983), pp. 577–728.

19
Attaining and Maintaining Integration

International organizations have often been seen as the best pathway for leading humanity out of the era of the nation-state. Beyond the actual international organizations which now exist, or have existed, there are the great projects for Atlantic Union or for Federal World Government which still promise much for supranational integration, if they could only get started. Against these visions of the future, it is worthwhile to consider the experiences of the past. What have been some of the actual cases of political integration, and what can be learned from them?

There are perhaps four dozen cases of political integration in the world from which something could be learned fairly directly that might help us better to deal with our similar present-day problems. Fourteen of these cases—ten from earlier history and four relatively recent ones—have been studied for the explicit purpose of making such comparisons to our contemporary problems, and some of the findings of these studies are worth summarizing here.[1]

[1]The historical studies dealt with the cases of successful integration of England; England and Wales; England and Scotland; the United States; Germany; Italy; and Switzerland; and with the failures of integration of Norway and Sweden; England and Ireland; and the Austro-Hungarian monarchy. The recent cases studied included the successes of the Nordic Council and of the European Economic Community, and the failures of the Federation of the West Indies and of the United Arab Republic. For details see K. W. Deutsch, S. A. Burrell *et al.*, *Political Community and the North Atlantic Area* (Princeton: Princeton University Press, 1957, 1968), and Amitai Etzioni, *Political Unification* (New York: Holt, Rinehart & Winston, 1965).

The main *tasks of integration* can be conveniently recalled under four headings: (1) maintaining peace; (2) attaining greater multipurpose capabilities; (3) accomplishing some specific task; and (4) gaining a new self-image and role identity.

All these tasks are operationally testable. Whether stable expectations of *peace* are being maintained within a community can be tested by the absence or paucity of specific preparation for war among the political units, regions, and populations within it. Evidence can be found in data on the deployment of troops, weapons, and military installations; in diplomatic records and in budgetary data; and in opinion data on the elite and mass levels. Whether a community has achieved greater *multipurpose capabilities* would be indicated at least roughly by its total gross national product, its per-capita GNP, and the scope and diversity of its current undertakings. Whether the community was fufilling *specific tasks* would be indicated by the existence, and perhaps by the growth, of appropriate joint functions, joint institutions, and joint resources and sacrifices devoted to these specific ends. Finally, whether the members of the community had attained a new *role identity*, or were in the process of attaining it, would be shown by the frequency of use of common symbols, and by the creation and wide adoption of new ones; by data on relevant elite and mass attitudes; and by relevant aggregate data on the actual behavior of the population, including popular acceptance of unrequired transfers of wealth or other benefits within the community, and of some degree of sharing benefits and burdens within it.

Whether the tasks envisaged for integration can in fact be fulfilled, and whether integration will succeed or fail, depends in part on the *background conditions* prevailing within and among the political units to be integrated. The conditions of integration can again be stated under four headings: (1) mutual relevance of the units to one another; (2) compatibility of values and some actual joint rewards; (3) mutual responsiveness; and (4) some degree of generalized common identity or loyalty. These four conditions interact and may strengthen one another, but in principle each can be verified separately.

Mutual relevance among the units is indicated by the relative volume and weight of transactions among them, such as trade, travel, and mail and other communications; by the extent to which such transactions exceed the levels which could be expected from mere chance and the size of the participating units; and by the extent of covariance between their effects on any two different participating political units.

The existence and extent of *joint rewards* for the partners in the prospective larger community can be attested to by the extent of the *positive* covariance of rewards for two or more of them, so that a reward for one is associated with the significant probability of a reward for the other.

The conditions for *mutual responsiveness* include the presence of significant capabilities and resources for communication, perception, and self-steering. A separate source of evidence consists in the actual performance in terms of speed, adequacy, and probability of responsive behavior.

Finally, *common generalized loyalty* can be indicated by the frequency and saliency of perceptions of joint interests, both in terms of distributions of attention and of parallel expectations of reward, as shown by survey data and by the content analysis of mass media and government communications. Another indication would be the objective compatibility or consonance of the major values of the participating populations, permitting cooperation among them to be perceived as legitimate. This could be supplemented by indications of common subjective feelings of the legitimacy of the integrated community, making loyalty to it also a matter of internalized psychic compulsion.

The goals and conditions of integration go far to determine the *processes and instruments* by which integration is approached. Once more, we can organize these instruments under four headings, as processes and techniques of: (1) value production; (2) value allocation; (3) coercion; and (4) identification. *Value production* and *value allocation* refer, respectively, to the production (or acquisition) and the allocation of goods, services, or relationships valued by the populations concerned. *Coercion* means primarily military or other enforcement; and *identification* means the deliberate promotion of processes and sentiments of mutual identification, loyalties, and "we"-feelings.

TYPES OF COMMUNITIES: AMALGAMATION VS. PLURALISM

The Process of Establishing an Amalgamated Security Community

If the main goal of integration is not only the preservation of peace among the integrated political units, but also the acquisition of greater power for general or specific purposes, or the acquisition of a common role identity, or some combination of all these, then a so-called *amalgamated political community* with a common government is likely to be preferred. If the main aim is peace, then a *pluralistic security community* may suffice, and in fact may be easier to attain.

An amalgamated community may also be an *amalgamated security community*, within which dependable expectations of peaceful change prevail, as attested by the absence of substantial specific preparations for large-scale warfare within it. Any reasonably well-integrated nation-state—such as Britain and the United States each were in 1986—is such an amalgamated security community—even though local violence among racial groups in American cities increased dramatically in the 1960s and erupted again sporadically in the 1970s, and even though such minority groups as the Welsh are striving for more cultural and social independence from British dominance in the United Kingdom by at times violent means. In both countries, however, these developments thus far have remained far short of civil war. But neither a common government nor common laws and institutions can ensure such internal peace and security to a country on the verge of civil war, such as the United States was in 1860–1861, India-Pakistan in 1946–1947, Nigeria in 1967, and perhaps Northern Ireland in the 1970s and 1980s. Indeed the very effort to maintain the amalgamated community or political union by force may bring on exactly that large-scale warfare which a security community was intended to prevent. The possible relationships between amalgamated communities and security communities are shown in Fig. 9.

The significance of these relationships is changing. Whereas large-scale civil wars and bloodshed could in the past be survived by the bulk of the warring population because they were waged with weapons of rather limited destructive potential, today the masses of those involved (and perhaps all humans) could be wiped out in a nuclear civil war fought on a fairly small scale. Accordingly, as the power of weapons has increased, the preserving of peace, and peaceful change and adjustment of conflicts, have become more important; unification for general-purpose power or for a sense of greater group prestige and identity has become less important. Similarly, as the legal distinction between international war and civil war has become less relevant, amalgamated but not integrated political communities have become more dangerous.

Though now more dangerous in case of failure, an amalgamated security community still will continue to look more desirable than its alternates, for if it succeeds, it will not only preserve peace but will provide greater strength for accomplishing both general and specific governmental services and purposes, and possibly a larger sense of identity and psychic reassurance for the elites and masses of its population. But though more desirable, like most better things, it will be harder to attain and keep.

Essential background conditions.   One study[2] lists twelve social and economic background conditions, within and among the participating units, which seem to be *necessary* (though perhaps not sufficient) if an amalgamated security community is to succeed:

1. Mutual compatibility of the main values relevant for political behavior
2. A distinctive and attractive way of life
3. Expectations of stronger and rewarding economic ties or joint rewards
4. A marked increase in the political and administrative capabilities of at least some of the participating units
5. Superior economic growth of at least some participating units (as compared to neighboring territories outside the area of prospective integration)
6. Some substantial unbroken links of social communication across the mutual boundaries of the territories to be integrated, and across the barriers of some of the major social strata within them
7. A broadening of the political elite within at least some political units, and for the emerging larger community as a whole
8. Relatively high geographic and social mobility of persons, at least among the politically relevant strata

[2]Deutsch, Burrell *et al., Political Community,* p. 58.

Figure 9   Political Amalgamation, Pluralism, and Security: Four Possible Patterns of Political Community

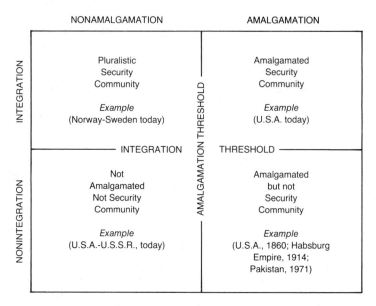

Note: All four cases involve a high degree of mutual relevance and, therefore, some degree of political unity. In each case, the countries, peoples, and governments concerned must take into account each other's behavior in making their own political decisions.
Source: Karl W. Deutsch, Sidney A. Burrell, *et al., Political Community and the North Atlantic Area: International Organization in the Light of Historical Experience* (Princeton: Princeton University Press, 1957, 1968), p. 7. Reprinted by permission of Princeton University Press.

9. Multiplicity of the scope of the flow of mutual communications and transactions

10. Some overall compensation of rewards in the flows of communications and transactions among the units to be integrated

11. A significant frequency of some interchange in group roles (such as being in a majority or a minority, benefactor or beneficiary, initiator or respondent) among the political units

12. Considerable mutual predictability of behavior.

Together, these background conditions provide much of the indispensable social, economic, and psychological environment for the more well-known political conditions for an amalgamated security community, which consist mainly in the willingness and ability of the preponderance of the politically relevant strata in all participating political units to:

1. Accept and support common governmental institutions

2. Extend generalized political loyalty to them and to the preservation of the amalgamated community

3. Operate these common institutions with adequate mutual attention and responsiveness to the messages and needs of all participating units.

Even if it has been established, an amalgamated security community, such as a federation or an empire, often is highly vulnerable to civil conflict or secession. Any one of half a dozen conditions is likely to make for its *disintegration:*

1. Any steep increase in economic, military, or political burdens on the community or on any participating unit (particularly if this increase in burdens comes at an early stage, before integration has become consolidated by the learning of deep political loyalties and habits)

2. A rapid increase in social mobilization and political participation, faster than the process of civic assimilation to the common political culture of the community.

3. A rapid increase in regional, economic, cultural, social, linguistic, or ethnic differentiation, faster and stronger than any compensating integrative process

4. A serious lag or decline in the political or administrative institutions and capabilities of the government and the political elite, relative to the current tasks and burdens with which they have to cope

5. A relative closure of the political elite, slowing drastically the entry of new members and ideas, and giving rise to hostile counterelites of frustrated potential elite members

6. A failure of the government and the elite to carry out in time needed reforms and adjustments wanted or expected by the population (and perhaps already demonstrated in some salient areas abroad); or failure to adjust in time to the imminent decline or loss of some privileged or dominant minority position (such as the position of the white minority in the former Federation of Rhodesia and Nyasaland).

The process of integration.   Amalgamated security communities, such as nation-states or federations, are not like organisms. They do not come into existence by a process of growth through a fixed sequence of stages, similar to the way in which a tadpole develops into a frog, or a kitten grows to be a cat. Rather, integration resembles an *assembly-line process.* Integrated communities are assembled in all their essential elements and aspects in the course of history, somewhat as an automobile is put together. It matters little for the performance of the finished car in what sequence each part is added, so long as all its necessary elements eventually are incorporated. Certain characteristics of the process of integration, however, have been observed in many past cases; and they will be worth watching for in present and future ones.

The process of integration often begins around a *core area* consisting of one or a few political units which are stronger, more highly developed, and in some significant respects more advanced and attractive than the rest. The governments and political elites of such potential core areas of a prospective larger political system then often act as active leaders, unifiers, or (in Etzioni's term) "elite" for the emerging integrated political system. England played this role in the British Isles; Piedmont did so in the unification of Italy, and Prussia in that of Germany; and Massachusetts, Virginia, Pennsylvania, and New York did so jointly in the integration of the thirteen American colonies into the United States.

Early in the course of the integrative process, a psychological "no-war" community often also develops. War among the prospective partners comes to be considered as illegitimate; serious preparations for it no longer command popular support; and even if some of the prospective partner countries find themselves on opposite sides in some larger international conflict, they conduct themselves so as to keep actual mutual hostilities and damage to a minimum—or else refuse to fight each other altogether. A virtual "no-serious-war" community of this kind emerged among the Swiss Cantons in the sixteenth century; among the Italian states since the mid-eighteenth century; among the American states since 1775; and among the German states since the mid-nineteenth century; and it may have emerged since 1950 among the EEC countries despite many memories of past wars among them.

Often also the most salient political divisions within the emerging amalgamated security community become weaker, and—still more important—they shift away from the boundaries of the participating units. Political life then becomes dominated by divisions cutting across the original political units and regions. The more varied and salient these mutually *cross-cutting divisions* are, the better for the acceptability of the emerging union. The history of such cross-cutting alignments of political parties, religions, and economic interests (all supplementing, modifying, and partly overriding the old ties to the original units and regions) can be traced in the history of the unification of Britain, Switzerland, Italy, Germany, and the United States.

Conversely, where cleavages among regions and political units are paralleled and reinforced by old or new cleavages of language, religion, ideology, economic interest, and social class, there integration is likely to be halted or reversed. This happened between Britain and most of Ireland; among the various parts of the Austro-Hungarian monarchy; and temporarily between the North and South in the United States. In each case, the amalgamated security community collapsed—only temporarily in the United States, but (so far) permanently in the other cases.

Finally, in the successful cases of integration by political amalgamation, the main cross-regional political factions or parties stood for something new. They were identified with one or several *major cross-regional innovations* which were both important and attractive at that place and time. The Reformation and the reforms of the Tudor kings both played a major part in the integration of England and Wales, and so did the reforms of the Whigs (and their substantial acceptance by the Tories) in the unification of England and Scotland. Liberals and Liberalism played a similar part in the unifications of Switzerland, Italy, and Germany in the nineteenth century, often aided by the acceptance and sponsorship of important reforms and innovations by enlightened conservatives such as Cavour and Bismarck. The United States were unified with the aid of the American Revolution, and both Hamilton's Federalists and Jefferson's Democratic Republicans stood for major (and in part unprecedented) innovations. By contrast, this element of major cross-regional innovation was weaker in the English-Irish Union of 1801; in the Habsburg monarchy after 1810; and in the Norwegian-Swedish Union after 1814; and all these unions eventually were dissolved.

The issue of functionalism as a path to integration. In contrast to these major aspects of the process, the much-debated issue of *functionalism* turns out to be much less important. Functionalism, we recall, means partial amalgamation. It works in this way: some specific tasks are handed over by the participating governments to some common agency. But these tasks are not very important and so usually do not transfer enough general-purpose power to the new agency to allow it to be, even "in effect," capable of any act requiring overall amalgamation. Thus, most of the time, it must settle for partial, or functional amalgamation. Such functional amalgamation sometimes *has* led step by step to overall amalgamation. This happened, for instance, in such cases as those of the German Customs Union in the nineteenth century, the common administration of the Western lands by the United States under the Articles of Confederation (1781–1791), and the Swiss Cantons since the late fourteenth and early fifteenth centuries; and between England and Wales and England and Scotland, preceding full amalgamation in each case.

On the other hand, Italy was unified without any significant preceding functional amalgamation; and the presence of functional amalgamation did not keep the Norwegian-Swedish Union from dissolving. Moreover, although a period of functional amalgamation preceded full amalgamation in the cases of England and Ireland, and of Austria, Bohemia, and Hungary, these amalgamated communities ultimately failed.

Functionalism and functional arrangements, we may conclude, have little effect by themselves upon the eventual success or failure of efforts to establish amalgamated security communities. The outcome in each case is most likely to depend on other conditions and processes, particularly on how rewarding or unrewarding were the experiences associated with functional arrangements. The most that can be said for functionalism is that it avoids the perils of premature overall amalgamation, and that it gives the participating governments, elites, and peoples more time gradually to learn the habits and skills of more far-reaching, stable, and rewarding integration.

The politics of integration: leaders and issues. As a political process, integration has a *takeoff point* in time, when it is no longer a matter of a few prophets or scattered and powerless supporters, but turns into a larger and more coordinated movement with some significant power behind it. Before takeoff a proposal for integration is a theory; after takeoff it is a force.

Such larger unification movements may aim mainly at peace, and hence at integration based upon consent to peaceful change and conflict management; or they may aim mainly at power for specific ends, or for general purposes, and hence at amalgamation which may also be accomplished by conquest or coercion. Often, indeed, political unification movements have been broad coalitions, some of whose supporters have chiefly cared for internal peace while others have wanted most of all collective power through this larger union; and still others have wanted both.

To become acute, the basic issue of integration must become salient to substantial interest groups and to large numbers of people. In the historic cases studied, this happened usually in the course of a threefold process of habit breaking. First and most important, a new and attractive *way of life* had to emerge, with common expectations for more good things to come and with enough experiences of recent improvements over the past, or over the standards of neighboring areas, so as to make these common expectations credible and to give the populations and political elites concerned at least some latent sense of unity of outlook and interests. Second, this latent sense of unity had to be aroused by some *external challenge* which clearly required some new and joint response. And third, a *new generation* had to arrive on the political scene, taking the earlier degree of common interest and outlook for granted, and ready to treat it as the starting point for new political actions. The third of these events, the arrival of a new generation in politics, is highly probable, since it occurs roughly every fifteen years. The second, the impact of some external challenge, is also rather probable, since fairly substantial political and economic challenges are likely to occur in a fast-changing world at least every twenty to twenty-five years, if not more often. Only the first process is improbable. It is the emergence of a rewarding new way of life, and with it, of a latent sense of unity and common interest in defending or extending it; and in most parts of the world this happens at most once in several generations.

Once this improbable combination of events occurs, political leadership toward unification usually is provided not by a single social class but by a *cross-class coalition*. Typically, such a coalition in our historical cases linked some marginal or partly alienated members and groups among the elite ("the most outside of the insiders") to some of the strongest and most vigorous groups among the nonelite ("the most inside of the outsiders") who were beginning to press for a larger share of political power.

From the outset, major *political compromises* will be needed to hold together these integrated movements and broad cross-class coalitions whose members are apt to be quite diverse in background, interests, and outlook. But they are likely to be special kinds of compromises. They will be designed not to frustrate all parties by giving each much less than what it wants most, but on the contrary to reward each by conceding it much or all of that demand which is most salient to it, in return for its concessions on other matters which are less urgent to it but more salient to other partners in the coalition. Such compromises imply political "log-rolling" instead of mutual obstruction; instead of frustrating one another, the partners must discover a way to exchange political favors and to dovetail genuine and substantial concessions to one another's vital interests.

This work of discovering and establishing viable patterns of mutual political accommodation often will take considerable time. Accordingly, many integration movements show a succession of three stages. At first, there is a stage of *leadership by intellectuals,* during which the movement is mainly supported by intellectuals (and not necessarily by a majority of these) and by relatively few and limited groups from other strata. Later on, there comes the stage of *great politicians,* when broader interest groups begin to swing behind the integration movement, and mutually rewarding political compromises are worked out. Finally, this stage shades over into the stage of *mass movements* and/or *large-scale elite politics,* when the issue of political unification becomes intensely practical. Even so, the movement is likely to have setbacks and failures. As Richard Merritt's study of the unification of the American colonies suggests,[3] integrative activities and popular support for them are likely to rise and then decline again in a manner somewhat resembling a learning curve. If the social learning process is successful, however, each peak and each trough on this curve will be higher than its corresponding predecessor, until the process crosses some critical threshold and some major step toward an amalgamated security community has been accomplished.

Appeals and methods. In the course of this social learning process, the relevant elites and populations have to learn to connect all or most of their important political concerns and issues with the issue of unification; and they must come to perceive this issue clearly as a single and relatively simple decision, uncluttered by too many competing alternative proposals. Most effective among the political appeals and interests to be harnessed to the cause of integration are appeals for new or greater *rights and liberties* for individuals or groups. Next in effectiveness to the appeals for greater liberty rank the appeals for more *equality*—political, social, and/or economic. Close to these two, there ranks the appeal of a rewarding *way of life,* often including some experience and/or promise of prosperity and material well-being. In contrast to these three effective appeals, the appeals of seeking greater collective power for its own sake, or of defending and preserving some special minority privileges of group or class, seem to have had little or no effect in deciding the outcome of an integrative process: in one historical study, these last two types of appeal occurred about as often in cases of failure of integration as in cases of success.[4]

To promote political amalgamation, all the usual political methods have been used, but not all have been equally effective. By far the most effective method, in terms of the relative frequency with which it was followed by success, was the enlistment of broad popular participation and support. Among the cases studied, every amalgamation movement that won such popular participation was eventually successful. The second most effective method was the acceptance of pluralism, and hence of the autonomy and sovereignty of the participating political units for substantial tran-

---

[3]R. L. Merritt, *Symbols of American Community, 1735–1775* (New Haven: Yale University Press, 1966).

[4]Deutsch, Burrell *et al., Political Community and the North Atlantic Area,* pp. 95–105.

sition periods. Next in terms of effectiveness ranked the large-scale use of propaganda; the promise to abolish specific items of unpopular legislation; and the promotion of political or administrative autonomy for the participating units.

By contrast, some methods had little or no effect in making amalgamation come about: they occurred about as often in cases of success as they did in cases of failure. Such relatively ineffective methods included the promotion of specific political institutions, the use of symbols, and the use of patronage for the appointment of purposefully selected individuals to political or administrative office. All these methods may have been necessary, but by themselves they seem to have contributed little or nothing to make success more likely.

Three methods turned out to be counterproductive—that is, they were significantly more often associated with the failure of amalgamation than with its success. These counterproductive methods were early insistence on overall amalgamation, early efforts to establish a monopoly of violence, and outright military conquest.

Opposition to amalgamation most often came from peasants, farmers, and other rural groups; and in the second place, from privileged groups or regions which feared to lose something from amalgamation. Peasant opposition seems to have made no significant difference to the success or failure of amalgamation movements, but active peasant support, though rare, was invariably associated with success. Privileged groups seem to have made no difference to the eventual success or failure of integration— neither by their opposition nor by their support—but they almost always gained some substantial concessions to their interest; and as far as the amalgamation movement in each case was concerned, the making of such concessions to the privileged groups seems to have had some small effect in favor of success.

In the end, amalgamation movements often succeeded through a combination of closure and creativity. They usually succeeded by closing out all competing proposals and alternatives, so as eventually to channel all political attention and action toward the single paramount issue and policy of amalgamation. But they often succeeded in doing so, and in maintaining and broadening their political coalition, only by means of the originality and resourcefulness with which the proponents of amalgamations invented and formulated specific plans for union and specific institutions to make it work. Often this element of political invention and innovation seems to have been critical. Many of the central institutions of successfully amalgamated security communities were original and relatively improbable at the time and place at which they were adopted. Conversely, several amalgamated security communities were wrecked by routine policies and views, and by obvious decisions, all of which were highly probable but inadequate at the time and place they occurred. In the politics of amalgamation, too, genius often consisted in discovering an improbable but highly relevant solution, or a sequence of solutions of this kind, and in turning them into reality.

The Process of Establishing a Pluralistic
Security Community

Pluralistic security communities are easier to establish and to maintain, and hence often are a more effective means to keep the peace among their members. They seem to require only three major conditions for their existence:

1. Compatibility of major political values

2. Capacity of the governments and politically relevant strata of the participating countries to respond to one another's messages, needs, and actions quickly, adequately, and without resort to violence

3. Mutual predictability of the relevant aspects of one another's political, economic, and social behavior (but these relevant aspects are far fewer in the case of a pluralistic security community than they would be in its much more tightly-knit amalgamated counterpart).

Just as a pluralistic security community requires fewer favorable background conditions for its success, so it requires simpler, though perhaps subtler, processes in order to come into existence.

The main process required seems to be an increasing unattractiveness and improbability of war among the political units of the emerging pluralistic security community, as perceived by their governments, elites, and (eventually) populations. A seond process, similar to that favoring the rise of amalgamated security communities, is the spread of intellectual movements and traditions favoring integration, and preparing the political climate for it. A third process, perhaps, is the development and practice of habits and skills of mutual attention, communication, and responsiveness, so as to make possible the preservation of the autonomy and substantial sovereignty of the participating units, and the preservation of stable expectations of peace and peaceful change among them. The difficulties in the way of these three processes are by no means trivial; but they are less than the difficulties in the path of outright amalgamation among almost any group of sovereign nation-states in today's world.

SOME EMERGING ISSUES OF INTEGRATION
AND WORLD POLITICS

Three broad philosophic issues emerge from our survey of the conditions and processes of integration. The first is the issue of the primary goal to be adopted. Is it to be *peace* within the integrated area, *or* is it to be some form of corporate *power,* perhaps for its defense against outsiders, or for some variety of other purposes? Or if both peace and power are emphasized as long-run goals, which is to be sought first, and what time-path toward the ultimate attainment of both goals is to be envisaged?

The second issue is that of the possible *hegemony* of one political unit (such as the most powerful nation-state) within the emerging security community, as against the substantial equality or near-equality of its more-or-less sovereign members. Related to this question is that of majority voting, as against negotiations and special concessions. Though majority voting looks like—and sometimes is—an equalitarian device, it also can be used to establish the hegemony of one great power, or of a few of them, with the help of the easily influenced or controlled votes of some lesser powers.

The result could be a pattern resembling a pyramid of holding companies. A power with great but limited resources could secure for itself a practically paramount role in the decisions of a small group of countries. This group—let us call it alliance *A*—could jointly command paramount influence within some larger alliance *B*. Alliance *B*, in turn, could be used to control alliance *C;* and so forth, until some alliance finally would lead to formal majority control of the United Nations, and to substantive control of much (and ideally all) of the world. Nothing quite like this has ever happened, but the possibility is there; and the almost instinctive resistance of many countries to far-reaching majority voting in international or supranational bodies, and their preference for mutual negotiations and responsiveness among sovereign units, may be related to these considerations. In the early and middle 1970s, a general opposition against the alleged policies of hegemony of either or both of the "superpowers"—the United States and the Soviet Union—had become a major theme in the foreign policy of the Chinese People's Republic and India; and these large states themselves appear to have become more careful in exercising hegemonial pressure upon such neighboring countries as Afghanistan, Nepal, Pakistan, Bangladesh, North Korea, and Taiwan; instead, China and India are encouraging their neighbors to consider themselves, as the two powers are, as "nonaligned" nations.

The third issue is related to the second. It is this: Can larger organizations be built up best by downgrading their components, so as to make them easier to control and cheaper to replace? Specifically, are federations to be built up by weakening their member states, and international organizations by weakening the nations of which they are composed?

For the near future, some tentative answers can be indicated. Keeping an uneasy but tolerable peace is likely to appear more urgent to most governments than creating large supranational organizations with vast powers for more or less general purposes. Sovereignty with only a few limitations will seem more attractive to most governments than submission to the hegemony of any great power or partial coalition of great powers. And the upgrading, rather than the downgrading, of the capabilities and the prestige of nation-states will look both more practical and more desirable to most of their governments and peoples.

An era of pluralism and, at best, of pluralistic security communities, may well characterize the near future. In the long term, however, the search for integrated political communities that command both peace and power, and that entail a good deal of amalgamation, is likely to continue until it succeeds. For such success, not only good will and sustained effort, but political creativity and inventiveness will be needed, together with a political culture of greater international openness, understanding, and compassion.

Without such a new political climate and new political efforts, humanity is unlikely to survive for long. But the fact that so many people in so many countries are becoming aware of the problem, and of the need for increasing efforts to deal with it, makes it likely that it will be solved.

20

Interdependence, Dependence, and Increased Equality: Which Way Is the World Going?

> The world is round and whole as a heart,
> And when it is riven in two halves apart,
> It must die.

These lines, written by the young Czech poet George Wolker after World War I, echo the feelings of many people to this day. After World War II, a former Presidential candidate of the Republican party in the United States, Wendell R. Willkie, summed up what he saw as the lessons of that war in a book he called simply *One World;* Walter Lippman and other writers published a book entitled *One World or None;* and a highly respected American economic expert, Bernard Baruch, in 1947 called the choice between national sovereignty and complete control by a single worldwide agency in the field of atomic energy a choice "between the quick and the dead."

Other people imagined that they saw the opposite. Nation-states and national power would remain the paramount reality in world politics for generations as they had been for generations in the past. In this regard at least, the respected scholar Hans Morgenthau suggested, the twentieth century would continue to resemble the nineteenth, and the statecraft of Alexander Hamilton, Camillo Count Cavour, and Prince Otto von Bismarck would still offer realistic lessons to leaders near the end of the present century and perhaps longer. Another well-informed observer has noted a paradox. "The world has shrunk," the United States Secretary of State, Henry Kissinger, told the United Nations Assembly in September 1976, "but the nations of the world have not come closer together. Paradoxically, nationalism has been on the rise at the precise time when the most serious issues we all face can only be resolved through the recognition of our interdependence. . . ."[1]

Who is right? Are the world's states, countries, and peoples moving toward becoming one, or are they drifting apart? What have been the facts during our century and particularly in the more recent decades? What are they now and where do they seem to be pointing?

INTERDEPENDENCE AND ITS DIMENSIONS

Two countries are *interdependent* if a change in country A, say a rise in the general price level, is followed by some predictable change in country B, such as perhaps also a rise in the level of prices there. If a change in country B has as big an effect in country A as the change in A had on B, then we may call their interdependence *symmetrical*.

Changes often make a difference to matters which people value. As we saw in Chapter 14 (see pp. 209–211), if a change occurs in country A that is experienced as rewarding there, and if it is followed by a rewarding change in B, and if changes that are bad for A are followed by changes that are bad for B, and vice versa, then we may speak of a *positive* interdependence, or, as it was termed in that earlier chapter, a positive covariance of rewards. But if interdependent changes that are good for A are bad for B, and vice versa, then we may speak of a negative covariance of rewards, and we call this kind of interpendence *negative*. As we saw in the earlier chapter, strong positive interdependence tends to support solidarity; strong negative interdependence tends to promote conflict; and weak interdependence tends to make but little difference either way.

Has the interdependence among the countries of the world been increasing or decreasing during this century? If it has been increasing, has it been doing so in a positive or negative direction? And what has become of the symmetry or asymmetry of these relationships?

In order to seek answers to these questions, the different dimensions of interdependence must be analyzed. Since interdependence has a greater or lesser power over the course of events within the states involved in it, we may think of its main dimensions as similar to those of power and of integration (as set forth in Chapters 3 and 15, pp. 20–45 and 203–211).

---

[1]Cited in James Reston, "Kissinger's 'Farewell' Addresses," *The New York Times* (October 1, 1976), p. A 27:1. © 1976 by The New York Times Company. Reprinted by permission.

Domain and Resources

Most conspicuously, the domain and the resources of interdependence have increased. As to its *domain*, there is hardly any inhabited territory left on our planet whose inhabitants are not involved in some transactions and most often some structural links with persons and organizations in other territories.

Such *resources* of interdependence include transport by air, sea, and land; trade and finance; mail, telegraph, telephone, news, films, radio, and television; business, recreation, travel, and the transnational movement of students, teachers, and scientists; and fashions in clothes, music, and life styles. All these are processes flowing across national boundaries, and in most cases these flows are supported by structural links, such as airlines, shipping lines, railroads, highways, hotels and motels, communication channels and organizations, export and import firms, banks, stock and commodity exchanges, multinational corporations, and governmental and nongovernmental international organizations. In absolute terms, such as personnel budgets and volume of activities, almost all of these interdependent structures and processes have grown a great deal during our century, and hence it is tempting to infer that the interdependence of the world has also grown.

But if the resources of interdependence have increased, so have the world's population, income, and activities, and most of these continue to depend mainly on processes *within* each nation-state. Commodities supplied from only a few countries but in great demand elsewhere—such as oil, wheat, various metals, timber, tropical products, computers, jet planes, and other products of highly specialized technology—all are objects of international trade, as well as international conflicts. But the spread of modern technology has enabled many countries to produce at home some of these goods, or acceptable substitutes for them. At the same time, moreover, the construction of domestic roads, harbors, schools, housing, hospitals, and sanitary systems all have increased, and often more quickly. So have public and private services within almost all countries, such as government, education, health, personal care, recreation, and entertainment. As a result, the *proportion* of goods and services directly involved in international transactions, as compared to the total gross national product, has declined in many countries, in comparison to what it was in 1913 or 1928.

Something similar may be true for the world as a whole. The proportion of world trade to the world's gross national product was about 19 percent in 1970. By 1974, however, the ratio of world trade to world GNP had jumped back to the 1913 level of 30 percent, and by 1980 had reached a level of almost 35 percent . This was due, in part, to the steep price increases in petroleum, wheat, and other internationally traded commodities in the late 1970s. Whether this represents a short-term deviation or long-term change or trend remains to be seen after data become available beyond the period of worldwide economic recession in the early 1980s.[2] Similarly, it has been estimated that a larger proportion of the world's savings was being invested abroad in about 1871 than was the case a hundred years later.[3]

What does this mean in terms of interdependence or in terms of power? Years ago, the American sociologist Daniel Lerner showed that French survey respondents who derived more than one-half of their income from international transactions were much more in favor of an internationalist policy—in that case, European integration—than were their compatriots who drew most of their income from domestic activities within France, and who turned out to prefer more nationally oriented policies.[4] If this finding should be an indication of a more general relationship, then the persons and resources employed in the international or transnational sector of a nation's economy would furnish a major potential base for the political support of more internationally oriented policies, in contrast to more domestically oriented ones. If other things were equal, a relative increase in this sector then should tend to favor international political integration, while a relative decline should tend to make such integration more difficult. Feelings take time to develop and to be maintained; and feelings of internationalism are not likely to remain strong among people whose daily lives include few or no salient international activities.

Other things, of course, are not necessarily equal. Even if the international sector in a country should shrink in relation to the domestic one, the firms and interest groups in it might be more highly concentrated and better connected and organized to exert political influence. In this manner, they may be able for a fairly long time—perhaps one or two generations—to compensate for their shrinking popular and economic power base and retain a major influence on the foreign and domestic policies of their country. But even these opportunities are limited; if most of a nation's population and capital are increasingly employed in the domestic sector, national attention and priorities sooner or later will tend to follow. Conversely, long-run real price increases of fuels and raw materials might bring about relative expansion of the international trade sectors in both the highly developed and the developing countries.

[2]Calculations for 1970 and 1980 by Peter Brecke, based on data from *World Bank Atlas 1981* (Washington, D.C.: The World Bank, 1981); *U.N. Statistical Yearbook 1981* (New York: United Nations, 1981); and *U.N. Yearbook of International Trade Statistics, 1975 and 1981* (New York: United Nations, 1975; 1981).

[3]Edward L. Morse, "Transnational Economic Processes," in R. O. Keohane and J. S. Nye, Jr., eds., *Transnational Relations and World Politics, International Organization*, 25, no. 3 (Summer 1971), pp. 373–398. Foreign investments by Arab countries of their "petroleum dollars" after the oil price rises of 1973–1974 may have increased this proportion of international to intranational investments; whether for a short or long time is not yet certain.

[4]Daniel Lerner, "French Business Leaders Look at E.D.C.: A Preliminary Report," *Public Opinion Quarterly*, 20, no. 1 (Spring 1956), pp. 212–220.

Range and Scope

For any one country—call it A—we may call the *range* of its *dependence* on another nation, B, the difference between the greatest value gain and the worst value loss—perhaps the highest gain or subsidy vs. the worst damage which A can experience from a depression, blockade, or war—as a result of its transactions with B. Thus international transactions after 1973 have brought vast sums of money to Saudi Arabia and Kuwait (and particularly to their rulers), while dependence on foreign markets and sources of supply have left such countries as Bolivia and Zaire in abysmal poverty. Similarly, the range of gains and losses that changes in B engender in A constitute the range of B's dependence upon A. The set of these two ranges then represents the *range of interdependence* between A and B.

Furthermore, the range of all the gains and losses which A can derive from its transactions with *all* other countries represents the range of its dependence upon the rest of the world, and the range of changes which events within A can produce in the rest of the world represents the range of the world's dependence upon A (which could be substantial if A were a large country or one in control of some particularly important and scarce commodity); and the set of these two ranges represents the interdependence between the world and country A.

In recent years, the range of international interdependence has probably increased. Countries now can bestow large benefits upon other countries, either through the national action of a single large country, as did the United States in 1948–1952 in its aid to the economic rehabilitation of Europe through the Marshall Plan, or through its large deliveries of grain to India in the 1960s and early 1970s under Public Law 480 or through the substantial economic aid given to its allies in the Middle East, notably Israel and Egypt, and the victims of famine in the Sahel region in Ethiopia in the mid-1980s. Or else they may bestow large benefits through international agencies, such as the World Health Organization (WHO) through its contributions to the eradication of malaria in many countries. But nations now also can do more terrible damage to each other, deliberately through weapons of mass destruction and nuclear warfare, or negligently through the pollution of the air, seas, and rivers—as in the accidental nuclear catastrophy at Chernobyl in the Soviet Union in mid-1986, with effects that spread across several international boundaries. And the dependence of nation-states on vital resources over which one or several countries may have a monopoly or controlling power—such as the Republic of South Africa and the Soviet Union over virtually all of the world's resources of manganese, chrome, platinum, and diamonds, or the relative scarcity of plutonium and uranium, concentrated in a few countries of the world, and the controlling power of the Arab countries over oil exports—may produce at best scarcities, worldwide economic recession, and inflation, if only temporarily. Recent years have experienced such successful and effective manipulation of the world's and single countries' dependence on vital natural resources and scarce commodities; but fortunately the full range of these negative international effects has not yet been turned into reality—but the grim possibilities are there, and they are still increasing.

The *scope* of dependence of one country, *A*, upon another, *B*, consists in the *kinds* of activities and institutions in *A* that can be significantly affected by changes that occur in *B*. Conversely, the set of kinds of processes and structures in *B* that are likely to change significantly in response to changes in *A* constitute the scope of *B*'s dependence upon *A*. The set of these two scopes then make up the *scope of interdependence* between *A* and *B*.

With the growing scope of human activities and of government actions, the scope of international interdependence has increased. The world of 1986 was interdependent in regard to practically all the goods, services, and activities as the world of 1913 had been, and a large array of new interdependent activities had been added, such as international radio and television links; large-scale trade in new products such as antibiotics, bananas, tranquilizers, vitamins, warplanes, computers, and uranium; large-scale exchange of new kinds of data on such new fields of knowledge as nuclear physics, space science, molecular biology, ecology, and the control of population growth (the efforts of some governments particularly in Britain and the United States to restrict for strategic reasons this international flow of new kinds of technology have slowed this trend, but not reversed it); newly prominent art forms such as motion pictures, folklore art and music, and many more. The more rapid spread of scientific knowledge, as well as of changing life styles, across national boundaries testifies to the considerable extent to which the scope of international interdependence has increased.

Gains and Costs

If interdependence is high, positive, and valued by the participants, it is likely to turn into integration. Many gains from integration are well known and have been widely publicized. Economic integration into a single market offers gains from greater specialization in a wider division of labor and often a better utilization of the comparative advantages of each region or population group. Political integration permits the mobilization of more money and labor for larger undertakings. Cultural integration offers a larger public to artists, and a wider choice of artists and their works to the public. In many such harmonious situations, almost everybody may be expected to gain, and nobody to lose.

Not all situations, however, are harmonious. Even in integrating two markets, the less efficient producers in one or both of them may be pushed out of business and into bankruptcy. Their employees, their suppliers, the owners of the land they rent, and the villages, towns, and provinces to which they paid taxes all may lose some income along with them—perhaps to the point where they suffer serious damage. Even if the sum of these losses from integration were smaller than the sum of gains resulting from it, these losses still may hit a larger number of people, or those less well-equipped to bear them. Thus, if the gainers from integration should be a relatively few rich individuals and groups, and the losers should be numerous and poor, then the aggregate marginal utility of the amounts lost by each loser might be greater than that of the gains to those that got them. Even if we should accept the doctrine of some economists, according to which utilities to different persons are forever incomparable and incommensurable—so that these economists would refuse to say whether the utility of a second lapdog to a rich person was greater than the utility of a critically needed medicine to a sick slum child and to his mother—we could still count the number of persons on each side, the presumable intensity of their feelings, and the likelihood of their taking action. And as students of politics we then could still ask in every case within a particular political system whether the marginal gains of the few powerful and rich carry more or less weight than the urgent needs of the many poor and weak, or of the many who are somewhere in between.

Answers to such questions will be largely matters of empirical facts and observations. Such answers may have to be sought not only in economic affairs but also in politics and culture. Whose political demands will tend to be more successful after integration, perhaps by now being able to call upon greater power resources to support them; and whose demands will only have diminished chances of success, perhaps due now to being met with less responsiveness by the larger integrated system? In regard to culture, which persons and groups will gain from integration through widened opportunities and choices, and which ones may tend to lose through being swamped by the products of an alien culture, and through a diminution of their sense of self-reliance, integrity, and self-respect?

Out of the empirical answers to all these questions, we must derive three kinds of rough cost-benefit estimates: (1) for the aggregate population of all the political units that are to be, or have been, integrated; (2) for the population of each unit that was or is separate and autonomous before integration; and (3) for particular subpopulations, groups, or classes within each such unit.

If people's interests were their sole and sufficient motive for action, and if they were simply identical with their expected value gains or losses, and further, if people were perfectly capable of perceiving accurately their true interests, then such rough cost-benefit estimates should tell us much about the probable opponents of any particular integration policy or project. As it is, we must also take into account many kinds of human feelings, memories, prejudices, and traditions; the dislike of most people for too great burdens of decision and thought; their distrust of the unfamiliar; the terrible force of habits of millions of people; the effects of conformity, fear, and rage. In short, we must consider all the many conditions that influence the real behavior of people in order to estimate whether a particular plan for political integration will succeed or fail, or whether a more-or-less integrated political community will remain so, or in what direction it is apt to change.

The Weight of Integration

This is something similar to the weight of power (see pp. 24—31). It is the change in the probability of political, social, or economic outcomes which is produced by increasing interdependence toward integration. The more of a difference integration makes to the outcome of events within the integrated area, the greater is its *internal weight*. Thus the existence of the United States, its Constitution, and its politics have made a large difference in the relations of North and South and of blacks and whites within this country; and it promises to make still more of a difference in the future. Similarly, the existence of an integrated Swiss political community has made a large difference to the relations among the different language groups within that country.

But the fact that two or more previously separate political units have become integrated may also make a difference to the peoples and nations outside them. This difference we may then call the *external weight* of integration. Thus, by 1608 when Cornwall, Wales, and Scotland had become to a large extent integrated into Great Britain, this new United Kingdom became a major power in world affairs and the conqueror of many overseas territories in the course of the next three centuries.

After a change has occurred in an interdependent relationship, its weight can be estimated by the changes that have followed in each of the participating countries. But how can we estimate the weight of interdependence for a country before the relationship has changed? As a first step, we can note the simple quantitative proportion—the statistical weight—of the interdependent activities in question within the total ensemble of relevant activities. How large a proportion does the foreign trade of a country represent as compared to its total economic activities, as indicated by its gross national product? The larger that proportion, the greater—so we may estimate—is the weight of a country's dependence on foreign trade; and the greater the proportion of that country's foreign trade to the total international trade of the world, the greater—so we may estimate—will be the world's dependence upon that country.

In general, then, the larger the proportion of the transactions between any two actors (which may be states or groups of states) to the sum total of their relevant activities, the greater we may expect to be the weight of their interdependence. This is likely to be true, even though this weight may be different for each of the two partners—most often lighter for the bigger or richer, and heavier for the smaller or poorer one.

This weight of interdependence is seen clearly when it changes, and particularly when existing links are reduced or cut. The weight of an increase in interdependence through the addition of a new interdependent relationship may be smaller than the weight—i.e., the effects—of interrupting that relationship once it has been established. The gradual increase of oil imports into the United States did not seem to have any spectacular effects there; however, the prospects of its sudden partial disruption by an Arab oil embargo in October 1973, and the subsequent fivefold rise in the price of oil did have significant effects on political and economic expectations and behavior in the United States.

But all these considerations are only a first stage in our analysis. In order to go further, we must ask not only about the mere size or volume of transactions that constitute interdependence between two international actors, but we must ask about their relative importance for the functioning, and perhaps the survival, of each actor. In the case of two nation-states, we must ask about the *sensitivity* of each country to any diminution or disruption of their mutual transaction flow. How badly needed were the goods and services which had been obtained from the partner country? How easily could substitutes be obtained for them, or other sources of supply be found and used, and at what cost? Otherwise, what would be the costs of doing without them, in terms of damage and disruption? It is the total of all these costs and the size of the changes needed to meet them that measure the sensitivity of each political system, each economy, and each society and culture to any reduction or disruption of its external transactions.

Obviously, this sensitivity varies with the economic, technological, and political structure of the state concerned, and with the type of transactions cut back or interrupted. Countries that use much oil, such as France or the Netherlands, may be more sensitive to its sudden scarcity or higher price than are countries which use little, such as Chad, Niger, or Nepal. Countries that produce too little food to feed their population are sensitive to interruptions of or price increases in their food supply. Such sensitivities need not be symmetrical. In early 1974, at the time of the Arab oil embargo, a French satirical weekly, *Charlie Hebdo,* published a wry cartoon with the caption: "The Dutch strike back—no more tulips for the Arabs!" Just as the Arabs could do more easily without tulips than the Dutch could do without oil, so the United States and Western Europe could do more easily without bananas than the countries of Central America and West Africa could do without the many industrial products and spare parts that they import from these highly industrialized countries. Such asymmetries can be one of the sources of dependence in international politics.

The Solidity of Integration

One integrated political community may survive severe strains, while another may collapse under them, or even under lesser ones. The solidity of interdependence, like that of integration, then can be measured, or estimated, by the severity of strains which it is likely to withstand, in the light of the past strains which it has survived. Thus Austria-Hungary broke apart in 1918 under the strains of World War I, and so did Pakistan in 1972 under the strains of large-scale social mobilization, political unrest, and economic difficulties. By contrast, no substantial movements toward voluntary political separation or secession arose in any region of Germany after World Wars I and II, although its political integration dated only from 1871, and despite the large sufferings and stresses which these World Wars had imposed on the country. The integration of Italy, dating in the main from 1860, proved similarly solid in 1945, despite the strains of World War II.

WHEN INTERDEPENDENCE IS HIGHLY UNEQUAL: IMPERIALISM AND DEPENDENCY

Interdependence, however, does not always lead to integration. The word "interdependence" suggests a two-way process. Among states or other international actors, it reminds us that this relationship is mutual—what happens to actor *A* makes a difference to *B*, but what happens to *B* also makes a difference to *A*. Beyond this, however, the word "interdependence" seems to suggest that these two effects somehow should be equal, and this is by no means necessarily the case.

When a large country and a smaller one are interdependent, relatively small changes in the big country may produce big changes in the small one. The United States and Canada are closely linked in many ways, but the United States has about nine times Canada's population and more than eleven times its income. "When the United States sneezes," a Canadian wrote, "Canada catches pneumonia." Yet Canada is as highly developed industrially, culturally, and politically as the United States, and in many ways it has successfully held its own in preserving the autonomy and self-direction of its political life and foreign policy, its own education system, and mass media.

Among many other countries, such as the United States and Guatemala, France and the Ivory Coast, Britain and Ghana, the Soviet Union and Outer Mongolia, or India and Nepal, interdependence has been still far more asymmetrical. The more unequal and one-sided the flow of influence and power, the more have people in the poorer and weaker countries been inclined to speak of "imperialism" and "dependency." In the world of today, just what do these words mean?

Imperialism: Dominance Through Old and New Controls

There are many means to make the fate of one country or people depend upon the actions of the rulers of another, and it seems that in the course of history all of them have been tried. One of the oldest has been direct military conquest and the incorporation of the defeated under direct political rule and command—the *imperium,* as the ancient Romans called it—of the victors. It is this *imperium* by naked power from which the later French and English word *empire* was derived, denoting the area of supreme political and military rule, usually combined with the exaction of taxes and tributes, by a supreme central government or ruler.

The empires of antiquity have all disappeared. But in the sixteenth century, several European states acquired fleets of sailing ships that could carry intercontinental voyagers and troops with muskets and artillery, so that they gained a decisive advantage in military power over many non-Western kingdoms and peoples, from the Aztecs in Mexico to the Incas in Peru, the Zulus of South Africa, the Hindus of India, and the Muslims of Algeria and Egypt. Most of these territories were turned into colonies within the empire of this or that Eurpean power. The colonial peoples then became its subjects, ruled and most often exploited by their new "mother country," often with the help of a small number of colonists of European stock and/or a small native elite of local Rajahs, Sultans, or chieftains collaborating with the imperial power.

By 1913, on the eve of World War I, the division of Asia and Africa among such empires was nearly complete, with only China, Japan, Thailand, Ethiopia, and Liberia the chief remaining exceptions. By that time, too, the Western overseas empires were paralleled by the land empires of Tsarist Russia in Central Asia and Siberia, Austria-Hungary in Central and Southeastern Europe, and the Ottoman Empire in the Near East; and Japan had begun to build an empire of her own with the conquest of Formosa (Taiwan) and Korea.

All these empires had certain similar characteristics. Each had a capital city and central government amidst a larger metropolitan region with more developed economic and industrial resources and higher levels of income, health, and education, surrounded by the outlying provinces and colonies, where the business executives of the metropolis enjoyed many privileges and often near-monopolies, and where the local people were much poorer, rarely literate, and with much higher rates of sickness and death. In maintaining and defending this state of affairs, the governments, bureaucracies, armed forces, and police of each empire also preserved, in effect, this state of inequality for generations and centuries, and sometimes they even worsened it. In the metropolitan areas, the empire was seen by many people as a source of prosperity and strength, but among the colonial populations, people came to see it as the source of alien rule, exploitation, and frustration.

For about half a century, roughly from 1875 to 1925, colonial empires flourished, each under the direct administrative and military control of a relatively more industrialized power, and accepted as "natural" and right by the majority of public opinion in the "mother country." The striving to acquire, preserve, and enlarge such an empire for one's own nation was called *imperialism.*

Conservative Advocates

This striving for empire was often counted a virtue, as if it were simply patriotism on a larger scale, and it often guided the actual policies of governments. It was justified by conservative theorists, such as Sir Charles Dilke and Sir John Robert Seeley in Britain; it was practiced by conservative leaders, such as Benjamin Disraeli, Lord Beaconsfield in Britain, and his compatriots, Lord Roseberry, Lord Curzon, and Cecil Rhodes; by Jules Ferry in France; by President William McKinley, Senator Albert Beveridge, and Rear Admiral Alfred Thayer Mahan in the United States; and by many others—all of whom scarcely suspected how radically they were subverting their own world by this practice. Rather, they insisted that imperialist policies were indispensable, if capitalism—the economic system of large-scale private enterprise—were to survive and with it, as they saw it, the very existence of their own nation.

Liberal Critics

Liberal theorists dissented. They agreed that capitalism was good, but they denied that imperialism and wars for colonies were necessary for its survival. The belief that wars and conquests would pay in the twentieth century simply was *The Great Illusion*, said the British writer Sir Norman Angell in a book of the same title. In another book, *Imperialism*, the British writer J. A. Hobson insisted that imperialism only benefitted a few special interest groups, mainly the big banks and brokerage houses of the City of London, but was unnecessary and indeed damaging for almost everybody else.

In 1918, the Austrian economist Joseph A. Schumpeter (who later moved to the United States) asserted that capitalism was inherently peaceful, and he proposed a sociological theory of imperialism.[5] If a country, he said, for whatever historical reason had acquired a strong warlike elite with military habits and values, that elite would seek to act out these values and habits under whatever pretext might be found. The security of every border district would then require the conquest of the district beyond it; and that district, in turn, so they would say, could only be made secure by further conquests. Despite such rhetoric of national security and defense, imperialism was, according to Schumpeter, simply "objectless expansion"—the mindless acting out of behavior patterns by an elite that had learned no others. Often such a warlike elite of aristocratic landowners and officers might be inherited from the precapitalist past, but it might also have become equipped by modern industry with much more destructive weapons. In such cases, said Schumpeter, "imperialism is atavism," and he believed this to be the case in Imperial Germany and Japan at the time of World War I. But such a powerful and warlike social class or major interest group could also come newly into being, perhaps by the need of a not particularly warlike society to resist a military attack from the outside. Whatever its origin, once such a strong military elite or interest group was established with substantial power over the entire society, it would then tend to press for more armaments, bases, territories, and expansionist policies in accordance with the political and cultural habits it had learned.

President Eisenhower's complaint in his Farewell Address of 1961 about the power of the "military-industrial complex" in the United States seemed strikingly similar to this line of Schumpeter's thinking. Yet the strength of imperialism in any industrial country depended on the extent and depth of its social and historic roots, and hence Schumpeter expected that Britain and the United States eventually would give up their empires and imperialist policies relatively easily, while continuing as predominantly capitalist welfare states. Within its own terms, this prediction seems not to have been proven wrong by the experiences of the last half century.

---

[5] J. A. Schumpeter, *Imperialism and Social Classes* (New York: Meridian, 1955).

Marxist Theories of Imperialism

From the first decade of our century onward, imperialism became a focus of attention of Marxist writers. In Germany, Rudolf Hilferding argued that the automatic working of capitalist competition would produce ever fewer and larger firms, ever more involved in financial operations rather than in mere production, and ever more tending to use the power of the nation-state to strengthen and expand their areas of economic empire and monopolistic privilege.[6] This coming of age of *finance capital* and monopolistic privilege, wrote Hilferding in 1909, would give rise to an ideology that would fit its increasingly bureaucratic structures: it would be a pseudo-biological ideology of racism and warfare. In this manner, young Hilferding predicted something like the coming of Nazism; and more than thirty years later, in World War II, he was murdered by the Nazis whose rise he had foreseen. But in his perspective on the future, Hilferding also had left open a more optimistic possibility: a "general cartel" might eventually unite all private business enterprises into one, and then rule and exploit the world economy in peace. A similar vision—that the world's empire and business monopolies eventually might all unite peacefully in an age of *ultraimperialism*—was proposed by the democratic Marxist Karl Kautsky.

A much more radical Marxist analysis was put forward in 1912 by Rosa Luxemburg.[7] All capitalist firms taken together, she argued, could only be profitable if they sold their output of goods and services for *more* money than they had paid out as wages, rent, and other costs in producing them. Hence, she deduced, capitalism inevitably must need to find more purchasing power in the market than it can create by itself, and a purely capitalist economy must necessarily stagnate or wreck itself in recurrent depressions. The only way out for capitalism, she thought, was unending penetration and conquest of noncapitalist territories and populations. Only the value of land and other properties in the not-yet-capitalistic peasant districts at home and in the precapitalistic colonial areas overseas could supply the additional markets and profits which capitalism needed to survive. Imperialism and its attendant wars, she concluded, were a necessity for capitalism; they would disappear with capitalism but not sooner.

World War I seemed to confirm this gloomy prospect. None except capitalist governments had existed at its outbreak. They had started it, were waging it, and seemed likely to start other wars in the future. Writing in 1916, in his Swiss exile, Lenin insisted that capitalism could not survive without the direct political administration and military occupation of colonial areas, and that under capitalism wars were certain and lasting peace impossible. He called his book *Imperialism: The Highest Stage of Capitalism.*[8] For the capitalists, he thought, would shift more and more investments to the colonies, particularly in the heavy industries, and thus make them

[6]R. Hilferding, *Das Finanzkapital* (Vienna: Brand, 1909, 1920).

[7]R. Luxemburg, *Die Akkumulation des Kapitals* (Leipzig: Frankes Verlag, 1921).

[8]V. I. Lenin, *Imperialism: The Highest Stage in Capitalism* (New York: Progress Publications, USSR, 1975).

potentially more powerful than the old metropolitan areas—while paying an "aristocracy of workers" in these "mother countries" somewhat better, so as to win their support for imperialist policies. In the long run, however, the metropolitan countries themselves, according to Lenin, would "decay," turning increasingly into golf courses and game preserves, and their working people into butlers and gamekeepers. Colonial revolutions and secessions from the old empires were therefore inevitable, leaving the old imperial centers prey to economic depression and mass unemployment. At the same time, these depressions and unending wars would bring so much suffering to the workers in the mother countries that they, too, would rise in revolt; and capitalism and imperialism—so he plainly suggested—would perish together in a chain of worldwide revolutions.

In some ways, the radical Marxists agreed with the conservatives. Both sides believed that capitalism needed imperial expansion, colonies, and therefore repeated wars in order to survive. But where Disraeli, Rhodes, and others had seen capitalism as good and viable, and hence well-worth the price of war, the revolutionary Marxists like Luxemburg and Lenin saw capitalism as bad and relatively fragile, and the hideous costs of modern war were for them one more reason to strive to end this economic system.

The liberal writers disagreed with both groups. Neither Hobson nor Angell nor Schumpeter considered capitalism in itself as bad. They all agreed that it did not need empires, colonies, or wars for its survival; and, as noted above, the liberal Marxist writers Hilferding and Kautsky did not exclude this possibility of a peaceful capitalist future.

Who Was Right?

Today, more than half a century after all these contending predictions, we still have no conclusive answer. A second World War has followed the first, and the governments that started it—those of Nazi Germany, Fascist Italy, and militarist Japan—all asserted at the time the conquest of larger empires and colonies as a major war aim. But their Western adversaries, Britain and the United States, neither sought nor gained any major new colonies. Britain gave up her empire, as did eventually France, Belgium, the Netherlands, Spain, and Portugal. The United States gave independence to the Philippines and a legal option of independence to Puerto Rico. Moreover, most of the former "mother countries," having lost their colonies, became more prosperous in the years from 1950 to 1987, and their populations were better fed, housed, and educated than ever before. The belief of both conservatives and radical Marxists, that capitalism needed the direct rule over colonies, thus far has not been confirmed. And the worldwide economic recession of the mid-1970s to the late 1980s with its considerable levels of high unemployment and expansion of the poorer strata of the societies of many highly industrialized countries was not deep enough to change this verdict. Moreover, no efforts to reconquer or acquire new colonies have been seriously suggested or undertaken by the former colonial powers.

Another radical prediction—that colonial empires would not endure—has fared somewhat better. In the decades between 1913 and the present, most imperial and colonial regimes became untenable. The imperial and would-be imperial powers fought each other over the colonies they held, or those they tried to get, and ended up by all making each other weaker. The metropolitan populations, at first mostly those below the middle-class level but later on growing proportions of all social classes, found that for most of them the colonies brought little gain and rather, through the wars, much suffering; and eventually they became less inclined to fight for them, or to have their children drafted to do so.

Britain's American colonies became independent in 1776, with the notable exception of Canada. In the nineteenth century, Spain's empire in Latin America was replaced by independent republics. Between 1890 and 1930, Canada, Australia, Ireland, and New Zealand became substantially independent from Britain; and in Central Europe and the Near East an array of successor states eventually emerged from the ruins of the empires of Austria-Hungary and Turkey. After World War II, finally, most of the rest of the world's former colonial areas turned into sovereign states. The age of imperialism seemed to be over.

But was it over? How could one tell?

Despite his insistence that capitalism needed to rule colonial countries directly, so as to safeguard there the investments from the "mother country," Lenin also admitted the existence of *"half-colonial countries,"* such as China, Iran, and the Latin American Republics. Such countries were legally independent, but were in fact, he thought, each ruled by one or more of the imperial countries through their dependence on foreign trade, banking and insurance, foreign shipping, foreign technology and military equipment, and experts and advisers. In such countries, a native upper and middle class of landowners, merchants, small industrialists, and high bureaucrats would safeguard the interests of capital—their own and often also that of foreigners—so as to keep their countries more or less safely within the worldwide chain of the imperialist economic and social system. From time to time, however, so Lenin thought, conflicts would arise between the capitalists of a semicolonial country and those of a metropolitan power, and in such cases the nationalism of the colonial countries would join its effects to those of the peasants' and workers' revolts and thus contribute to that eventual collapse of the imperialist system which Lenin so confidently expected and so ardently desired.

The modern theories of "dependency" have continued from the 1950s onward some of the themes and some of the vocabulary of Lenin's thought but with important modifications.

DEPENDENCY: IMPERIALISM BY OTHER MEANS?

These theories take up in part an old theme of a minority of nineteenth-century economic theorists, such as the German Friedrich List and the American Henry Carey, according to which free trade might be good for highly industrialized countries but bad for relatively underdeveloped ones, since the latter would need to protect their "infant industries," as List called them, against their stronger foreign competitors. Lack of such protection would make the underdevelopment of the less industrialized countries worse and condemn them to long-run backwardness and poverty. In their own time, List and Carey lost the argument in economic theory and in most textbooks. There the "classic" theory prevailed, according to which free trade was supposed to benefit everyone, since it would lead each country to specialize in those activities in which it had a comparative advantage, such as port wine for Portugal and textiles and machinery for England. In reality, however, the industries in which England specialized under free trade in the nineteenth century were intensive in both using and rewarding industrial capital and skill and in making them in time more abundantly available to other branches of industry, fostering economic growth throughout most of the country.

Portugal's specialty, wine producing, did next to nothing of that kind. Most of Portugal's industries remained underdeveloped, with only a few exceptions such as fisheries and sardine canning; and Portugal in time became one of the poorhouses of Western Europe. Nineteenth-century free trade between England and Ireland seemed to have similar results: Britain and the six counties of today's Northern Ireland specialized in industry while Southern Ireland—today's Ireland—was left to specialize in poverty.

Most major countries on the European continent, as well as the United States, however, rejected in economic practice the advice of classic free-trade theory and the textbooks. They each used tariffs and other measures to protect their own industries against the competition of more advanced countries, and their industrial economies developed far more powerfully than those of countries that continued to cling to free trade. Today, some countries officially proclaim free-trade doctrines, as does the United States, and in part Britain, the Netherlands, and a few others, but in practice almost all countries also use many methods of intervention and protection, direct and indirect, so as to modify the flow of international trade in favor of their own influential industrial and other interest groups. Some governments, however, try harder than others; among those who do try hard, the bigger, richer, and stronger countries are more likely to succeed; and the absolute gap between most of the highly developed countries and most of the underdeveloped ones has in fact increased.

Why is this so? Some Latin American and Arab economists have sought an answer in their theory of *dependency*. Developed by such theorists as André Gunder Frank, Osvaldo Sunkel, Anouar Abdel Malek, and Samir Amin, and appealingly summarized by Johan Galtung,[9] the theory says that the poverty of the underdeveloped countries is the result of the present

---

[9]Johan Galtung, "A Structural Theory of Imperialism," *Journal of Peace Research* 8, no. 2 (1971), pp. 81–118.

international economic system which by its automatic operation has "under-developed" the poorer nations of the world, keeping them as poor as if they were still colonies. This system, say these theorists, is by its very structure the equivalent of the old system of colonial empires. In its results it is imperialism, they insist, even though it operates through other means.

Center vs. Periphery

A few highly industrialized countries, so the theory goes, form the social and economic *center* of the world. Each of these is rich, commands a diversified technology, produces a wide variety of goods and services, and trades with many different partner countries throughout the world. Since such a "center" country does not depend on the sale or supply of any one commodity, nor on trade with any one country, it cannot easily be compelled to accept unfavorable terms of trade, and rather will come out better in most international bargains. In trading with much less highly industrialized countries, moreover, each center country will mainly develop its capital-intensive and skill-intensive industries, a large supply of capital and managerial talent, a diversified and sophisticated technology, a resourceful and highly skilled workforce, and a large pool of engineers, scientists, and technicians—in short, all the conditions for further industrial and economic growth.

The many less industrialized countries of the world, according to the same theory, are in the opposite condition. They are in effect at the *periphery* of the international political and economic system. Poor in capital, credit, technology, skilled industrial labor, technical and scientific personnel, and competent managers, they are constrained to exporting only one or a few kinds of agricultural or mining products, and to trading in the main only with a single "partner" country, on which they depend for sales, credit, shipping, banking, and insurance, as well as for industrial products, equipment, and spare parts, together with scientific and technological information and know-how and higher-level technical and managerial personnel. Since they have only one or a few kinds of goods to sell, and only one major country to sell to and to borrow money from, they will get the worst of most bargains, and in the "free" market the terms of trade will be most often highly unfavorable for them—i.e., they will have to give much of their own simple goods for relatively little of the technically more complex goods from the richer center country. Moreover, their simple economic activities will produce but little capital, skills, and other resources for the development of other industries. As a result, the peripheral countries will tend to stay poor, while the center countries will tend to get richer.

Centers vs. Peripheries Within Nation-States

A similar contrast, still according to this theory, will be found in the internal structure of each of the two types of countries. Within each center country, there is again a center region, usually the capital city and the regions where the most advanced industries are located, and a periphery, mostly rural, where the less technically developed activities and the poorer and less skilled people are found. But since the center countries are rich and getting richer, say the theorists of dependency, the center regions of the center countries can afford to make concessions to their own peripheral regions and populations, and to share a little of their wealth with them, thus purchasing their political acquiescence or support.

In every periphery country, in this view, the opposite conditions hold. Here the population of the national center region will refuse to share any of the country's meager wealth with the national periphery; rather, they will tend to make themselves into little enclaves of Western-level wealth and Western-style standards of living and material consumption, guarding their automobiles, air conditioners, and refrigerators against the people of the periphery who continue to live in grass huts or hovels. The result, according to this theory, is a much deeper social division in the underdeveloped, peripheral countries than in the highly developed, center ones, giving rise in the former to much more bitter and violent social conflicts, riots, guerilla activities, terrorism from the political right and left, civil wars, frequent military dictatorships, and, less often, revolutions. Such revolutions are rare and rarely successful, says the theory, because most of the people in the urban, industrialized, and middle-class central sectors of each peripheral country are being rewarded for siding with the status quo at home and with the international system of unequal exchange, its multinational corporations, and its political, cultural, and economic privileges against the poverty-stricken majority of their own people who remain underemployed or unemployed, scattered in the hungry rural hinterlands or huddled in the slums and shanty towns at the periphery of the big cities.

Capital and talents are being drained out of these peripheries and out of the peripheral countries as a whole, according to this view, and hence the international system of inequality and exploitation in the world market and the related inequality within each peripheral country, all remain self-perpetuating, with no objective process of economic or historical development in sight to aid those who would change this situation in its basic structure. Only a subjective change of consciousness and will among the masses of the poor on the periphery of the peripheral countries could bring about a revolutionary struggle to end this "imperialist" system, forcing the local middle classes to choose between continuing to support their foreign imperial allies or turning against them and siding with their poor compatriots.

The contrast to Lenin's theory stands out, even though both groups of theorists invoke his name. According to Lenin and his followers, industrialization and economic growth themselves are huge and potentially liberating forces. They tend to increase the numbers, discipline, capabilities, and social awareness of workers, and through the growing contacts with workers, he thought, also the political capabilities and awareness of the poorer part of the peasants, who can become their allies. Moreover, imperialism, as he saw it, will bring capital and industry, including heavy industry, to the colonial and half-colonial countries; it must strive for direct military conquest and control. This in turn, he thought, will bring it into recurrent conflicts with the native middle classes of the developing countries, so that eventually workers, poor peasants, and, from time to time, these native middle classes all will be united in a broad coalition to resist and finally to destroy the imperialist system.

The "New Left of the 1970s," using much of the same vocabulary, saw a radically different prospect, and this perspective has continued to be maintained by some proponents of dependency theory in the 1980s. Most capital will remain in the center countries; the underdeveloped countries will remain poor, backward, and economically, culturally, and, in effect, even politically subjected; their workers will feel relatively privileged and become conservative; and only their unemployed, poor-rural, and "marginal" groups will long for change but may be powerless to achieve it.

CONTENDING THEORIES AND THE SEARCH FOR EVIDENCE

Both these perspectives correspond to some elements of reality but neither corresponds to all of it. In the course of history, industrialization has led to more than one social system. In some previously nonindustrial countries— Japan, Russia, Finland, Sweden, Norway, Denmark, Iceland, Australia, some countries in Eastern Europe and the Balkans, and parts of India, China, and Brazil—industry has grown in the course of our century. In this same period, revolutions and civil wars in Russia, China, Yugoslavia, Cuba, and Vietnam eventually led to the establishment of communist regimes, but in Japan, Germany, Italy, and Scandinavia thorough industrialization has occurred alongside constitutional governments or the establishment of democratic systems which soon took root and eventually commanded the loyalty of the great majority of the populations. On the other hand, in many countries in Latin America, Africa, and Asia, repressive native military regimes have emerged which defend local patterns of extreme economic inequality and social privilege while remaining more or less subservient to foreign creditors and corporations.

Where earlier stages of development had reduced or decreased social inequality, industrialization eventually strengthened mass purchasing power and created a significant domestic market with mass production and consumption of goods. These factors seem to have favored domestic investments and constitutional and democratic systems in the early industrializing countries of the West. Where, on the contrary, social cleavages and mass poverty remained extreme and hence the domestic market relatively unimportant—with very little investment taking place—industry became concentrated in the export sector where the local population functioned as a source of cheap labor rather than as important customers. Under these conditions, social cleavages and antagonisms remained extreme, and industry remained largely restricted to limited enclaves oriented to the world market—somewhat as the dependency theorists had predicted. In this manner, formerly "peripheral" countries of Western Europe such as Scandinavia, Ireland, Greece, or southern Italy still found a way to a broader national industrialization and democratic constitutions, while such countries as Iran, Peru, or Senegal did not. The forms and consequences of industrial development and economic growth were thus determined by political developments creating conditions in favor of greater or lesser mass purchasing power.[10]

What specific conditions decide the outcome of a country's entry into the world market and the age of industrialization? What decides whether it will outgrow the state of dependency relatively gradually and more or less peacefully, or whether its dependency on one or several richer countries will endure for several generations or even centuries, only to be ended, if at all, by a bloody revolution?

Perhaps six conditions are decisive. The first two are cultural and may have developed in earlier centuries:

1. a cultural interest in things and materials such as wood and metal, in tools, in inanimate sources of energy, such as water power and wind power;

2. cultural habits of diligence and thrift, of accuracy and reliability, and an interest in time.

The next two are matters of economic history:

3. the availability of capital for investment within the country, as against its non-accumulation, or dissipation through tribute, flight abroad, or through exploitation and luxury consumption through a small elite at home; and

4. a relatively large domestic market based on the purchasing power of a broader base of the population, often resulting from their success in earlier social struggles.

The last two conditions are closely connected with the previous four, but arise in the early stages of industrialization itself;

5. a multiplicity of different trades and skills in manufacturing and transport instead of the growth of only a very few branches of industry; and

6. a balance among the many and various branches of industrial development.

Of course, these six conditions interact, and each can contribute to the further development of the others. But where all or almost all of them are present, dependency can be outgrown sooner and autonomous growth can be combined with growing interactions with the world economy.

To what extent is the theory of dependency borne out by observable data? The information presented in Table 20 offers a mixed picture. Four highly industrialized countries—the United States, the Federal Republic of

[10]See Dieter Senghaas, *The European Experiment: A Historical Critique of Development Theory*, Dover, NH: Longwood Pub. Group, 1985; Ulrich Menzel, *In der Nachfolge Europas— Autozentrierte Entwicklung in den ostasiatischen Schwellenländern Südkorea und Taiwan*, München, Verlag Simon & Magiera KG, 1985; Ulrich Menzel and Dieter Senghaas, *Europas Entwicklung und die Dritte Welt*, especially chapter 6, II 'Indikatoren zur Bestimmung von Schwellenländern. Ein Vorschlag zur Operationalisierung, edition suhrkamp, Suhrkamp Verlag Frankfurt am Main, 1986.

TABLE 20   Center and Periphery: Highly Developed vs. Less Developed Countries, c. 1975

	1 US	2 FRG	3 UK	4 USSR	5 ARG	6 BRAZ	7 ECUAD	8 GHANA	9 INDON	10 TANZAN	11 CHINA	12 INDIA	WORLD Mean	Med
1. TPOP (mil)	214.0	53.0	56.0	255.0	25.0	110.0	7.0	10.0	136.0	15.0	839.0	613.0	26.0	6.0
2. GNP/C (1978$)	9770.0	8880.0	5720.0	3710.0	2030.0	510.0	950.0	380.0	340.0	240.0	230.0	180.0	2466.0	930.0
3. ENERG/C (= kgs coal equiv)	10999.0	3939.0	5268.0	5050.0	1763.0	668.0	416.0	169.0	184.0	68.0	672.0	208.0	2047.0	583.0
4. GPCH (1970–1978) %	2.3	3.1	1.9	4.3	1.5	6.0	5.6	–3.0	5.3	1.7	5.2	1.6	2.2	2.3
5. ENERCH (1950–1975) %	1.7	3.0	0.7	4.2	3.5	4.1	5.1	2.5	5.5	3.0	5.4	4.3		
6. NONA	97.0	90.0	98.0	81.0	86.0	58.0	53.0	46.0	40.0	16.0	37.0	27.0	47.0	50.0
7. LIT	99.0	99.0	99.0	100.0	93.0	66.0	74.0	30.0	62.0	66.0	82.0	36.0	58.0	60.0
8. NEWS/1000	287.0	214.0	388.0	397.0	154.0	39.0	49.0	51.0	7.0	3.0	n.d.	16.0	115.0	49.0
9. RADIO/1000	1879.0	344.0	699.0	481.0	838.0	155.0	100.0	107.0	37.0	15.0	12.0	23.0	199.0	122.0
10. TRD/GNP %	14.0	34.0	46.0	11.0	18.0	20.0	44.0	27.0	41.0	46.0	6.0	13.0	65.0	50.0
11. COMCONC	10.0	9.0	10.0	17.0	17.0	11.0	41.0	38.0	58.0	21.0	n.d.	6.0	31.0	21.0
12. PARCONC	11.0	9.0	6.0	7.0	7.0	10.0	30.0	12.0	30.0	7.0	n.d.	11.0	20.0	15.0
13. CALOR/C	3576.0	3434.0	3336.0	3460.0	3347.0	2562.0	1983.0	2272.0	2063.0	2453.0	2021.0	2578.0	2431.0	
14. PROT/C	104.0	98.0	92.0	108.0	107.0	62.0	47.0	53.0	44.0	47.0	64.0	48.0	68.0	62.0
15. INFD	16.0	10.0	16.0	28.0	59.0	84.0	115.0	107.0*	125.0	96.0*	109.0*	134.0	79.0	51.0

Notes: Numbers in parentheses refer to pages in Taylor and Jodice. Key to abbreviations:

TPOP = total population (pp. 91–94)

GNP/C = gross national product per capita 1978 in U.S.$ (pp. 110–113)

ENERG/C = per-capita energy consumption in equivalents of kilograms of coal (pp. 114–117)

GPCH = average annual growth rate of per-capita GNP, c. 1970–1978, in percent (pp. 110–113)

ENERCH = average annual growth rate of per-capita energy consumption, c. 1950–1975, in percent (pp. 114–117)

NONA = percent of labor force *not* employed in agriculture, 1977 (from data in pp. 208–210)

LIT = percent of literates in population aged 15 and above (pp. 169–172)

NEWS = newspaper circulation per 1000 population (pp. 175–177)

RADIO = radio receivers per 1000 population (pp. 178–180)

TRD/GNP = foreign trade (imports plus exports) as percent of GNP (pp. 226–229)

COMCONC = index of concentration of kinds of commodities exported × 100 (pp. 230–232)

PARCONC = index of concentration of export-receiving partner countries × 100 (pp. 233–235)

CALOR/C = average food calories per capita per day, c. 1977 (pp. 142–145)

PROT/C = average grams of food protein per capita per day, c. 1974 (pp. 146–149)

INFD = infant death rate in first year, per 1000 live births (pp. 156–159)

n.d. = no data available

Source: From data in C. L. Taylor and D. A. Jodice, *World Handbook of Political and Social Indicators,* 3rd ed. (New Haven, CT: Yale Univ. Press, 1983).
*1970 data from *World Bank Atlas* (Washington, D.C.: The World Bank, 1985).

Germany, Great Britain, and the Soviet Union—as well as a country at an intermediate level of development, Argentina, all are much higher in per-capita gross national product and in per-capita consumption of energy than are the seven less developed countries—Ghana, Brazil, Ecuador, China, India, Indonesia, and Tanzania. The same contrasts of 2:1 or more in favor of the highly developed countries are found in the average levels of economic growth, nonagricultural occupations, literacy, scientific contributions, newspaper circulation, radio listening, and average nutrition. In their exports, the highly developed countries have very low degrees of concentration on particular commodities or partner countries, while the less developed most often show higher degrees of concentration in both respects—somewhat as the theory of dependency predicts. Finally, as an indicator of popular well-being or suffering, the infant death rates in the four rich countries are only one-third or less of those in the six poorer countries in the table, for which such data are available. All this information tends to confirm in part the assertion that extreme inequality and in some sense injustice continue to characterize the international system, even after the age of formal empires has ended.

But some of the data are less conclusive than the dependency theory would assert. Argentina, for example, does not fit well into this statistical picture; on the average it is too rich, too high in energy consumption, too literate, too well-supplied with newspapers and radios, too well-fed, and too little dependent on foreign trade in general or on any one partner country in particular to be counted as a "Third World" country—and yet its infant death rate is appalling. The distinct division of the world into "center" and "periphery" areas is thus becoming increasingly obsolete, and a more complex analytical approach incorporating the features of the so-called newly industrializing countries (NICs) such as Argentina, Brazil, Mexico, Taiwan, and perhaps Turkey, needs to be developed. Other countries, too, no longer show the clear-cut characteristics of exploitation and dependency of the traditional two-way division. The majority of oil-exporting countries since the 1970s are in many ways closer to being center countries in terms of per-capita gross national product, per-capita consumption of energy and rates of economic growth, but at the same time show development characteristics more typical of periphery countries, such as a high trade concentration on particular commodities, and a generally lower standard of living for the entire population. The long-term prediction of dependency theorists of the self-perpetuating persistence of inequality and exploitation as well as dependency by the highly developed over the developing countries thus will need to be modified to take account of such dynamic and autonomous changes in the world economy.

There are other things that do not fit the dependency theory. China and India are so big and have such small sectors of foreign trade, compared to their total GNP, that it is difficult to see how these could make them truly dependent on any worldwide imperialistic system. Moreover, China's political and social institutions for nearly forty years have been radically different from those of the other developing countries, yet the levels of her people in regard to nutrition in both protein and calories, to per-capita income, to access to radio listening, and to scientific contributions are not impressively better than are those in other less developed countries (LDCs) in the table. Finally, for most of the eight LDCs, the levels of nonagricultural occupations and of literacy are higher, and the indices of partner country concentration lower, than the theory of self-perpetuating dependency would seem to suggest.

Clearly, the last word in this discussion has not yet been spoken. More recently, Marxist-oriented dependency theorists have developed an analytical perspective that stresses the importance of worldwide exchange relations rather than the underlying social relations of worldwide capitalist production; these worldwide exchange relations, the world-system theoretical approach argues, structure the world economy by generating the international division of labor and the specialization of production. Trade relations thus determine the hierarchical order and the exploitation of peripheral by center or core areas at the world market level, and hence create "world classes" of the bourgeoisie and proletariat—with the world being stratified into zones of nations or groups of nations, rather than national units. In this market system, nations are peripheralized by being incorporated into the worldwide division of labor, and the process of "development" in this context merely signifies the attainment of a more advantageous position in the world system at the expense of other, more peripheral states.

Major conflicts and tensions arise over the disjuncture between these global economic system processes and political arrangements, which tend to be defined by individual nation-states. These, and world politics in general, tend to distort the normal operation of the world market. The stronger a state and its apparatus of control, the better it can influence the world market and its position in it, while weaker states will tend to produce patterns of dependency, which in turn will lower the strength of these states even further. Thus, the strength of a nation's state apparatus will parallel the position of the society within the global division of labor: core areas will spawn strong states, and peripheral areas are likely to be characterized by weak states. World-system theorists predict that the expansionist logic of the world capitalist system and the antagonistic structure of the world economy versus individual nation-states will eventually lead to competition among the core-states themselves—in addition to conflict between weak and strong states, as well as conflicts between state and private capitalist interests at the subnational level. These structural contradictions will eventually lead to the breakup of the world system and as the factors of production become freed and the limits of structural expansion reached, the doom of world capitalism will be followed by a "postcapitalist" system.[11]

[11]For more extensive discussions of the world-systems theoretical approach, see Immanuel Wallerstein, *The Capitalist World Economy* (Cambridge: Cambridge Univ. Press, 1979); Albert Bergesen (ed.), *Studies of the Modern World System* (New York: Academic Press, 1980); W. L. Hollist and James N. Rosenau (eds.), *World System Debates*, special issue of *International Studies Quarterly* 25 (March 1981); and Bruce Andrews, "The Political Economy of World Capitalism: Theory and Practice," *International Organization* 36, no. 1 (Winter 1982), pp. 135–163.

Schematic as much as this theory still is, it does attempt to take into account some of the structural political and economic changes that have occurred in recent decades, such as the declining importance of national boundaries and national economic decision-making in a world of increasing economic interdependence. Particularly the less developed countries have experienced radical changes and developments in their political and social systems following their exposure to the world market and international economic influences which very often reached far beyond the control of their state apparatus. How far these changes have been autonomous, however, and how far they were tied to, or produced by, world capitalist modes of production is still in need of much further empirical testing.

In most of the world's less developed countries, the new administrative and military organization and personnel are now native, not foreign. The predominant ideology now is nationalism, not imperialism. There is now a larger native middle class and often a noticeable increase in local industries. There are more workers in industry and transport and more labor unions. Schools and universities often are greatly expanded, and the new masses of students often are a source of political unrest, and so are the expanded cities. Despite efforts of the local dictators and of their foreign backers, the political and social situation in many of these newly industrializing countries looks more precarious and less stable and self-perpetuating than the theories of dependency assume; this situation may indeed indicate that what states and their ruling governments try to unify, the world economy system tears asunder. Above all, the capabilities of the local populations have changed and are continuing to change, including their growing capabilities for more nearly full emancipation.

The further emancipation of these developing countries may well involve considerable political changes within them. It may bring higher prices for their exports and stiffer demands upon the highly developed countries, rather than a perpetuation of the pattern of exploitation experienced so far in the world's socioeconomic setting. For a time some of the peripheral countries may well reduce their trade and financial links with the center ones, and instead increase the collaboration and interchange among the peripheral countries—the Third World. Later only, on a basis of greater equality and increased mutual aid, may the present level of world interdependence be restored and eventually even be increased, to benefit all participants in the world economy and eventually reduce the dangerous division of the world into a dominating and profiting group of rich nation-states and an exploited and underprivileged larger part of humankind, the Third World.

21

Some Prospects for the Future

"The future," the Nobel Prize winning physicist and philosopher Percy W. Bridgman once said, "is a program." What did he mean by that?

Every scientific prediction is based on the extrapolation of some earlier events or observations. We derive our guesses about the future by projecting ahead some time-series of events and experiences from the past. But there are many such series: they may run parallel, or converge or diverge; they may cross over so as to make relatively small what once was big, and to make what was small in the past big in the future. We do not want to project, then, single time-series in isolation, but rather the *configuration* of several of the most important series of data and events in their changing patterns of interactions and proportions.

As a strategist may try to read the future positions and capabilities of an army from the present deployment of its troops, so we can try to estimate at least some of the expectable patterns of the future of world politics from the present distribution and deployment of the world's populations, needs, resources, hopes, and efforts. It is in this sense that the world trends of today in their joint configuration add up to a program that can suggest to us something of the probable shape of things to come.

Even then we cannot foresee the future with any certainty. It involves too many probabilities, singly and in combination. But though we cannot foresee precisely or reliably, we can try to *provide* some plans, preparations, and resources for some of the most likely risks, constraints, and opportunities for at least a limited span of time ahead.

FOUR TIME HORIZONS

Most large changes in human behavior require time and effort. Large organizations and social, economic, and political systems behave with something similar to momentum: when they receive messages to change their course, they still need time to accept them and more time to respond. In many respects, therefore, there is a time span of lag or momentum for which much of their behavior can be foretold but not controlled: we can only say that for that period they will largely continue to act the way they did before. During this time span, the system cannot be effectively steered on any new course, although steering efforts may be made, which may have visible effects at a later stage. Taking as a date of departure the year 1986, this period so dominated by momentum that it cannot be currently steered may well extend until about 1990–1995; and this then becomes the nearest time horizon for our projections. Here we can perhaps foresee but not control, and this is the stuff out of which tragedies are made.

Beyond that period, however, there begins a new one which is far enough away so that large-scale efforts of governments to change the course of events would have time enough to take effect, and which is yet near enough so that much about it still can be foreseen. This is that portion of the future which in principle can be to a significant degree predicted and controlled; it is that part of the future for which we have at least a somewhat better chance to provide long-range policies. For the purposes of this chapter, this will be first of all the period until A.D. 2010—that is, if there is no great war, most of the active lifetime of the present generation of college and university students. In the second place, and for a more modest ensemble of probable developments, it will be the epoch until A.D. 2050—that is, the active lifetime of the children of the college students of today.

A very few matters, including some important ones, can be gauged for a still longer period, up to A.D. 2100, or until the retirement of the grandchildren of the present generation of university students; and, accordingly, we may through suitable public policies exercise at least some degree of specific control over these aspects of our future. Beyond 2100, however, almost all foresight of which we are now capable grows so dim, and the consequences of our present-day policy decisions become so uncertain, that we cannot realistically undertake any policy steps today that could promise us any substantial degree of guidance over the course of events in the twenty-second century. What will be likely to happen more than one century from now is something we now can neither foresee nor control.[1]

Our time horizons, then, will be the years around 1995, 2010, 2050, and 2100, respectively. And the first trends of development we look for are

---

[1] I am indebted to John R. Platt for the line of reasoning that has led to the foregoing section. For what I have made here of his insights, however, I alone must be responsible.

the numbers of people on our planet and the amounts of food, energy, and capital which they are likely to need to live.

PEOPLE, FOOD, ENERGY, AND CAPITAL

By 1986, the world population had grown to 5 billion, increasing at a rate of 1.7 percent per year. At this rate, our number should double in about 41 years, so that we should be 8 billion in 2010 or shortly thereafter.

Birth rates and death rates between them determine most of population growth; and though they have declined in Europe and the United States, they are still high in many countries of Africa, Latin America, and Asia. Moreover, in most of these countries, death rates are likely to fall as modern medical and public health techniques are being adopted; but the family patterns and reproductive habits of hundreds of millions of Third World villagers and poor townsfolk will not quickly change. For these reasons it seems realistic to expect that on the average the 1.7 percent rate of population growth is likely to persist until 2010, and that accordingly we should count on a world population of 8 billion by or near that year.

In the next period, 2010–2050, however, birth rates should fall and the world's rate of population increase should decline, perhaps to an average of 1 percent for the forty-year period, leading to a world population of about 12 billion in 2050 A.D..

After that date, another decline in birth and population growth rates seems likely; perhaps to an average of 0.5 percent for the 2051–2100 epoch, resulting in a world population of about 15.4, or less than 16 billion around the latter year. After 2100, then, the world population might attain zero growth, or come close to it—if we can make any reasonable estimate of trends beyond 2100.

The reasons for the rates assumed in the preceding paragraphs cannot be discussed in detail here. They include such points as these: by 2010, the majority of humanity, including the majority of the world's women, will be literate city dwellers who are no longer occupied with agriculture; the life expectancy of children will have grown; in many countries other provisions against sickness and old age will have taken the place of the large family; and as the motivations for family planning and birth control increase, more and more varied means for these purposes will be available. There may well be some local and temporary countertrends and eddies, but this gradual slowdown of population growth seems to be the direction in which the mainstream of world development will be most likely to go. Five billion people in 1986, 8 billion in 2010, 12 billion in 2050, and close to 16 billion in 2100—where is the food for all these people to come from?

From the mid-1950s through the mid-1980s, world food production approximately has kept pace with population growth. Today, the world population is on the whole neither better nor worse fed than it was in the 1950s, nor is the distribution of food or famine in the world much more or less unequal and unjust than it was two decades ago. But where is twice as much food for twice as many people to be found?

Most fertile tillable land is already under cultivation. The main gains can come only from more intensive agriculture: raising much bigger crops on but little more land. This will mean a "green revolution" through the use of the high-yielding strains of maize, wheat, and rice that have been developed in recent decades. But these "miracle strains" of food plants in turn require much more water and fertilizer per acre. Large-scale irrigation, in turn, will take much more energy for building dams and digging reservoirs, canals, and ditches, and later for dredging them from time to time; additional energy for pumping water where it is needed; still more energy for the chemical fertilizer plants; and finally, energy for the transport and distribution of the grain supplies and for the construction of adequate facilities for their storage. A greater supply of energy for agriculture is likely to become a condition for the survival of millions.

To produce energy, people must use capital, and as the next three decades go on, they will need ever more of it, for most of the easily accessible deposits of coal, oil, and natural gas have already been found and exploited. Most of the new mineral fuels must now come from ever deeper layers of the earth or from the bottom of the sea, requiring ever more elaborate machines, drilling towers, pipe shafts for their production, pipe lines, gas works, cracking plants, and thermal power stations for their use. There is still some electric energy to be obtained from water power, but this requires new dams and turbines, and here the capital costs per megawatt (though not the fuel costs) are higher than in thermal power stations. Nuclear power stations with their shielding require still more capital per unit, and the safe disposal of their fission products tends to create additional capital requirements. At present, and probably for the next 25 years, thermonuclear power stations, using the much higher energy levels of nuclear fusion processes, seem likely to require still more capital, if they should become practical within that time at all. Finally, solar energy, vast but spread out over large areas, will require still more capital for the mirrors, batteries, and other devices for its collection, storage, and transmission. There is today no realistic prospect for getting much more energy by 2010 except at a higher cost of capital per unit of power.

Twice as many people, at least twice as much food, more energy per unit of food, and more capital per unit of energy—all this may well add up to a world need for about four times as much capital as is being used today. And this is not yet the whole story.

THE SOCIAL MOBILIZATION OF THE WORLD'S MEN AND WOMEN

People are not only growing in numbers; they are changing in important characteristics and qualities. Many forms of *social mobilization* make people available for new patterns of behavior. Already today the majority of humans have become exposed to the demonstration effects of airplanes, automobiles, electric lights, and many other items of modern technology, enhancing their sense of power and of possibilities of change. They have learned to use money and to deal with relative strangers. They have become part of the audience of modern mass media of communication, such as radio, motion pictures, television, posters, newspapers, and books, which show them how other people live and act, and what they themselves may be missing. Every decade, perhaps another 20 percent of humanity becomes exposed to these effects. By 2010, more than 90 percent of the human population will have their imagination stirred up by these processes.

The fast mobilization of people's imaginations is accompanied or followed by a slower but more basic mobilization of their experiences and capabilities. The majority of the world's adults (those over fifteen years) had become literate by 1955—for the first time since the invention of writing. Every ten years, another 7 percent are shifting into the literate sector of the population. Thus by 1980, more than two-thirds had become literate; by 2010, more than 90 percent of the people over fifteen will have this capability.

In 1986, about one-half of the world's population was no longer occupied with agriculture. This, too, was for the first time in several thousand years. Every ten years, another 7 percent of the world's workforce, on the average, is moving out of agriculture into nonagricultural pursuits, or into unemployment. By the end of the century, over 70 percent of the world's working-age population will no longer be in agriculture; by 2010, this proportion may be close to 75 percent, outnumbering the world's remaining peasants about three to one.

Somewhat similarly, in 1987, more than one-half of the people in the world were living in cities and towns. Many of these lived in small towns under 20,000 inhabitants, but even so this worldwide majority of town dwellers was the first since the first cities were built about 3000 b.c. Every decade, another 5 percent, on the average, are moving into towns or are engulfed by towns and cities spreading out into the countryside. By 2010, about two-thirds of humanity will be urban.

Perhaps more than one-fifth of the world's working-age population (fifteen to sixty-four years) in 1987 was employed in industry and transport; and about another 4 percent of that age group is joining them in each decade. By 2010, one-third of the world's workforce may be working in industry and transport, and by 2050 they may well form the majority of the world's working-age population.

The total share of wage and salary earners, including clerical and service workers, is much higher. They were more than one-third of the world's workforce in 1987 and they are likely to be its majority by 2010. Employers, peasants, and other self-employed people in town and country will be a minority on this planet.

In all these respects, and many others, the patterns of thousands of years are breaking in our lifetime. Some of these changes seem slow on the time scale of a busy year or two, but they are dramatically swift when seen on a scale of decades and generations. Faster than ever before, humanity is being transformed in its social and economic structures and informed by its mass communications. The transformation includes the experiences of many millions of people and their expanding needs for public services, economic security, and social welfare. And it includes their inner needs for identity, for belonging to a place and to a group of people, and for some clear and simple orientation in a too-fast-changing and too-complicated world. When these needs are no longer answered automatically by social tradition, they turn into political needs—needs that often seem to be answered most readily by nationalism, by class alignments, and by simplifying political ideologies or leaders.

The upshot of many of these changes is a thrust of people toward politics. Sometimes people then demand the vote in the hope to use it; at other times they may refuse to vote, despairing of its usefulness in a political system which they have found unresponsive and from which they have become alienated. But having become mobilized socially, having left behind many old habits and relationships, they are now available for new demands, new commitments, and new activities.

Worldwide we are witnessing a decline of fatalism and submissiveness to deprivation and oppression. The age-old mass apathy on which the old empires were founded is going irretrievably. We are living in an age of declining tolerance for frustration, for alien rule, and for government from a great distance. This is an age of rising costs of foreign intervention and of its declining effectiveness.

REDUCING INEQUALITY: THROUGH GROWTH OR THROUGH CONFLICT

The world as a whole is still poor and very unequal, but it is already to some extent ungovernable, and it may be on the way toward becoming more so. In the rich countries, many of the working people and the poorer people expect that at some time in the future they and their children will be better off. These hopes can only be fulfilled in one of two ways: either by redistribution of some part of the national income, so as to take it from the middle and upper classes and give it to their poorer compatriots; or else by economic growth. But mere redistribution is not practical. Those who now are better off would resist tooth and nail, even by force of arms, any attempt to take from them a substantial part of what they now have and are used to having. The result would be violence and civil war, the costs of which might well make everybody poorer, including those who were supposed to be benefited at the outset. Only continued economic growth could bring substantial improvements to the poor without subjecting the middle and upper middle classes to sacrifices which they would refuse to accept.

The same principle holds on the international level. Improving the lot of the people of the world's poor countries would require either transferring to them a good deal of capital and income from their richer neighbors—something which the latter would fight rather than accept—or else there would have to be continued economic growth, so as to permit everyone to gain without anyone losing. So long as people's material needs are still so large and so urgent, economic growth will remain a major precondition for peace among nations and within them.

How much economic growth is likely to be needed to maintain a chance for international and civil peace until the year 2010? Between 1870 and 1970, average per-capita income in many countries grew by about 3 percent per year, doubling every twenty-three years, despite the destruction caused by wars and revolutions during that period. Even this growth rate did not suffice by itself to ensure peace; yet we now are looking for the smallest growth rate that still might give peace a chance, if it were combined with other peace-preserving measures. Perhaps the smallest politically acceptable annual growth rate per capita for the world's highly industrialized and developed countries (DCs)—let us recall that they now comprise 20 percent of world population, enjoying 80 percent of world income—might be 1.5 percent, doubling their per-capita income in fifty years. This would permit the per-capita income share of the world's less developed countries (LDCs) to grow much faster, at 4 percent per year, doubling every 17.5 years. Since the LDCs have 80 percent of world population but only 20 percent of world income, even this rapid growth rate would at first add to the world's total income only 0.8 percent per year, while the slower growth rate of 1.5 percent, applied to the DCs' 80 percent share would at first add only an annual 1.2 percent, leaving the total annual growth rate of per-capita world income at 2 percent—close to the average of the 1950–1975 period.

We cannot go into details here. But even these provisional and illustrative figures suggest that with a moderate continuing growth of per-capita DC income and a moderately accelerated growth in the corresponding rate for the LDCs, a moderate and manageable average economic growth rate for the world could be sustained. If the present-day proportions were maintained, the average per-capita incomes of LDCs and DCs might become equal within less than fifty-five years, or by about 2040, with the DCs twice as rich per capita as they are today, the LDCs eight times so, and total per-capita income for the world nearly three times what it is today.

For the shorter period 1986–2011, per-capita world income would be close to twice that of the 1980s, with LDC per-capita income increased fourfold, the corresponding figure for 1986 DCs increased by about 70 percent, and today's proportional gap of about 16:1 between the DC and LDC per-capita incomes reduced to less than 7:1, or cut down to less than one-half—a change that should at least help somewhat to maintain mutual trust and peace among nations. An opposite development seems also possible, wherein elites in a number of rich and powerful DCs might use their political power to increase not only the concentration of wealth in their own upper strata—and correspondingly reduce the shares of their poorer countrymen—but also to increase their countries' shares of the world's resources and reduce correspondingly the shares of other nations. If this changing of relative shares should occur while humankind as a whole gets much richer, world stability could nevertheless be maintained, as it has been in the past. But if the world's income should stagnate or substantially decline over longer periods of time, prospects for peaceful change and the nonviolent transition of such shares of wealth will decrease accordingly.

Now, however, we see our requirements add up. To the doubled world population by 2011 and its increased requirements of food, energy, and capital, discussed earlier, we now must add the effects of a doubled average per-capita income. Taken together, these considerations suggest that the world's capital requirements by 2011 may well be between six and eight times the level of the mid-1980s. If this should be indeed the direction of approximate magnitude of world developments over the next thirty-five years, the politics of this relatively near future may be in large part the politics of capital formation and the public and private guidance of capital investment.

OTHER PRESSURES TOWARD CONFLICT

Social mobilization, as we have seen, makes people less tolerant of fate, frustrations, and extreme inequality, and more often ready to raise political demands and to take action to press for them. At the same time, more people are learning to form organizations and to act in an organized manner to promote their interests.

A century ago, farmers, workers, and business executives in the United States were for the most part unorganized. Most of them were engaged in something close to what economists call "perfect competition." They competed in the market as individuals and accepted farm prices, wage rates, and market demand as given, to be adapted to, but not susceptible to change by their own actions. By the 1980s most of this had changed. Farmers, workers, and business executives all had become organized and were themselves trying to set, directly or with the help of the government, the prices and conditions at which their goods or services were to be sold. Each organized group now was trying to act as if it were a single monopolist, or, more accurately, as if it were an oligopolist, one among a very few competitors, able to gain a quasi-monopolistic advantage in the market. In short, each group now was trying to offer less in the market and to charge more for it.

This will work quite well, so long as only some groups are organized and others are not. The organized groups will get higher prices or wages for offering fewer goods and services; and the unorganized groups will be paying more and getting less.

But what happens when nearly everyone is organized? Then everyone will try to charge more and offer less. With higher prices and fewer goods, money will lose some of its purchasing power, and people will complain about inflation. With everyone trying to limit output for goods and services in the market, there will be fewer jobs offered and there will be fewer good investment opportunities for people's savings; and people will speak of recession or stagnation; and they may speak of "stagflation" when they notice how inflation and stagnation sometimes seem to go together.

In this situation, everyone is tempted to wish that the other groups' organizations could be weakened or destroyed, so as to permit the profitable continuation of one's own oligopolistic practices. Every interest group may now try to increase its political power among the electorate, within the government, and in many countries even with the help of the armed forces and police. Eventually the power of some groups to bargain in an organized manner may be weakened or destroyed, as has happened to labor unions at various times in many countries, and other groups may then expect to become more prosperous at their expense.

Something similar may happen in the world market. In the 1860s, most groups and most countries were unorganized in their buying and selling. "Perfect" competition was considered normal. The products of unorganized European and American industry and labor were exchanged for the products of equally unorganized farmers and overseas countries. By the 1920s and 1930s, people in most of the industrialized countries had learned to organize. The eight-hour day, legal minimum wages, union bargaining, and government taxes for social welfare and military spending all increased the prices of manufactured goods, while oil, coffee, bananas, and other products of unorganized overseas labor and peasants remained cheap.

But now, in the 1980s, the overseas countries are learning to organize, and so are the interest groups within them. Between 1970 and 1984 American wheat prices almost tripled, automobile prices more than doubled, and oil prices increased more than twenty-fold. In mid-1986, after a weakening of the OPEC oil cartel, oil prices remained about ten times as high as they had been in 1970. Here, too, there has been a temptation to use political power and even military force to compel "the others" to give up some or all of their organized bargaining power. Big countries importing oil hinted for a time at their option of using military force to keep its price from rising further. Some oil-exporting countries bought arms and built up their own military forces, which had the effect of making the use of force against them less attractive.

The result has been a tendency toward a militarization of world politics. In much of South Asia, Africa, and Latin America, military regimes have risen to power. Many conventional weapons, such as tanks, artillery, short-range rockets, and aircraft have been acquired by many non-Western governments; and submachine guns, grenades, mortars, and flame throwers are now in the hands of guerillas, as well as of police, in many countries. The days from 1500 to 1950, when the Western countries—and indeed, any highly industrialized country—had a decisive military advantage over any less developed nation are past. In China, Korea, Algeria, and Vietnam, long military deadlocks have testified to the fact that now the world's peoples fight in more nearly equal terms, with few or no quick, cheap victories in sight for anyone.

But will not nuclear weapons restore the military superiority of a few great powers? There is little chance that they will do so. Even today, the nuclear weapons of one big power are in large part balanced by those of another, with no conspicuous gains for any of them. And the trend toward proliferation of nuclear technology and nuclear weapons, though it may be slowed down for a while by international agreements, will eventually dilute even the military advantages which some nuclear powers still have today, leaving all countries more vulnerable.

NUCLEAR PROLIFERATION: HOW FAST, HOW FAR?

In 1945, the United States was the only nation possessing nuclear weapons. In 1986 there were at least six nations who admitted to have such weapons—the United States, Britain, the Soviet Union, France, China, and India—and it was widely believed that Israel, South Africa, and perhaps also some Arab country possessed some nuclear warheads. If so, the number of nations with nuclear weapons has been doubling about every ten years, or four times in less than forty years. If this pace should continue, there should be fifteen or sixteen countries with nuclear weapons around the year 2000, about twenty-five in 2010, and about a hundred by 2050.

Many of the "candidate countries" are well known—those who could acquire nuclear weapons even today, if their governments chose to do so. Such "candidate countries" include West Germany, Japan, Canada, Australia, Italy, Sweden, Switzerland, Brazil, Pakistan, New Zealand and perhaps Taiwan, Egypt, and Iran. By 2010, if not sooner, Indonesia, Argentina, Algeria, Iraq, and other countries will probably have followed suit. Already today the two countries with the largest numbers of mouths to feed—China with over 1 billion and India with more than 700 million—have nuclear weapons. Within the lifetime of today's students, most of the world's larger and potentially hungry countries will be so armed, unless that lifetime should be drastically shortened.

An Imaginary Conversation

Let us imagine a possible conversation in 1997 at the White House on the occasion of the visit of India's prime minister; let us call him Minoo M. Gandhi III, with the president of the United States, Ronald Bush Mondale.

"Mr. President," says the Indian guest, "you know that my government has done everything to consolidate peace and friendship between our two countries. Now, however, the failure of this year's monsoon rains threatens to make 1995 the worst year of famine in our history, just as our population has risen past the 900 million mark. We shall need food relief, Mr. President, on a larger scale than ever before."

"Our grain reserves are limited," answers the President, "and I cannot be sure how our Congress would respond to a very large request."

"Mr. President," says the Prime Minister, "if we do not get adequate relief and our people start dying in the famine, my government will fall and my moderate policies will disappear with it. As you know, our most likely successors in office will be the new conservative-revolutionary movement whose followers worship Kali, the Hindu goddess of death, and look forward to the fiery dance of the god Shiva that will destroy the world for its later renewal. They say that we should rather die fighting than starve quietly. They have adherents among the personnel of our nuclear submarine and rocket forces; and no one in India will be able to stop them, once my government has fallen. Mr. President, can you risk letting me fall?"

If any of us were the American partner in a conversation of this kind, ten years hence, what answer should we give—and what would be its consequences?

What Price Recklessness?

Thus far we have only imagined a rational conversation among rational states. Since the 1930s, however, there usually have been three or more governments in the world that were suicidally irrational. In the 1930s and early 1940s, Hitler's Germany, Mussolini's Italy, and the militarists' Japan had such governments which took their nations into war and destroyed themselves by so doing.

The reckless governments of the late 1970s luckily ruled smaller states, but the governments of Colonel Qaddafi's Libya, General Amin's Uganda, and the Ayatollah Ruhollah Khomeini's Iran seemed capable of taking their countries across the brink of self-destruction, and no one could exclude the possibility that in other years and other countries desperado governments might come to power. If a number of recklessly irrational governments remain in the world while the number of countries with nuclear weapons increases, it becomes ever more probable that some day a recklessly irrational government will acquire nuclear weapons, and political psychopathology will combine with nuclear physics to injure or destroy humankind.

THE CLASH OF SOCIAL ORDERS

About 150 nations in the world carry on most of their economic and social activities under institutions of private enterprise and the private property of land and large-scale productive equipment and resources. In these countries, children are taught to see these institutions as free and reasonable, and to see collective property and comprehensive state planning as inefficient, unreasonable, and oppressive. But in the sixteen communist-ruled countries of the world, comprising nearly one-third of humanity, children are taught the opposite. Collectivism and communism, they learn, stand for freedom and goodness, and capitalism for evil, oppression, and decline. Western ideas and practices seem almost mad to many of them, as their ideas and practices seem almost mad to many of us. There is little true communication between "East" and "West," and what there is remains precarious. Under these conditions, almost any serious clash or conflict, any revolution or civil war in one or another "Third World" country could escalate into an ideological war that could spread like a forest fire but with more devastating consequences.

At the same time, each ideological camp is deeply split within itself, the East between the rival communist doctrines of the Soviet Union and

China, the noncommunist world between the efforts of the highly developed countries to retain their large economic advantages and the resentment of their underprivileged neighbors.

Altogether, there is today more than enough social and psychological dynamite in the world to match its ample stocks of TNT, uranium, and plutonium.

WHAT CAN BE DONE?

Though we cannot predict for certain, we can provide for risks.

We can provide stocks of food in many parts of the world against climatic catastrophes, crop failures, and famines.[2]

We can explore, develop, try out, and apply on a large scale old and new methods to increase *capital formation* in all countries, in both the public and private sectors. We can include here also the formation of invisible capital in the form of scientific and technological *research and development* as well as the formation of productive skills and work habits through education.

We can greatly increase our efforts to develop particular branches of technology which are likely to prove crucial in the coming decades. These urgently needed developments include:

1. Utilization of *solar energy* and other alternative sources to fossil fuels.

2. The *long distance transfer* of large amounts of *electric energy* so as to permit the location of nuclear and conventional power stations far from concentrations of human settlement, e.g., in the polar regions.

3. The producing of goods and equipment with *higher information ratios*, i.e., with more decisions per unit of material, weight, or energy, such as transistors, printed circuits, microchips, miniaturization, and similar devices for "doing more with less."

4. The *recycling* of used metals and other scarce materials without excessive use of energy.

5. The substantial *reduction of pollution* associated with industrial production and the use of energy.

6. *Biotechnologies* of land restoration after strip mining or soil erosion.

New technologies are not everything that will be needed. Beyond them, we shall need changes in our culture and our values, particularly in the world's highly developed countries and their favored skilled and professional strata. There today we still gauge increases in popular living stan-

[2]This was one of the recommendations of an international symposium of the Nobel Foundation at Stockholm in September, 1974. See *Nobel Symposium 29. Man, Environment, and Resources*, T. Segerstedt and S. Nilsson, eds. (Stockholm, Sweden: Trycksaksservice A.G., 1975). The United Nations Food Conference in Rome in 1974 was spurred by the decrease in world grain production in 1972 and several severe famines in the wake of worldwide droughts and floods. Consequently, the International Fund for Agricultural Development (IFAD), a specialized agency within the United Nations system, was established in 1976 to counter such disastrous shortages in the production and supply of food.

dards almost entirely in tangible quantitative terms of matter and energy: more automobiles and bigger ones; bigger and stronger outboard motors; more machines in our homes; more traffic lanes and bigger superhighways. This cannot go on indefinitely, particularly if we are to move toward greater international equality and a greater share of the world's good things for everyone. But how could we go on with no more hope for further improvement? Perhaps we may have to learn that improvement need not always be enlargement. We may have to take many of our future gains in terms of services and their better quality, rather than of things and greater bulk. Perhaps we shall learn to want more cross-country skis and fewer motor sleds, more camp sites and bicycle paths and fewer outboard motors, more chamber music and more municipal symphony orchestras and fewer expressways.

In our collective sense of belonging, we may learn to seek more for human solidarity and wisdom, and less for national power and prestige, more for the community of a family or friendship group, and less for the peck order of a chicken yard.

In world politics, we may learn to outgrow the fascination of a pseudo-conservatism which for thousands of years has trapped people into that futile path which the ancient writers of Greek tragedies called *koros*, the hero's pride in success; *hybris*, tragic arrogance and overreaching; and *até*, the eventual madness of doom which drives the hero to rush toward self-destruction. Rather, we may yet learn that only through growth, change, adaptation, and partial self-transformation can persons, groups, and peoples preserve their own identity so that true conservatism becomes possible.

Will enough of us learn all these things and in time? There is no way of knowing for certain; we shall have to try. It seems likely that humanity is going soon to "shoot the rapids" in the stream of its development so far. Perhaps the first four-fifths of our century will look quiet and idyllic in comparison with the decades that are coming.

Yet we know at least something about the tasks that are coming and the problems that are staring us in the face. Humanity has met other challenges before; and it has been said that knowing what a problem is means already to be half-way toward its solution. We have been learning to recognize the problems of our common survival on this planet; and if we take them seriously now, we have reasons to hope that solutions will be found and acted on in time.

To Explore Further

GENERAL SURVEYS

CARR, E. H., *The Twenty Years' Crisis: An Introduction to the Study of International Relations*, In new ed. of 1946 rev. ed. New York: Harper & Row, 1964.

DEUTSCH, K. W., *Tides Among Nations*. New York: Free Press, 1979.

GREENSTEIN, F. I., AND N. W. POLSBY (EDS.), *The Handbook of Political Science*, 8 vols. Vol. 8: *International Politics*. Reading, MA: Addison-Wesley, 1975.

HAAS, E. B., AND A. S. WHITING, *Dynamics of International Relations*, repr. of 1956 ed. Westport, CT: Greenwood, 1975.

HOLSTI, K. J., *International Politics: A Framework for Analysis*, 4th ed. Englewood Cliffs, NJ: Prentice-Hall, 1983.

JENSEN, L., *Explaining Foreign Policy*. Englewood Cliffs, NJ: Prentice-Hall, 1982.

KEGLEY, C. W., AND E. WITTKOPF, *World Politics: Trend and Transformation*. New York: St. Martin's Press, 1981.

LABARR, D. F., AND J. D. SINGER, *The Study of International Politics: A Guide to the Sources for the Student, Teacher, and Researcher*. Santa Barbara, CA: ABC-Clio, 1976.

LIGHT, M., AND A.J.R. GROOM (EDS.), *International Relations: A Handbook of Current Theory*. Boulder, CO: Lynne Rienner, 1985.

MACRIDIS, R. C., (ED.), *Foreign Policy in World Politics*, 6th ed. Englewood Cliffs, NJ: Prentice-Hall, 1985.

MORGENTHAU, H. J., *Politics Among Nations: The Struggle for Power and Peace*, 6th rev. ed. New York: Knopf, 1985.

MORGENTHAU, H. J., AND K. W. THOMPSON, (EDS.), *Principles and Problems of International Politics: Selected Readings*. Lanham, MD: Univ. Press of America, 1982.

PETTMAN, R., *Human Behavior and World Politics: An Introduction to International Relations.* New York: St. Martin's Press, 1975.

ROSENAU, J. N., *International Politics and Foreign Policy,* 2nd ed. New York: Free Press, 1969.

ROSENAU, J. N., *et al., World Politics.* New York: Free Press, 1976.

SONDERMANN, F. C., *et al.* (eds.), *The Theory and Practice of International Politics,* 6th ed. Englewood Cliffs, NJ: Prentice-Hall, 1983.

STOESSINGER, J. G., *The Might of Nations,* 8th ed. New York: Random House, 1986.

SULLIVAN, M., *International Relations: Theories and Evidence.* Englewood Cliffs, NJ: Prentice-Hall, 1976.

WRIGHT, Q., *The Study of International Relations.* New York: Irvington, 1984.

BASIC QUANTITATIVE DATA

BANKS, A. S., AND R. B. TEXTOR, *A Cross-Polity Survey.* Cambridge, MA: M.I.T. Press, 1963.

BURGESS, P. M., AND R. W. LAWTON, *Indicators of International Behavior: An Assessment of Events Data Research.* Beverly Hills, CA: Sage, 1972.

MICKIEWICZ, E. (ED.), *Handbook of Soviet Social Science Data.* New York: Free Press, 1973.

Military Balance, 1981–1982, The. London: International Institute for Strategic Studies, 1981–1982, and Boulder, CO: Westview Press, 1981.

RUMMEL, R. J., *The Dimensions of Nations,* Vol. 1. Beverly Hills, CA: Sage Publications, 1972.

SINGER, J. D. (ED.), *Quantitative International Politics: Insights and Evidence.* New York: Free Press, 1968.

SINGER, J. D., AND M. SMALL, *The Wages of War: 1816 to 1965.* Ann Arbor, MI: Inter-university Consortium for Political and Social Research, 1974.

SIVARD, R. L., *World Military and Social Expenditures 1987–88.* Washington, D.C.: World Priorities, 1987.

TAYLOR, C. L., AND D. JODICE, *World Handbook of Political and Social Indicators.* 2 vols., 3rd ed. New Haven, CT: Yale Univ. Press, 1983.

U.S. ARMS CONTROL AND DISARMAMENT AGENCY, *World Military Expenditures and Arms Transfers 1969–1978.* Ann Arbor, MI: Inter-university Consortium for Political and Social Research, 1982.

VASQUEZ, J. A., "Statistical Findings in International Politics: A Data-Based Assessment," *International Studies Quarterly,* 20, no. 2 (June 1976), 171–218.

World Development Report 1985. New York: Oxford Univ. Press, for the World Bank, 1985.

BASIC THEORY AND RESEARCH METHODS

ALKER, H. R., JR., AND T. J. BIERSTEKER, "The Dialects of World Order: Notes for a Future Archeologist of International Savoir Faire," *International Studies Quarterly,* 28 (1984), 121–142.

ALKER, H. R., *et al.* (eds.), *Mathematical Approaches to Politics.* New York: Elsevier, 1973.

ALMOND, G. A., AND S. VERBA (EDS.), *The Civic Culture Revisited.* Boston: Little, Brown, 1980.

ARON, R., *Peace and War: A Theory of International Relations,* repr. of 1966 ed. Melbourne, FL: Krieger, 1981.

ASHLEY, R. K., "Political Realism and Human Interests," *International Studies Quarterly,* 25, no. 2 (June 1981), 204–236.

BALDWIN, D. A., "Power Analysis and World Politics: New Trends versus Old Tendencies," *World Politics,* 31, no. 2 (January 1979), 161–194.

BELL, D., "Twelve Modes of Prediction. A Preliminary Sorting of Approaches in the Social Sciences," *Daedalus,* 93, no. 3 (Summer 1964), 845–880.

BRUCAN, S., *The Dissolution of Power: A Sociology of International Relations and Politics.* New York: Knopf, 1971.

BULL, H., *The Anarchical Society: A Study of Order in World Politics.* New York: Columbia Univ. Press, 1977.

BUNDY, W. P., "Elements of Power," *Foreign Affairs,* 56, no. 1 (October 1977), 1–26.

BUZAN, B., AND R. J. BARRY JONES (EDS.), *Change and the Study of International Relations: The Evaded Dimension.* New York: St. Martin's Press, 1981.

CALLAHAN, P., *et al.* (eds.), *Describing Foreign Policy.* Beverly Hills, CA: Sage Publications, 1982.

COHEN, R., *International Politics: The Rules of the Game.* New York: Longman, 1981.

DAHL, R. A., "The Concept of Power," *Behavioral Science,* 2 (1957), 201–215.

DAHL, R. A., *Modern Political Analysis,* 4th ed. Englewood Cliffs, NJ: Prentice-Hall, 1984.

DEUTSCH, K. W., *Politics and Government: How People Decide Their Fate,* 3rd ed. Boston: Houghton Mifflin, 1980.

DOUGHERTY, J. E., AND R. L. PFALTZGRAFF, JR., *Contending Theories of International Relations: A Comprehensive Survey,* 2nd ed. New York: Harper & Row, 1980.

DUDLEY, L., "Foreign Aid and the Theory of Alliances," *Review of Economics and Statistics,* 61 (1979), 564–571.

EAST, M., *et al.* (eds.), *Why Nations Act,* Beverly Hills, CA: Sage, 1978.

EUSTON, D., *A Systems Analysis of Political Life.* Chicago: Univ. of Chicago Press, 1979.

EULAU, H., *Micro-Macro Political Analysis: Accents of Inquiry.* Chicago: Aldine, 1969.

FOX, W. T. (ED.), *Theoretical Aspects of International Relations.* Notre Dame, IN: Univ. of Notre Dame Press, 1959.

FROHLICH, N., *et al., Political Leadership and Collective Goods.* Princeton, NJ: Princeton Univ. Press, 1971.

FROMKIN, D., *The Independence of Nations.* New York: Praeger Publishers, 1981.

GALTUNG, J., *Theory and Methods of Social Research.* London: Allen & Unwin, 1967.

GOLDMANN, K., AND G. SJOSTEDT (EDS.), *Power, Capabilities, Interdependence: Problems in the Study of International Influence.* Beverly Hills, CA: Sage, 1979.

HART, J., "Three Approaches to the Measurement of Power in International Relations," *International Organization,* 30, no. 2 (Spring 1976), 289–305.

HARTMANN, F. H., *The Conservation of Enemies: A Study in Enmity.* Westport, CT: Greenwood Press, 1982.

HERZ, H., "Political Realism Revisited," *International Studies Quarterly,* 25, no. 2 (June 1981), 182–197.

HOFFMAN, S., *Janus and Minerva: Essays on the Theory and Practice of International Politics.* Boulder, CO: Westview Press, 1986.

HOFFMAN, S. (ED.), *Contemporary Theory in International Relations,* repr. of 1960 ed. Westport, CT: Greenwood, 1977.

HOLSTI, K. J., *The Dividing Discipline: Hegemony and Diversity in International Theory.* Winchester, MA: Allen & Unwin, 1985.

HOLSTI, O. R., *et al.* (eds.), *Change in the International System.* Boulder, CO: Westview, 1980.

JOYNT, C. B., AND P. E. CORBETT, *Theory and Reality in World Politics.* Pittsburgh: Univ. of Pittsburgh Press, 1978.

KAPLAN, M., *System and Process in International Politics.* New York: Wiley, 1957.

KNORR, K., *The Power of Nations.* New York: Basic Books, 1975.

KNORR, K., *The War Potential of Nations,* repr. of 1956 ed. Westport, CT: Greenwood, 1978.

KNORR, K., AND J. N. ROSENAU (EDS.), *Contending Approaches to International Politics.* Princeton, NJ: Princeton Univ. Press, 1969.

KNORR, K., AND S. VERBA (EDS.), *The International System: Theoretical Essays,* repr. of 1960 ed. Westport, CT: Greenwood, 1982.

KRATOCHWIL, F., "On the Notion of 'Interest' in International Relations," *International Organization,* 36, no. 1 (Winter 1982), 1–30.

LAMPERT, D. E., *et al.,* "Is There an International System?," *International Studies Quarterly,* 22, no. 1 (March 1978), 143–166.

LASSWELL, H. D., *World Politics and Personal Insecurity.* New York: Free Press, 1965.

LASSWELL, H. D., *Politics: Who Gets What, When and How.* New York: World, 1966.

LASSWELL, H. D., AND A. KAPLAN, *Power and Society.* New Haven, CT: Yale Univ. Press, 1950.

LEPAWSKY, A., *et al.* (eds.), *The Search for World Order: Studies by Students and Colleagues of Quincy Wright.* New York: Irvington, 1971.

LIEBER, R. J., *Theory and World Politics.* Boston: Little, Brown, 1977.

McCLELLAND, C. A., *Theory and the International System.* New York: Macmillan, 1966.

MANSBACH, R. W., AND J. A. VASQUEZ, *In Search of Theory: A New Paradigm for Global Politics.* New York: Columbia Univ. Press, 1981.

MERRITT, R. L. (ED.), *Foreign Policy Analysis.* Lexington, MA: Lexington Books, 1975.

MORGAN, P. M., *Theories and Approaches to International Politics,* 4th ed. New Brunswick, NJ: Transaction Books, 1985.

NUECHTERLEIN, D. E., "The Concept of 'National Interest': A Time for New Approaches," *Orbis,* 23 (Spring 1979), 73–92.

OLIVER, J. K., "The Balance of Power Heritage of 'Interdependence' and 'Traditionalism'," *International Studies Quarterly,* 26, no. 3 (Sept. 1982), 373–396.

OLSON, M., JR., *The Logic of Collective Action: Public Goods and the Theory of Groups,* 2nd rev. ed. Cambridge, MA: Harvard Univ. Press, 1971.

OLSON, M., JR., AND R. ZECKHAUSER, "An Economic Theory of Alliance," *Review of Economics and Statistics,* 48 (1966), 266–279.

OLSON, M., *The Rise and Decline of Nations.* New Haven: Yale Univ. Press, 1982.

OPPENHEIM, F. E., " 'Power' Revisited," *Journal of Politics,* 40 (August 1978), 589–608.

PARSONS, T., *Societies: Evolutionary and Comparative Perspectives.* Englewood Cliffs, NJ: Prentice-Hall, 1966.

PRAGER, C.A.L., "Taking Theory For Granted in International Politics," *Political Studies,* 26 (March 1978), 15–29.

RIKER, W. H., *The Theory of Political Coalitions.* Westport, CO: Greenwood, (1962), 1984.

ROSECRANCE, R. N., *Action and Reaction in World Politics: International Systems in Perspective,* repr. of 1963 ed. Westport, CT: Greenwood, 1977.

ROSECRANCE, R. N., "International Theory Revisited," *International Organization,* 35, no. 4 (Autumn 1981), 691–713.

ROSEN, S. J., AND W. S. JONES, *The Logic of International Relations,* 3rd ed. Boston: Little, Brown, 1980.

ROSENAU, J. N., "Pre-theories and Theories of Foreign Policy," in R. Barry Farrell (ed.), *Approaches to Comparative and International Politics.* Evanston: Northwestern Univ. Press, 1966, pp. 27–92.

ROSENAU, J. N., *The Scientific Study of Foreign Policy,* 2nd ed. New York: Nichols Pub., 1980.

ROSENAU, J. N., *The Study of Political Adaptation.* New York: Nichols Pub., 1981.

ROSENAU, J. N., "A Pre-Theory Revisited: World Politics in an Era of Cascading Interdependence," *International Studies Quarterly,* 28 (1984), 245–305.

RUSSETT, B. M., AND J. D. SULLIVAN, "Collective Goods and International Organization," *International Organization,* 25 (Autumn 1971), 853.

RUSSETT, B. M., *Power and Community in World Politics.* San Francisco: W. H. Freeman, 1972.

RUSSETT, B. M., *International Regions and the International System,* repr. of 1967 ed. Westport, CT: Greenwood, 1975.

RUSSETT, B. M., AND H. STARR, *World Politics: The Menu for Choice.* San Francisco: W. H. Freeman, 1981.

SCHUMAN, F. L., *International Politics: Anarchy and Order in the World Society.* 7th ed., New York: McGraw-Hill, 1969.

SULLIVAN, M. P., *International Relations: Theories and Evidence.* Englewood Cliffs, NJ: Prentice-Hall, 1976.

TANTER, R., AND R. H. ULLMANN (EDS.), *Theory and Policy in International Relations.* Princeton, NJ: Princeton Univ. Press, 1971.

TAYLOR, M., *Community, Anarchy, and Liberty.* Cambridge: Cambridge Univ. Press, 1982.

TAYLOR, T. (ED.), *Approaches and Theory in International Relations.* London: Longman, 1978.

VASQUEZ, J. A., AND R. W. MANSBACH, "The Issue Cycle: Conceptualizing Long-Term Global Political Change," *International Organization,* 37, no. 2 (Spring 1983), 257–279.

VERBA, S., *et al., Participation and Political Equality.* Cambridge: Cambridge Univ. Press, 1978.

WALTZ, K. N., *Theory of International Politics.* New York: Random House, 1979.

WEBER, M., *Economy and Society: An Outline of Interpretive Sociology.* Berkeley, CA: Univ. of California Press, 1979.

WRIGHT, Q., *Problems of Stability and Progress in International Relations,* repr. of 1954 ed. Westport, CT: Greenwood, 1976.

YOUNG, O. R., *Systems of Political Science.* Englewood Cliffs, NJ: Prentice-Hall, 1968.

YOUNG, O. R., "Anarchy and Social Choice: Reflections on the International Polity," *World Politics*, 30, no. 2 (January 1978), 241–263.

YOUNG, O. R., "International Regimes: Problems of Concept Formation," *World Politics*, 32, no. 3 (April 1980), 331–356.

ZINNES, D. A., *Contemporary Research in International Relations: A Perspective and Critical Appraisal.* New York: Free Press, 1976.

CONTRIBUTIONS FROM PSYCHOLOGY AND THE BEHAVIORAL SCIENCES

ATKINSON, J. W. (ED.), *Motives in Fantasy, Action, and Society,* Princeton, NJ: Van Nostrand, 1958.

BRECHER, M. (ED.), *Studies in Crisis Behavior.* New Brunswick, NJ: Transaction, 1979.

DE RIVERA, J. (ED.), *The Psychological Dimension of Foreign Policy.* Columbus, OH: Merrill, 1968.

DRUCKMAN, D. (ED.), *Negotiations: Social-Psychological Perspectives.* Beverly Hills, CA: Sage, 1977.

ELDRIDGE, A. F., *Images of Conflict.* New York: St. Martin's Press, 1979.

EULAU, H., *The Behavioral Persuasion in Politics.* New York: Random House, 1963.

FALKOWSKI, L. S. (ED.), *Psychological Models of International Politics.* Boulder, CO: Westview Press, 1979.

FEIERABEND, I. K., *et al., Anger, Violence and Politics: Theories and Research.* Englewood Cliffs, NJ: Prentice-Hall, 1972.

FISHER, R. (ED.), *International Conflict and Behavioral Science.* New York: Basic Books, 1965.

GAMSON, W., AND A. MODIGLIANI, *Untangling the Cold War: A Strategy for Testing Rival Theories.* Boston: Little, Brown, 1971.

GEORGE, A., "The 'Operational Code': A Neglected Approach to the Study of Political Leaders and Decision-Making," *International Studies Quarterly*, 13, no. 2 (1969), 190–222.

GREENSTEIN, F., *Personality and Politics.* Chicago: Markham, 1969.

GUETZKOW, H. (ED.), *Groups, Leadership, and Men.* New York: Carnegie Press, 1951.

HAAS, M. (ED.), *International Systems: A Behavioral Approach.* New York: Chandler, 1974.

HERMAN, C. F. (ED.), *International Crises.* New York: Free Press, 1973.

HERMANN, M. (ED.), *A Psychological Examination of Political Leaders.* New York: Free Press, 1977.

HERMANN, M. "Explaining Foreign Policy Behavior Using the Personal Characteristics of Political Leaders," *International Studies Quarterly*, 24 (1980), 7–46.

HOLSTI, O. (ED.), "The 'Operational Code' as an Approach to the Analysis of Belief Systems," Final Report to the National Science Foundation, Grant NO. SOC 75–15368, Duke University.

INKELES, A., AND D. J. LEVINSON, "National Character: The Study of Modal Personality and Sociocultural Systems," in G. Lindzey and E. Aronson (eds.), *Handbook of Social Psychology*, 2 vols., 3rd ed. Reading, MA: Addison-Wesley, 1985.

KELMAN, H. C. (ED.), *International Behavior: A Social-Psychological Analysis.* New York: Holt, Rinehart & Winston, 1965.

KLINEBERG, O., *The Human Dimension in International Relations.* New York: Holt, Rinehart & Winston, 1964.

LARSON, D. W. *Origins of Containment: A Psychological Explanation.* Princeton, NJ: Princeton Univ. Press, 1985.

MACK, J. E., "Toward a Collective Psychopathology of the Nuclear Arms Competition," *Political Psychology*, 6, no. 2 (June 1985), 291–321.

NISBETT, R., AND L. ROSS, *Human Inference: Strategies and Shortcomings of Social Judgment.* Englewood Cliffs, NJ: Prentice-Hall, 1980.

RANNEY, A. (ED.), *Essays on the Behavioral Study of Politics.* Urbana: Univ. of Illinois Press, 1962.

SIMON, H. A., "Human Nature in Politics: The Dialogue of Psychology with Political Science," *American Political Science Review*, 79, no. 2 (June 1985), 293–304.

SINGER, J. D. (ED.), *Human Behavior and International Politics.* Chicago: Rand McNally, 1965.

STAGNER, R., *Psychological Aspects of International Conflict.* Monterey, CA: Brooks-Cole, 1967.

STEIN, H. F., "Psychological Complementarity in Soviet-American Relations," *Political Psychology*, 6, no. 2 (June 1985), 249–261.

WALKER, S. G., "The Motivational Foundations of Political Belief Systems: A Re-Analysis of the Operational Code Conduct," *International Studies Quarterly*, 27 (1983), 179–201.

ZAWODNY, J. K., *Man and International Relations*, 2 vols. New York: Chandler, 1966.

SPECIALIZED STUDIES ON INTEREST GROUPS, CLASSES, AND LEADERS

BAUER, R. A., *et al.*, *American Business and Public Policy: The Politics of Foreign Trade*, 2nd ed. Hawthorne, NY: Aldine Pub., 1972.

BOTTOMORE, T. B., *Classes in Modern Society*. New York: Random, 1968.

BRODER, D. S., *Changing of the Guard: Power and Leadership in America*. New York: Simon & Schuster, 1980.

BURNS, J. M., *Leadership*. New York: Harper & Row, 1978.

CAMPBELL, C., *Governments Under Stress: Political Executives and Key Bureaucrats in Washington, London, and Ottawa*. Toronto: Univ. of Toronto Press, 1983.

DAHRENDORF, R., *Class and Class Conflict in Industrial Society*. Stanford, CA: Stanford Univ. Press, 1961.

EDINGER, L. J. (ED.), *Political Leadership in Industrialized Societies*. New York: Wiley, 1967.

EDSALL, T. B., *The New Politics of Inequality*. Philadelphia: West, 1985.

ETHEREDGE, L. S., "Personality Effects on American Foreign Policy 1898–1968: A Test of Interpersonal Generalization Theory," *American Political Science Review*, 72 (June 1978), 434–451.

FALKOWSKI, L. S., *Presidents, Secretaries of State, and Crises in U.S. Foreign Relations: A Model and Predictive Analysis*. Boulder, CO: Westview Press, 1978.

GEORGE, A., "The 'Operational Code': A Neglected Approach to the Study of Political Leaders and Decision-Making," *International Studies Quarterly*, 13, no. 2 (1969), 190–222.

HARGROVE, E. C., AND M. NELSON, *Presidents, Politics and Policy*. Baltimore: Johns Hopkins Univ. Press, 1984.

HERMANN, M. (ED.), *A Psychological Examination of Political Leaders*. New York: Free Press, 1977.

HOLSTI, O. R., AND J. N. ROSENAU, "Vietnam, Consensus, and the Belief Systems of American Leaders," *World Politics*, 32, no. 1 (October 1979), 1–56.

HOPPLE, G. W., *Political Psychology and Biopolitics: Assessing and Predicting Elite Behavior in Foreign Policy Crises*. Boulder, CO: Westview Press, 1980.

HUGHES, B. B., *The Domestic Context of American Foreign Policy*. San Francisco: W. H. Freeman, 1978.

KRITZER, H. M., "Ideology and American Political Elites," *Public Opinion Quarterly*, 42 (Winter 1978), 484–502.

LASSWELL, H. D., AND D. LERNER (EDS.), *World Revolutionary Elites: Studies in Coercive Ideological Movements*, repr. of 1965 ed. Westport, CT: Greenwood, 1980.

LLOYD WARNER, W., *Social Class in America: A Manual of Procedure for the Measurement of Social Status*. Gloucester, MA: P. Smith, 1957.

LLOYD WARNER, W., *The Status System of a Modern Community*. New Haven, CT: Yale Univ. Press, 1959.

LOWI, T. J., *The Personal President: Power Invested, Promise Unfulfilled*. Ithaca, NY: Cornell Univ. Press, 1985.

LUTTWAK, E. N., *The Pentagon and the Art of War*. New York: Simon & Schuster, 1985.

MARSHALL, T. H., *Class, Citizenship, and Social Development*. Chicago: Univ. of Chicago Press, 1977.

MATHIAS, C. McC., "Ethnic Groups and Foreign Policy," *Foreign Affairs*, Summer 1981, 975–998.

NEUSTADT, R. E., *Presidential Power: The Politics of Leadership with Reflections on Johnson and Nixon*. New York: Wiley, 1976.

PAIGE, G. D., *The Scientific Study of Political Leadership.* New York: The Free Press, 1977.

PARKIN, F., *Class Inequality and Political Order.* New York: Holt, Rinehart & Winston, 1971.

PATCHEN, M., "Social Class and Dimensions of Foreign Policy Attitudes," *Social Science Quarterly,* 51 (December 1970), 649–667.

PETERSON, M., *International Interest Organizations and the Transmutation of Postwar Society,* Stockholm: Almqvist and Wiskell, 1979.

PREWITT, K., AND A. STONE, *The Ruling Elites: Elite Theory, Power, and American Democracy.* New York: Harper & Row, 1973.

GLAZER, N. AND D. P. MOYNIHAN, EDS. *Ethnicity: Theory and Experience.* Cambridge: Harvard Univ. Press, 1975.

RUSSETT, B. M., AND E. C. HANSON, *Interest and Ideology: The Foreign Policy Beliefs of American Businessmen.* San Francisco: W. H. Freeman, 1975.

STUART, D., AND H. STARR, "The 'Inherent Bad Faith Model' Reconsidered: Dulles, Kennedy, and Kissinger," *Political Psychology,* 3, nos. 3–4 (Fall/Winter 1981/1982), 1–33.

TUCKER, R. C., *Politics as Leadership.* Columbia: Univ. of Missouri Press, 1981.

VOSLENSKY, M., *Nomenklatura: The Soviet Ruling Class.* New York: Doubleday, 1984.

WILLETTS, P. (ED.), *Pressure Groups in the Global System.* New York: St. Martin's Press, 1982.

NATIONALISM AND MODERN NATIONS AND EMPIRES

BENDIX, R., *Nation-Building and Citizenship: Studies of Our Changing Social Order,* 2nd rev. ed. Berkeley, CA: Univ. of Calif. Press, 1977.

BLACK, C. E., *The Dynamics of Modernization: A Study in Comparative History.* New York: Harper & Row, 1967.

BROWN, P. G., AND H. SHUE (EDS.), *Boundaries: National Autonomy and Its Limits.* Totawa, NJ: Rowman & Littlefield, 1981.

CLAUDE, I. L., *National Minorities: An International Problem.* Westport, CT: Greenwood, 1955.

COBBAN, A., *The Nation State and National Self-Determination,* New York: Apollo Editions, 1970.

COHEN, B. J., *The Question of Imperialism: The Political Economy of Dominance and Dependence.* New York: Basic Books, 1973.

COLINVAUX, P., *The Fate of Nations.* New York: Simon & Schuster, 1980.

CONNOR, W., "Nation-Building or Nation-Destroying," *World Politics,* 24 (1972), 319–355.

DAVIS, H. B., *Nationalism and Socialism: Marxist and Labor Theories of Nationalism to 1917.* New York: Monthly Review Press, 1967.

DEUTSCH, K. W., *Nationalism and Social Communication: An Inquiry into the Foundations of Nationality,* 2nd ed. Cambridge, MA: M.I.T. Press, 1966.

DEUTSCH, K. W., *Tides Among Nations.* New York: Free Press, 1979.

DEUTSCH, K. W., AND W. J. FOLTZ (EDS.), *Nation-Building,* 2nd ed. New York: Atherton, 1966.

DEUTSCH, K. W., AND R. L. MERRITT, *Nationalism and National Development: An Interdisciplinary Bibliography.* Cambridge, MA: M.I.T. Press, 1970.

EISENSTADT, S. N., *The Political Systems of Empires,* New York: Free Press, 1969.

EMERSON, R., *From Empire to Nation.* Boston: Beacon Press, 1962.

FANON, F., *The Wretched of the Earth.* New York: Grove Press, 1965.

HANRIEDER, W. F., "Dissolving International Politics: Reflections on the Nation-State," *American Political Science Review,* 72 (December 1978), 1276–1287.

HENDERSON, G., et al., *Divided Nations in a Divided World.* New York: McKay, 1974.

HERZ, J. H., *The Nation-State and the Crisis of World Politics: Essays on International Politics in the Twentieth Century.* New York: Longman, 1976.

HOLBRAAD, C., *Middle Powers in International Politics.* New York: St. Martin's Press, 1984.

ISAACS, H. R., *Idols of the Tribe.* New York: Harper & Row, 1977.

ISAACS, H. R., *Power and Identity: Tribalism in World Politics.* New York: Foreign Policy Association, 1979.

KAHLER, M., *Decolonization in Britain and France: The Domestic Consequences of International Relations.* Princeton: Princeton Univ. Press, 1984.

KOHN, H., *The Age of Nationalism: The First Era of Global History,* repr. of 1962 ed. Westport, CT: Greenwood Press, 1976.

KOHN, H., *American Nationalism: An Interpretative Essay*, repr. of 1957 ed. Westport, CT: Greenwood Press, 1980.

KOHN, H., *Nationalism: Its Meaning and History*, rev. ed. Melbourne, FL: Krieger, 1982.

LENIN, V. I., *Imperialism, the Highest Stage of Capitalism*. New York: Progress Publications, USSR, 1975.

LIJPHART, A., *The Trauma of Decolonization: The Dutch and West New Guinea*. New Haven, CT: Yale Univ. Press, 1966.

LIPSET, S. M., *The First New Nation: The United States in Historical and Comparative Perspective*. New York: Norton, 1979.

MACFARLANE, S. N., *Superpower Rivalry and Third World Radicalism: The Idea of National Liberation*. Baltimore: Johns Hopkins Univ. Press, 1985.

MERRITT, R. L., AND B. M. RUSSETT (EDS.), *From National Development to Global Community: Essays in Honor of Karl W. Deutsch*. London: Allen & Unwin, 1981.

PATTERSON, O., *Ethnic Chauvinism: The Reactionary Impulse*, Briarcliff Manor, NY: Stein & Day, 1977.

PERHAM, M. F., *The Colonial Reckoning: End of Imperial Rule in Africa in the Light of British Experience*, repr. of 1962 ed. Westport, CT: Greenwood, 1976.

PYE, L. W. (ED.), *Communication and Political Development*. Princeton, NJ: Princeton Univ. Press, 1963.

PYE, L. W., AND S. VERBA (EDS.), *Political Culture and Political Development*. Princeton, NJ: Princeton Univ. Press, 1965.

RICHMOND, A. H., *Immigration and Ethnic Conflict: Canadian Comparative Perspectives*. London: Macmillan, 1987.

ROSEN, S. J., AND J. R. KURTH, *Testing Theories of Economic Imperialism*. Lexington, MA: Lexington Books, 1974.

SAID, A. A., AND L. R. SIMMONS (EDS.), *Ethnicity in an International Context*. New Brunswick, NJ: Transaction Books, 1976.

SCHUMPETER, J., *Imperialism and Social Classes*. New York: Meridian, 1955.

SHAFER, B. C., *Faces of Nationalism*, 2nd ed. New York: Harcourt, 1974.

SHAFER, B. C., *Nationalism: Its Nature and Interpreters*, 4th ed. Washington, D.C.: American Historical Association, 1976.

SHAFER, B. C., *Nationalism and Internationalism: Belonging*. Melbourne, FL: Krieger, 1982.

SHEPHERD, G. W., JR., *et al.*, *Race Among Nations: A Conceptual Approach*. Lexington, MA: Heath, 1970.

SMITH, A. D., *The Ethnic Revival*. Cambridge: Cambridge Univ. Press, 1981.

SMITH, A. D., *State and Nation in the Third World: The Western State and African Nationalism*. New York: St. Martin's Press, 1983.

SMITH, A. D., *Theories of Nationalism*, 2nd ed. New York: Holmes & Meier, 1983.

SMITH, T., *The Pattern of Imperialism: The United States, Great Britain, and the Late-Industrializing World since 1815*. New York: Cambridge Univ. Press, 1981.

COMMUNICATION AND DECISION MAKING

ALLISON, G. T., *Essence of Decision: Explaining the Cuban Missile Crisis*. Boston: Little, Brown, 1971.

ART, R., "Bureaucratic Politics and American Foreign Policy: A Critique," *Policy Sciences*, no. 4 (1973), 467–490.

AXELROD, R., *Structure of Decision: The Cognitive Maps of Political Elites*. Princeton, NJ: Princeton Univ. Press, 1976.

AXELROD, R., "The Rational Timing of Surprise," *World Politics*, 31, no. 2 (January 1979), 228–246.

AXELROD, R., *The Evolution of Cooperation*. New York: Basic Books, 1985.

BUTOW, R.J.C., *Japan's Decision to Surrender*, 2nd ed. Stanford, CA: Stanford Univ. Press, 1965.

CHRISTOPHER, W., WITH P. H. KREISBERG (EDS.), *American Hostages in Iran: The Conduct of a Crisis*. New Haven, CT: Yale Univ. Press, 1985.

COHEN, R., *Threat Perception in International Crisis*. Madison: Univ. of Wisconsin Press, 1979.

COWHEY, P. F., AND D. D. LAITIN, "Bearing the Burden: A Model of Presidential Responsibility in Foreign Policy," *International Studies Quarterly*, 22, no. 2 (June 1978), 267–296.

DAVISON, W. P., AND J. BOYLAN, *Mass Media: Systems and Effects.* New York: Praeger, 1976.

DAVISON, W. P., AND L. GORDENKER (EDS.), *Resolving Nationality Conflicts: The Role of Public Opinion Research.* New York: Praeger, 1980.

DAVISON, W. P. *et al., News from Abroad and the Foreign Policy Public.* New York: Foreign Policy Association, 1980.

DE SOLA POOL, I. (ED.), *The Prestige Press: A Comparative Study of Political Symbols.* Cambridge, MA: M.I.T. Press, 1970.

DEUTSCH, K. W., *Nerves of Government: Models of Political Communication and Control,* 2nd ed. New York: The Free Press, 1966.

DIXON, W. J., "Measuring Interstate Affect," *American Journal of Political Science,* 7, no. 4 (November 1983), 828–851.

DOWTY, A., *Middle East Crisis: U.S. Decision-Making in 1958, 1970, and 1973.* Berkeley, CA: Univ. of California Press, 1984.

FREI, D., *Assumptions and Perceptions in Disarmament.* New York: United Nations Publications, 1984.

GELB, L. H., *The Irony of Vietnam: The System Worked.* Washington, D.C.: Brookings Inst., 1979.

GEORGE, A., *Presidential Decisionmaking in Foreign Policy. The Effective Use of Information and Advice.* Boulder, CO: Westview, 1980.

HALPERIN, M., *Bureaucratic Politics and Foreign Policy.* Washington, D.C.: Brookings Inst., 1974.

HAMSON, F. O., "The Divided Decision-Maker: American Domestic Politics and the Cuban Crises," *International Security,* 9, no. 3 (Winter 1984/1985), 130–165.

HANDEL, M. I., "The Yom Kippur War and the Inevitability of Surprise," *International Studies Quarterly,* 21, no. 3 (September 1977), 461–502.

HEAD, R. G., *et al., Crisis Resolution: Presidential Decision Making in the Mayaguez and Korean Confrontations.* Boulder, CO: Westview Press, 1979.

HERMAN, C. F., *Crises in Foreign Policy: A Simulation Analysis.* Indianapolis, IN: Bobbs-Merrill, 1969.

HERMAN, C. F. (ED.), *International Crises.* New York: Free Press, 1973.

HIRSCHMAN, A. O., *Exit, Voice, and Loyalty: Responses to Decline in Firms, Organizations, and States.* Cambridge, MA: Harvard Univ. Press, 1970.

HOLSTI, O. R., *et al., Unity and Disintegration in International Alliances.* Melbourne, FL: Krieger, 1973.

HOOPES, T., *The Limits of Intervention: An Inside Account of How the Johnson Policy of Escalation Was Reversed in Vietnam,* rev. ed. New York: Longman, 1973.

HUSBAND, W. B., "Soviet Perceptions of U.S. 'Positions of Strength' Diplomacy in the 1970s," *World Politics,* 31 (July 1979), 495–517.

JANIS, I., *Victims of Groupthink: A Psychological Study of Foreign-Policy Decisions and Fiascoes.* Boston: Houghton Mifflin, 1973.

JERVIS, R., *The Logic of Images in International Relations.* Princeton, NJ: Princeton Univ. Press, 1970.

JERVIS, R., *Perception and Misperception in International Politics.* Princeton, NJ: Princeton Univ. Press, 1976.

KANE, S. N., "Reassessing the Bureaucratic Dimension of Foreign Policy Making: A Case Study of the Cuban Sugar Quota Decision, 1954–1956," *Social Science Quarterly,* 64, no. 1 (March 1983), 46–65.

KENNEDY, R. F., *Thirteen Days: A Memoir of the Cuban Missile Crisis.* New York: Norton, 1971.

KEOHANE, R. O., "Reciprocity in International Relations," *International Organization,* 40, no. 1 (Winter 1986), 1–27.

KRASNER, S. D., "Are Bureaucracies Important? Or Allison Wonderland," *Foreign Policy,* no. 7 (Summer 1972), 159–179.

LEBOW, R. N., "The Cuban Missile Crisis: Reading the Lessons Correctly," *Political Science Quarterly,* 98, no. 3 (Fall 1983), 431–458.

LENCZOWSKI, J., *Soviet Perceptions of U.S. Foreign Policy.* Ithaca, NY: Cornell Univ. Press, 1982.

LENG, R. J., "Reagan and the Russians: Crisis Bargaining Beliefs and the Historical Record," *American Political Science Review,* 78, no. 2 (June 1984), 338–355.

LEWIS, W. H., *et al.,* "The Press and Foreign Policy," *Washington Quarterly,* no. 2 (Spring 1979), 31–38.

MERRITT, R. L. (ED.), *Communication in International Politics.* Champaign, IL: Univ. of Illinois Press, 1972.

ONEAL, J. R., *Foreign Policy Making in Times of Crisis.* Columbus, OH: Ohio State Univ. Press, 1982.

PAIGE, G. D., *The Korean Decision.* New York: Free Press, 1968.

PRESSMAN, J. L., AND A. WILDAVSKY, *Implementation: How Great Expectations in Washington Are Dashed in Oakland,* 3rd ed. Berkeley, CA: Univ. of California Press, 1984.

PUTNAM, R. D., AND N. BAYNE, *Hanging Together: The Seven-Power Summits.* Cambridge, MA: Harvard Univ. Press, 1984.

ROSATI, J. A., "Developing a Systematic Decision-Making Framework: Bureaucratic Politics in Perspective," *World Politics,* 33, no. 2 (January 1981), 234–252.

SCHELLING, T. C., "Confidence in Crisis," *International Security,* 8, no. 4 (Spring 1984), 55–66.

SEBENIUS, J. K., "Negotiation Arithmetic: Adding and Subtracting Issues and Parties," *International Organization,* 37, no. 2 (Spring 1983), 281–316.

SIGAL, L. V., "The 'Rational Policy' Model and the Formosa Straits Crises," *International Studies Quarterly,* 14, no. 2 (June 1970), 121–156.

SIVERSON, R. M., "International Conflict and Perceptions of Injury: The Case of the Suez Crisis," *International Studies Quarterly,* 14, no. 2 (June 1970), 157–165.

SLATER, J., *Intervention and Negotiation: The United States and the Dominican Revolution.* New York: Irvington, 1970.

SNYDER, R. C., *et al.* (eds.), *Foreign Policy Decision-Making.* New York: Free Press, 1962.

STEINER, M., "The Search for Order in a Disorderly World: Worldviews and Prescriptive Decision Paradigms," *International Organization,* 37, no. 3 (Summer 1983), 373–413.

WEINSTEIN, B., *The Civic Tongue: Political Consequences of Language Choices.* New York: Longman, 1983.

WENDZEL, R. L., *International Relations: A Policy-maker Focus,* 2nd ed. New York: John Wiley & Sons, 1980.

YOUNG, R. A. (ED.), "International Crisis: Progress and Prospects for Applied Forecasting and Management," special issue of *International Studies Quarterly,* 21, no. 1 (March 1977).

ZIMMERMAN, W. AND R. AXELROD, "'The Lessons' of Vietnam and Soviet Foreign Policy," *World Politics,* 34, no. 1 (October 1981), 1–24.

COMPARATIVE FOREIGN POLICY

ADOMEIT, H., *Soviet Risk-Taking and Crisis Behavior: A Theoretical and Empirical Analysis.* Winchester, MA: Allen & Unwin, 1982.

ALLEN, D. AND M. SMITH, "Europe, the United States and the Middle East: A Case Study in Comparative Policy Making," *Journal of Common Market Studies,* 22, no. 2 (December 1983), 125–146.

ALMOND, G. A. *et al., Comparative Politics Today: A World View,* 3rd ed. Boston: Little, Brown, 1984.

ANDRIOLE, S. J. *et al.,* "A Framework for the Comparative Analysis of Foreign Policy Behavior," *International Studies Quarterly,* 19 (June 1975), 160–198.

BARNETT, D. A., *The Making of Foreign Policy in China: Structure and Process.* Boulder, CO: Westview Press/Washington, D.C.: Johns Hopkins Foreign Policy Institute, 1985.

BISHOP, W. J., AND D. S. SORENSEN, "Superpower Defense Expenditures and Foreign Policy," *Sage International Yearbook of Foreign Policy Studies,* 7 (1982), 163–182.

BLACK, J. E. AND K. W. THOMPSON (EDS.), *Foreign Policies in a World of Change,* repr. of 1963 ed. Salem, NH: Ayer Co., 1975.

BOBROW, D. B., *et al., Understanding Foreign Policy Decisions: The Chinese Case.* New York: Free Press, 1979.

BURGESS, P. M., *et al., International and Comparative Politics: A Handbook.* Boston: Allyn, 1978.

DADDIEH, C. K. AND T. M. SHAW, "The Political Economy of Decision-Making in African

Foreign Policy. Recognition of Biafra and the Popular Movement for the Liberation of Angola (MPLA)," *International Political Science Review*, 5, no. 1 (1984), 21–46.

DEUTSCH, K. W., *et al.*, *Comparative Government: Politics of Industrialized and Developing Nations.* Boston: Houghton Mifflin, 1981.

DOMINGUEZ, J. I. (ED.), *Cuba: Internal and International Affairs.* Beverly Hills, CA: Sage, 1982.

DOMINGUEZ, J. I., AND J. LINDAU, "The Primacy of Politics. Comparing the Foreign Policies of Cuba and Mexico," *International Political Science Review*, 5, no. 1 (1984), 75–101.

GRIFFITH, W. E., *The Superpowers and Regional Tensions: The USSR, the United States, and Europe.* Lexington, MA: Heath, 1982.

HANRIEDER, W. F. (ED.), *Comparative Foreign Policy: Theoretical Essays.* New York: McKay, 1971.

HANSEN, P. AND N. PETERSEN, "Motivational Bases of Foreign Policy Attitudes and Behavior: An Empirical Analysis," *International Studies Quarterly.* 22, no. 1 (March 1978), 49–77.

HOFFMANN, E. P., AND F. J. FLERON, JR. (EDS.), *The Conduct of Soviet Foreign Policy*, 2nd ed. Hawthorne, NY: Aldine Pub., 1980.

HOLSTI, K. J. (ED.), *Why Nations Realign: Foreign Policy Restructuring in the Postwar World.* Winchester, MA: Allen & Unwin, 1982.

IRISH, M. D., AND E. FRANK, *Introduction to Comparative Politics: Thirteen Nation States*, 2nd ed. Englewood Cliffs, NJ: Prentice-Hall, 1978.

JÖNSSON, C., "The Ideology of Foreign Policy," *Sage International Yearbook of Foreign Policy Studies*, 7 (1982), 91–110.

KATZENSTEIN, P. J. (ED.), *Between Power and Plenty: Foreign Economic Policies of Advanced Industrial States.* Madison, WI: Univ. of Wisconsin Press, 1978.

KEGLEY, C., JR., AND P. MCGOWAN (EDS.), *Foreign Policy: USA/USSR.* Beverly Hills, CA: Sage Publications, 1982.

KENNEDY, P., *Strategy and Diplomacy, 1870–1945: Eight Studies.* Winchester, MA: Allen & Unwin, 1984.

KIM, S. S. (ED.), *China and the World: Chinese Foreign Policy in the Post-Mao Era.* Boulder, CO: Westview Press, 1984.

KNUDSEN, B. B., "Europe between the Superpowers: An All-European Model for the End of the 20th Century," *Cooperation and Conflict*, 20, no. 2 (1985), 91–112.

LEBOVIC, J. H., "Capabilities in Context: National Attributes and Foreign Policy in the Middle East," *Journal of Peace Research*, 22, no. 1 (1985), 47–67.

LENCZOWSKI, J., *Soviet Perceptions of U.S. Foreign Policy.* Ithaca, NY: Cornell Univ. Press, 1982.

MACFARLANE, S. N., "Africa's Decaying Security System and the Rise of Intervention," *International Security*, 8, no. 4 (Spring 1984), 127–151.

MACRIDIS, R. C., AND B. E. BROWN (EDS.), *Comparative Politics: Notes and Readings*, 5th ed. Homewood, IL: Dorsey, 1977.

MACRIDIS, R. C., *Modern Political Systems: Europe*, 5th ed. Englewood Cliffs, NJ: Prentice-Hall, 1983.

MACRIDIS, R. C., *Foreign Policy in World Politics*, 6th ed. Englewood Cliffs, NJ: Prentice-Hall, 1985.

MCGOWAN, P. AND C. W. KEGLEY, JR. (EDS.), *Foreign Policy and the Modern World System.* Beverly Hills, CA: Sage Publications, 1983.

MAZRUI, A. A., *Africa's International Relations: The Diplomacy of Dependency and Change.* Boulder, CO: Westview Press, 1977.

MUNOZ, H., AND J. TULCHIN (EDS.), *Latin American Nations in World Politics.* Boulder, CO: Westview Press, 1984.

OSGOOD, R. E., *The Weary and the Wary: U.S. and Japanese Security Policies in Transition.* Baltimore, MD: Johns Hopkins Univ. Press, 1972.

POTTER, W. C., "Issue Area and Foreign Policy Analysis," *International Organization*, 34, no. 3 (Summer 1980), 405–427.

RAPOPORT, A., *The Big Two: Soviet-American Perceptions of Foreign Policy,* New York: Irvington, 1972.

ROSENAU, J. N. (ED.), *Comparing Foreign Policies: Theories, Findings, and Methods.* New York: Halsted Press, 1974.

SHAW, T. M. AND O. AMKO (EDS.), *The Political Economy of African Foreign Policy.* New York: St. Martin's Press, 1984.

STOESSINGER, J. G., *Nations in Darkness: China, Russia, and America*, 4th ed. New York: Random House, 1986.

TINT, H., *French Foreign Policy Since the Second World War*. New York: St. Martin's Press, 1973.

ULAM, A. B., *Expansion and Coexistence: Soviet Foreign Policy, 1917–1973*. New York: Holt, Rinehart & Winston, 1974.

ULAM, A. B., *Dangerous Relations: The Soviet Union in World Politics, 1970–1982*. New York: Oxford Univ. Press, 1983.

VALENTA, J., AND W. C. POLTER (EDS.), *Soviet Decision Making for National Security*. Winchester, MA: Allen & Unwin, 1984.

WALTZ, K. N., *Foreign Policy and Democratic Politics*. Boston: Little, Brown, 1967.

WELCH, W. AND J. F. TRISKA, "Soviet Foreign Policy Studies and Foreign Policy Models," *World Politics*, 23, no. 4 (July 1971), 704–733.

UNITED STATES FOREIGN POLICY

ARON, R., *The Imperial Republic: The United States and the World, 1945–1973*, repr. of 1974 ed. Lanham, MD: Univ. Press of America, 1982.

ART, R. J., *et al.* (eds.), *Reorganizing America's Defense: Leadership in War and Peace*. Elmsford, NY: Pergamon, 1985.

BALL, G. W., *The Discipline of Power*. Boston: Little, Brown, 1968.

BARBER, J. D., *The Presidential Character: Predicting Performance in the White House*, 2nd ed. Englewood Cliffs, NJ: Prentice-Hall, 1977.

BAUER, R. A., *et al.*, *American Business and Public Policy: The Politics of Foreign Trade*, 2nd ed. Hawthorne, NY: Aldine Pub., 1972.

BENOIT, E. AND K. BOULDING, EDS., *Disarmament and the Economy*. Repr. Westwood, CT: Greenwood, 1978.

BERES, L. R., *Reason and Realpolitik: U.S. Foreign Policy and World Order*. Lexington, MA: Heath, 1984.

BERGSTEN, C. F., *The International Economic Policy of the United States: Selected Papers of C. Fred Bergsten, 1977–1979*. Lexington, MA: Lexington Books., 1980.

BERGSTEN, C. F., *The United States in the World Economy: Selected Papers of C. Fred Bergsten, 1981 to 1982*. Lexington, MA: Lexington Books., 1983.

BROWN, S., *The Faces of Power: Constancy and Change in United States Foreign Policy from Truman to Reagan*, 2nd ed. New York: Columbia Univ. Press, 1983.

CALLEO, D. P. AND B. M. ROWLAND, *America and the World Political Economy: Atlantic Dreams and National Realities*. Bloomington, IN: Indiana Univ. Press, 1973.

CRAIG, G. A., "The United States and the European Balance," *Foreign Affairs*, 55, no. 1 (October 1976) 187–198.

DAHL, R. A., *Congress and Foreign Policy*. Repr. of 1950 ed., Westwood CT: Greenwood, 1983.

DAHL, R. A., *Controlling Nuclear Weapons: Democracy vs. Guardianship* Syracuse, NY: Syracuse U.P., 1985.

DALLEK, R., *The American Style of Foreign Policy: Cultural Politics and Foreign Affairs*. New York: Knopf, 1983.

DESTLER, I. M., *et al.*, *Our Own Worst Enemy: The Unmaking of American Foreign Policy*. New York: Simon & Schuster, 1984.

Documents From the U.S. Espionage Den. Qum (Tran): Inti-Sharat-T. Islami, 1983.

DOMINGUEZ, J. I., *U.S. Interests and Policies in the Caribbean and Central America*. Washington, D.C.: Am. Enterprise, Institute for Public Policy Research, 1982.

DOMINGUEZ, J. I., "It won't go away. Cuba on the US foreign policy agenda," *International Security*, 8, no. 1 (Summer 1983), 113–128.

DOMINGUEZ, J. I. (ED.), *Economic Issues and Political Conflict: U.S.-Latin American Relations*. Woburn, MA: Butterworths, 1982.

EPSTEIN, E. J., "Secrets from the CIA Archive in Teheran, *Orbis*, 31:1 (Spring 1987), pp. 33–42.

FEINBERG, R., *The Intemperate Zone: The Third World Challenge to U.S. Foreign Policy.* New York: Norton, 1983.

FELD, W. J., *American Foreign Policy: Aspirations and Reality.* New York: Wiley, 1984.

FRANCK, T. M. AND E. WEISBAND, *Foreign Policy by Congress.* New York: Oxford Univ. Press, 1979.

FROMKIN, D. AND J. CHASE, "What *Are* the Lessons of Vietnam?" *Foreign Affairs,* 63, no. 4 (Spring 1985), 722–746.

FULBRIGHT, J. W., *The Arrogance of Power.* New York: Random House, 1967.

GADDIS, J. L., *Strategies of Containment: A Critical Appraisal of Postwar American National Security Policy.* New York: Oxford Univ. Press, 1982.

GADDIS, J. L., "The Rise, Fall and Future of Detente," *Foreign Affairs,* 62, no. 2 (Winter 1983/1984), 354–377.

GARTHOFF, R. L., *Detente and Confrontation: American-Soviet Relations from Nixon to Reagan.* Washington, D.C.: Brookings Inst., 1985.

GIRLING, J.L.S., *America and the Third World: Revolution and Intervention.* Boston: Routledge & Kegan Paul, 1980.

HALBERSTAM, D., *The Best and the Brightest.* New York: Penguin Books, 1983.

HALBERSTAM, D., *The Reckoning: The Challenge to America's Greatness.* Philadelphia: Morrow, 1986.

HALPERIN, M. H. AND A. KANTER (EDS.), *Readings in American Foreign Policy: A Bureaucratic Perspective.* Boston: Little, Brown, 1973.

HALPERIN, M. H., *et al., Bureaucratic Politics and Foreign Policy.* Washington, D.C.: The Brookings Inst., 1974.

HOFFMAN, S., *Gulliver's Troubles, or the Setting of American Foreign Policy.* New York: McGraw-Hill, 1968.

HOFFMAN, S., *Primacy or World Order: American Foreign Policy Since the Cold War.* New York: McGraw-Hill, 1980.

HOFFMAN, S., *Dead Ends: American Foreign Policy in the New Cold War.* Cambridge, MA: Bazzinge, 1983.

HOLSTI, O. R., AND J. N. ROSENAU, *American Leadership in World Affairs: Vietnam and the Breakdown of Consensus.* Winchester, MA: Allen & Unwin, 1984.

HOYT, E. C., *Law and Force in American Foreign Policy.* Washington, D.C.: Univ. Press of America, 1985.

HSIAO, G. T. (ED.), *Sino-American Normalization and Its Policy Implications,* 2nd ed. New York: Praeger, 1983.

HUGHES, B. B., *The Domestic Context of American Foreign Policy.* San Francisco: W. H. Freeman, 1978.

IRISH, M. D., AND E. FRANK, *U.S. Foreign Policy: Context, Conduct, Content.* New York: Harcourt, 1975.

JENTLESON, B. W., "From Consensus to Conflict: The Domestic Political Economy of East-West Energy Trade Policy," *International Organization,* 38, no. 4 (Autumn 1984), 625–660.

JERVIS, R., *The Illogic of American Nuclear Strategy.* Ithaca, NY: Cornell Univ. Press, 1985.

JORDAN, R. S., *et al., The United States and Multilateral Resource Management: Marine Minerals, Food, and Energy.* New York: Praeger, 1984.

KEGLEY, C. W., JR. AND P. J. McGOWAN (EDS.), *Challenges to America: United States Foreign Policy Studies.* Beverly Hills, CA: Sage Publications, 1979.

KEGLEY, C. W., AND E. R. WITTKOPF, *American Foreign Policy Pattern and Process.* New York: St. Martin's Press, 1979.

KENNAN, G. F., *Realities of American Foreign Policy,* 2nd ed. New York: Norton, 1966.

KENNAN, G. F., *The Nuclear Delusion: Soviet-American Relations in the Atomic Age.* New York: Pantheon, 1982.

KISSINGER, H. A., *American Foreign Policy: A Global View.* Brookfield, VT: Gower Pub. Co., for Inst. of Southeast Asian Studies, 1982.

KISSINGER, H. A., *The Necessity for Choice: Prospects of American Foreign Policy,* repr. of 1961 ed. Westport, CT: Greenwood, 1984.

KNORR, K. (ED.), *NATO and American Security,* repr. of 1959 ed. Westport, CT: Greenwood, 1984.

Krasner, S. D., *Defending the National Interest: Raw Materials, Investments, and U.S. Foreign Policy.* Princeton, NJ: Princeton Univ. Press, 1978.

Litwok, R. S., *Detente and the Nixon Doctrine.* Cambridge: Cambridge Univ. Press, 1984.

May, E. R., *"Lessons" of the Past: The Use and Misuse of History in American Foreign Policy.* New York: Oxford Univ. Press, 1973.

Morgenthau, H. J., *In Defense of the National Interest: A Critical Examination of American Foreign Policy.* Lanham, MD: Univ. Press of America, 1983.

Nie, N. H., *et al., The Changing American Voter.* Cambridge, MA: Harvard Univ. Press, 1976.

Nye, J. S., Jr., *The Making of America's Soviet Policy.* New Haven, CT: Yale Univ. Press, 1984.

Osgood R. E., *Ideals and Self-Interest in America's Foreign Relations.* Chicago: Univ. of Chicago Press, 1953.

Osgood, R. E., *Alliances and American Foreign Policy.* Baltimore, MD: Johns Hopkins Univ. Press, 1968.

Osgood, R. E., *Containment, Soviet Behavior, and Grand Strategy.* Berkeley, CA: Univ. of California, Institute of International Studies, 1981.

Osgood, R. E., *The Successor Generation: Its Challenges and Responsibilities.* New Brunswick, NJ: Transaction Books, 1983.

Osgood, R. E., *et al., America and the World: From the Truman Doctrine to Vietnam.* Baltimore, MD: Johns Hopkins Univ. Press, 1970.

Oye, K. R., J. Lieber, and D. Rothchild, *Eagle Defiant: U.S. Foreign Policy in the 1980s.* Boston: Little, Brown, 1983.

Pfaltzgraff, R. L., Jr., *Energy Issues and Alliance Relationships: The United States, Western Europe and Japan.* Cambridge, MA: Institute for Foreign Policy Analysis, 1980.

Powers, T., *The Man Who Kept the Secrets.* New York: Kropf, 1979.

Rielly, J. E. (ed.), *American Public Opinion and U.S. Foreign Policy 1979.* Chicago: Chicago Council on Foreign Relations, 1979.

Rieselbach, L. N., *Congressional Politics.* New York: McGraw-Hill, 1973.

Rothstein, R. L., *The Third World and U.S. Foreign Policy: Cooperation and Conflict in the 1980s.* Boulder, CO: Westview Press, 1981.

Russett, B. M., *What Price Vigilance? The Burdens of National Defense.* New Haven, CT: Yale Univ. Press, 1970.

Russett, B. M. and E. C. Hanson, *Interest and Ideology: The Foreign Policy Beliefs of American Businessmen.* San Francisco: W. H. Freeman, 1975.

Schlesinger, A., Jr., *The Imperial Presidency.* Boston: Houghton Mifflin, 1973.

Serfaty, S., *American Foreign Policy in a Hostile World.* New York: Praeger, 1984.

Sewell, J. W., *et al.* (eds.), *U.S. Foreign Policy and the Third World: Agenda 1985–1986.* New Brunswick, NJ: Transaction Books (for the Overseas Development Council), 1985.

Sheehan, N. and E. W. Kenworthy, *The Pentagon Papers.* New York: Times Books., 1971.

Spanier, J. and E. M. Uslaner, *American Foreign Policy Making and the Democratic Dilemmas,* 4th ed. New York: Holt, Rinehart & Winston, 1985.

Spanier, J. and J. Nogee, *Congress, the Presidency and American Foreign Policy.* Elmsford, NY: Pergamon, 1981.

Stoessinger, J. G., *Crusaders and Pragmatists: Movers of Modern American Foreign Policy,* 2nd ed. New York: Norton, 1985.

Sullivan, M. P., *The Vietnam War: A Study in the Making of American Policy.* Lexington, KY: Univ. Press of Kentucky, 1985.

Tucker, R. W., "The Purposes of American Power," *Foreign Affairs,* 59, no. 2 (Winter 1980/ 1981), 241–274.

"U.S. Defense Policy in the 1980s," special issue of *Daedalus,* 109, no. 4 (Fall 1980).

Verba, S. and N. Nie, *Participation in America: Political Democracy and Social Equality.* New York: Harper & Row, 1972.

THEORY OF GAMES AND ANALYSIS OF CONFLICTS

Adeniran, T. and Y. Alexander (eds.), *International Violence.* New York: Praeger, 1983.

ART, R. AND R. JERVIS (EDS.), *International Politics: Anarchy, Force, Political Economy and Decision Making*, 2nd ed. Boston: Little, Brown, 1985.

AXELROD, R., *The Evolution of Cooperation*. New York: Basic Books, 1984.

BLECHMAN, B. M. (ED.), *Preventing Nuclear War: A Realistic Approach*. Bloomington: Indiana Univ. Press/Washington, D.C.: Center for Strategic and International Studies, 1985.

BOULDING, K. E., *Conflict and Defense: A General Theory*. New York: Harper & Row, 1968.

BRAMS, S. J., *Superpower Games: Applying Game Theory to Superpower Conflict*. New Haven, CT: Yale Univ. Press, 1985.

BRAMS, S. J., AND M. P. HESSEL, "Threat Power in Sequential Games," *International Studies Quarterly*, 28 (1984), 23–44.

BRECHER, M. (ED.), *Studies in Crisis Behavior*. New Brunswick, NJ: Transaction Books, 1979.

BRITO, D. L., AND M. D. INTRILIGATOR, "Conflict, War, and Redistribution," *American Political Science Review*, 79, no. 4 (December 1985), 943–957.

CHRISTOPHER, W. WITH P. H. KREISBERG (ED.), *American Hostages in Iran: The Conduct of a Crisis*. New Haven, CT: Yale Univ. Press, 1985.

CHOUCRI, N. AND R. C. NORTH, *Nations in Conflict*. San Francisco: W. H. Freeman, 1975.

CLINE, W., *Reciprocity: a New Approach to World Trade Policy?*, Washington, D.C.: Institute for International Economics, 1982.

CONYBEARE, J.A.C., "Public Goods, Prisoners' Dilemmas and the International Political Economy," *International Studies Quarterly*, 28, no. 1 (March 1984), 5–22.

DEUTSCH, M., *The Resolution of Conflict: Constructive and Destructive Processes*. New Haven, CT: Yale Univ. Press, 1973.

DORAN, C. F., AND W. PARSONS, "War and the Cycle of Relative Power," *American Political Science Review*, 74, no. 4 (December 1980), 947–965.

DOUGHERTY, J. E., et al., *Ethics, Deterrence, and National Security*. Elmsford, NY: Pergamon, 1985.

DOWNS, G. W., et al., *Arms Races and Cooperation*, special issue of *World Politics*, 38, no. 1 (October 1985).

DYSON, F., *Weapons and Hope*. New York: Harper & Row, 1984.

ETZIONI, A., *The Hard Way to Peace*. New York: Colliers, 1962.

Explaining Cooperation under Anarchy: Hypotheses and Strategies, special issue of *World Politics*, 38, no. 1 (October 1985).

FERRIS, W. H., *The Power Capability of Nation-States*. Lexington, MA: Lexington Books, 1973.

FISCHER, G. W, "Conceptual Models, Judgment, and the Treatment of Uncertainty in Nuclear Threat Assessment," *Journal of Social Issues*, 39, no. 1 (1983), 87–116.

FISHER, R. (ED.), *International Conflict and Behavioral Science*. New York: Basic Books, 1965.

FRASER, N. M., *Conflict Analysis: Models and Resolutions*. New York: North-Holland, 1984.

GALTUNG, J., *Peace and War Defense*. Atlantic Highlands, NJ: Humanities Press, 1976.

GALTUNG, J., *Peace and Social Structure*. Atlantic Highlands, NJ: Humanities Press, 1978.

GALTUNG, J., *Peace and World Structure*. Atlantic Highlands, NJ: Humanities Press, 1980.

GALTUNG, J., *Peace Problems: Some Case Studies*. Atlantic Highlands, NJ: Humanities Press, 1980.

GEORGE, A. AND R. SMOKE, *Deterrence in American Foreign Policy: Theory and Practice*. New York: Columbia Univ. Press, 1974.

GOMPERT, D. C., et al., *Nuclear Weapons and World Politics*, 1980's Project, Council on Foreign Relations. New York: McGraw-Hill, 1977.

GURR, T. R., *Why Men Rebel*. Princeton, NJ: Princeton Univ. Press, 1970.

GURR, T. R. (ED.), *Handbook of Political Conflict: Theory and Research*. New York: Free Press, 1980.

HART, D. M., "Soviet Approaches to Crisis Management: The Military Dimension," *Survival*, 26, no. 5 (September/October 1984), 214–223.

HARTMANN, F. H., *The Conservation of Enemies: A Study in Enmity*. Westport, CT: Greenwood, 1982.

HERZ, J. H., *International Politics in the Atomic Age*. New York: Columbia Univ. Press, 1959.

HOOPES, T., *The Limits of Intervention*, 2nd ed., New York: Longman, 1973.

HUTH, P. AND B. RUSSETT, "What Makes Deterrence Work? Cases from 1900 to 1980," *World Politics*, 36, no. 4 (July 1984), 496–526.

JERVIS, R., "Cooperation under the Security Dilemma," *World Politics*, 30 (January 1978), 167–214.

JERVIS, R., *The Illogic of American Nuclear Strategy.* Ithaca, NY: Cornell Univ. Press, 1985.

JERVIS, R., *et al., Psychology and Deterrence.* Baltimore, MD: Johns Hopkins Univ. Press, 1985.

KAHLER, M., "Rumors of War: The 1914 Analogy," *Foreign Affairs*, 58, no. 2 (Winter 1979/1980), 374–396.

KAHN, H., *On Escalation: Metaphors and Scenarios.* New York: Praeger, 1965.

KAPLOWITZ, N., "Psychopolitical Dimensions of International Relations: The Reciprocal Effects of Conflict Strategies," *International Studies Quarterly*, 28 (1984), 374–406.

KNORR, K. (ED.), *Historical Dimensions of National Security.* Lawrence, KS: Univ. Press of Kansas, 1976.

KNORR, K. (ED.), *Power, Strategy, and Security: A World Politics Reader.* Princeton, NJ: Princeton Univ. Press, 1983.

LAWSON, F. H., "Using Positive Sanctions to End International Conflicts: Iran and the Arab Gulf Countries," *Journal of Peace Research*, 20, no. 4 (1983), 311–328.

LEBOW, R. N., *Between Peace and War: The Nature of International Crisis*, 2nd ed., Baltimore, MD: Johns Hopkins Univ. Press, 1984.

LIPSON, C., "International Cooperation in Economic and Security Affairs," *World Politics*, 37 (October 1984), 1–23.

LOCKHART, C., *Bargaining in International Conflicts*, New York: Columbia Univ. Press, 1979.

LUCE, R. D., AND H. RAIFFA, *Games and Decisions: Introduction and Critical Survey.* New York: Wiley, 1957.

MACK, A.J.R., "Why Big Nations Lose Small Wars: The Politics of Asymmetric Conflict," *World Politics*, 27, no. 2 (January 1975), 175–200.

MANDEL, R., "Political Gaming and Foreign Policy Making During Crises," *World Politics*, 24, no. 4 (July 1977), 610–625.

MANDELBAUM, M., *The Nuclear Revolution: International Politics Before and After Hiroshima.* New York: Cambridge Univ. Press, 1981.

NEWHOUSE, J., *Cold Dawn: The Story of SALT.* New York: Holt, Rinehart, & Winston, 1973.

PENNOCK, J. R. AND J. W. CHAPMAN (EDS.), *Coercion.* New York: Lieber-Atherton, 1972.

PFALZGRAFF, R. L., JR., AND J. K. DAVIS, *SALT II: Promise or Precipice.* Washington, D.C.: Advanced International Studies Institute, in Association with the Univ. of Miami, 1976.

RAPOPORT, A., *Fights, Games, and Debates.* Ann Arbor, MI: Univ. of Michigan Press, 1960, 1974.

RAPOPORT, A., *Strategy and Conscience.* New York: Harper & Row, 1964.

RAPOPORT, A. AND A. M. CHAMMAH, *The Prisoner's Dilemma.* Ann Arbor, MI: Univ. of Michigan Press, 1970.

RAPOPORT, A., *et al., The Two X Two Game.* Ann Arbor, MI: Univ. of Michigan Press, 1976.

REMINGTON, R. A., *The Warsaw Pact: Case Studies in Communist Conflict Resolution.* Cambridge, MA: M.I.T. Press, 1971.

RIKER, W. H., *The Theory of Political Coalitions*, repr. of 1962 ed. Westport, CT: Greenwood, 1984.

ROTHSTEIN, R. L. "Consensual Knowledge and International Collaboration: Some Lessons from the Commodity Negotiations," *International Organization*, 38, no. 4 (Autumn 1984), 733–762.

RUMMEL, R. J., *Understanding Conflict and War*, 5 vols. Beverly Hills, CA: Sage Publications, 1976–1981.

RUSSETT, B., *Power and Community World Politics.* San Francisco: W. H. Freeman, 1974.

RUSSETT, B., "Defense Expenditures and National Well-being," *American Political Science Review*, 76, no. 4 (December 1982), 767–777.

RUSSETT, B., *The Prisoners of Insecurity: Nuclear Deterrence, the Arms Race, and Arms Control.* San Francisco: W. H. Freeman, 1983.

RUSSETT, B., "The Mysterious Case of Vanishing Hegemony; or, is Mark Twain Really Dead?", *International Organization*, 39, no. 2 (Spring 1985), 207–231.

SCHELLING, T. C., *The Strategy of Conflict.* Cambridge, MA: Harvard Univ. Press, 1960.

SCHELLING, T. C., *Arms and Influence*, repr. of 1966 ed., Westport, CT: Greenwood, 1976.

SCHELLING, T. C., *Micromotives and Macrobehavior.* New York: Norton, 1978.

SCHELLING, T. C., "Confidence in Crisis," *International Security*, 8, no. 4 (Spring 1984), 55–66.

SCHELLING, T. C., *Choice and Consequence*. Cambridge, MA: Harvard Univ. Press, 1985.

SCHELLING, T. C., AND M. H. HALPERIN, *Strategy and Arms Control*. Elmsford, NY: Pergamon, 1985.

Security and Confrontation in the Nuclear Age, special issue of *P.S.*, 17, no. 1 (Winter 1984), 10–40.

SHARP, G., *The Politics of Nonviolent Action*. Boston, MA: Porter Sargent, 1973, 1974.

SHUBIK, M., *Game Theory in the Social Sciences: Concepts and Solutions*. Cambridge, MA: M.I.T. Press, 1982.

SHUBIK, M., *Mathematics of Conflict*. New York: Elsevier, 1983.

SHUBIK, M., *A Game Theoretical Approach to Political Economy*. Cambridge, MA: M.I.T. Press, 1984.

SIPRI Yearbook: World Armaments and Disarmament, 1985. Stockholm: International Peace Research Institute, and Philadelphia: Taylor and Francis, 1985.

SIVERSON, R. M. AND M. R. TENNEFOSS, "Power, Alliance, and the Escalation of International Conflict, 1815–1965," *American Political Science Review*, 78, no. 4 (December 1984), 1057–1069.

SNIDAL, D., "Coordination Versus Prisoners' Dilemma: Implications for International Cooperation and Regimes," *American Political Science Review*, 79, no. 4 (December 1985), 923–942.

SNYDER, G. H., "The Security Dilemma in Alliance Politics," *World Politics*, 36, no. 4 (July 1984), 461–495.

SNYDER, G. H. AND P. DIESING, *Conflict Among Nations: Bargaining, Decision Making and System Structure in International Crisis*. Princeton, NJ: Princeton Univ. Press, 1977.

SNYDER, J. L., "Rationality at the Brink: The Role of Cognitive Processes in Failures of Deterrence," *World Politics*, 30, no. 3 (April 1978), 345–365.

STOLL, R. J., "Bloc Concentration and Dispute Escalation Among the Major Powers, 1830–1965," *Social Science Quarterly*, 65, no. 1 (March 1984), 48–59.

STONE, J., *Conflict Through Consensus: United Nations Approaches to Aggression*. Baltimore, MD: Johns Hopkins Press, 1977.

TALBOTT, S., *Endgame: The Inside Story of SALT II*. New York: Harper, 1979.

TALBOTT, S., *Deadly Gambits: The Reagan Administration and the Stalemate in Nuclear Arms Control*. New York: Knopf, 1984.

TAYLOR, M., *Anarchy and Cooperation*. London: Wiley, 1976.

TAYLOR, M., *Community, Anarchy and Liberty*. Cambridge: Cambridge Univ. Press, 1982.

TUCKER, R. W., *The Nuclear Debate: Deterrence and the Lapse of Faith*. New York: Holmes & Meier, 1985.

VON NEUMANN, J. AND O. MORGENSTERN, *Theory of Games and Economic Behavior*. Princeton, NJ: Princeton Univ. Press, 1980.

WAGNER, R. H., "The Theory of Games and the Problem of International Cooperation," *American Political Science Review*, 77, no. 2 (June 1983), 330–346.

WALKER, S. G. *et al.*, "Evidence of Learning and Risk Orientation During International Crises: The Munich and Polish Cases," *British Journal of Political Science*, 14, no. 1 (January 1984), 33–51.

WALLACE, M. D., "Armaments and Escalation. Two Competing Hypotheses," *International Studies Quarterly*, 26, no. 1 (March 1982), 37–56.

Weapons in Space, special issues of *Daedalus* (Spring and Summer 1985).

WILKENFELD, J. AND M. BRECHER, "Superpower Crisis Management Behavior," *Sage International Yearbook of Foreign Policy Studies*, 7 (1982), 185–212.

WILKENFELD, J. *et al.*, *Foreign Policy Behavior: The Interstate Behavior Analysis Model*. Beverly Hills, CA: Sage, 1980.

WILLRICH, M. AND J. B. RHINELANDER, *SALT: The Moscow Agreements and Beyond*. New York: Free Press, 1975.

WOLFE, T. W., *The SALT Experience*. Cambridge, MA: Ballinger, 1979.

WRIGHT, Q., *et al.* (eds.), *Preventing World War III*. New York: Simon and Schuster, 1962.

YOUNG, O. R., *The Politics of Force: Bargaining During International Crises*. Princeton, NJ: Princeton Univ. Press, 1969.

YOUNG, O. R. (ED.), *Bargaining: Formal Theories of Negotiation*. Champaign, IL: Univ. of Illinois Press, 1975.

ZAGARE, F. C., *Game Theory: Concepts and Applications*. Beverly Hills, CA: Sage Publications, 1984.

ZARTMAN, W. I., *Ripe for Resolution: Conflict and Intervention in Africa.* New York: Oxford Univ. Press, 1985.

WAR AND ITS ASPECTS

ART, R. J. AND K. N. WALTZ (EDS.), *The Use of Force: International Politics and Foreign Policy,* 2nd ed. Lanham, MD: Univ. Press of America, 1983.

BEER, F. A., *Peace Against War: The Ecology of International Violence,* San Francisco: W. H. Freemann, 1981.

BLAINEY, G., *The Causes of War.* New York: Free Press, 1975.

BRAMSON, L. AND G. W. GOETHALS (EDS.), *War: Studies from Psychology, Sociology, Anthropology,* rev. ed. New York: Basic Books, 1968.

BUENO DE MESQUITA, B., *The War Trap.* New Haven, CT: Yale Univ. Press, 1981.

BUENO DE MESQUITA, B., "The Costs of War: A Rational Expectations Approach," *American Political Science Review,* 77, no. 2 (June 1983), 347–357.

CHOUCRI, N. (ED.), *Multidisciplinary Perspectives on Population and Conflict,* Syracuse, NY: Syracuse Univ. Press, 1984.

CHOUCRI, N. AND R. NORTH, *Nations in Conflict: National Growth and International Violence.* San Francisco: W. H. Freeman, 1975.

CLAUSEWITZ, K. VON, *On War.* J. J. Graham (trans.). New York: Barnes & Noble, 1902.

COHEN, E. A., "Constraints on America's Conduct of Small Wars," *International Security,* 9, no. 2 (Fall 1984), 151–181.

ECKSTEIN, H. (ED.), *Internal War: Problems and Approaches,* repr. of 1964 ed. Westport, CT: Greenwood, 1980.

The Economic Foundations of War, special issue of *International Studies Quarterly,* 27, no. 4 (December 1983).

FALK, R. A. AND S. S. KIM (EDS.), *The War System: An Interdisciplinary Approach.* Boulder, CO: Westview, 1980.

FALK, R. A. AND S. H. MENDLOVITZ (EDS.), *The Strategy of World Order,* 3 vols. Vol. 1: *Toward a Theory of War Prevention.* New York: World Policy Journal, 1966.

FAY, S. B., *The Origins of the World War,* 2 vols. New York: Macmillan, 1928.

The Great War and the Nuclear Age, special issue of *International Security,* 9, no. 1 (Summer 1984).

HALLE, L. J., "Does War Have a Future?", *Foreign Affairs,* 52, no. 1 (October 1973), 20–34.

HALPERIN, M. H., *Limited War in the Nuclear Age,* repr. of 1963 ed. Westport, CT: Greenwood, 1978.

HERKEN, G., *Counsels of War.* New York: Knopf, 1985.

HOFFMAN, S., *The State of War.* New York: Praeger, 1965.

HOLSTI, O. R., *Crisis Escalation War.* Montreal: McGill-Queen's Univ. Press, 1972.

HOLSTI, R., *The Relation of War to the Origin of the State,* repr. of 1913 ed. Philadelphia: Porcupine Press.

IKLE, F. C., *Every War Must End.* New York: Columbia Univ. Press, 1971.

KAHN, H., *On Escalation.* New York: Praeger, 1965.

KAHN, H., *On Thermonuclear War,* repr. of 1961 ed. Westport, CT: Greenwood, 1978.

KAHN, H., *Thinking About the Unthinkable in the 1980s.* New York: Simon & Schuster, 1984.

KNORR, K., *On the Uses of Military Power in the Nuclear Age.* Princeton, NJ: Princeton Univ. Press, 1966.

KNORR, K., *Military Power and Potential.* Lexington, MA: Heath, 1970.

KNORR, K., *The War Potential of Nations,* repr. of 1956 ed. Westport, CT: Greenwood, 1978.

LEVY, J. S., "Theories of General War," *World Politics,* 37, no. 3 (1985), 344–374.

MIDLARSKY, M. I., *The Disintegration of Political Systems: War and Revolution in Comparative Perspective.* Columbia: Univ. of South Carolina Press, 1986.

MILWARD, A. S., *War, Economy, and Society, 1939–1945.* Berkeley, CA: Univ. of California Press, 1977.

MOST, B. A. AND H. STARR, "Diffusion, Reinforcement, Geopolitics, and the Spread of War," *American Political Science Review,* 74, no. 4 (December 1980), 932–946.

Most, B. A. and H. Starr, "Conceptualizing 'War': Consequences for Theory and Research," *Journal of Conflict Resolution*, 27, no. 1 (1983), 137–159.

North, R. C. and M. Willard, "The Convergence Effect: Challenge to Parsimony," *International Organization*, 37, no. 2 (Spring 1983), 340–358.

Organski, A.F.K. and J. Kugler, *The War Ledger*. Chicago: Univ. of Chicago Press, 1980.

Osgood, R. E., *Limited War Revisited*. Boulder, CO: Westview Press, 1979.

Pillar, P. R., *Negotiating Peace: War Termination as a Bargaining Process*. Princeton, NJ: Princeton Univ. Press, 1983.

Richardson, L. F., *Arms and Insecurity*. Chicago: Quandrangle Books, 1960.

Russett, B. M. (ED.), *Peace, War and Numbers*. Beverly Hills, CA: Sage Publications, 1972.

Singer, D. J. (ED.), *The Correlates of War I: Research Origins and Rationale*. New York: Free Press, 1979.

Singer, D. J. (ED.), *The Correlates of War II: Testing Some Realpolitik Models*. New York: Free Press, 1980.

Singer, D. J. and M. Small, *The Wages of War, 1816–1965: A Statistical Handbook*. Ann Arbor, MI: Inter-university Consortium for Political and Social Research (ICPSR), 1974.

Small, M. and D. J. Singer, *Resort to Arms: International and Civil Wars, 1816–1980*. Beverly Hills, CA: Sage, 1982.

Stoessinger, J. G., *Why Nations Go to War*, 3rd ed. New York: St. Martin's Press, 1982.

Waltz, K. N., *Man, the State and War: A Theoretical Analysis,* New York: Columbia Univ. Press, 1959.

Walzer, M., *Just and Unjust Wars: A Moral Argument with Historical Illustrations*. New York: Basic Books, 1977.

Wilkinson, D., *Deadly Quarrels: Lewis F. Richardson and the Statistical Study of War*. Berkeley, CA: Univ. of California Press, 1980.

Wright, Q., *The Role of International Law in the Elimination of War*. Dobbs Ferry, NY: Oceana, 1962.

Wright, Q., *A Study of War*, 2nd ed. Chicago: Univ. of Chicago Press, 1983.

Zinnes, D. A., "An Analytical Study of the Balance of Power Theories," *Journal of Peace Research*, 4, no. 3 (1967), 270–288.

DIPLOMACY

Acheson, D., *Present at the Creation: My Years in the State Department*. New York: New American Library, 1970.

Bell, C., *The Diplomacy of Detente: The Kissinger Era*. New York: St. Martin's Press, 1977.

Blechman, B. and S. Kaplan, *Force Without War*. Washington, D.C.: Brookings, 1978.

Cleveland, H., *et al., The Overseas Americans*, repr. of 1960 ed. Salem, NH: Ayer Co. Publishers, 1980.

Craig, G. A. and G. L. Alexander, *Force and Statecraft: Diplomatic Problems of Our Time*. New York: Oxford Univ. Press, 1983.

Etzold, T. H., *The Conduct of American Foreign Relations: The Other Side of Diplomacy*. New York: New Viewpoints, 1978.

Falkowski, L. S., *Presidents, Secretaries of State, and Crisis Management in U.S. Foreign Relations: A Model and Predictive Analysis*. Boulder, CO: Westview Press, 1978.

George, A. L., "Crisis Management: The Interaction of Political and Military Considerations," *Survival*, 26, no. 5 (September/October 1984), 223–234.

George, A. L., *et al., The Limits of Coercive Diplomacy*. Boston: Little, Brown, 1971.

George, A. L. (ED.), *Managing U.S.–Soviet Rivalry: Problems of Crisis Prevention*. Boulder, CO: Westview Press, 1983.

Giniger, H., *Diplomacy: How Nations Negotiate*. New York: Harper & Row, 1973.

Iatridis, J. O. (ED.), *Ambassador MacVeagh Reports: Greece, 1933–1947*. Princeton, NJ: Princeton Univ. Press, 1980.

Ikle, F. C., *How Nations Negotiate*, repr. of 1964 ed. Washington, D.C.: Georgetown Univ. School of Foreign Service, 1982.

ISAACSON, W. AND E. THOMAS, *Wise Men: Architects of The American Century.* New York: Simon and Schuster, 1986.

JACKSON, H. M., SENATOR (ED.), *The Secretary of State and the Ambassador. Jackson Subcommittee Papers on the Conduct of American Foreign Policy.* New York: Praeger, 1964.

JOHNSON, E.A.J. (ED.), *The Dimensions of Diplomacy.* Baltimore, MD: Johns Hopkins Univ. Press, 1964.

KENNAN, G. F., *American Diplomacy: 1900–1950,* enl. ed. Chicago: Univ. of Chicago Press, 1985.

KENNEDY, P., *Strategy and Diplomacy, 1870–1945: Eight Studies.* Winchester, MA: Allen & Unwin, 1984.

KISSINGER, H. A., *The White House Years.* Boston: Little, Brown, 1979.

KISSINGER, H. A., *Years of Upheaval.* Boston: Little, Brown, 1982.

LAUREN, P. G. (ED.), *Diplomacy: New Approaches in History, Theory, and Policy.* New York: Free Press, 1979.

Negotiation and Statecraft, U.S. Congress, Senate, Committee on Government Operations, 91st Congress, 2nd session, 1970.

NEUSTADT, R. E., *Alliance Politics.* New York: Columbia Univ. Press, 1970.

NICOLSON, H., "The 'Old' and the 'New' Diplomacy," in R. L. Pfaltzgraff (ed.), *Politics and the International System,* 2nd ed. Philadelphia: Lippincott, 1972.

PLISCHKE, E., *Modern Diplomacy: The Art and the Artisans.* Washington, D.C.: American Enterprise Institute, 1979.

RUBIN, B., *Secrets of State: The State Department and the Struggle over U.S. Foreign Policy.* New York: Oxford Univ. Press, 1985.

SAPIN, B. M., *The Making of United States Foreign Policy.* New York: Praeger, 1966.

SEMMEL, A. K., "Some Correlates of Attitudes to Multilateral Diplomacy in the U.S. Department of State," *International Studies Quarterly,* 20, no. 2 (June 1976), 301–324.

Soviet Diplomacy and Negotiating Behavior: Emerging New Context for U.S. Diplomacy, Washington, D.C.: Congressional Research Service for the House Committee on Foreign Affairs, G.P.O., 1979.

WATSON, A., *Diplomacy.* New York: McGraw-Hill, 1982.

WEBSTER, C. K., *The Art and Practice of Diplomacy.* New York: Barnes & Noble, 1962.

ZELIKOW, P. D., "Force Without War, 1975–82," *Journal of Strategic Studies,* 7, no. 1 (March 1984), 29–54.

INTERNATIONAL LAW

BLACK, C. E. AND R. A. FALK (EDS.), *The Future of International Legal Order.* Vol. 4: *The Structure of the International Environment.* Princeton, NJ: Princeton Univ. Press, 1972.

BRIERLY, J. L., *The Law of Nations: An Introduction to the International Law of Peace,* new ed. London: Oxford Univ. Press, 1963.

CORBETT, P. E., *Law in Diplomacy.* Gloucester, MA: Peter Smith, 1967.

CUTLER, L. N., "The Right to Intervene," *Foreign Affairs,* 64, no. 1 (Fall 1985), 96–112.

DEUTSCH, K. W. AND S. HOFFMAN (EDS.), *The Relevance of International Law.* Garden City, NY: Doubleday Anchor Books, 1971.

DORE, I. I., *International Law and the Superpowers: Normative Order in a Divided World.* New Brunswick, NJ: Rutgers Univ. Press, 1984.

FALK, R. A., *The Vietnam War and International Law,* 4 vols. Princeton, NJ: Princeton Univ. Press, 1967–1976.

FALK, R. A., *Human Rights and State Sovereignty.* New York: Holmes & Meier, 1981.

FALK, R. A., *The End of World Order: Essays on Normative International Relations.* New York: Holmes & Meier, 1983.

FALK, R. A., "The Role of the International Court of Justice," *Journal of International Affairs,* 37, no. 2 (Winter 1984), 253–268.

FALK, R. AND S. KIM, *An Approach to World Order Studies and the World System.* New York: World Policy Journal, 1982.

FALK, R. A. AND S. H. MENDLOVITZ (EDS.), *The Strategy of World Order,* 4 vols. Vol. 2: *International Law.* New York: World Policy Journal, 1966.

FALK, R. A., *et al., Studies on a Just World Order,* 3 vols. Vol. 2: *International Law: A Contemporary Perspective.* Boulder, CO: Westview, 1985.

GOULD, W. L. AND M. BARKUN, *International Law and the Social Sciences.* Princeton, NJ: Princeton Univ. Press, 1970.

International Law and Development: Perspectives for the 1980s, special issue of *Journal of African Law,* 26, no. 1 (Spring 1982), 1–93.

LOWE, A. V., "Do General Rules of International Law Exist?", *Review of International Studies,* 9, no. 3 (July 1983), 207–213.

O'BRIEN, W. V., *The Conduct of Just and Limited War.* New York: Praeger, 1981.

ONUF, N. G. AND V. S. PETERSON, "Human Rights from an International Regimes Perspective," *Journal of International Affairs,* 37, no. 2 (Winter 1984), 329–342.

OSGOOD, R. E. AND R. W. TUCKER, *Force, Order, and Justice,* repr. of 1967 ed. Baltimore, MD: Johns Hopkins Univ. Press, 1971.

PERKINS, J. A., *The Prudent Peace: Law as Foreign Policy,* Chicago: Univ. of Chicago Press, 1981.

POLEBAUM, B. M., "National Self-Defense in International Law: An Emerging Standard for a Nuclear Age," *New York University Law Review,* 59, no. 1 (April 1984), 187–229.

RUBIN, A. P., "Terrorism and the Laws of War," *Denver Journal of International Law and Policy,* 12, no. 2–3 (Spring 1983), 219–235.

RUGGIE, J. G., "Human Rights and the Future International Community," *Daedalus,* 112, no. 4 (Fall 1983), 93–110.

SANDERS, D., *Lawmaking and Cooperation in International Politics: The Idealist Case Re-examined.* New York: Macmillan, 1985.

SCHACHTER, O., "Self-help in International Law: U.S. Action in the Iranian Hostage Crisis," *Journal of International Affairs,* 37, no. 2 (Winter 1984), 231–246.

SCHWARZENBERGER, G., "The Credibility of International Law," *Yearbook of World Affairs,* 37 (1983), 292–301.

STONE, J., *Visions of World Order: Between State Power and Human Justice.* Baltimore, MD: Johns Hopkins Univ. Press, 1984.

SUTER, K., *An International Law of Guerilla Warfare.* New York: St. Martin's Press, 1984.

TORNEY, J. V. (ED.), *Human Rights: International Perspectives,* special issue of *International Studies Quarterly,* 23, no. 2 (June 1979).

The United States Action in Grenada, special issue of *American Journal of International Law,* 78, no. 1 (January 1984), 131–175.

WALZER, M., *Just and Unjust Wars.* New York: Basic Books, 1977.

WESTON, B. H., "Nuclear Weapons and International Law: Illegality in Context," *Denver Journal of International Law and Policy,* 13, no. 1 (Fall 1983), 1–15.

WRIGHT, Q. *The Role of International Law in the Elimination of War.* Dobbs Ferry, NY: Oceana, 1962.

WRIGHT, Q., *International Law and the United Nations,* repr. of 1960 ed. Westport, CT: Greenwood, 1976.

INTERNATIONAL ORGANIZATIONS

ALKER, H. R. AND B. M. RUSSETT, *World Politics in the General Assembly.* New Haven, CT: Yale Univ. Press, 1965.

BARROS, J. (ED.), *The United Nations: Past, Present, and Future.* New York: Free Press, 1973.

BENNETT, A. L., *International Organizations: Principles and Issues,* 3rd ed. Englewood Cliffs, NJ: Prentice-Hall, 1984.

BLOOMFIELD, L. P. AND C. W. YOST, *What Future for the U.N.?* New Brunswick, NJ: Transaction Books, 1977.

BULL, H. AND A. WATSON (EDS.), *The Expansion of International Society.* New York: Clarendon Press/Oxford, 1984.

CLAUDE, I. L., JR., *Swords into Plowshares: The Problems and Progress of International Organization,* 4th ed. New York: Random, 1971.

DIXON, W. J., "The Emerging Image of U.N. Politics," *World Politics*, 34, no. 1 (October 1981), 47–61.

FALK, R. A. AND S. H. MENDLOVITZ (EDS.), *The Strategy of World Order*. Vol. 3: *The United Nations*. New York: World Policy Journal, 1966.

FARLEY, L. T., *Change Processes in International Organizations*. Cambridge, MA: Schenkman Publishing, 1982.

FELD, W. J., *Multinational Enterprises and U.N. Politics: The Quest for Codes of Conduct*. Elmsford, NY: Pergamon, 1980.

FELD, W. J. AND R. A. COATE, *The Role of International Nongovernmental Organizations in World Politics*. New York: Learning Resources in International Studies, 1976.

FELD, W., *et al.*, *International Organizations: A Comparative Approach*. New York: Praeger, 1983.

FRANCK, T. M., *Nation Against Nation: What Happened to the U.N. Dream and What the U.S. Can Do About It*. New York: Oxford Univ. Press, 1985.

FULBRIGHT, J. W., *et al.*, *The Future of the United Nations*. Washington, D.C.: American Enterprise Institute for Public Policy Research, 1977.

GOODRICH, L. M., *The United Nations in a Changing World*. New York: Columbia Univ. Press, 1976.

GOODRICH, L. M., *Korea: A Study of U.S. Policy in the United Nations*, repr. of 1956 ed. Westport, CT: Greenwood, 1979.

GOODRICH, L. M. AND D. A. KAY (EDS.), *International Organization: Politics and Process*. Madison, WI: Univ. of Wisconsin Press, 1973.

GOODRICH, L. M. AND A. P. SIMONS, *The United Nations and the Maintenance of International Peace and Security*, repr. of 1955 ed. Westport, CT: Greenwood, 1974.

GORDENKER, L. (ED.), *The United Nations in International Politics*. Princeton, NJ: Princeton Univ. Press, 1971.

HAAS, E. B., *Tangle of Hopes*. Englewood Cliffs, NJ: Prentice-Hall, 1969.

HAAS, E. B., "Regime Decay: Conflict Management and International Organizations, 1945–1981," *International Organization*, 37, no. 2 (Spring 1983), 189–256.

HAAS, E. B., *et al.*, *Conflict Management by International Organizations*. Morristown, NJ: General Learning Press, 1972.

HAAS, E. B., *et al.*, *Scientists and World Order: The Uses of Technical Knowledge in International Organizations*. Berkeley, CA: Univ. of California Press, 1978.

HILL, M., *The United Nations Systems*. New York: Cambridge Univ. Press, 1978.

HOFFMAN, S., "International Organization and the International System," *International Organization*, 24, no. 3 (Summer 1970), 389–413.

JACOBSEN, K., *The General Assembly of the United Nations: A Quantitative Analysis of Conflict, Inequality, and Relevance*. New York: Columbia Univ. Press, 1978.

JORDAN, R. S. (ED.), *International Administration: Its Evolution and Contemporary Applications*. London: Oxford Univ. Press, 1971.

MORGENTHAU, H. J. (ED.), *Peace, Security, and the United Nations*, repr. of 1946 ed. Salem, NH: Ayer Co. Publications, 1973.

MURPHY, J. F., *The United Nations and the Control of International Violence: A Legal and Political Analysis*, Totowa, NJ: Allanheld, 1983.

NICHOLAS, H. G., *The United Nations as a Political Institution*, 5th ed. New York: Oxford Univ. Press, 1975.

PUCHALA, D. J., "American Interests and the United Nations," *Political Science Quarterly*, 97, no. 4 (Winter 1982–1983), 571–588.

SCHMITTER, P. C., "The 'Organizational Development' of International Organizations," *International Organization*, 25 (Autumn 1971), 918.

SEWELL, J. P., *Functionalism and World Politics: A Study Based on United Nations Programs Financing Economic Development*, Princeton, NJ: Princeton Univ. Press, 1966.

SEWELL, J. P. *UNESCO and World Politics: Engaging in International Relations*. Princeton, NJ: Princeton Univ. Press, 1975.

SINGER, J. D. AND M. D. WALLACE, "Intergovernmental Organization in the Global System, 1815–1964: A Quantitative Description," *International Organization*, 24, no. 2 (Spring 1970), 239–287.

SKJELSBAEK, K., "The Growth of International Nongovernmental Organization in the Twentieth Century," *International Organization*, 25 (Summer 1971), 420–442.

STOESSINGER, J. G., *The United Nations and the Super-Powers: China, Russia, and America,* 4th ed. New York: Random, 1977.

THARP, P. A., JR., "Transnational Enterprises and International Regulation: A Survey of Various Approaches in International Organizations," *International Organization,* 30, no. 1 (Winter 1976), 47–73.

WRIGHT, Q., *International Law and the United Nations,* repr. of 1960 ed. Westport, CT: Greenwood, 1976.

Yearbook of International Organizations 1985–1986, 3 vols., 22nd ed. New York: K.G. Saur, 1985.

POLITICAL INTEGRATION

BIRCH, A. H., "Minority Nationalist Movements and Theories of Political Integration," *World Politics,* 30, no. 3 (April 1978), 325–344.

BRADA, J. C., AND J. A. MENDEZ, "Economic Integration Among Developed, Developing and Centrally Planned Economies: A Comparative Analysis," *Review of Economics and Statistics,* 57, no. 4 (1985), 549–556.

COCKS, P., "Towards a Marxist Theory of European Integration," *International Organization,* 34, no. 1 (Winter 1980), 1–40.

DAHRENDORF, R., "International Power: An European Perspective," *Foreign Affairs,* 56, no. 1 (October 1977), 72–88.

FALK, R. A., *A Global Approach to National Policy.* Cambridge, MA: Harvard Univ. Press, 1975.

FALK, R. A. AND S. H. MENDLOVITZ (EDS.), *Regional Politics and World Order.* San Francisco: W. H. Freeman, 1973.

HAAS, E. B., *Beyond the Nation-State: Functionalism and International Organization.* Stanford, CA: Stanford Univ. Press, 1964.

HAAS, E. B., *The Obsolescence of Regional Integration Theory.* Berkeley, CA: Univ. of California Press, 1976.

HAAS, M., "Paradigms of Political Integration and Unification: Applications to Korea," *Journal of Peace Research,* 21, no. 1 (1984), 47–60.

HALLSTEIN, W., *Europe in the Making.* New York: Norton, 1973.

HUGHES, B. B. AND J. E. SCHWARZ, "Dimensions of Political Integration and the Experiences of the European Community," *International Studies Quarterly,* 16 (September 1972), 263–294.

IONESCU, G. (ED.), *Between Sovereignty and Integration.* New York: Halsted Press, 1973.

JACOB, P. E. AND J. V. TOSCANO (EDS.), *The Integration of Political Communities.* Philadelphia: Lippincott, 1964.

LINDBERG, L. N., *The Political Dynamics of European Economic Integration.* Stanford, CA: Stanford Univ. Press, 1963.

LINDBERG, L. N. AND S. A. SCHEINGOLD, *Europe's Would-Be Polity.* Englewood Cliffs, NJ: Prentice-Hall, 1970.

LINDBERG, L. N. AND S. A. SCHEINGOLD (EDS.), *Regional Integration: Theory and Research.* Cambridge, MA: Harvard Univ. Press, 1970.

MACRIDIS, R. C., *Modern Political Systems: Europe,* 5th ed. Englewood Cliffs, NJ: Prentice-Hall, 1983.

MERRITT, R. L. AND B. M. RUSSETT (EDS.), *From National Development to Global Community: Essays in Honor of Karl W. Deutsch.* London: Allen & Unwin, 1981.

MITRANY, D., *A Working Peace System.* Chicago: Quadrangle Books, 1966.

NAU, H. R., "From Integration to Interdependence: Gains, Losses, and Continuing Gaps," *International Organization,* 33, no. 1 (Winter 1979), 119–147.

NYE, J. S., JR., *International Regionalism.* Boston: Little, Brown, 1968.

NYE, J. S., JR., *Peace in Parts: Integration and Conflict in Regional Organization.* Boston: Little, Brown, 1971.

O'LEARY, J. P., *Systems Theory and Regional Integration: The "Market Model" of International Politics.* Washington, D.C.: Univ. Press of America, 1978.

OLSON, M., *The Logic of Collective Action.* Cambridge, MA: Harvard Univ. Press, 1965.

PENTLAND, C., *International Theory and European Integration.* New York: Free Press, 1973.

Regional Integration: Theory and Research, special issue of *International Organization,* 24, no. 4 (Autumn 1970).

RUSSETT, B. M., *International Regions and the International System,* repr. of 1967 ed. Westport, CT: Greenwood, 1975.

THOMPSON, W. R., "The Regional Subsystem: A Conceptual Explication and a Propositional Inventory," *International Studies Quarterly,* 17, no. 1 (March 1973), 89–117.

CASES OF REGIONAL INTEGRATION

AXLINE, W. A., "Underdevelopment, Dependence, and Integration: The Politics of Regionalism in the Third World," *International Organization,* 31 (Winter 1977), 83–105.

AXLINE, W. A., "Integration and Development in the Commonwealth Caribbean: the Politics of Regional Negotiations," *International Organization,* 32, no. 4 (Autumn 1978), 953–973.

BACH, D. C., "The Politics of West African Economic Cooperation: CEAO and ECOWAS," *Journal of Modern African Studies,* 21, no. 4 (December 1983), 605–623.

BANERJI, M., "Institutionalization of the Non-aligned Movement," *International Studies,* 20, no. 3/4 (July/December 1981), 549–563.

BOND, R. D., "Regionalism in Latin America: Prospects for the Latin American Economic System (SELA)," *International Organization,* 32, no. 2 (Spring 1978), 401–423.

CAPORASO, J. A., "The External Consequences of Regional Integration for Pan-European Relations: Inequality, Dependence, Polarization, and Symmetry," *International Studies Quarterly,* 20, no. 3 (September 1976), 341–392.

DE PORTE, A. W., *Europe between the Superpowers: The Enduring Balance.* New Haven, CT: Yale Univ. Press, 1979.

DE PORTE, A. W., *The Atlantic Alliance at 35,* Philadelphia: Foreign Policy Association, Headline Series No. 268, 1984.

DEUTSCH, K. W., et al., *France, Germany, and the Western Alliance. A Study of Elite Attitudes on European Integration and World Politics.* New York: Scribner's, 1967.

DEUTSCH, K. W., et al., *Political Community and the North Atlantic Area: International Organization in the Light of Historical Experience.* Princeton, NJ: Princeton Univ. Press, 1957, 1968.

DOWNEN, R. L. AND B. J. DICKSON (EDS.), *The Emerging Pacific Community: A Regional Perspective.* Boulder, CO: Westview Press, 1984.

EL-AYOUTY, Y. AND I. W. ZARTMAN (EDS.), *The OAU after Twenty Years.* New York: Praeger, 1984.

ESTERLINE, J. J., "ASEAN: A Model of Third World Integration," *Southeastern Political Review,* 11, no. 2 (Fall 1983), 3–34.

ETZIONI, A., *Political Unification: A Comparative Study of Leaders and Forces.* New York: Holt, Rinehart & Winston, 1965.

FEDDER, E. H., *NATO: The Dynamics of Alliance in the Post-war World.* New York: Dodd, Mead, 1973.

FELD, W. J., *The European Community in World Affairs: Economic Power and Political Influence.* Boulder, CO: Westview, 1985.

FELD, W. J. (ED.), *Western Europe's Global Reach: Regional Cooperation and Worldwide Aspirations.* Elmsford, NY: Pergamon, 1980.

FELD, W. J. AND G. BOYD (EDS.), *Comparative Regional Systems: West and East Europe, North America, the Middle East and Developing Countries.* Elmsford, NY: Pergamon, 1980.

FELD, W. J. AND J. K. WILDGEN, *Domestic Political Realities of European Unification: A Study of Mass Public and Elites in the European Community Countries,* new ed. Boulder, CO: Westview, 1977.

FELD, W. J. AND J. K. WILDGEN, *NATO and the Atlantic Defense. Perceptions and Illusions.* New York: Praeger, 1982.

FERRIS, E. G., "National Political Support for Regional Integration: The Andean Pact," *International Organization,,* 33, no. 1 (Winter 1979), 83–104.

FOLTZ, W. J., *From French West Africa to the Mali Federation.* New Haven, CT: Yale Univ. Press, 1965.

GALTUNG, J., *The European Community: A Superpower in the Making.* London: Allen & Unwin, 1973.

GRUHN, I. V., *Regionalism Reconsidered: The Economic Commission for Africa.* Boulder, CO: Westview Press, 1979.

HAAS, E. B., *The Uniting of Europe: Political, Social, and Economic Forces, 1950–1957,* rev. ed. Stanford, CA: Stanford Univ. Press, 1968.

HOLLOWAY, D. AND J.M.O. SHARP (EDS.), *The Warsaw Pact: Alliance in Transition?* Ithaca, NY: Cornell Univ. Press, 1984.

IONESCU, G. (ED.), *The European Alternatives: An Inquiry into the Policies of the European Community.* Rockville, MD: Sijthoff & Noordhoff, 1979.

JORDAN, R. S. AND W. J. FELD, *Europe in the Balance: The Changing Context of European International Politics.* Winchester, MA: Faber & Faber, 1985.

KAPLAN, L. S., *The United States and NATO: The Formative Years.* Lexington: Univ. Press of Kentucky, 1984.

KAPLAN, L. S. AND R. W. CLAWSON, *NATO After Thirty Years.* Wilmington, DE: Scholarly Resources, 1981.

KATZENSTEIN, P., *Disjoined Partners: Austria and Germany since 1815.* Berkeley: U of Cal Press, 1976.

KATZENSTEIN, P., *Corporatism and Change: Austria, Switzerland and the Politics of Industry.* Ithaca: Cornell U.P., 1984.

KATZENSTEIN, P., *Small States in World Markets: Industrial Policy in Europe.* Ithaca: Cornell U.P., 1985.

KISSINGER, H. A., *The Troubled Partnership: A Re-appraisal of the Atlantic Alliance,* repr. of 1965 ed. Westport, CT: Greenwood, 1982.

KITZINGER, U. W., *The Politics and Economics of European Integration,* repr. of 1963 ed. Westport, CT: Greenwood, 1976.

MERRITT, R. L., *Symbols of American Community, 1735–1775,* repr. of 1966 ed. Westport, CT: Greenwood, 1976.

MERRITT, R. L. AND D. J. PUCHALA (EDS.), *Western European Perspectives on International Affairs: Public Opinion Studies and Evaluations.* New York: Praeger, 1968.

MORAWETZ, D., *The Andean Group: A Case Study in Economic Integration among Developing Countries.* Cambridge: M.I.T. Press, 1974.

MORRIS, B. AND K. BOEHM, *The European Community,* 2nd ed. New York: Stockton Press, 1985.

NYE, J. S., JR., *Pan-Africanism and East African Integration.* Cambridge, MA: Harvard Univ. Press, 1965.

OKOLO, J. EMEKA, "Integrative and Cooperative Regionalism: The Economic Community of West African States," *International Organization,* 39 no. 1 (Winter 1985), 121–153.

OSGOOD, R. E., *NATO, the Entangling Alliance.* Chicago: Univ. of Chicago Press, 1962.

ROBERTSON, A. H., *European Institutions,* 3rd ed. New York: M. Bender, 1973.

RUSSETT, B. M., *Community and Contention: Britain and America in the Twentieth Century,* repr. of 1963 ed. Westport, CT: Greenwood, 1983.

SEERS, D. AND C. VAITSOS (EDS.), WITH MARJA-LIISA KILJUNEN, *Integration and Unequal Development: The Experience of the EEC.* New York: St. Martin's Press, 1980.

SIMON, S. W., *The ASEAN States and Regional Security.* Stanford, CA: Hoover Institution Press, 1982.

TAYLOR, P., "The European Communities as an Actor in International Society," *Revue d'Integration europeene,* 6, no. 1 (Autumn 1982), 7–41.

TAYLOR, P., "Intergovernmentalism in the European Communities in the 1970s: Patterns and Perspectives," *International Organization,* 36, no. 4 (Autumn 1982), 741–766.

TUCKER, R. W. AND L. WRIGLEY (EDS.), *The Atlantic Alliance and Its Critics.* New York: Praeger, 1983.

INTERDEPENDENCE AND DEPENDENCE

ALKER, H. R., *et al., Analyzing Global Interdependence,* Cambridge, MA: M.I.T. Center for International Studies, 1974.

AMIN, S., *Accumulation on a World Scale: A Critique of the Theory of Underdevelopment*, 2nd ed., New York: Monthly Review Press, 1978.

AMIN, S., *Imperialism and Unequal Development*. New York: Monthly Review Press, 1979.

ANDREWS, B., "The Political Economy of World Capitalism: Theory and Practice," *International Organization*, 36, no. 1 (Winter 1982), 135–163.

ARNDT, H. W., "The 'Trickle-Down' Myth," *Economic Development and Cultural Change*, 32, no. 1 (October 1983), 1–10.

BAKER-FOX, A., *et al.*, *Canada and the United States: Transnational and Transgovernmental Relations*, special issue of *International Organization*, 28, no. 4 (Autumn 1974).

BALDWIN, D. A., "Interdependence and Power: A Conceptual Analysis," *International Organization*, 34, no. 4 (Autumn 1980), 471–506.

BALL, G. W. (ED.), *Global Companies: The Political Economy of World Business*. Englewood Cliffs, NJ: Prentice-Hall, 1975.

BARNET, R. J. AND R. E. MÜLLER, *Global Reach: The Power of the Multinationals*. New York: Simon & Schuster, 1974.

BAUER, P. T., "The Economics of Resentment: Colonialism and Underdevelopment," *Journal of Contemporary History*, 4, no. 1 (January 1969), 51–71.

BEHRMAN, J. N., *The Role of International Companies in Latin American Integration: Autos and Petrochemicals*. Lexington, MA: Committee for Economic Development, 1972.

BERGESEN, A. (ED.), *Studies of the Modern World System*. New York: Academic Press, 1980.

BERGSTEN, C. F., *Managing International Economic Interdependence: Selected Papers of C. Fred Bergsten*. Lexington, MA: Lexington Books, 1977.

BERGSTEN, C. F., *The International Economic Policy of the United States: Selected Papers of C. Fred Bergsten, 1977–1979*. Lexington, MA: Lexington Books, 1980.

BERSTEN, C. F., *The United States in the World Economy: Selected Papers of C. Fred Bergsten, 1981 to 1982*. Lexington, MA: Lexington Books, 1983.

BERGSTEN, C. F., *et al.*, *American Multinationals and American Interests*. Washington, D.C.: Brookings Institution, 1978.

BHAGWATI, J. N., *Essays in Development Economics*, 2 vols. Cambridge, MA: M.I.T. Press, 1985.

BHAGWATI, J. N. (ED.), *The New International Economic Order: The North-South Debate*. Cambridge, MA: M.I.T. Press, 1977.

BLAKE, D. H. AND R. S. WALTERS, *The Politics of Global Economic Relations*, 2nd ed. Englewood Cliffs, NJ: Prentice-Hall, 1983.

BLOOMFIELD, L. P. AND I. C. BLOOMFIELD, *The U.S., Interdependence and World Order*. New York: Foreign Policy Association, 1975.

BORNSCHIER, V. AND T. H. BALLMER-CAO, "Income Inequality: A Cross-National Study of the Relationships Between MNC-Penetration, Dimensions of the Power Structure and Income Distribution," *American Sociological Review*, 44 (June 1979), 487–506.

BOULDING, K. E. AND E. BOULDING, *Introduction to the Global Society: Interdisciplinary Perspectives*. New York: Learning Resources in International Studies, 1977.

BRADA, J. C. AND J. A. MENDEZ, "Economic Integration Among Developed, Developing and Centrally Planned Economies: A Comparative Analysis," *Review of Economics and Statistics*, 67, no. 4 (1985), 549–556.

BRANDT, W., *et al.*, *North-South: A Program for Survival*, Cambridge, MA: M.I.T. Press, 1980.

BRESSAND, A., "Mastering the 'Worldeconomy'," *Foreign Affairs*, 61, no. 4 (Spring 1983), 745–772.

BROWN, L. R., *World Without Borders*. New York: Random House, 1973.

BURNS, A. C., *In Defense of Colonies*. London: Allen and Uncoin, 1957.

CAPORASO, J. A., "Dependency Theory: Continuities and Discontinuities in Development Studies," *International Organization*, 34, no. 4 (Autumn 1980), 605–628.

CAPORASO, J. A., "Industrialization in the Periphery: The Evolving Global Division of Labor," *International Studies Quarterly*, 25, no. 3 (September 1981), 347–384.

CAPORASO, J. A. (ED.), *Dependence and Dependency in the Global System*, special issue of *International Organization*, 32, no. 1 (Winter 1978).

CHASE-DUNN, C., "Interstate System and Capitalist World Economy: One Logic or Two?", *International Studies Quarterly*, 25 (March 1981), 19–42.

CLARK, C. AND D. BAHRY, "Dependent Development: A Socialist Variant," *International Studies Quarterly*, 27 (1983), 271–293.

COHEN, B. J., *The Question of Imperialism: The Political Economy of Dominance and Dependence,* New York: Basic Books, 1973.

COOPER, R. N., "Trade Policy as Foreign Policy," Cambridge, MA: Harvard Institute for Economic Research, *Discussion Paper No. 1160, 1985.*

COWHEY, P. F., *The Problems of Plenty: Energy Policy and International Politics.* Berkeley, CA: Univ. of California Press, 1985.

COWHEY, P. F. AND E. LONG, "Testing Theories of Regime Change: Hegemonic Decline or Surplus Capacity?", *International Organization,* 37, no. 2 (Spring 1983), 157–188.

COX, R. W., "IDEOLOGIES AND THE NEW INTERNATIONAL ECONOMIC ORDER: REflECTIONS ON SOME RECENT LITERATURE," *International Organization,* 33, no. 2 (Spring 1979), 257–302.

DEUTSCH, K. W. AND A. ECKSTEIN, "National Industrialization and the Declining Share of the International Economic Sector, 1890–1959," *World Politics,* 13, no. 2 (January 1961), 267–299.

DEUTSCH, K. W., *et al.,* "Population Sovereignty, and the Share of Foreign Trade," *Economic Development and Cultural Change,* 10 (July 1962), 353–366.

DEUTSCH, K. W., *et al., Comparative Government: Politics of Industrialized and Developing Nations.* Boston: Houghton Mifflin, 1982.

DOLAN, M. B. AND B. W. TOMLIN, "First World–Third World Linkages: External Relations and Economic Development," *International Organization,* 34, no. 1 (Winter 1980), 41–63.

DOS SANTOS, T. "The Structure of Dependence," *American Economic Review,* 60, no. 2 (May 1970), 231–236.

DUDLEY, L., "Foreign Aid and the Theory of Alliances," *Review of Economics and Statistics,* 61 (1979), 564–571.

FEINBERG, R. AND K. OYE, "After the Fall: U.S. Policy Toward Third World Regimes," *World Policy,* 1, no. 1 (1983), 201–215.

FRANK, A. G., *On Capitalist Underdevelopment.* New York: Oxford Univ. Press, 1975.

FRANK, A. G., *Dependent Accumulation and Underdevelopment.* New York: Monthly Review Press, 1979.

GALBRAITH, J. K., *Economic Development.* Cambridge, MA: Harvard Univ. Press, 1964.

GALTUNG, J., "A Structural Theory of Imperialism," *Journal of Peace Research,* 8, no. 2 (1972), 81–118.

GALTUNG, J., "On the Relation Between Military and Economic Non-alignment," *Non Aligned World,* 1, no. 2 (April/June 1983), 192–202.

GILPIN, R., *U.S. Power and the Multinational Corporation: The Political Economy of Foreign Direct Investment.* New York: Basic Books, 1975.

GILPIN, R., *War and Change in World Politics.* New York: Cambridge Univ. Press, 1981.

GOUREVITCH, P., "The Second Image Reversed: The International Sources of Domestic Politics," *International Organization,* 32, no. 4 (Autumn 1978), 881–911.

HAAS, E. B., *The Web of Interdependence.* Englewood Cliffs, NJ: Prentice-Hall, 1970.

HAAS, E. B., "Why Collaborate? Issue-Linkage and International Regimes," *World Politics,* 32, no. 3 (April 1980), 357–405.

HAYTER, T., *The Creation of World Poverty: An Alternative View to the Brandt Report.* New York: Pluto Press, 1981.

HAYTER, T. AND C. WATSON, *Aid: Rhetoric and Reality.* New York: Pluto Press, 1985.

HIRSCH, F., "Is there a New International Economic Order?", *International Organization,* 30, no. 3 (Summer 1976), 521–531.

HIRSCHMAN, A. O., *National Power and the Structure of Foreign Trade,* reissue of 1945 ed. Berkeley, CA: Univ. of California Press, 1981.

HOLLIST, W. L. AND J. N. ROSENAU (EDS.), *World System Debates,* special issue of *International Studies Quarterly,* 25, no. 1 (March 1981).

HOLSTI, K. J., "A New International Politics? Diplomacy in Complex Interdependence," *International Organization,* 32, no. 2 (Spring 1978), 513–530.

HUNTINGTON, S. P., "Transnational Organizations in World Politics," *World Politics,* 25, no. 3 (April 1973), 338–368.

JACKMAN, R. W., "Dependence on Foreign Investment and Economic Growth in the Third World," *World Politics,* 34, no. 2 (January 1982), 175–196.

KADAR, B., *Structural Changes in the World Economy.* New York: St. Martin's Press, 1984.

KATZENSTEIN, P. (ED.), *Between Power and Plenty: Foreign Economic Policies of Advanced Industrial States*. Madison, WI: Univ. of Wisconsin Press, 1978.

KEOHANE, R. O., *After Hegemony: Cooperation and Discord in the World Political Economy*. Princeton, NJ: Princeton Univ. Press, 1984.

KEOHANE, R. O., "Reciprocity in International Relations," *International Organization*, 40, no. 1 (Winter 1986), 1–27.

KEOHANE, R. O. AND J. S. NYE, JR., *Transnational Relations and World Politics*. Cambridge, MA: Harvard Univ. Press, 1972.

KEOHANE, R. O. AND J. S. NYE, JR., *Power and Interdependence: World Politics in Transition*. Boston: Little, Brown, 1977.

KINDLEBERGER, C. P., *Power and Money: The Politics of International Economics and the Economics of International Politics*. New York: Basic Books, 1970.

KINDLEBERGER, C. P., *America in the World Economy*. New York: Foreign Policy Association, 1977.

KINDLEBERGER, C. P., "Dominance and Leadership in the International Economy: Exploitation, Public Goods, and Free Rides," *International Studies Quarterly*, 25, no. 2 (June 1981), 242–254.

KINDLEBERGER, C. P., "International Public Goods Without International Government," *American Economic Review*, 76, no. 1 (March 1986), 1–13.

KINDLEBERGER, C. P. AND D. B. AUDRETSCH (EDS.), *The Multinational Corporation in the 1980s*. Cambridge, MA: M.I.T. Press, 1983.

KRASNER, S. D., "Regimes and the Limits of Realism," *International Organization*, 36 (Spring 1982), 497–510.

KRASNER, S. D., "Third World Vulnerabilities and Global Negotiations," *Review of International Studies*, 9, no. 4 (October 1983), 235–249.

KRASNER, S. D., *Structural Conflict: The Third World Against Global Liberalism*. Berkeley, CA: Univ. of California Press, 1985.

KRASNER, S. D. (ED.) *International Regimes*, special issue of *International Organization*, 36, no. 2 (Spring 1982).

LAKE, D. A., "Beneath the Commerce of Nations: A Theory of International Economic Structures," *International Studies Quarterly*, 28 (1984), 143–170.

MAGDOFF, H., *Imperialism: From the Colonial Age to the Present*. New York: Monthly Review Press, 1979.

MALEK, A. A., *Sociologie de l'imperialisme*. Paris: Armand Colin, 1971.

MALEK A. A., *Le developpement inegal*. Paris: Editions Minuit, 1973.

MANSBACH, R. W. AND Y. H. FERGUSON, *The Web of World Politics: Non-state Actors in the Global System*. Englewood Cliffs, NJ: Prentice-Hall, 1976.

MANSBACH, R. W. AND J. A. VASQUEZ, *In Search of Theory: A New Paradigm for Global Politics*. New York: Columbia Univ. Press, 1981.

MITSUO, O., "The Sociology of Development and Issues Surrounding Late Development," *International Studies Quarterly*, 26, no. 4 (December 1982), 596–622.

MORSE, E. L., *Foreign Policy and Interdependence in Gaullist France*. Princeton, NJ: Princeton Univ. Press, 1973.

MORSE, E. L., *Modernization and the Transformation of International Relations*. New York: Free Press, 1976.

MYRDAL, G., *Asian Drama: An Inquiry into the Poverty of Nations*, 3 vols. Millwood, NY: Kraus Reprint, 1968.

MYRDAL, G., *An International Economy: Problems and Perspectives*, repr. of 1956 ed. Westport, CT: Greenwood, 1978.

MYRDAL, G. *Beyond the Welfare State: Economic Planning and Its International Implications*, repr. of 1960 ed. Westport, CT: Greenwood, 1982.

NAU, H. R., "From Integration to Interdependence: Gains, Losses, and Continuing Gaps," *International Organization*, 33, no. 1 (Winter 1979), 119–147.

OLSON, M., *The Rise and Decline of Nations*. New Haven, CT: Yale Univ. Press, 1982.

PERHAM, M., *The Colonial Reckoning*. repr. of 1962 ed., Westwood, CT: Greenwood, 1976.

PIRAGES, D. (ED.), *International Politics of Scarcity*, special issue of *International Studies Quarterly*, 21, no. 4 (December 1977).

RICHARDSON, N. R., *Foreign Policy and Economic Dependence*. Austin and London: Univ. of Texas Press, 1978.

ROBINSON, J., *Multinational Corporations and Political Control*. New York: St. Martin's Press, 1983.

RODNEY, W., *How Europe Underdeveloped Africa*, 2nd rev. ed. Washington, D.C.: Howard Univ. Press, 1982.

ROEDER, P. G., "The Ties That Bind: Aid, Trade, and Political Compliance in Soviet–Third World Relations," *International Studies Quarterly*, 29, no. 2 (June 1985), 191–216.

ROSECRANCE, R. AND A. STEIN, "Interdependence: Myth or Reality?," *World Politics*, 26 (October 1973), 1–27.

ROSENAU, J. N., *In Search of Global Patterns*, New York: Free Press, 1976.

ROSENAU, J. N., *The Study of Global Interdependence: Essays on the Transnationalization of World Affairs*. New York: Nichols Pub., 1980.

RUBINSON, R., "The World-Economy and the Distribution of Income Within States: A Cross-national Study," *American Sociological Review*, 41 (August 1976), 638–659.

RUGGIE, J. G. (ED.), *The Antinomies of Interdependence: National Welfare and the International Division of Labor*. New York: Columbia Univ. Press. 1983.

RUSSETT, B., "Dimensions of Resource Dependence: Some Elements of Rigor in Concept and Policy Analysis," *International Organization*, 38, no. 3 (Summer 1984), 481–499.

SCHUMPETER, J. A., *Imperialism and Social Classes*. New York: Meridian, 1955.

SCHUMPETER, J. A., *Capitalism, Socialism and Democracy*. Magnolia, MA: Peter Smith, 1983.

SCOTT, A. M., "The Logic of International Interaction," *International Studies Quarterly*, 21, no. 3 (September 1977), 429–459.

SELIGSON, M. A. (ED.), *The Gap Between Rich and Poor: Contending Perspectives on the Political Economy of Development*. Boulder, CO: Westview, 1984.

SENGHAAS, D., *The European Experience: A Historical Critique of Development Theory*. Dover, NH: Longwood Pub. Group, 1985.

SINGER, M. M., *Weak States in a World of Powers: The Dynamics of International Relationships*. New York: Free Press, 1972.

SMITH, T., "The Underdevelopment of Development Literature: The Case of Dependency Theory," *World Politics*, 31, no. 2 (January 1979), 247–288.

SMITH, T., *The Pattern of Imperialism: The United States, Great Britain and the Late-Industrializing World Since 1815*. New York: Cambridge Univ. Press, 1981.

SPERO, J., *Politics of International Economic Relations*, 3rd ed. New York: St. Martin's Press, 1985.

SPIEGEL, S. L., *Dominance and Diversity: The International Hierarchy*. Lanham, MD: Univ. Press of America, 1980.

STALLINGS, B., *Economic Dependency in Africa and Latin America*. Beverly Hills, CA: Sage, Comparative Politics Professional Paper 31, 1972.

STRANGE, S., "Reactions to Brandt: Popular Acclaim and Academic Attack," *International Studies Quarterly*, 25, no. 2 (June 1981), 328–342.

STRANGE, S., "The Global Political Economy, 1959–1984," *International Journal*, 39, no. 2 (Spring 1984), 267–283.

SUNKEL, O., "Big Business and 'Dependencia': A Latin American View," *Foreign Affairs*, 50, no. 3 (April 1972), 517–531.

TAYLOR, M. J. AND N. J. THRIFT (EDS.), *The Geography of Multinationals*. Kent, England: Croom Helm, 1982.

THOMPSON, W. R. (ED.), *Contending Approaches to World System Analysis*. Beverly Hills, CA: Sage Publications, 1983.

TOLLISON, R. D. AND T. D. WILLETT, "International Integration and Interdependence of Economic Variables," *International Organization*, 27, no. 2 (Spring 1973), 255–271.

VERNON, R., *Sovereignty at Bay: The Multinational Spread of U.S. Enterprises*. New York: Basic Books, 1971.

VERNON, R., *Storm Over the Multinationals: The Real Issues*. Cambridge, MA: Harvard Univ. Press, 1977.

VERNON, R., "Multinationals: No Strings Attached," *Foreign Policy*, 33 (Winter 1978/1979), 121–134.

VERNON, R., *Two Hungry Giants: The United States and Japan in the Quest for Oil and Ores*. Cambridge, MA: Harvard Univ. Press, 1983.

VERNON, R., *Exploring the Global Economy*. Lanham, MD: Univ. Press of America, 1985.

VOLGY, T. J. AND H. KENSKI, "Systems Theory and Foreign Policy Restructuring: Distance Change in Latin America, 1953–1970," *International Studies Quarterly*, 26, no. 3 (September 1982), 445–474.

WALLERI, R. D., "The Political Economy Literature on North-South Relations: Alternative Approaches and Empirical Evidence," *International Studies Quarterly*, 22, no. 4 (December 1978), 587–624.

WALLERSTEIN, I., *The Capitalist World Economy*. Cambridge: Cambridge Univ. Press, 1979.

WARD, B., *The Rich Nations and the Poor Nations*. New York: Norton, 1962.

WEAVER, J. H. AND K. P. JAMESON, *Economic Development: Competing Paradigms—Competing Parables*, DSP Occasional Paper No. 3. Washington, D.C.: The Agency for International Development, 1978.

WEEDE, E. AND H. TIEFENBACH, "Some Recent Explanations of Income Inequality: An Evaluation and Critique," *International Studies Quarterly*, 25, no. 2 (June 1981), 255–282.

WILBER, C. K. (ED.), *The Political Economy of Development and Underdevelopment*, 2nd ed. New York: Random House, 1979.

YERGIN, D. AND M. HILLENBRAND (EDS.), *Global Insecurity: A Strategy for Energy and Economic Upheaval*. Boston, Houghton Mifflin, 1982.

ZARTMAN, I. W., "Europe and Africa: Decolonization or Dependency?", *Foreign Affairs*, 54, no. 2 (1976), 325–343.

AN AGENDA FOR THE FUTURE

ALLISON, G. T., *et al.*, (eds.), *Hawks, Doves, and Owls: An Agenda for Avoiding Nuclear War*. New York: Norton, 1985.

ASHLEY, R. K., "The Eye of Power: The Politics of World Modeling," *International Organization*, 37, no. 3 (Summer 1983), 495–535.

BELL, D., *The Coming of Post-Industrial Society: A Venture in Social Forecasting*, 2nd ed. New York: Basic Books, 1976.

BERGSTEN, C. F., *The World Economy in the Nineteen Eighties: Selected Papers of C. Fred Bergsten, 1980*. Lexington, MA: Lexington Books, 1981.

BHAGWATI, J. N. (ED.)., *Economics and World Order: From the 1970s to the 1990s*. New York: Free Press, 1972.

BHAGWATI, J. N. AND J. G. RUGGIE (EDS.), *Power, Passions and Purpose: Prospects for North–South Negotiations*. Cambridge, MA: M.I.T. Press, 1984.

BROWN, L. R. AND E. P. ECKHOLM, *By Bread Alone*. Washington, D.C.: Overseas Council Development, 1974.

BROWN, L. R. AND P. SHAW, *Six Steps to a Sustainable Society*. Washington, D.C.: Worldwatch Institute, 1982.

BROWN, L. R., *et al.*, *State of the World, 1985: A Worldwatch Institute Report on Progress Toward a Sustainable Society*. New York: Norton, 1985.

CHOUCRI, N. AND T. W. ROBINSON (EDS.), *Forecasting in International LOAD Relations: Theory, Methods, Problems, Prospects*. San Francisco: W. H. Freeman, 1978.

COATE, R. A., *Global Issue Regimes*. New York: Praeger Publishers, 1982.

COLE, H.S.D., *et al.* (eds.), *Models of Doom: A Critique of The Limits to Growth*. New York: Universe Books, 1973.

DEUTSCH, K. W., *et al.* (eds.), *Problems of World Modeling*. Cambridge, MA: Ballinger, 1977.

FALK, R. A., *This Endangered Planet: Prospects and Proposals for Human Survival*. New York: Random House, 1972.

FALK, R. A., *Future Worlds*. New York: Foreign Policy Assn., 1976.

FRITSCH, B., *Growth Limitation and Political Power*. Cambridge, MA: Ballinger Pub., 1976.

GALTUNG, J., *The True Worlds: A Transnational Perspective*. New York: Free Press, 1980.

GALTUNG, J., *There Are Alternatives: Four Roads to Peace and Security*. Chester Springs, PA: Dufour, 1984.

HEILBRONER, R. L., *An Inquiry into the Human Prospect: Updated and Reconsidered for the 1980s*. New York: Norton & Co., 1980.

HERRERA, A. O., *et al., Catastrophe or New Society? A Latin American Model.* Ottawa: International Development Research Centre, 1976.

HIRSCH, F., *Social Limits to Growth.* Cambridge, MA: Harvard Univ. Press, 1976.

INKELES, A., "The Emerging Social Structure of the World," *World Politics,* 27, no. 4 (July 1975), 467–495.

INKELES, A. AND D. H. SMITH, *Becoming Modern: Individual Change in Six Developing Countries.* Cambridge, MA: Harvard Univ. Press, 1974.

INKELES, A., *et al., Exploring Individual Modernity.* New York: Columbia Univ. Press, 1983.

KAHN, H. *et al., World Economic Development: Projections from 1979 to the Year 2000.* New York: Morrow, 1979.

MEADOWS, D. L. (ED.), *Alternatives to Growth.* Vol. 1: *A Search for Sustainable Futures.* Cambridge, MA: Ballinger Pub., 1978.

MEADOWS, D. L. AND D. H. MEADOWS, *The Limits to Growth, A Report for the Club of Rome's Project on the Predicament of Mankind,* 2nd ed. New York: New American Library, 1972.

MEADOWS, D. L. AND D. H. MEADOWS (EDS.), *Toward Global Equilibrium: Collected Papers.* Cambridge, MA: M.I.T. Press, 1973.

MEADOWS, D. L., *et al., Dynamics of Growth in a Finite World.* Cambridge, MA: M.I.T. Press, 1974.

MEADOWS, D. H., *et al.* (eds.), *Groping in the Dark: The First Decade of Global Modeling.* New York: John Wiley & Sons, 1982.

MESAROVIC, M. AND E. PESTEL, *Mankind at the Turning Point.* New York: New American Library, 1976.

MYRDAL, A., *The Game of Disarmament: How the United States and Russia Run the Arms Race,* 2nd ed. New York: Pantheon Books, 1982.

MYRDAL, G., *The Challenge of World Poverty: A World Anti-Poverty Program in Outline.* New York: Random, 1971.

NYE, J. S., JR., "Multinational Corporations in World Politics," *Foreign Affairs,* 53, no. 1 (October 1974), 153–175.

OLSON, M., "Increasing the Incentives for International Cooperation," *International Organization,* 25, no. 4 (Autumn 1971), 845–865.

PIRAGES, D. (ED.), *International Politics of Scarcity,* special issue of *International Studies Quarterly,* 21, no. 4 (December 1977).

REPETTO, R. (ED.), *The Global Possible: Resources, Development, and the New Century.* New Haven, CT: Yale Univ. Press, 1986.

SCHMIDT, H., *A Grand Strategy for the West.* New Haven, CT: Yale Univ. Press, 1985.

SHAKHNAZAROV, G., *The Destiny of the World: The Socialist Shape of Things to Come.* Moscow: Progress Publishers, 1979.

SINGER, J. D. AND R. J. STOLL (EDS.), *Quantitative Indian World Politics: Timely Assurance and Early Warning.* New York: Praeger, 1984.

SINGER, J. D. AND M. D. WALLACE (EDS.), *To Augur Well: Early Warning Indicators in World Politics.* Beverly Hills, CA: Sage, 1979.

SKOLNIKOFF, E. B., *The International Imperatives of Technology: Technological Development and the International Political System.* Berkeley, CA: University of California, Institute of International Studies, 1972.

SNYDER, R. C., *et al.,* "A Global Monitoring System: Appraising the Effects of Government on Human Dignity," *International Studies Quarterly,* 20, no. 2 (June 1976), 221–260.

STOBAUGH, R. AND D. YERGIN (EDS.), *Energy Future: Report of the Energy Project at the Harvard Business School.* New York: Random, 1979.

THOMAS, L., "Scientific Frontiers and National Frontiers: A Look Ahead," *Foreign Affairs,* 62, no. 4 (Spring 1984), 966–994.

TOMPKINS, E. B. (ED.), *Peaceful Change in Modern Society.* Stanford, CA: Hoover Institution Press, Stanford Univ., 1971.

WARD, B. AND R. DUBOS, *Only One Earth: The Care and Maintenance of a Small Planet,* 2nd ed. New York: Norton, 1983.

WILLRICH, M., *Energy and World Politics,* 2nd ed. New York: Free Press, 1978.

WRIGHT, Q., *On Predicting International Relations: The Year 2000.* Denver, CO: Monograph Series, 1969.

YOUNG, O. R., *Resource Management at the International Level: The Case of the North Pacific.* New York: Nichols, 1977.

Index